1000
new designs

1000

new designs
and where to find them
A 21st Century Sourcebook

Jennifer Hudson

Laurence King Publishing

LAURENCE KING

Published in 2006 by
Laurence King Publishing Ltd
361-373 City Road
London EC1V 1JJ
e-mail: enquiries@laurenceking.co.uk
www.laurenceking.co.uk

A catalogue record for this book is available
from the British Library

ISBN-13: 978 1 85669 466 7
ISBN-10: 1 85669 466 6

Designed by Struktur Design Limited.
Printed in China.

Front cover:
Chair, Hara. Giorgio Guriolo, Kundalini srl, Italy.
Back cover:
Teaspoon, DB. Ed Annink, Droog Design,
the Netherlands.
Rug, Salim. Alfredo Häberli, Ruckstuhl AG,
Switzerland.
Bookcase, Shelf X. Naoto Fukasawa,
B&B Italia SpA, Italy.
Fabric, London Toile. Timorous Beasties, UK.
Late Sofa. Ronan and Erwan Bouroullec,
Vitra, Switzerland.
Kettle, Morrison. Jasper Morrison, Rowenta, UK.
Bowl, Rabbit. Hella Jongerius, Nymphenburg
Porcelain, Germany.
Bookcase, Lotus. Karim Rashid, Tonelli srl, Italy.
Armchair, MT Rocker. Ron Arad, Driade SpA and
Marzorati Ronchetti, Italy.
Chaise longue, Fly. Ora-Íto, B&B Italia SpA, Italy.
Breeding Table. Clemens Weisshaar and Reed Kram,
Moroso SpA, Italy.
Saddle, Rebel. Propeller, Linear, Sweden.
Seating, Osorom. Konstantin Grcic, Moroso SpA, Italy.
Chandelier, Vortexx. Zaha Hadid and Patrick
Schumacher, Sawaya & Moroni, Italy.
Kitchen, K12. Norbert Wangen, Boffi SpA, Italy.
Tableware, Editor. Miguel Vieira Baptista, Portugal.
Chair, Sushi. Fernando and Humberto Campana,
Edra SpA, Italy.
Bookshelf, Hey, chair, be a bookshelf! Maarten Baas,
the Netherlands.

Acknowledgements

I would like to dedicate *1000 New Designs and Where
to Find Them* to my son Willoughby, and to thank the
following people for their invaluable help in the
making of this book: Laurence King for having faith
in me; all the designers who are featured (especially
those who have taken the time to be interviewed),
as well as the manufacturers who have supplied
information and visual material; Max Fraser for his
comprehensive listing of international design outlets
and for his general advice and encouragement;
Roger Fawcett-Tang for his patience and his skill in
organizing over 1000 designs into some kind of order
and making the book look good as well; John Jervis,
my editor at Laurence King Publishing, for his
unflinching hard work in getting all to a publishable
state and Krystyna Mayer for her professional copy-
editing; Felicity Awdry for her production expertise;
Mandi Arculis and Andy Prince for their help in the
earlier stages of the book; and Laura Willis, whose
marketing know-how will surely make the books fly
off the shelves. But, over and above all, I would like
to thank Fredrika Lökholm for her hours and hours of
dedication and without whom I didn't have a hope in
hell of compiling this sourcebook – 'deep breaths and
it won't take long Fredrika'.

Introduction

The following pages comprise a sourcebook of over 1000 designs since the turn of the century. It is intended as a tool not only for the consumer, but also for those seeking inspiration in their own design work. Each object is presented with a caption providing full technical details, as well as the websites of the manufacturers, or designers where relevant. Commentaries throughout shed light on the work of personalities and on trends, making the book more than just a catalogue of desirable objects.

Thirty-three designers were interviewed. They were all asked the same ten questions, of which they were requested to answer at least six. The topics covered varied from how they and others view their work, to where they think design is heading. Their replies, some light-hearted and others more thoughtful, provide a change of pace for the reader, but more importantly they have thrown up some interesting themes. Not the least of these is the fact that many wonderful products never reach the marketplace in a current manufacturing climate that is 'playing it safe', with manufacturers pandering to a media society by providing an overabundance of products that are conceived to look good in today's design magazines.

Design since the millennium has witnessed a liberating pluralism, and for the past six years the design community has been in a state of flux, with no one style or trend being dominant. There has been a slow breaking down of the barriers between disciplines, cultures, roles and skills: this is a period in which there is a place for craft-based, low-tech, individualistic approaches, as well as for mass-produced high tech. Despite an unhealthy economic climate in the West, this lack of specific design protocol has led to an increase in experimentation and the rise of conceptual design – design as communication, interactive objects and products that could be considered 'too close to the art gallery' (Tom Dixon) for comfort, but that nonetheless aim to redefine our perception of design and stimulate international discussion.

Advanced production methods and the growing use of CADs in the development of objects have given birth to research into the use of new, more pliant materials that can be moulded into the softened and rounded shapes created by these digitalized programs. This ISDN revolution has promoted a greater sophistication of products and has accelerated the speed not only of the manufacturing process, but also of change itself. The computerized production chain that originally resulted in the destruction of individuality can now be customized to allow designs to be manipulated and personalized – a 'smart' industrial process that allows for individualism on a commercial, mechanized scale.

Stereolithography, a technique originally invented by Chuck Hall in 1986 for

Blob
Designed for Magis, not produced
Karim Rashid
www.karimrashid.com

Net
'Floating' bed
Xavier Lust and
Bruno Fattorini
www.xavierlust.com

Martini glass
Created for Bombay Sapphire design competition but not produced
Tokujin Yoshioka
www.tokujin.com

Martini glass
Created for Bombay Sapphire design competition but not produced
Karim Rashid
www.karimrashid.com

Flat Mode
Sewing machine
Itay Potash
www.itaypotash.com

rapid prototyping, allows objects to 'grow' organically. Designs created on CAD programs are translated from the virtual to the physical by using a 3D layering system to build up successive sheets of the material being used, each individually cut and photochemically hardened by laser before adding the next layer. The idea is to eventually create bespoke products, with customers selecting from a range of colours, forms, textures and materials that are then gestated in a studio lab into whatever item is desired, and delivered shortly afterwards. In its early stages at present, 'desktop manufacturing' is a phenomenon that will allow consumers to become designers by creating their individualized pieces on the computer. This will be an Internet Revolution facilitating a whole new form of Industrial Revolution.

The concept of 'design for all' introduces trends that have grown steadily in recent years: the increased democratization of design, the rise of superficial styling and the birth of the design personality.

Throughout the 1960s and 70s, retailers such as Habitat and IKEA succeeded in bringing affordable contemporary design to the masses, yet it took the design press a little while to catch on. With big names such as Arad, Starck, Rashid, Dixon, Alessi and Swatch taking design from the showcase and on to the high street, the majority of fashion magazines and leading newspapers began to include dedicated lifestyle sections. The specialized press now religiously covers the latest trends, no matter how tenuous they may be, and more perniciously has made celebrities out of a few.

This is a dangerous development. One of the questions I posed to the people interviewed for this book was whether they considered that the cult of the personality was taking over the design world. The response came, time and time again, that it is a risky path we are following when the designer is becoming more of a talking point than the design itself. Matali Crasset makes the significant point that the 'superstardom' of some is resulting in students taking up design for the wrong reasons, while Jasper Morrison is concerned that the increased media interest in design and designer personalities is creating a demand for styling

Take Away
Foldable writing desk – unfolded
Beat Karrer
beat@beatkarrer.net

Take Away
Foldable writing desk – folded
Beat Karrer
beat@beatkarrer.net

Nino Rota e None Rota
Chair and armchair designed for Cap Design SpA but not produced
Ron Arad
www.ronarad.com

Transparent Cakes
Glass containers
RADI Designers
www.radidesigners.com

Bowling set
Designed as part of Magis's Post Computer Games series but not produced
Ross Lovegrove
www.rosslovegrove.com

Lily Eau
Floating outdoor lamp, energy-efficient light commissioned by Luceplan for Greenlight prize
Willem van der Sluis and Hugo Timmermans
www.luceplan.com

Cornici wallpaper
Compose your own works of art
Jordi Pigem de Palol and Enrico Azzimonti
www.enricoazzimonti.it

Black out
Torch/lamp
Lorenzo Damiani
Lorenzo.damiani@tin.it

the 'look', as he calls it, which, if steps are not taken soon, will result in design becoming no more than another form of entertainment or fashion accessory.

The design world is facing a crucial crossroads and there is a growing urgency to take serious stock of the present situation. Design has a ubiquitous presence. James Irvine is often quoted as saying that 'everything that is manufactured has been designed by somebody ... even if they are not called designers'. The objects with which we choose to surround ourselves, from the chair we sit on, the bed we sleep in, the car we drive and the electronics we use, to the humble milk carton we pick up from the supermarket every day, define not only us, but also, eventually in retrospect, the era in which we live. Design underlines our everyday actions and moulds our consciousness. It is the social responsibility of the 'designer' to produce only that which will improve life, to try to ignore media hype and the panacea of advertising, and to conceive products that will last the vagaries of time and make our world a better place. There is an ever-increasing need for a move away from 'statement' design to more 'normal' design. It may not look as good in the glossies, but it will have more honesty and integrity, and will reverse the trend away from overproduction of the unnecessary towards a more thoughtful and anonymous design.

The design industry, too, is in the process of having to reinvent itself. With Asia's rise as a major design and production powerhouse, Western manufacturers are having to examine how they can compete with sophisticated and cost-effective product-sketching and rendering skills, as well as with advanced engineering and manufacturing techniques that can produce a mature product quickly and at one-fifth of the price.

According to the Chinese National Bureau of Statistics, a sales boom in China has resulted in a market expected to grow to £0.75 trillion ($1.3 trillion) in ten years. Not only China but also countries like Taiwan, South Korea and Thailand are following a path similar to that of Japan in the 1970s and 80s, and are experiencing both a qualitative change in their manufacturing industry and a rise in interest in the design process. The former vice-president of Industrial Design for

Textiles with an industrial aesthetic
Claire Lane
claired.lane@aol.com

Tantalight
Plastic and aluminium light
Andreas Krause and Jonas Upton-Hansen
www.kuh-design.com

Hammock/deckchair
for inside or outside use
Marc Krusin
mkrusin@hotmail.com

Rose Line
Shelving developed as a prototype for VIA
Jörg Gessner
www.via.fr

Triband telephone in pen form
Capable of translating written word into SMS messages
Produced as a prototype for Siemens
www.siemens.com

PS Chair
Made from nylon 'protective sleeve' packaging material
Joohee Lee
info@jooheelee.co.uk

Shelflife
Bookshelf with integral chair and table
Charles Trevelyen
charles.trevelyen@blue yonder.co.uk

Standing Hanger
Magnus Long
www.magnuslong.com

the New York-based Smart Design, Scott Henderson, poses the questions: 'Where in our world is the vast majority of manufacturing taking place? Where has the Internet played a major role in the proliferation of a global design aesthetic? Where has entrepreneurship and new wealth created the fastest-growing and second-largest economy in the world over the shortest period of time?'

Chinese shoppers are buying like they have never done before. Sales at restaurants and retail outlets are growing even faster than the spectacular 9.4 per cent annual expansion of the economy. China has overtaken the US in sales of televisions and mobile phones and is soon to surpass it in the sales of computers, while a double-digit rise in urban incomes has drawn the likes of Cartier, Prada and Armani to expand here faster than anywhere else in the world. According to Merrill Lynch, only 2 per cent of China's population can afford luxury goods, but by 2009 China will account for 20 per cent of the world market in high-end luxury products.

Not content any longer with being the workbench of the world, Asian countries are steadily building up their own design language and, to an increasing extent, products are being engineered to appeal to an international audience as well as to the Asian market. There are now over 400 design schools in China alone, churning out more than 8000 graduates a year, including many who flock to the best US and European graduate design programmes to continue their education. China has long had a history of producing copies of designs drawn up elsewhere, but now, as the Chairman of the Industrial Design Department at Hunan University points out, it is 'our goal to make the transition from "Made in China" to "Designed in China".'

Asia is, for now, a nascent threat. Its education system is still very much of the 'I teach, you listen' style, with an emphasis placed on examinations. An atmosphere that discourages questions, experimentation and

the challenging of opinions stifles its creativity. Asia's culture is also a very traditional one, and design professors are more often than not selected from among their own design graduates. Faith is placed on established relationships, which only hinders diversity. Added to this is the fact that design works closely with manufacturing in Asia, which results in an emphasis on producing products with speed and efficiency rather than with individuality and innovation.

Faced with a plethora of objects, all of which are probably comparable as far as product performance is concerned, original and pioneering design has become a principal tool for differentiation. What the West needs to counter the economic and technical domination of Asia is governments and manufacturers willing to risk investment in skills, research and innovation for the future. Playing it safe is only a short-term option for profitability and is detrimental to integrity. International design firms should be seeking collaborative projects with fast-growing Asian businesses – a cross-pollination between the East and West, between a long-established tradition and a burgeoning economy. In the end, maybe what we currently perceive as a threat could be an opportunity for the future, with new manufacturing creating a demand for more designers from around the world who are willing to expand their horizons.

The pages that follow feature some of the best designs of the last five years. The design world has been in stasis for a good while now and it will be interesting to see what will develop from the opening up of new markets and from technological innovation by the end of the decade. It has been a mammoth task to put this book together, but I would like to take this opportunity to thank the designers whose work is featured for shaping the world we live in.

Having worked on the *International Design Yearbook* for over ten years, what I found most restricting when compiling this book was the fact that I had to limit my choice to items in production, a constraint that was not placed on guest editors of the *Yearbook*. Much of the experimental, conceptual and craft work we are seeing more of today had to be exorcized, as did items that have not yet been fully developed – this introduction is illustrated with such products, which couldn't make it into the pages of this book.

We have witnessed the formation of the more economically viable but maybe less innovative manufacturing conglomerates over the past couple of years. These include, for example, Cap Design, Gufram and Gebrüder Thonet coming under the umbrella of Poltrona Frau (financed by the Ferrari-backed Charme Group) and B&B Italia selling the majority of its shares to the Bulgari-financed Opera group. This has led to a shift to a marketing policy aligned more to the fashion and car industries, which has resulted in a streamlining of backlist products to create design brands that are not always compatible with originality. Thus numerous excellent products that have been taken out of production also had to go.

I have taken some liberties. It would not make sense to cover design over the last six years without representing Droog Design. They have recently set up Droog BV, an affordable edition of 185 pieces in the Droog Design Collection, yet much of their output has been developed for themed exhibitions and produced in very limited batches (see pages 103, 117, 180, 199, 272 and 287). Patrick Jouin's 'Solid' furniture (see page 68) is in the process of development. It can be ordered through his studio and through Moss in New York as a limited-edition piece retailing for £8920 ($15,650), but it is not exactly readily available; it does, however, represent a technological development that will revolutionize design manufacturing.

Glassware is difficult. The designs of Anu Penttinen (see page 200), Takahide Sano (see page 193) and Massimo Micheluzzi (see page 179), for example, are one-offs or limited batch, but I have chosen to include them because if you cannot order the exact items illustrated here, they are still working in a similar style. In the same vein, the textile designs of Claudy Jongstra (see page 213) and Yoshiki Hishinuma (see page 224) are generic.

Ensemble
Mobile phone headset developed as a 'dream project' with Orange
Jérôme Olivet
www.jeromeolivet.fr

Design By Pressure
Table formed from pressed branches
Front Design
www.frontdesign.se

Ghost table
Decorative tabletop using DuPont patented SentryGlas Expressions interlayer
Samuele Mazza
www.samuelemazza.com

Shuffle Door
A door with a secret
Marjet Wessels Boer
www.marjetwessels boer.com

Linea and Corso
Fluorescent wallpapers made with luminescent pigments
Gruppe RE
www.gruppe-re.de

Design by Reflection
Vase with a permanent reflection in its glaze
Front Design
www.frontdesign.se

Bookshelf
Developed as a prototype for VIA
Philippe Nigro
www.via.fr

Curtain of Light
Fibre optics and LEDs embedded in polyester textile
Developed as a prototype for VIA
Clementine Chambon
www.via.fr

Ross Lovegrove's staircase (see page 329) was developed for his own studio. It is an iconic design and represents both his fascination with the organic and his experimental use of materials; he is in the process of researching ways of remodelling it to manufacture the product for commercial applications. Marcel Wanders's 'Can of Gold' is included. It does still exist in the marketplace, and although there are only a few remaining, it is important because it is more than just a designed item – it is also an act of social activism, linking the art world, the consumer and the local homeless (see page 339).

Emmanuel Babled's 'Joker Lounge' series (see page 35) was never produced, Marcel Wanders's 'Fish Net Chair' (see page 52) was taken out of production and Natanel Gluska's work (see page 53) is individually created by chainsaw, but all of these designers would make the items to order. Constantin and Laurene Leon Boym's 'Salvation Ceramics' (see page 174) was discontinued by Moooi, but there are a dozen or so sets still available and there is a plan to make special editions.

I have allowed myself the indulgence of including Denis Santachiara's 'Mister Tesla' (see page 260) because it is such an innovative concept and I wanted a reason to include a short commentary on his work. There are items of his in this book that are in production, but this light sculpture visually represents the spirit of the man. Joris Laarman's concrete radiator is featured (see page 334) because if it is not in production it should be, and it also gave rise to a new typology – the 'designed' radiator. However, the vast majority of designs you will look at here are waiting for you to buy them. There are actually over 1000, so I hope the odd 'cheat' will only help to whet your appetite.

For reasons of availability, and to keep the book as fresh as possible, of the 1000-plus products illustrated, more than half are designs from the twelve months before the book went to print; the remaining items are balanced to the more recent, and only iconic pieces date from as far back as 2000. There are bound to be omissions, and for those I apologize.

Tables and Chairs

Table, Snow
Nendo
Plywood, glass
H: 30cm (11 ¾in)
W: 70cm (27 ½in)
D: 125cm (49in)
Swedese Möbler
AB, Sweden
www.swedese.se

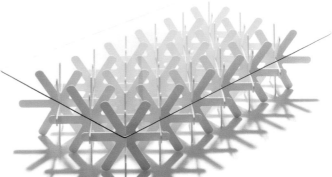

**Coffee table,
Fresh Fat**
Tom Dixon
Extruded woven plastic
H: 43cm (16 ⅞in)
W: 56cm (22in)
L: 90cm (35in)
Tom Dixon, UK
www.tomdixon.net

Tom Dixon's **'Fresh Fat'** table was born from an experiment he carried out for the Milan Furniture Fair 2001, when he collaborated with Domus to create an installation that involved both performance art and instant creativity. Set against the ornate backdrop of the deconsecrated church of San Paolo Converso, Dixon's plastic extrusion machine was visited by a host of designers, all of whom produced extraordinary feats of plastic engineering from the spaghetti-like strands of hot, fresh, fat polymer strands the machine pumped out. Tom's table was created by the same process. The malleable material hardens almost immediately, so that the design is created instantaneously, each design being slightly different from the others. The Provista plastic takes on a glass-like clarity as it solidifies into extraordinary constructions. Each unique and precious object is made to order, and challenges the preconception of plastic as a throwaway material.

Table, 36-24-36
Studioilse
MDF, turned
rubberwood,
polyurethane lacquer
W: 90cm (35in)
L: 260cm (102in)
Ferrious, UK
www.ferrious.com
www.studioilse.com

Table, Surf series
Carlo Colombo
MDF, polyurethane
H: 75cm (29 ½in)
W: 160, 180, 200 or 220cm
(63, 71, 79 or 87in)
D: 100, 105, 115 or 120cm
(39, 41, 45 or 47in)
Zanotta SpA, Italy
www.zanotta.it

Low table, Blade
Christian Ghion
Corian ®
H: 35cm (13 ³/₄in)
W: 42cm (16 ¹/₂in)
L: 180cm (71in)
Christian Ghion, France
www.christianghion.com

Table, 4SPR
Jean Nouvel
Coach hide
H: 72cm (28 ³/₈in)
W: 120cm (47in)
D: 60cm (23 ⁵/₈in)
Matteograssi, Italy
www.matteograssi.it

Table, Digitable
Patricia Urquiola
Water jet drilled bleach
H: 42cm (16 ¹/₂in)
W: 43cm (16 ⁷/₈in)
D: 38.5cm (15 ³/₈in)
B&B Italia SpA, Italy
www.bebitalia.it

Tables, I Was Here
Jason Miller
Recycled plastic lumber
H: 43–46cm
(16 ⁷/₈–18 ¹/₈in)
W: 51–56cm
(20 ¹/₈–22in)
L: 51–56cm
(20 ¹/₈–22in)
Miller Studio, USA
www.millerstudio.us

Legalized graffiti:
'I Was Here' is a series
of small tables inscribed
with found scribblings.
The pieces are
constructed from plastic
lumber, a material made
from 100 per cent post-
consumer waste. The
graffiti is digitalized
and engraved into the
surface by a CNC
milling machine.

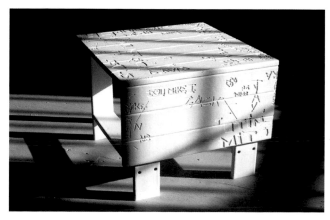

Table, PS
Garth Roberts
Chrome-plated metal,
leather
H: 39cm (15 3/8in)
Diam: 62cm (24 3/8in)
Fasem, Italy
www.fasem.it

**Above and right:
Table, Oval**
Tord Boontje
Powder-coated steel
H: 76cm (29 7/8in)
W: 220cm (87in)
D: 126cm (50in)
Moroso SpA, Italy
www.moroso.it

Table, Lebeau
Patrick Jouin
Stainless steel,
sandblasted glass,
polyurethane
H: 75cm (29 1/2in)
Diam: 140 or 160cm
(55 1/8 or 63in)
Cassina SpA, Italy
www.cassina.com

**Side table, T-table
series**
Patricia Urquiola
PMMA
Various dimensions
Kartell SpA, Italy
www.kartell.it

Table, Big Bombo
Stefano Giovannoni
Polyurethane leg and
top, stamped steel base
H: 76cm (29 7/8in)
W: 110cm (43in)
L: 170cm (67in)
Magis SpA, Italy
www.magisdesign.com

Stefano Giovannoni

Which of your designs to date would you like to be remembered by?
Whoever knows me knows me as the father of many different products, such as the 'Girotondo' family, the 'Mami' pots, the 'Bombo' stool, the 'Merdolino', 'Cico', the 'Magic Bunny', the 'Mary Biscuit', and so on. How could I choose one of them to represent me?

How do you think others view your work?
I have always been seen as the designer of 'funny' ironic products because those kinds of objects were so radical and innovative when they came out that they immediately became both cult products and bestsellers. Other people say I am the most marketable designer (first of all my clients). Alberto Alessi in an interview once referred to me as 'the champion of super and popular' because I have managed to bridge the gap between elitist design and design for the mass market, reaching the broadest audience. Andrea Branzi wrote 'Giovannoni's signs belong to the people, but their origin is certainly very sophisticated and part of the kind of modernity that believes that it is the future that works to better the present, and not vice versa.' Alessandro Mendini said that my 'neo-pop attitude transforms the contemporary world in a kind of hyper-realistic world characteristic of virtuality, managing a matter like design that from a rhetoric discipline has become a liberating process.' What I think is that I bypassed the culture of design, moving to a new culture related to mass consumption and communication, filtering the popular culture and the taste of the common people. This is the reason why I have designed a larger number of bestsellers than any other designer, but the official culture of design cannot tolerate it and considers my work to be on the border of the design context.

Which designer has influenced you the most and why?
My maestro was Remo Buti; thirty years ago he was a real conceptual and minimalist architect and designer, not so well known but so important for everybody who met him! During the 1980s I collaborated with the big masters: Ettore Sottsass, Alessandro Mendini and Andrea Branzi; of course I consider them so important for our design culture, they were so charismatic! But the strongest influence on my design approach came from reading Jean Boudrillard's essays about the consumer society and the concept of merchandise.

If you were not a designer, what would you like to be and why?
If I were not a designer I would have two options: to be a cook or a fisherman. Or both. Because I like fish, I like to fish and I like to cook fish.

What role do you think the designer has in society today?
The most important role for a designer is economic. I think my main task as an industrial designer should be to create products that will be successful for myself and for the company I work with, and that contribute positively to the economy of my country. I have always thought that the quality of a product is directly proportional to the appeal of the product itself on the market, and I always verify this through the concrete results, achieving clear parameters of evaluation. Still, there are a lot of designers and architects who prefer to discuss what is nice and what is not, teaching the customers what they should desire.

Do you buy a lot of design pieces?
In my home I have several wonderful pieces from the Bharata Collection by Ettore Sottsass; the big 'On the rocks' sofa by Edra; many lamps by Marcel Wanders for Cappellini; a couple of pieces by Johanna Grawunder; the Alessandro Mendini 'Proust' chair of the 1970s; a sofa-bed by Magistretti; a group of products from the 1960s like the 'Mies' armchair of Archizoom; Marco Zanuso's mirrored television cube by Brionvega; a couple of lamps by Castiglioni and 'Il pratone'. I definitely have many design objects in my house, but I also have some old Chinese furniture, a big table carved by hand from a single tree, some Indian, Moroccan and Japanese objects, and of course many products for the table and for the kitchen, and some furniture designed by my wife and myself and custom-made for the house. I very much enjoy mixing objects from different periods and cultures.

Is there a design in your home that you couldn't live without?
My sons are absolutely the best products I did, and the only ones I couldn't live without!

Where do you think design is heading? Is there someone we should be watching out for?
There is an important new element that probably will change the design context a lot in the next future. Design has in the past been confined to a very small territory with very special items strictly connected to furniture but isolated from mass production and big distribution. From the moment that the big international companies, especially those in the consumer electronics business, needed to specialize the image of their products according to new consumer categories, they started to work more and more intensely with designers. Currently the decreasing cost of Chinese production is pushing the big distribution towards design. Design will become the important added value and the element that differentiates the companies operating in big distribution from the lower end of the market dominated by Chinese companies.

In the near future design will probably be more and more connected with mass production and big distribution. I have always wanted to design for the supermarkets but never succeeded in doing so before the last two years. In a moment where design companies have increasing economic problems, 80 per cent of my new clients in the last year came from big distribution and big international companies. I think we have reached a very significant turning point representing a new context for design.

Is the cult of the personality taking over the design world?
In the last years the designer on the top of the wave has been burnt within the next six months. I think it might be better to stay a little bit away from the big waves!

Table, Bieder
Emaf Progetti
MDF
H: 74cm (29 ⅛in)
Diam: 100, 115 or 128cm
(39, 45 or 50in)
Zanotta SpA, Italy
www.zanotta.it

Coffee table, Acca
Tom Kühne
Steel
H: 46cm (18 ⅛in)
W: 43cm (16 ⅞in)
D: 36cm (14 ⅛in)
Zanotta SpA, Italy
www.zanotta.it

Container Table
Marcel Wanders
Thermosetting resins
reinforced with wood
fibre, polyurethane
H: 70cm (27 ½in)
Diam: 30 or 56cm
(11 ¾ or 22in)
Moooi, the Netherlands
www.moooi.nl

Table, Flare
Marcel Wanders
Injection-moulded ABS
legs, HPL laminate top
H: 76cm (29 ⅞in)
W: 80cm (31in)
L: 160 or 80cm
(63 or 31in)
Magis SpA, Italy
www.magisdesign.com

Low table, Hub
Piero Lissoni
Glass
H: 35cm or 40cm
(13 ³⁄₄in or 15 ³⁄₄in)
Diam: 50cm (19 ⁵⁄₈in)
Glas Italia, Italy
www.glasitalia.com

Table, ill_bill
Kijode (Kai, Johannes,
Denise)
Rigid foamed plastic
slab, varnished
W: 80 or 100cm
(31 or 39in)
L: 140 or 220cm
(55 or 87in)
Kijode®, Austria
www.kijode.com

Dining table
Matthew Sindall
Satinated steel,
metacrilate
H: 79cm (31 ¹⁄₈in)
W: 200cm (78 ³⁄₄in)
D: 100cm (39 ³⁄₈in)
Sawaya & Moroni, Italy
www.sawayamoroni.it

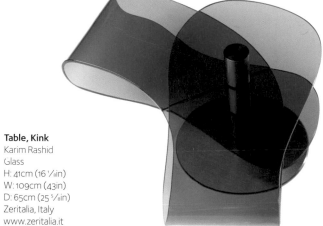

Table, Kink
Karim Rashid
Glass
H: 41cm (16 ¹⁄₈in)
W: 109cm (43in)
D: 65cm (25 ⁵⁄₈in)
Zeritalia, Italy
www.zeritalia.it

Coffee table, Layers
Rodolfo Dordoni
Smoked curved glass
H: 45cm (17 ³/₄in)
W: 120cm (47in)
D: 120cm (47in)
Fiam Italia SpA, Italy
www.fiamitalia.it

Table, Gahan
Eero Koivisto
Oak wood
H: 70cm (27 ¹/₂in)
W: 90cm (35in)
L: 200 or 250cm
(79 or 98in)
David design, Sweden
www.daviddesign.se

Claesson, Koivisto and Rune

Which of your designs to date would you like to be remembered by?
'Pebbles' by Cappellini .

How do you think others view your work?
Maybe as contemporary Scandinavian?

Which designer has influenced you the most and why?
Achille Castiglioni. Spiritual, idea-based and beautiful.

If you were not a designer, what would you like to be and why?
Musicians or chefs. Seems fun.

What role do you think the designer has in society today?
Interpreter of changes in society.

Do you buy a lot of design pieces?
Not really.

Is there a design in your home that you couldn't live without?
Apple Powerbook.

What do you consider to be the best piece of design since the millennium?
The iPod.

Where do you think design is heading? Is there someone we should be watching out for?
More human, less ironic. Naoto Fukasawa.

Is the cult of the personality taking over the design world?
No.

Coffee table, Basilia
Eero Koivisto and
Ola Rune
Laminated plywood
H: 28cm (11in)
W: 100–120cm
(39 ³/₈–47 ¹/₄in)
L: 100–120cm
(39 ³/₈–47 ¹/₄in)
Swedese Möbler AB,
Sweden
www.swedese.com

Table, MY 082
Michael Young
Injection-moulded
polypropylene,
chromed steel, MDF
H: 70.5cm (28in)
W: 140 or 180cm
(55 or 71in)
D: 75 or 80cm
(29 ½ or 31in)
Magis SpA, Italy
www.magisdesign.com

Table, Ipsilon
Raul Barbieri
Aluminium, fabric
H: 74cm (29 ⅛in)
W: 150cm (59in)
D: 85cm (33in)
Ycami SpA, Italy
www.ycami.com

**Table, bench and
ancillary top, CU**
Monica Graffeo
Moulded rigid
polyurethane with low-
density internal core
Various dimensions
Kristalia srl, Italy
www.kristalia.it

Side table, Toki
Setsu and Shinobu Ito
Float glass
H: 60cm (23 ⅝in)
W: 52cm (20 ½in)
D: 43cm (16 ⅞in)
Fiam Italia SpA, Italy
www.fiamitalia.it

**Set of coffee/side
tables, The Twins**
Gary van Broekhoven
Bent plywood, various
finishes
Each,
H: 40cm (15 ¾in)
W: 64cm (25 ¼in)
D: 40cm (15 ¾in)
GVB Ltd, UK
www.gvb-uk.com

Modular table system with embedded chair, Birth
Aziz Sariyer
Wood or compact laminate
H: 72cm (28 ³/₈in)
Derin, Turkey
www.derindesign.com

The **'Birth' table** is a modular chair and table system. Eight chairs fit closely into eight individual compartments that can be used separately or fitted together in various configurations.

Coffee table, Flatpack Furniture
Maarten Baas
Wood, glass
H: 40cm (15 ³/₄in)
Diam: 110cm (43in)
Maarten Baas,
the Netherlands
www.maartenbaas.com

Maarten Baas's **'Flatpack'** table is a more refined example of the exercise in reclamation he began with the 'Hey, chair, be a bookshelf!' in development since 2001 (see page 116). In his earlier work assorted pieces of rubbish were gathered and given new life by adding an epoxy resin coating and re-forming them into a functioning piece of furniture. With 'Flat Pack', disassembled flat-pack IKEA furniture has been given a similar treatment.

Table, Kino
Christian Ghion
Dacryl PMMA
H: 51cm (20in)
W: 42cm (16 ¹/₂in)
D: 42cm (16 ¹/₂in)
Sawaya & Moroni, Italy
www.sawayamoroni.it

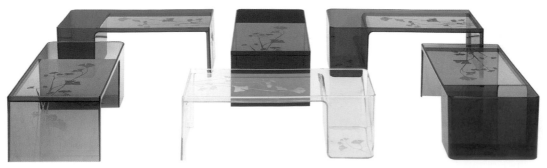

Side table and magazine holder, Usame
Patricia Urquiola
PMMA polymethyl methacrylate
H: 30cm (11 ³/₄in)
W: 85cm (33in)
D: 40cm (15 ³/₄in)
Kartell SpA, Italy
www.kartell.it

We are living in a world of increasing globalization and the breaking down of economic, cultural and artistic barriers. This may be good for us in terms of transcending and integrating the world's major economic regions through global finance, industry, communication and international migration, but there is bound to be a backlash when we are faced with diminishing self-determination and the loss of national identity. Politically we are beginning to recognize it in the post-9/11 condemnation of America's high-handed attitudes and actions, the threat of international terrorism and the rejection of the proposed new European Union constitution in both France and the Netherlands. Culturally, a critique is evident in the increasing importance internationally of recognizable national schools of cinema, literature, art and crafts. In the design world, the boundaries may be blurring in countries with a well-developed design consciousness and manufacturing industry. However, there is a growing popularity in the importance of those nations that have not previously enjoyed a defined design culture and where designers are now building up their own language through experimentation, conceptual design and a combination of a low-tech aesthetic with high-tech production methods.

Another attempt to assert a sense of **national identity** is visible in the trend of using recognizable topographical imagery in design. This book features rugs with city motifs – Harry Allen's New York street map (see page 214) and Hive's 'Cityscape' carpet (see page 206). Karim Rashid has produced interconnecting tableware with an Istanbul skyline (see page 176) and Timorous Beasties gave us their Glasgow and London toiles (see page 230). In 2005 Edra decided to show two pieces of furniture separately from their main collection. Both the Campanas' 'Brasilia Table' and Ezri Tarazi's 'New Baghdad Table' take as their theme capital cities. The first is a chaotic assemblage of splintered Reflex, each one different from the other. The Campanas have long been interested in fragmentation, and their work on Brasilia symbolizes the multi-faceted concentration of humanity in their native country, and also denotes the hard stones on

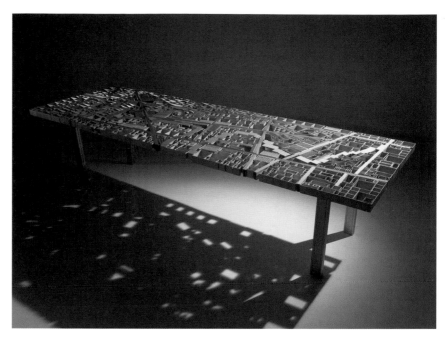

which Brasilia is built; rocks that are meant to have magical powers and still today attract esoteric communities to the area. The 'New Baghdad Table' (surely a political statement, conceived as it is by an Israeli designer) is constructed from many individual industrial aluminium profiles, which make up a map of the city with the River Tigris running through it. Each piece has its own identity, but together they make a cohesive plan out of diversity. Tables represent the ritual dimension of hospitality, while the use of fragments sends the message that out of chaos can come harmony and peace.

Table, New Baghdad
Ezri Tarazi
Aluminium
Various dimensions
Edra SpA, Italy
www.edra.com

Table, Brasilia
Fernando and
Humberto Campana
Reflex
Various dimensions
Edra SpA, Italy
www.edra.com

Table, A table with a drinking problem
Laurens van Wieringen
PU, steel
H: 74.5cm (29 ⅛in)
W: 80cm (31in)
D: 80cm (31in)
Studio Laurens van
Wieringen,
the Netherlands
www.laurensvan
wieringen.nl

Coffee table, Acca II
Christoph Böninger
Chromium-plated steel,
American walnut or
ash veneer
H: 50cm (19 ⁵/₈in)
W: 125cm (49in)
D: 102cm (40in)
ClassiCon GmbH,
Germany
www.classicon.com

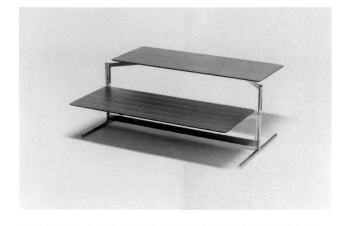

**Table with two levels,
Wogg 32 Level Two**
Atelier Oï
Chrome, honeycomb
alucore
H: 51 and 73cm
or 43 and 73cm
(20 ¹/₈ and 28 ³/₄in
or 16 ⁷/₈ and 28 ³/₄in)
Diam: 100 or 120cm
(39 or 47in)
Wogg AG, Switzerland
www.wogg.ch

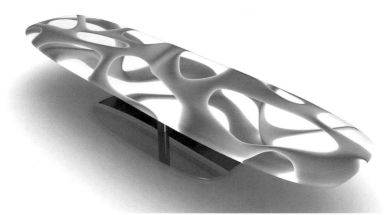

Table, Bac
Jasper Morrison
Oak, grey oak or Santos
H: 72.2cm (28 ³/₈in)
W: 240cm (94in)
D: 85cm (33in)
Cap Design SpA, Italy
www.cappellini.it

Low table, Blade
Christian Ghion
Corian®
H: 34cm (13 ³/₈in)
W: 180cm (71in)
D: 45cm (17 ³/₄in)
Créa Diffusion, France
www.christianghion.com

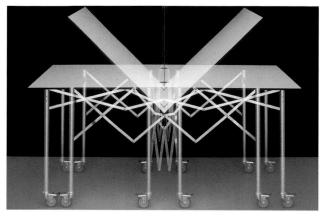

**Folding table,
Scissor table, Alu 1**
Benjamin Thut
Synthetic resin,
refined steel
W: 80cm (31 ½in)
L: 160cm (63in)
Sele 2, Switzerland
www.sele2.ch

**Side table,
O Livro Mesa**
Miguel Vieira Baptista
Cardboard, fabric, glass
H: 40cm (15 ¾in)
Diam: 40cm (15 ¾in)
Miguel Vieira Baptista,
Portugal
www.mvbfactory.com

A successful symbiosis
of the conceptual with
the functional, this little
reading table, '**O Livro
Mesa**', reappropriates
the book, using it as a
recognizable support.
The content is
temporarily abandoned
whilst the memory of
the original remains.

Table, Pallas
Konstantin Grcic
Powder-coated metal
H: 72cm (28 ¾in)
W: 75cm (29 ½in)
L: 240cm (94in)
ClassiCon GmbH,
Germany
www.classicon.com

Konstantin Grcic makes an interesting analogy
between bullfighting and design. Each, he says, is a
strict formal process with very firm rules, yet just as
the bull has to be killed within fifteen minutes and
a design has to have a final outcome, the process
involved in the successful culmination of each is
fraught with unforeseeable obstacles that have to
be adjusted for, and reacted to. It is this element of
chance that he finds both exciting and rewarding.
'It is always the risk, the not knowing, the adventure
that attracts me as a designer.' All his designs come
from orders. At the start of a project he likes to be
left alone, quietly working out how best to fulfil the
client's brief, conceptually developing ideas with a
minimum of visual and technical assistance – 'getting
to grips with how things are manufactured and how
they function is the wellspring of my creativity'.

Konstantin started his career at the Academie
Oskar Kokoschka in Salzburg, where he became
interested in carpentry and cabinet making. He
followed this up with a period at the Parnham College
in Dorset, UK before taking a Master's degree at the
Royal College in London. His earlier works all share a
rationalist design language, but more recently he has
become interested in experimenting with computer-
design software that has resulted in products with
more fluid forms. For the 'Stool_One' and 'Chair_One',
both manufactured by Magis (see pages 43 and 64),
Grcic deliberately set out to create a strange form in
die-cast aluminium, a material new for both him and
Magis at the time; the graphic end product grew from
an investigation of flat planes and angles built up into
3D form. Grcic likes to reduce all his designs to the
basics, reassembling them in intriguing and innovative
ways. 'Pallas' found its beginnings in the aesthetics
of the Citroën DS car. Reduced to its three basics,
two trestle-like uprights and a board in-between,
it is a reworking of a typology that fascinates Grcic.
Tables are important to him. They have strong
anthropological meaning: they are objects around
which we communicate, from which we eat and,
according to Grcic, on which we can sleep if
absolutely necessary.

Software dynamically generating tables, Breeding Table
Clemens Weisshaar
and Reed Kram
Steel ST37, laser cut
and powder coated
Various dimensions
Moroso SpA, Italy
www.moroso.it

One of the more interesting exhibitions during the 2005 Designmai in Berlin was a group show on the work of the young German designers who have made such an impact on the design world over recent years. The show was successful in bringing out some of the features that characterize much of their output: the importance of new technologies and materials, the search for a modern German identity, a current re-examination of minimalism, and the design of objects for mass production. Works by Konstantin Grcic, Jerszy Seymour, Vogt and Weizenegger, Werner Aisslinger and Re Design all illustrate these trends, but it is probably in the 'Breeding Tables' by **Kram and Weisshaar** where many of these factors overlap.

Kram and Weisshaar's backgrounds are very different. Kram, born in Ohio, specializes in media design, having cut his teeth designing video games before co-founding the Aesthetics and Computation Group led by John Meada. Weisshaar's background is in product design and he was assistant to Konstantin Grcic before setting up his own company. Their studio was founded in 2002, yet the duo work in different cities (Stockholm and Munich respectively), and

collaborate by means of frequent meetings and the latest communication technology. They like the idea of a two-centre office because it allows them to build up more contacts, experiences and potential for growth.

The 'Breeding Table' project came out of the designers' disillusionment on having walked around the Milan Furniture Fair in 2002 and seeing that design was moribund. With their varying backgrounds and expertise in IT and advanced technological manufacturing methods, they were disappointed that not enough companies were harnessing these two very important developments to produce something completely different. On their return from the fair, they started to look at different computer programs, experimenting with algorithmic modelling to produce subtle repeats of a table shape. The couple are often quoted as describing the computer and software they use (Rhino – much beloved of industrial designers) as their 'digital sweatshop'. From the information it is given, it churns out hundreds of unimaginable designs that the duo then select, construct on laser-cutting and steel-bending machines, and pass on to highly trained technicians to finish by hand. Their intention is

to prove that mass-manufacture and craftsmanship can co-exist, which they believe is the only way that the European design industry will be able to compete with the threat from the production lines of the Far East.

Kram and Weisshaar are not alone in their desire to combine personalization with mass production. Ron Arad (see page 40) and Ross Lovegrove (see page 329) have long worked with stereolithography. Patrick Jouin is also experimenting in this field (see page 68). Marcel Wanders's 'Snotty' vases for Cap Design trace the trajectory of a sneeze digitally and re-create it industrially (see page 198 for full explanation), and each item of Gaetano Pesce's 'Nobody's Perfect' range of resin furniture for Zerodisegno (see page 56) is unique, although mass-produced. What differentiates Kram and Weisshaar, however, is their total examination of the design process from concept to realization: from how to get the most out of a digitized cutting machine normally used merely for repetitions, to the eventual effect tapping into such a manufacturing potential will have on the future design economy. I think we will be hearing a lot more from this resourceful pair.

Table, Arc
Ashley Hall,
Matthew Kavanagh
Aluminium tube frame,
float glass top with
methacrylate supports
H: 75cm (29 ½in)
W: 178cm (70in)
D: 91cm (36in)
Zeritalia, Italy
www.zeritalia.it

Table, Tango series
Stefano Giovannoni
Frame in bent steel
plate, top in
tempered glass
Various dimensions
Magis SpA, Italy
www.magisdesign.com

Table, Keramik table range
Bruno Fattorini
Matt-lacquered aluminium, laminated porcelain, glass panel
Various dimensions
MDF Italia srl, Italy
www.mdfitalia.it

Table, Wood Table
Maarten Van Severen
Solid oak
H: 72.5cm (28 ³⁄₄in)
W: 200cm (79in)
D: 75cm (29 ¹⁄₂in)
Vitra, Switzerland
www.vitra.com

Table, La Grande Table
Xavier Lust
Anodized aluminium
H: 73cm (28 ³⁄₄in)
L (max.): 440cm (173in)
MDF Italia srl, Italy
www.mdfitalia.it

Table, Herbarium
Mats Theselius
Glass, lacquered steel
H: 73cm (28 ³⁄₄in)
L: 150cm (59in)
Källemo AB, Sweden
www.kallemo.se

Jasper Morrison

Which of your designs to date would you like to be remembered by?
I'd prefer to be remembered by the sum of the work rather than any one thing. I don't think I'm trying to achieve anything spectacular really – rather the opposite these days. I've decided to call it supernormal.

If you were not a designer, what would you like to be and why?
I'd like to be a postman, delivering by bicycle. I think that would be a nice life.

What role do you think the designer has in society today?
We should be the guardians of the man-made environment, along with architects and graphic designers. Unfortunately, design (in general) has taken another course and become a source of visual pollution, the collective effect of so many creative egos all trying to make a statement to be noticed by.

Do you buy a lot of design pieces?
I love well-designed things and I buy them whenever I see something good.

Is there a design in your home that you couldn't live without?
There are quite a few I'd be sad to lose, like my Dieter Rams shelving, 'Wegner' chair, some old wine glasses, a Castiglione desk from De Padova ...

Is the cult of the personality taking over the design world?
I think so, exaggerated by media coverage. It's a pity because better designer objects tend not to have too much ego attached to them. Unfortunately, design has become a big media subject and it sells a lot of expensive magazines. The media have very little interest in whether a design is useable or not. Instead, all their focus is on the 'look'. This distorts everyone's opinion into a parallel of the fashion world.

Rectangular table, ATM (Advanced Table Module)
Jasper Morrison
Powder-coated MDF, polished chrome tubular steel, powder-coated die-cast aluminium, nylon, plastic
H: 72–78cm (28 ³/₈–31in)
W: 90cm (35in)
L: 180cm (71in)
Vitra, Switzerland
www.vitra.com

Table, Simplon
Jasper Morrison
Anodized aluminium legs and polished lacquered oak top
H: 72cm (28 ³/₈in)
W: 90cm (35 ¹/₂in)
L: 200cm (78 ⁷/₈in)
Cap Design SpA, Italy
www.cappellini.it

TV unit, table and bookcase with doors, Simplon
Jasper Morrison
Aluminium shelves or case, anodized aluminium legs
TV unit,
H: 49cm (19 ¹/₄in)
W: 48cm (18 ⁷/₈in)
L: 80cm (31in);
Table,
H: 72cm (28 ³/₈in)
W: 90cm (35in)
L: 200cm (79in);
Bookcase with doors,
H: 78cm (31in)
W: 44cm (17 ³/₈in)
L: 240cm (94in)
Cap Design SpA, Italy
www.cappellini.it

Modular table system, Joyn
Ronan and Erwan Bouroullec
Powder-coated MDF, melamine-faced particleboard, powder-coated aluminium, powder-coated sheet shell, fabrics, leather, polyurethane, polypropylene
H: 72cm (28 ³⁄₈in)
W: 180cm (71in)
L: 440cm (173in)
Vitra, Switzerland
www.vitra.com

Although **Corian**, an advanced blend of mineral and pure acrylic polymer, was launched in 1966, it is only in recent years that it has been coming into its own as architects and designers increasingly turn to it to create furniture, lighting and interiors for a wide range of sectors. The new, complex design shapes now being produced by CAD programs are demanding increasingly more malleable materials. Corian appears to be the perfect answer to such demands: it can be worked into virtually any shape or design, whether a softly rounded ergonomic table or a long reception desk. The Bouroullec brothers have been especially innovative in their use of what they term a 'monochromatic monomaterial', sculpting vases, platters and mirrors out of the body of their 'Console with Mirror' and 'Console with Bowl' designs, both for Cap Design SpA.

Console with Mirror
Ronan and Erwan Bouroullec
Corian®
H: 80cm (31 ¹⁄₄in)
W: 200cm (78in)
D: 45cm (17 ¹⁄₄in)
Cap Design SpA, Italy
www.cappellini.it

Desk and office accessories, Più
Catharina Lorenz and Steffen Kaz, Lorenz*Kaz
Bent sheet metal
Various dimensions
Zoltan Gruppo De Padova, Italy
www.zoltan.it

Product desk, Scriba
Claudio Bellini
Anodized aluminium, Plexiglas
H: 87cm (34 ¹⁄₄in)
W: 155 or 185cm (61 or 72 ⁷⁄₈in)
D: 90cm (35 ³⁄₈in)
Ycami SpA, Italy
www.ycami.com

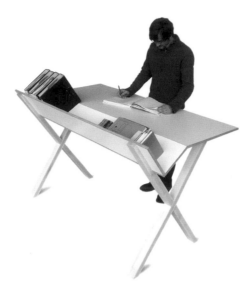

Office table, Kant
Patrick Frey and
Markus Boge
White foil-covered
beech plywood and
solid maple
H: 74 or 111cm
(29 1/8 or 44in)
W: 190cm (75in)
D: 105cm (41in)
Nils Holger Moormann
GmbH, Germany
www.moormann.de

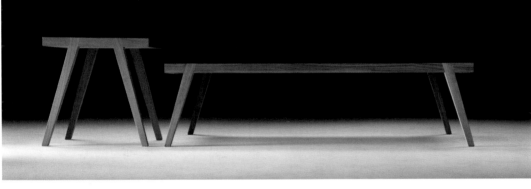

Tables, Artwood
Antonio Citterio
Solid wood
Various dimensions
Flexform SpA, Italy
www.flexform.it

**Retractable wall table,
Clino Once Again**
Mario Mazzer
Stainless steel tube
frame, white Werzalit
top
H: 103cm (41in)
W: 110cm (43in)
D (closed): 10cm (3 7/8in)
D (open): 76cm (29 7/8in)
Magis SpA, Italy
www.magisdesign.com

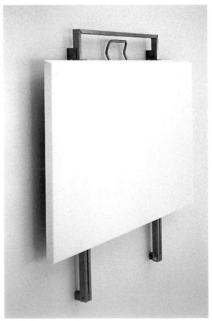

Table, Two Tops
Marcel Wanders
Solid oak, MDF with
oak veneer
H: 76cm (29 ⁷⁄₈in)
Secretary,
W: 120cm (47in)
D: 60cm (23 ⁵⁄₈in);
Table,
W: 90cm (35in)
D: 180, 220 or 260cm
(71, 87 or 102in)
Moooi, the Netherlands
www.moooi.com

When I first met **Marcel Wanders** during the Milan Furniture Fair 2003, it was with a view to sounding him out as a possible future guest editor for the *International Design Yearbook*. Immediately striking was his utter dedication to what he does and his passion to contribute objects that mean something in everyday life. He looks on his works as narratives: 'For me, designing revolves around this idea, around the fact that what I make means something to other people, around the notion that a design communicates.' For this reason, the objects and interiors he produces do not alienate. They are timeless and classical, but also innovative and surprising. As he likes to say: 'My designs are humorous but never a joke.' He likes to stretch archetypes to the limit, to give birth to the unexpected, yet he never slips into parody. His inventiveness lies in the way he manipulates materials (especially natural substances) and techniques, as well as the standard aesthetics we associate with certain objects. He recycles ideas and typologies and recreates the ordinary, but produces designs that

would not seem out of place in anyone's front room. When he was selecting for the *Yearbook* in 2004, his conversation often returned to his worry that today the West is too preoccupied with invention and does not value enough the lessons it has learned from the past. He believes that there are too many designers trying too hard to invent the new – products that may have an appeal for a season or two, but that in the end will be redundant, as 'nothing ages so quickly as something that looks too new'. Wanders is strongly of the opinion that the consumer likes variety but needs security. We like to be surprised, but we want to feel comfortable with the objects we choose to fill our environment.

In the end, designs have to be commercial, and it is the balance between the experimental and the saleable that informs much of Wanders's work and ensures his continuing success. Ironically, however, he recognizes an imbalance of these two factors in Dutch design generally, and considers this to be at the heart of the crisis in the design industry in the Netherlands

at the moment (see page 116). Wanders's design collaborative, Moooi, is the first step in addressing this problem. In control of both the design and the manufacturing process, it provides the opportunity to reconsider artistic aesthetics and produce objects in a realistic and industrial way. The company has also instigated a training programme to encourage younger designers to make items that can be mass produced while retaining a unique appearance. Marcel says: 'I want Moooi to be a business. I think that so many designers run their companies like artistic free places. I think in the end it won't grow, it won't reach a lot of people because it's an academic enterprise, where it's more done for the designers than the people.'

Writing for *Icon* magazine in April 2004, Alex Wiltshire summed up Marcel Wanders perfectly: 'Marcel Wanders is an inventive and highly original designer, but at the same time a theatrical marketing man and a practical business man with a conscience.'

Table, Frame table
Alberto Meda
Aluminium top, die-cast
aluminium alloy legs
H: 73.6cm (29 ¹⁄₈in)
L: 190cm (75in)
D: 95cm (37in)
Alias SpA, Italy
www.aliasdesign.it

Table, Sandra
Thomas Sandell
Oak, micro-lacquered
top
H: 72cm (28 ³⁄₈in)
W: 80cm (31in)
L: 180cm (71in)
Asplund, Sweden
www.asplund.org

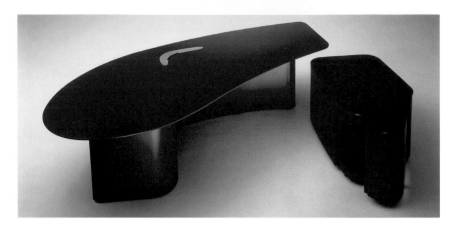

Executive workplace, MEG – Meda Executive Group
Alberto Meda
Powder-coated MDF, glass-fibred plastic, aluminium
H: 72cm (28³/₈in)
W: 115cm (45in)
L: 260cm (102in)
Vitra, Switzerland
www.vitra.com

Table, Pigreco
Emmanuel Babled
Polyurethane, solid oak, steel
H: 74cm (29¹/₈in)
W: 92cm (36in)
L: 200cm (79in)
Felicerossi srl, Italy
www.felicerossi.it

Chair, YU
Setsu and Shinobu Ito
Rotationally moulded polyethylene
H: 72cm (28³/₈in)
W: 58cm (22⁷/₈in)
D: 55cm (21⁵/₈in)
Felicerossi srl, Italy
www.felicerossi.it

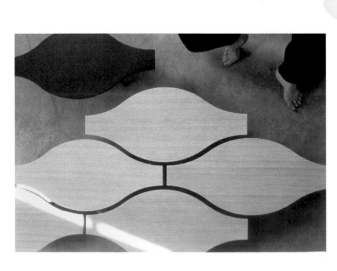

Coffee table, Grande Foglia
Marco Romanelli and Marta Laudani
Oak plywood top and epoxy powder-coated iron or aluminium frame
H: 18cm (7¹/₈in)
W: 54cm (21¹/₄in)
D: 38cm (15in)
Montina srl, Italy
www.montina.it

Seating, Easy Rider
Danny Venlet
In section-moulded
frame in EPS, covered
with 3D knitted fabrics
H: 74.5cm (29 ¹/₂in)
Diam: 120cm (47in)
Bulo, Belgium
www.bulo.com

**Mobile table-seating
combination, PicNik**
Dirk Wynants,
Xavier Lust
Aluminium
H: 74.5cm (29 ¹/₂in)
H (seat): 43.5cm (17 ³/₈in)
W: 147cm (58in)
D: 92cm (36in)
Extremis, Belgium
www.extremis.be

**Mobile table-seating
combination, DoNuts**
Dirk Wynants
Rubber, nylon, polyester
H: 75cm (29 ¹/₂in)
Diam: 190cm (75in)
Extremis, Belgium
www.extremis.be

**Swivelling media
auditorium chair, Alfa**
Jouni Leino
Formed birch plywood,
epoxy-coated tubular
steel, upholstery
H: 85cm (33in)
W: 44cm (17 ³/₈in)
D (seat): 54cm (21 ¹/₄in)
Diam: 100cm (39in)
Avarte Oy, Finland
www.avarte.it

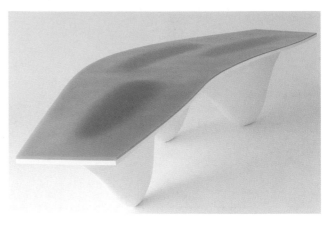

Writing desk with drawer and concealed light, Writing Desk
Michael Young
Die-cut aluminium, wood, felt, Bakelite
H: 115cm (45in)
H (desk): 75.5cm (29 7/8in)
W: 160cm (63in)
D: 68cm (26 3/4in)
Established & Sons, UK
www.established
andsons.com

One of the most exciting shows offsite during the Milan Furniture Fair 2005 was the debut exhibition of a new British furniture-design and manufacturing company, **Established & Sons**. Founded by a team of people who, through various backgrounds, all have strong connections to the design world, it has a healthy chance of surviving in a very competitive market. Alasdhair Willis (CEO) has been working in design marketing and brand strategy for many years, first as publisher of *Wallpaper** magazine, and later as head of his own creative consultancy with clients such as Adidas and Estée Lauder. Mark Holmes (design director) is a designer in his own right, having collaborated with e15, among others, while Sebastian Wrong (operations director) was head of his own manufacturing company before chancing his arm at entrepreneurship. The team is bound to get its marketing and PR well organized under the capable hands of Tamara Caspersz, who was manager of the London-based contemporary furniture trade showrooms Viaduct. Together they envisioned a company that would produce and sell objects created by the best of British talent, in a range of prices, and financially supported by the best of British manufacturing. Their backer, Angad Paul, is

director of the Caparo Group, which specializes in steel and engineering products and already had a network of factories based throughout the Midlands, as well as plants in North America and India.

For their first collection, Established & Sons approached Barber Osgerby, Future Systems (see page 86), Zaha Hadid, Mark Holmes, Michael Marriott (see page 121), Alexander Taylor (see page 270), Sebastian Wrong and Michael Young, who all immediately, as a vote of confidence, agreed to collaborate. The line mixes sophistication alongside the utilitarian, spectacular with the minimal and avant-garde with high-street collectibles. The name of the company was cleverly conceived to recall the heyday of British manufacturing, and to differentiate from the one-name brands such as Edra and Cassina. It also highlights the fact that the company plan to use both recognized designers and up-coming talent, a fact emphasized by the logo, which mixes historical and contemporary fonts with an elaborate and old-fashioned ampersand.

Dining/conference table, Aqua Table
Zaha Hadid
Laminated polyurethane resin, silicon
H: 85cm (33in)
W: 250cm (98in)
D: 150cm (59in)
Established & Sons, UK
www.established
andsons.com

Stacking chair, Pinch
Mark Holmes
Aluminium frame, leather/fabric upholstered ply
H: 80cm (31in)
W: 45cm (17 3/4in)
D: 45cm (17 3/4in)
Established & Sons, UK
www.established
andsons.com

Low table, Zero-in
Barber Osgerby
Pressed aluminium, glass
H: 35 or 40cm
(13 3/4 or 15 3/4in)
D: 90 or 120cm
(35 or 47in)
L: 90 or 120cm
(35 or 47in)
Established & Sons, UK
www.established
andsons.com

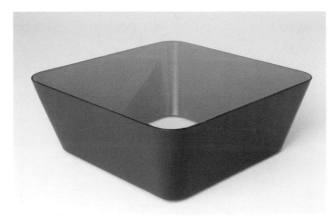

Seating collection, TT
Alfredo Häberli
Polyurethane, fabric
Chair,
H: 98cm (39in)
W: 71cm (28in)
D: 71cm (28in)
Alias SpA, Italy
www.aliasdesign.it

Table, Table#2
Fredrikson Stallard
Birch, steel
H: 40cm (15 ¾in)
Diam: 45cm (17 ¾in)
Limited batch production,
Fredrikson Stallard, UK
www.fredriksonstallard.com

Series of tables and chairs, Hex Family
Marc Newson
Die-cast aluminium,
beech plywood
Various dimensions
Magis SpA, Italy
www.magisdesign.com

Stool/table, Plank
Thomas Heatherwick
Wood
H: 40cm (15 ¾in)
W: 51cm (20 ⅛in)
D: 46cm (18 ⅛in)
Benchmark Furniture,
UK
www.benchmark-
furniture.com

**Series of furniture,
New Antiques**
Marcel Wanders
Lacquered wood
Chair,
H: 78cm (31in)
W: 48cm (18 ⁷⁄₈in)
D: 47cm (18 ¹⁄₂in)
Cap Design SpA, Italy
www.cappellini.it

**Table unit with 12
seats, X.12**
Franco Poli
Ash, wool-fabric
H: 75cm (29 ¹⁄₂in)
W: 308cm (121in)
D: 108cm (43in)
Bernini SpA, Italy
www.bernini.it

**Seat with built-in
desk, Solitaire**
Alfredo Häberli
Wood, cold foam with
flame fibre, fabric,
chrome lacquer
H: 71cm (28 in)
W: 93cm (36 ⁵⁄₈in)
D: 62cm (24 ³⁄₈in)
OFFECCT, Sweden
www.offecct.se

Seating, Osorom
Konstantin Grcic
Multi-layered
technopolymer
composite
Diam: 120cm (47in)
Moroso SpA, Italy
www.moroso.it

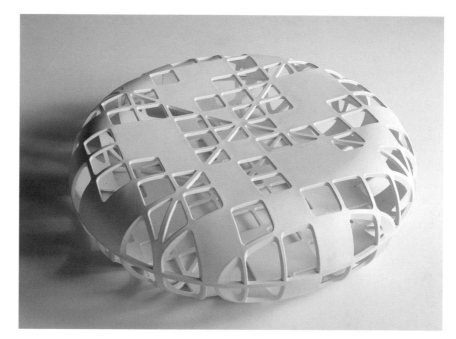

Konstantin Grcic

Which of your designs to date would you like to be remembered by?

Naturally I'd think that my more recent pieces would represent me best, like 'Chair_One' (Magis) or 'Miura' (Plank). But then there are older projects, like 'MAYDAY' (Flos) or my glasses for Iittala, which have been milestones in my career. I find it hard to extract singular items from the whole body of work. All of it is part of a larger meta-project – including the failures.

How do you think others view your work?

It always amazes me when people say that they can recognize certain handwriting or a recurring gesture in my work. The most common attribute that people see in my work is that of simplicity and rigour. It surprises me that the work comes across so clear and seemingly evident, since the process of designing it is rather difficult and unclear.

Which designer has influenced you the most and why?

There have been so many – and I still continue to be inspired by a lot of other designers. There are the 'larger than life' ones, like Joe Colombo, Achille Castiglioni, Ettore Sottsass, Dieter Rams and Philippe Starck. And then there are the 'life-size' ones, designers who I know personally, designers I collaborate with, friends. I guess I have always been influenced by both types. If I have to name just one it has to be Jasper Morrison. He was the first real

designer I met (when I was still a student), which means that I have known him for all my professional life. Jasper is important to me, because he taught me to think before designing. His work is always driven by the intelligence of how he approaches a project.

What role do you think the designer has in society today?

This question shouldn't really be discussed from within the design world. Our perspective tends to slightly overrate the importance of what design is. Anyway, as designers we create products which become part of people's lives. So I guess our role is definitively very close to society. Ideally, design should be adding quality to life – often, though, quite the opposite is true!

Do you buy a lot of design pieces?

I don't buy a lot, because I generally don't care much about possessing things. However, if I buy an object or a piece of furniture my choice is usually for contemporary design. The last piece I bought was Philippe Starck's 'La Marie' chair (Kartell).

Is there a design in your home that you couldn't live without?

I have a small wooden chair that is a present from a friend, designer Mats Theselius. What makes the chair so special is that it is somehow shrunk to an awkwardly narrow proportion and painted beige with fake wood grain drawn on top. I love this chair and I would never trade it for any other.

What do you consider to be the best piece of design since the millennium?

Jean Nouvel's 'Less' table for Unifor is sensational. For me it is the table of all time.

Is there someone we should be watching out for?

Definitively Kram/Weisshaar and definitively Stefan Diez.

Is the cult of the personality taking over the design world?

In principle I think there is nothing wrong with it. Design is made by people for people. I am finding it relevant to talk not only about products, but also about the people who are behind the work. Star-cult may be an extreme, but I don't think it will ever threaten to take over the design world. In fact, I am really glad we have overcome those times when design was an anonymous industry that had recipes and rules. It's good that today's design world has real people with real attitude!

Joker Lounge range
Emmanuel Babled
Corian®
Game table,
H: 35cm (13 ³/₄in)
D: 150cm (59in);
Chair,
H: 45cm (17 ³/₄in)
W: 80cm (31in)
L: 90cm (35in);
Stool,
H: 28cm (11in)
D: 60cm (23 ⁵/₈in);
Lamp, H: 20cm (7 ⁷/₈in)
Diam: 100cm (39 ³/₈in)
Emmanuel Babled, Italy
www.babled.net

Stool, Corks
Jasper Morrison
Cork
Table,
H: 34cm (13 ³/₈in)
Diam: 32cm (12 ⁵/₈in);
Stool,
H: 25cm (9 ⁷/₈in)
Diam: 45cm (17 ³/₄in)
Moooi, the Netherlands
www.moooi.nl

Two chairs from Foomy Collection
Markus Benesch
EVA-foam
Various dimensions
Money for Milan,
Germany
www.moneyformilan.com

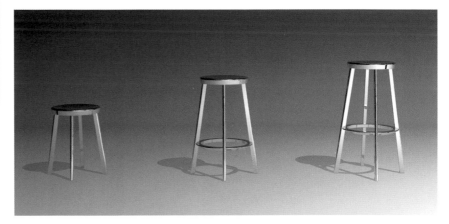

Stools, Déjà-vu series
Naoto Fukasawa
Aluminium
Various dimensions
Magis SpA, Italy
www.magisdesign.com

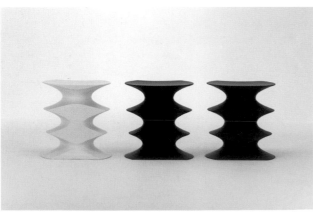

Seat, Hocker
Herzog and de Meuron
Multiple laminated
layers
H: 42cm (16 ¹/₂in)
W: 39.5cm (15 ³/₄in)
D: 30cm (11 ³/₄in)
Vitra, Switzerland
www.vitra.com

Armchair, Dora
Ludovica and Roberto
Palomba
Polyethylene
H: 74cm (29 1/8in)
W: 70cm (27 1/2in)
D: 63cm (24 3/8in)
Zanotta SpA, Italy
www.zanotta.it

Coffee table, Tod
Todd Bracher
Polypropylene
H: 52cm (20 1/2in)
W: 55cm (21 5/8in)
D: 43cm (16 7/8in)
Zanotta SpA, Italy
www.zanotta.it

Stool, 10 degrees
Morph
Rotationally moulded
polyethylene
H: 48cm (18 7/8in)
Diam: 42cm (16 1/2in)
Modus, UK
www.modusfurniture.co.uk

Seat, Pill
Jan Melis and
Ben Oostrum
Polyethylene foam,
rubber-like coating
H: 35cm (13 3/4in)
Diam: 60cm (23 5/8in)
MNO Design,
the Netherlands
www.mnodesign.nl

Stool, Qoffee
Rainer Spehl
Polyethylene
H: 47cm (18 ¹/₂in)
D: 35cm (13 ³/₄in)
Wydale Plastics, UK
www.rainerspehl.com

Seat, Pony
Eero Aarnio
Polyurethane foam,
steel tube
H: 70cm (27 ¹/₂in)
W: 60cm (23 ⁵/₈in)
L: 100 cm (39 ³/₈in)
Adelta, Germany
www.adelta.de

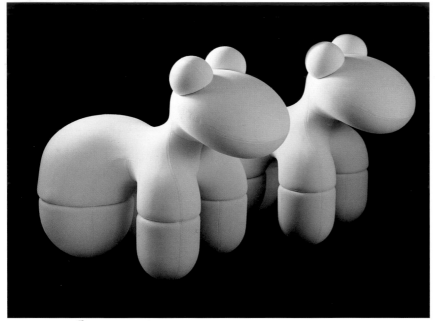

When I asked **Eero Aarnio** what role he would like to play as a designer in today's society, he replied, 'I play no "role" at all. When designing these items I have been very honest to myself. I'm transparent; my designs are like my signature, they can be executed only one way, my way. I have no fine explanations for my works; I just design items I like. To answer briefly, I love to create.'

Probably most famous for his hanging 'Bubble' chair of 1968, Aarnio was a pioneer in the use of plastics, which invaded the market during the mid-1960s, reigned supreme until the mid-1970s and are now enjoying renewed popularity. Plastic set designers free to make any shape and use any colour. The resulting creations were both fun and functional. Aarnio was born in Helsinki in 1932 and studied at the Institute of Industrial Arts. He became a household name following his collaboration with the Asko manufacturing company, who shared his vision that design means 'constant renewal, realignment and growth'. The organic form of the 'Globe' chair liberated Scandinavian design from its reputation for serene minimalist elegance. Here was a design that was fun and futuristic (the chair came complete with built-in telephone or stereo speakers), and summed up the swinging 1960s.

Today Aarnio works mainly for Adelta, who manufacture re-editions of the famous pieces as well as his new designs. The 'Pony' seat is a reissue of a 1970 classic, and is constructed in polyurethane foam. Aarnio comments, 'My cold-foamed designs get people to laugh and remember the best time of their childhood. They grow younger as they rediscover how funny and exciting it is to play. Inside every person there is still a little boy or girl who is curious and creative. I hope these designs will survive in the same way that blowing a soap bubble interests every new generation.'

Seat, Innovation C
Fredrik Mattson
Lacquered steel,
polyether foam, fabric
H: 75cm (29 ¹/₂in)
W: 70cm (27 ¹/₂in)
D: 65cm (25 ⁵/₈in)
Blå Station, Sweden
www.blastation.se

Chair, Fish chair
Satyendra Pakhalé
Fibre-reinforced plastics
H: 71.7cm (28 ³/₈in)
W: 55cm (21 ⁵/₈in)
D: 87.3cm (34in)
Cap Design SpA, Italy
www.cappellini.it

Stackable stool, Miura
Konstantin Grcic
Polypropylene
H: 81cm (32in)
W: 53cm (20 ⁷/₈in)
D: 55cm (21 ⁵/₈in)
Plank, Italy
www.plank.it

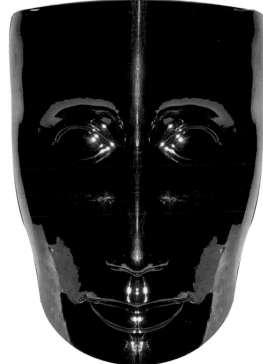

Stool, Bonze
Philippe Starck
Ceramic in gold
H: 45.5cm (18 ¹/₈in)
W: 33.5cm (13 ³/₈in)
D: 45.5 cm (18 ¹/₈in)
XO, France
www.xo-design.com

Barstool, Fizz
James Irvine
Chrome
H: 78cm (31in)
W: 50cm (19 ⁵/₈in)
D: 32cm (12 ⁵/₈in)
Plank, Italy
www.plank.it

Body props
Olivier Peyricot
Polyurethane, elastic
varnish
Various dimensions
Edra SpA, Italy
www.edra.com

**Coffee table,
Lo-rez-dolores table**
Ron Arad
Corian®, fibre optics,
mirror, media
H: 40cm (15 ³/₄in)
D: 160cm (63in)
Ron Arad Associates, UK
www.ronarad.com

Ron Arad is internationally known for his own unique style language and innovative use of techniques and materials. His collaboration with DuPont Corian at the Milan Furniture Fair 2004 did not disappoint. The 'Lo-rez-dolores-tabula-rasa' installation at the Gallery Gio'Marconi is the result of his research into the creative possibilities of working with Corian. Going beyond Corian's practical uses, Arad wanted to experiment with, and exploit, the translucency of the material, bringing large sheets of blank white Corian to sudden life with film, music and images. Designed in collaboration with the Belgium-based company Barco, specialists in imaging technology and visualization, 'Lo-rez-dolores' is a lens-shaped coffee table into which 22,000 fibre-optic pixels have been embedded. The table shows moving images and issues sounds from the user's choice of media, but when switched off, the table is once again a smooth seamless white orb. Most plasma screens are black and unwelcoming when not in use; with Corian the 'screen' is a beautiful object in itself.

**Small armchair,
Dummy**
Konstantin Grcic
Polyurethane foam,
expanded polyethylene
coupled with heat-
sealed fabric
H: 81cm (32in)
D: 40cm (15 ³/₄in)
W: 50cm (19 ⁵/₈in)
Moroso SpA, Italy
www.moroso.it

Rocking chair, Voido
Ron Arad
Blow-moulded
polyethylene
H: 78.4cm (31in)
W: 60.1cm (23 ⁵/₈in)
D: 114.8cm (45in)
Magis SpA, Italy
www.magisdesign.com

Ron Arad

Which of your designs to date would you like to be remembered by?
I'm still working on it. I don't work to be remembered.

How do you think others view your work?
I can't give a uniform answer. Architects see my work as design or architecture, designers see my work as art, artists see it as architecture. It's sometimes praised, and sometimes dismissed as art. It's a debate I wouldn't want to have with many people. Sometimes I'm approached by someone who is completely enthused by what I do, but then I see what else they admire and I'm not heartened. Individuals have different ways of appraising, different memories, associations, different ideas about what makes a piece interesting. There can never be just one reading, some are judging on technical innovation, others on how an object looks ...

Which designer has influenced you the most and why?
Many. It could be Achille Castiglioni, Enzo Mari, Carlo Colombo, but then again it could be Bob Dylan. I'm not only influenced by the physical but also by an approach, a mood.

If you were not a designer, what would you like to be, and why?
A dancer because I'm jealous of dancers. Actually having said that I probably wouldn't want to be a dancer because I wouldn't want to use my body as my tool. Maybe a Parkours as they train themselves to be different creatures.

What role do you think the designer has in society today?
Design is a big word. I don't want to know what its role is. Are we judging furniture or arms? There is such a big range. Sometimes success of design is measured by performance, sometimes sales and marketing. The creation of wealth. For example, Italian design's role is to save itself. Ten years ago they used only Italian designers, now they commission designers from other countries in order to keep selling. The role of design could be to cure, entertain, delight. It's a wide world. It could be one role but there again it could be the opposite.

Do you buy a lot of design pieces?
I can't help it. If I walk down the street and I see a Eero Saarinen chair, it can't just stay there. It can't be ignored. I recently bought the 'Womb Chair'. It was designed two years before I was born yet it's more advanced than anything I've done to date – false modesty!!

Is there a design in your home that you couldn't live without?
No, not really. There are objects but not particular ones. My coffee maker, but not necessarily the one I've actually got.

What do you consider to be the best piece of design since the millennium?
It would have to be something to do with IT. MP3 files are better than CDs. This century all the important new stuff is to do with the IT revolution. It's too early to say. Technological advancement is come and go, forever evolving. Did you know that today people make as many phone calls in one day as they did during the whole year in 1981?

Armchair, MT Rocker
Ron Arad
Stainless steel mirror polished
H: 79cm (31in)
W: 81cm (32in)
D: 105cm (41in)
Driade SpA
and Marzorati
Ronchetti, Italy
www.driade.com
and www.marzorati
ronchetti.it

Where do you think design is heading? Is there someone we should be watching out for?
I think it's important to ignore trends and look for individuals. Don't think in terms of minimalism but in terms of Herzog and de Meuron; don't think of decoration but of William Morris or Timorous Beasties. We should also be looking for a replacement for plastic. It took a long time for it to be accepted domestically. It's still the best mass-producible industrial material but its tyranny is at an end.

Is the cult of the personality taking over the design world?
What all five of them? It's not the designers' fault but over-enthusiastic client PR companies who urge journalists to pursue designers with request upon request for interviews. It shouldn't be that journalists work this way. They shouldn't be waiting for PR people to tell them what to do. I don't know how to reverse the trend, short of failing to comply with the demands.

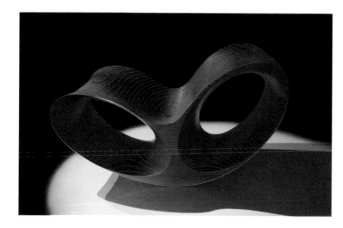

Rocking daybed,
Oh Void 2
Ron Arad
Corian®, coloured glue
H: 123cm (48in)
W: 47cm (18 ½in)
D: 193cm (76in)
Ron Arad Associates, UK
www.ronarad.com

Satyendra Pakhalé has refined an ancient metal-casting technique to produce contemporary objects. A core is made with a mixture of fine clean sand and clay. Traditionally, goat's dung is then soaked in water and ground and mixed with clay in equal proportions. This soft mixture forms the base mould. Once dried, it is used to create a wax pattern. A special natural wax is melted over an open fire and strained through a fine cloth into a basin of cold water, where it becomes solid. Care has to be taken to keep the wax absolutely clean and free of impurities. Next, it is squeezed through a sieve and recovered in the form of wax 'wires' (thick or thin as desired). Each of these wires is wrapped around the core, one after another, until the whole surface is covered. Originally, the artisan would have sat in the sun to let the clay core and the wax coating warm up uniformly. The whole form is finally covered in a mixture of equal parts clay, sand and cow dung, and fired. Base metals – brass, bronze, copper and so on – are melted together and poured in the fired clay mould to form the metal objects, the wax being lost in the process.

Chair, Horse chair
Satyendra Pakhalé
Bell Metal (lost-wax casting process) with sandblasted surface coating.
H: 96cm (38in)
W: 55cm (21⅝in)
D: 85cm (33in)
Atelier Satyendra Pakhalé, the Netherlands
www.satyendra-pakhale.com

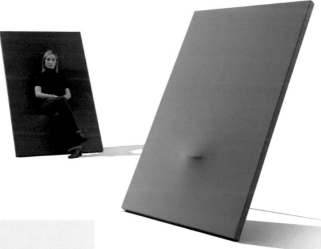

Seat/frame, Ram
No Picnic
Elastic lycra, enamelled steel frame, leather seat
H: 159cm (62in)
L: 106cm (41³⁄₈in)
D: 84cm (32³⁄₄in)
Felicerossi srl, Italy
www.felicerossi.it

Stool, Muku
Naoto Fukasawa
Mahogany solid wood
H: 70cm (27½in)
W: 37cm (14⅝in)
D: 38cm (15in)
Driade SpA, Italy
www.driade.com

High stool, LEM
Shin and Tomoko Azumi
Steel, plywood
H: 65–75cm (25⅝–29½in)
W: 39cm (15³⁄₈in)
D: 42cm (16½in)
Lapalma, Italy
www.lapalma.it

Chair, C 07
Pol Quadens
Carbon fibre,
honeycomb
H: 82cm (32in)
W: 38cm (15in)
D: 42cm (16 ½in)
Pol design studio,
Belgium
www.poldesign.com

Stool, Stool_One
Konstantin Grcic
Anodized aluminium,
die-cast aluminium
H: 83.9cm (33in)
W: 55.8cm (22in)
D: 44.2cm (17 ³/₈in)
H (seat): 76.3cm
(29 ⅞in)
Magis SpA, Italy
www.magisdesign.com

**Adjustable bar stool,
Al Bombo**
Stefano Giovannoni
Die-cast aluminium
H: 61–84cm (24–33in)
W: 44cm (17 ³/₈in)
D: 37cm (14 ⅝in)
Magis SpA, Italy
www.magisdesign.com

**Height-adjustable
stool, Spoon**
Antonio Citterio
Thermoplastic and
anodized aluminium
H: 55–75cm (21 ⅝–29 ½in)
W: 42cm (16 ½in)
D: 54cm (21 ¼in)
Kartell SpA, Italy
www.kartell.it

Chair, LCP Chair
Maarten Van Severen
PMMA
H: 70cm (27 $^1/_2$ in)
W: 48.5cm (19in)
D: 80cm (31in)
Kartell SpA, Italy
www.kartell.it

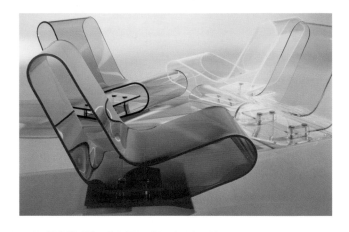

**Modular seating
system for indoors
and outdoors, Frame**
Francesco Rota
Aluminium, fabric
H: 68cm (26 $^3/_4$ in)
W: 83cm (33in)
D: 153cm (60in)
Paola Lenti srl, Italy
www.paolalenti.com

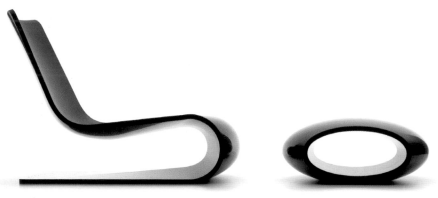

**Chaise longue,
Nouvelle Vague**
Christophe Pillet
Thermoplastic
Chaise longue,
H: 74cm (29 $^1/_8$ in)
W: 64cm (25 $^1/_4$ in)
D: 100cm (39in);
Footstool,
H: 26.8cm (10 $^5/_8$ in)
W: 63cm (24 $^3/_4$ in)
D: 64cm (25 $^1/_4$ in)
Porro srl, Italy
www.porro.com

LED Bench
Ingo Maurer
Moulded glass with
288 white LEDs inside,
emitting light on
both sides.
H: 40cm (15 $^3/_4$ in)
L: 200cm (79in)
D: 50cm (19 $^5/_8$ in)
Ingo Maurer GmbH,
Germany
www.ingo-maurer.com

Armchair, Ombra
Charlotte Perriand
Steel, upholstered
in fabric or leather
H: 65cm (25 ⅝in)
L: 70cm (27⅛in)
D: 82cm (32in)
Cassina SpA, Italy
www.cassina.it

A major part of Cassina's 2004 collection was devoted to re-editions by the modernist designer **Charlotte Perriand**: an addition to their 'I Maestri' series, which since the mid-1960s has re-edited design classics by Le Corbusier, Gerrit Thomas Rietveld, Charles Rennie Mackintosh, Erik Gunnar Asplund and Frank Lloyd Wright. Cassina argue that choosing to produce re-editions has less to do with a conservative attitude being the safest approach to the present unsettled economic climate, and more to do with their genuine conviction that works by masters of the Modern Movement can become fertile soil for designers today.

Perriand's work has a contemporary feel. In 1937, after having spent ten years in Le Corbusier's studio, where she was in charge of the furniture and fittings programme, she was invited by the Ministry of Trade and Industry of Japan to advise on industrial design. Once in Japan, Perriand was influenced by the tradition of Japanese furniture making, which appeared close to her own taste for the standardization of elements, harmony of forms and volumes, architectural flexibility and the care given to the environment. It is the East meets West style of the designs that followed that lends Perriand's work such an immediate appeal to young designers today.

The 'Ombra' armchair, which she originally designed in Tokyo in 1953 for her husband's house, combines a minimalist language and structure with maximum functionality and is the result of what Perriand described as 'a synthesis of the arts' of European and Japanese cultures. This contemporary version has introduced a steel structure and square cushions for seating and backrests, interlinked by a zipper, rather than a single sheet of curved ply board, yet the result retains the qualities of density and lightness of the reference piece.

Chair and pouf, Super Elastica
Marco Zanuso Jr and
Giuseppe Raboni
Indian cane
Chair,
H: 88cm (35in)
W: 100cm (39in)
D: 85cm (33in);
Pouf,
H: 43cm (16⅞in)
W: 60cm (23⅝in)
D: 85cm (33in)
Vittorio Bonacina, Italy
www.bonacinavittorio.it

Flower chair
Marcel Wanders
Matt chromed steel
H: 64cm (25in)
W: 78cm (30⅜in)
D: 71cm (27⅞in)
Moooi, the Netherlands
www.moooi.nl

**Easy chair, BD
Superstructure**
Björn Dahlström
Oak and cushion,
leather/fabric
H: 88cm (35in)
W: 108cm (43in)
D: 108cm (43in)
Cbi Design AB, Sweden
www.cbidesign.se

**Lounge chair and
footstool, Brasilia**
Ross Lovegrove
Painted polyurethane
Chair,
H: 83cm (32 ³/₄in)
W: 58cm (22 ⁷/₈in)
D: 100cm (39 ³/₈in);
Footstool,
H: 38cm (14in)
W: 55cm (21 ⁵/₈in)
D: 46cm (18 ¹/₈in)
Zanotta SpA, Italy
www.zanotta.it

Armchair, Lovenet
Ross Lovegrove
Galvanized and
powdered steel, PE,
stainless steel
H: 90cm (35 ⁵/₈in)
W: 150cm (59in)
D: 80cm (31 ¹/₂in)
Moooi, the Netherlands
www.moooi.nl

**Lounge chair,
Prince Chair**
Louise Campbell
Laser-cut metal,
water-cut EPDM, felt
H: 80cm (31in)
W: 100cm (39in)
D: 80cm (31in)
Hay, Denmark
www.hay.dk

Chair, Dragonfly
Karim Rashid
Chrome-plated steel,
leather- or fabric-
covered expanded
polyurethane
H: 79cm (31in)
W: 46cm (18 ¹⁄₈in)
D: 74cm (29 ¹⁄₈in)
D (expanded):
127cm (50in)
Bonaldo SpA, Italy
www.bonaldo.it

Chair, Tabasco
Jorge Pensi
Wood, polyurethane,
metal
H: 93cm (37in)
W: 70cm (27 ¹⁄₂in)
D: 88cm (35in)
Perobell, Spain
www.perobell.com

Chair, Go
Ross Lovegrove
High-pressure injection-
moulded magnesium
H: 77.5 cm (30 ¹⁄₂in)
W: 58.4 (23in)
D: 68.6 (27in)
Bernhardt Design, USA
www.bernhardtdesign.com

Chair, Air One
Ross Lovegrove
Polypropylene foam
H: 53cm (20 ⁷⁄₈in)
D: 115 cm (45in)
Edra SpA, Italy
www.edra.com

Fabricated from a polypropylene foam normally used
in packing, Ross Lovegrove's '**Air One**' stackable chair
and stool (not shown) in disco blue and silver recapture
the zeitgeist of the 1970s. They are extremely light
and can be transported and stacked easily.

Armchair, Smock
Patricia Urquiola
Steel, injected flame-
retardant polyurethane
foam
H: 68cm (26 ³/₄in)
W: 100cm (39in)
D: 80cm (31in)
Moroso SpA, Italy
www.moroso.it

Armchair, Sections
Luca Bonato
Acrylic
H: 108cm (42 ¹/₂in)
W: 120cm (47 ¹/₄in)
D: 86cm (33 ⁷/₈in)
Fusina srl, Italy
www.fusina-italy.com

Cocoon chair
Ann Tiukinhoy
Pamintuan
Wire
H: 74cm (28 ⁷/₈in)
W: 74cm (28 ⁷/₈in)
D: 86.5cm (33 ³/₄in)
The Gilded Expressions,
the Philippines
gildex@mozcom.com

**Easy chair, S.T.
Strange Thing**
Philippe Starck
Titanium, fabric
upholstery
H: 79cm (31in)
W: 98cm (38 ¹/₂in)
D: 76cm (29 ⁷/₈in)
Cassina SpA, Italy
www.cassina.it

Chair, Mars
Konstantin Grcic
Synthetic resin,
removable cover in
fabric or leather
H: 75cm (29 ¹/₂in)
W: 47cm (18 ¹/₂in)
D: 54cm (21 ¹/₄in)
ClassiCon GmbH,
Germany
www.classicon.com

Lounge chair, Easy
Rock Galpin
Solid hardwood, silk
chromed metal rod,
foam, fabric
Chair,
H: 91cm (36in)
W: 84cm (33in)
D: 85cm (33in);
Stool,
W: 64cm (25 1/4in)
D: 43cm (16 7/8in)
Designers Guild, UK
www.designersguild.com

Rock Gilpin's **'Easy'
lounge chair** was the
winner of the 2005
Laurent Perrier Design
Award. The well-thought-
out and elegant profile is
enhanced by the use of
a state-of-the-art foam
composite which moulds
around the body, as well
as a built-in lumbar
cushion for extra comfort.

Armchair, Slot
Sebastian Bergne
Steel, plywood
H: 70cm (27 1/2in)
H (seat): 36cm (14 1/8in)
W: 79cm (31in)
D: 82cm (32in)
Varaschin, Italy
www.varaschin.it

Chair, Sit
Michael Sodeau
Ply/oak wood, aluminium
H: 75cm (29 1/2in)
W: 70cm (27 1/2in)
D: 64.5cm (25 5/8in)
Modus, UK
www.modusfurniture.co.uk

**Various types of
seating element, Lazy**
Patricia Urquiola
Metal, fabric
Various dimensions
B&B Italia SpA, Italy
www.bebitalia.it

Armchair, 41 Paimio
Alvar Aalto
Birch wood, bent birch
plywood
H: 64cm (25 ¼in)
W: 60cm (23 ⅝in)
D: 80cm (31in)
Artek, Finland
www.artek.fi

Armchair, Fjord
Patricia Urquiola
Steel, flame-retardant
polyurethane foam
H: 102cm (40 ⅛in)
W: 95cm (37 ⅜in)
D: 80cm (31½in)
Moroso SpA, Italy
www.moroso.it

Armchair, 402
Alvar Aalto
Birch wood, PU,
sheepskin
H: 76cm (29 ⅞in)
W: 61cm (24in)
D: 70cm (27½in)
Artek, Finland
www.artek.fi

In 2004 Tom Dixon took over the creative direction of
Artek, injecting life back into a company that in the
1930s had been one of the most innovative furniture
manufacturers, set up to market the furniture,
lighting and textiles of Alvar Aalto. The company
is now owned by Art & Technology design group,
formed by Proventus (former backer of Artek) and
the Tom Dixon company. Quoting Aalto's maxim,
'Nothing old is ever reborn, but neither does it totally
disappear. And that which has once been, will always
reappear in new form,' Mirkku Kullberg, Artek's new
managing director, wants to maximize the company's
original manifesto of '... *monidal aktivitet*'. Her aim is
to secure, once again, Artek's position as a world
leader by telling its story in a fresh way as part of a
rigorous marketing programme. The 2005 range
offers a new take on its classic collection, bringing
back original modernist colours, upholstery fabrics
and materials (petrol blue, oak and sheepskin) that
have been out of production for years.

**Chair/couch/bed,
Hypnos**
Alfredo Häberli
Chromium-plated steel,
polyurethane with
polyester filling, artificial
leather, cover in fabric
or leather
H: 102cm (40in)
W: 80cm (31in)
L: 87–100cm
(34–79in)
ClassiCon GmbH,
Germany
www.classicon.com

Foldable seat/chair, Instantlounge
Stefan Diez and Christophe de la Fontaine
Textile, polypropylene
H: 57cm (22 ½in)
W: 87cm (34in)
D: 60cm (23 ⁵/₈in)
Elmar Flötotto, Germany
www.elmarfloetotto.de

Armchair, Butterfly Kiss
Christian Ghion
Upholstered heat-moulded plywood structure, fabric/leather, chromed steel
H: 86cm (34in)
H (seat): 35cm (13 ³/₄in)
W: 116cm (46in)
D: 78cm (31in)
Sawaya & Moroni, Italy
www.sawayamoroni.com

Sofa, Victoria and Albert Collection
Ron Arad
Polyester resin, steel polyurethane foam
H: 85–145cm (33 ½–57in)
W: 180–290cm (70 ⁷/₈–114 ¹/₈in)
Moroso SpA, Italy
www.moroso.it

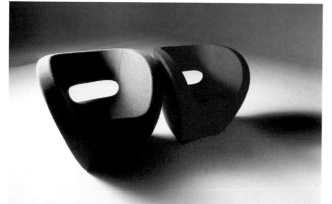

Armchair, Victoria and Albert Collection
Ron Arad
Polyester resin, steel, polyurethane foam
H: 75cm (29 ½in)
W: 74cm (29 ¼in)
Moroso SpA, Italy
www.moroso.it

Ron Arad's **'Victoria and Albert' sofa** for Moroso is named after the London museum, where an exhibition of Arad's work ran from June to October 2000. It is formed from a single band of tempered steel that is clad in foam and upholstered in a washable but irremovable cover in primary colours. It can be made in any size, although the bigger the better. Javier Mariscal said just after he had seen the sofa at the Moroso show in Milan that its size, luxuriance and sensuous curves gave it an indecent air – 'it is a love couch to be played on and enjoyed'. This is a rather pertinent comic comment, given that Professor David Starkey (one of the UK's most outspoken historians) revealed, while making a documentary on the life of Queen Victoria, that contrary to popular belief, the queen had enjoyed a boisterous, fun-loving attitude to sex.

Chair, Witch
Tord Boontje
Steel, injected flame-
retardant polyurethane
foam, leather
H: 87cm (34in)
W: 54cm (21 ¹⁄₄in)
D: 51cm (20 ¹⁄₈in)
Moroso SpA, Italy
www.moroso.it

Armchair,
Fish Net Chair
Marcel Wanders
Graphitic carbon rope
H: 74cm (28 ⁷⁄₈in)
W: 82cm (32in)
D: 75cm (29 ¹⁄₄in)
Cap Design SpA, Italy
www.cappellini.it

Lounge chair, Dragnet
Kenneth Cobonpue
Outdoor fabric,
galvanized wire,
stainless steel
H: 136cm (54in)
W: 84cm (33in)
D: 105cm (41in)
Interior Crafts of
the Islands, Inc,
the Philippines
www.kenneth
cobonpue.com

Chair, Hara
Giorgio Gurioli
UV-protected
lacquered fibreglass
H: 74cm (29 ⅛in)
W: 88cm (35in)
L: 74cm (29 ⅛in)
Kundalini srl, Italy
www.kundalini.it

Chair, Ripple
Ron Arad
Multi-layered techno-
polymer composite,
steel
H: 80cm (31in)
W: 68cm (26 ¾in)
D: 59cm (23 ¼in)
Moroso SpA, Italy
www.moroso.it

Armchair, MT1
Ron Arad
Rotational moulding
polyethylene
H: 83cm (33in)
H (seat): 42cm (16 ½in)
W: 73.5cm (29 ⅛in)
D: 74cm (29 ⅛in)
Driade SpA, Italy
www.driade.com

Chair
Natanel Gluska
Beech
Made to order
Natanel Gluska,
Switzerland
www.natanelgluska.com

Natanel Gluska's chairs
are all unique. He attacks
a virgin tree stump with
a chainsaw and fashions
from it a one-piece
hybrid of sculpture and
functional item. Here
market-led inhibitions
are shed, allowing the
designer real freedom
of expression.

Chair, Ginko
Ann Tiukinhoy
Pamintuan
Welded metal wire
H: 60cm (23 ⅗in)
W: 120cm (47in)
D: 120cm (47in)
The Gilded Expressions,
Philippines
gildex@mozcom.com

Armchair, Twin
Mario Cananzi
Metal tube, rattan core
H: 66cm (26in)
W: 75cm (29 ½in)
D: 64cm (25 ¼in)
Vittorio Bonacina, Italy
www.bonacinavittorio.it

Armchair, Corallo
Fernando and Humberto
Campana
Iron
H: 140cm (55in)
W: 100cm (39in)
D: 90cm (35in)
Edra SpA, Italy
www.edra.com

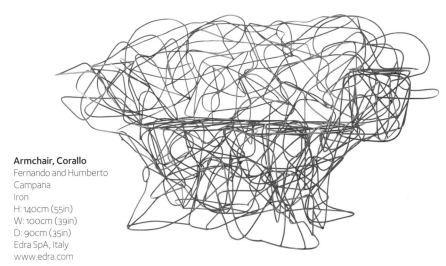

Chair, Sushi
Fernando and
Humberto Campana
Plastic, felt, fabric,
carpeting. Also available
in Swarovski crystal
fabric (below).
H: 65cm (25 ⁵/₈in)
W: 95cm (37in)
D: 85cm (33in)
Edra SpA, Italy
www.edra.com

In September 2005
Edra consolidated its
collaboration with
Swarovski by launching a
series of its most iconic
pieces in crystal. 'Sushi'
was one such, a little
ironic given the humble
concept behind its
original design

It would be fair to say that Edra discovered **Fernando and Humberto Campana**. In 1996 the company produced the 'Vermelha' knotted chair, which put them well and truly on the design map. Almost a decade later, in 2005, the brothers received the Nombre d'or prize from the Italian Minister of Culture to consecrate this business relationship, which has seen Edra successfully industrialize the designs of the Campanas without losing the unique appeal of their work – preserving the aura of 'genius loci' without allowing it to stray into ethnicity.

The Campanas' designs mix native Brazilian low-tech craftsmanship and recycled or raw materials, but translate this seemingly humble combination into a formula suitable for Italian manufacturing. The brothers consider that the otherwise technically competent Brazilian furniture industry lacks daring and is divorced from the contemporary design market, and for this reason they currently prefer to collaborate with foreign companies, although they remain domiciled and much influenced by their native country. All the Campanas' furniture is characterized by a blend of the artisanal and the industrial. Much of their work, for example, combines natural fibres such as sisal, straw, wood and rattan with synthetic materials and surfaces. Their aim is to borrow techniques from the traditional crafts to make modern designs, or else to use simple folk material in industrial processes. 'We are not interested in naive, romantic primitivism,' they claim, 'progress cannot be stopped. The problem is to coexist with the transformation without losing the knowledge contained in the materials and techniques.'

Armchair, Anemone
Fernando and Humberto
Campana
Stainless steel,
plastic tubing
H: 70cm (27 ⁵/₈in)
W: 100cm (43 ³/₈in)
D: 80cm (31 ¹/₂in)
Edra SpA, Italy
www.edra.com

Chair, Glove
Patricia Urquiola
Steel, polyurethane
rubber
H: 79cm (31in)
W: 52cm (20 ½in)
D: 51cm (20 ⅛in)
Molteni & C. SpA, Italy
www.molteni.it

Chair, La Sfogliata
Gaetano Pesce
Fibreglass, aluminium,
rubber, PVC, fabric
H: 11cm (4 ⅜in)
W: 52cm (20 ½in)
D: 58cm (22 ⅞in)
Meritalia SpA, Italy
www.meritalia.it

**Armchair,
Nobody's Perfect**
Gaetano Pesce
Polyurethane resin
H: 88cm (34 ⅝in)
W: 50cm (19 ⅝in)
D: 45cm (17 ⅛in)
Zerodisegno,
Quattrocchio, Italy
www.zerodisegno.com

Zerodisegno, in collaboration with Gaetano Pesce, has
developed a line called 'Nobody's Perfect', as an
expression of the diversities of people and regions of
the world. Each item is unique, cast in a multi-coloured
resin that sometimes completely fills the mould and
sometimes not, creating anthropomorphic shapes
that are not fully formed until they are released and
harden. Each piece includes a date that has been
hand-cast inside its own skin, and every example, in
its own 'imperfection', represents something that is
unique, different and extraordinary: each one
contains an act of creativity.

**Folding armchairs,
Outdoor**
Ronan and Erwan
Bouroullec
Nickel-coloured epoxy
satin lacquer-coated
steel, PVC,
polystyrene, EPDM
H: 99.7cm (39 ¼in)
W: 78.1cm (30 ¾in)
D: 69.2cm (27 ¼in)
Ligne Roset, France
www.ligne-roset.com

Large sculptural seating unit, It Seating
Jakob + MacFarlane
Fibreglass, resins, lacquer
H: 150cm (59in)
H (seat): 44cm (17 ³⁄₈in)
W: 190cm (75in)
D: 170cm (67in)
Sawaya & Moroni, Italy
www.sawayamoroni.com

Chair, Crystal
Zaha Hadid
Plastic and wood
agglomerate, car paint
H: 84cm (33in)
W: 62cm (24 ³⁄₈in)
D: 60cm (23 ⁵⁄₈in)
Sawaya & Moroni, Italy
www.sawayamoroni.com

Chair, IKEA PS Vägö
Thomas Sandell
Polypropylene
H: 71cm (28in)
W: 74cm (29 ¹⁄₈in)
D: 92cm (36 ¹⁄₄in)
IKEA, Sweden
www.ikea.com

Armchair, Sponge
Peter Traag
Polyurethane,
fluorocarbon polyester
thread fabric
H: 75cm (29 ½in)
W: 85cm (33in)
D: 94cm (37in)
Edra SpA, Italy
www.edra.com

**Armchair and
two-seater sofa,
Rive Droite**
Patrick Norguet
Plywood, polyurethane
steel, Pucci fabric
Armchair,
H: 69cm (26 ⅞in)
W: 98cm (38 ¼in)
D: 76cm (29 ⅝in);
Sofa,
H: 69cm (26 ⅞in)
L: 180cm (70 ¼in)
D: 76cm (29 ⅝in)
Cap Design SpA, Italy
www.cappellini.it

**Armchair in plastic,
The Big E**
Ron Arad
Thermal-shock and
sunlight-resistant
polyethylene
H: 98cm (39in)
W: 124cm (49in)
D: 92cm (36in)
Moroso SpA, Italy
www.moroso.it

**Armchair,
Metropolitan**
Jeffrey Bernett
Steel frame,
polyurethane, textile
H: 73cm (28 ¾in)
W: 84cm (33in)
D: 83cm (33in)
B&B Italia SpA, Italy
www.bebitalia.it

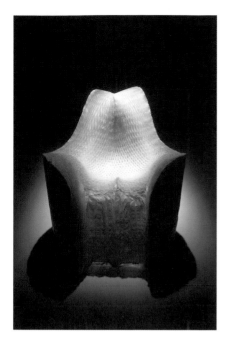

Chair, Honey-Pop
Tokujin Yoshioka
Paper
H: 83cm (32 ⅝in)
W: 80cm (31 ½in)
D: 83cm (32 ⅝in)
Tokujin Yoshioka Design,
Japan
www.tokujin.com

Armchair, Bloomy
Patricia Urquiola
Steel, flame-retardant
cold-expanded foam
H: 75cm (29 ½in)
H (seat): 46cm (18 ⅛in)
W: 58cm (22 ⅞in)
D: 58cm (22 ⅞in)
Moroso SpA, Italy
www.moroso.it

**Swivelling armchair,
Igloo**
Eero Koivisto
Chromed steel,
polyurethane,
polyurethane foam
H: 61.5cm (24 ⅜in)
W: 85cm (33in)
D: 76.5cm (30in)
Cap Design SpA, Italy
www.cappellini.it

Only a handful of objects impressed during the Milan
Furniture Fair 2002, and one of the most lasting
memories was provided at the Driade show on Via
Montepoleone. Against a pristine white background,
Tokujin Yoshioka had created a magical snowscape
that actually crunched under foot. You had to pass by
his 'Tokyo Pop' series (see page 61) before reaching
the inner sanctum, where the lights were dimmed
and spots outlined the ephemeral spectre of the
'Honey-Pop' chair. Tokujin states that 'One of the
standards by which I assess myself is whether I can
create a design that touches and amazes me. Design
should express emotions such as surprise, joy and
wonder. I strongly hope to create a design that I have
never seen and which I want to see.'

The construction of 'Honey-Pop' is reminiscent
of the 1950s concertina Christmas decorations, but
in reality it is a cellulose version of the exceptionally
strong and light honeycomb material used in the
aeronautical industry. This has been cut to a thickness
of one centimetre (⅜ inch) unfolded, and is sat on to
form an ergonomic shape that could only result from
the pressure of bottom on paper. It certainly does
surprise (at the freshness of the concept), and fill you
with joy (at the sheer poetry of its aesthetic) and
wonder (at how something that light and delicate
can take the weight of a fully grown man). The chair
reflects Yoshioka's interest in new materials, or
using materials adaptively, lifting them beyond their
conventional potential. The material suggests the
form, which he then liberates from it. 'Material is not
an end to itself. It is only after examining and studying
it closely that I can envisage giving it concrete form.
How it can be made even more interesting.'

Chair, Flo chair (red)
Patricia Urquiola
Steel, rattan
H: 86cm (34in)
H (seat): 45cm (17 ¾in)
W: 53cm (20 ⅞in)
D: 53cm (20 ⅞in)
Driade SpA, Italy
www.driade.com

Chair, Trono
Sottsass Associati
Technopolymers
H: 76cm (29 ⁷⁄₈in)
H (seat): 45cm (17 ³⁄₄in)
W: 52cm (20 ¹⁄₄in)
D: 55cm (21 ⁵⁄₈in)
Segis SpA, Italy
www.segis.it

**Indoor/outdoor
armchair, MB 1**
Mario Bellini
One-piece roto-
moulded polymer
H: 65cm (25 ⁵⁄₈in)
W: 78cm (31in)
D: 84cm (33in)
Heller, USA
www.helleronline.com

Armchair, Calla
Stefano Giovannoni
Fabric-covered moulded
polyurethane with
die-cast
aluminium base
H: 102cm (40in)
W: 87–169cm (34–67in)
D: 83cm (33in)
Modular srl, Italy
www.domodinamica.com

Armchair, Mist
Rodrigo Torres
Polyurethane, elastic
fabrics
H: 79cm (31in)
W: 73cm (28 ³⁄₄in)
D: 77cm (30in)
Modular srl, Italy
www.domodinamica.com

**Stackable armchair,
Toy**
Philippe Starck
Polypropylene
H: 78cm (31in)
H (seat): 43cm (16 ⁷⁄₈in)
W: 61.5cm (24 ³⁄₈in)
D: 57.5cm (22 ⁷⁄₈in)
Driade SpA, Italy
www.driade.com

Lounge chair, PET
Brian Kane
Steel, polyethylene
terephthalate (PET)
shell
H: 77cm (30in)
W: 72cm (28 ³⁄₈in)
D: 70cm (27 ¹⁄₂in)
Turnstone by Steelcase,
USA
www.steelcase.com

When first shown a piece of moulded felt, the San
Franciscan industrial designer **Brian Kane** found it to
be very unsophisticated – like the insulation in a car
boot. He did, however, recognize the potential of this
fully recyclable material. The source of the felt was
PET – polyethylene terephthalate, a plastic resin
commonly used in the manufacture of water bottles.
It is lightweight and strong, but more importantly it
is recyclable, and therefore poses no threat to the
environment. The 'PET Lounge Chair' was developed
in collaboration with Turnstone and is made by
inexpensively compressing two sheets of PET on
to a steel frame and reducing the fabric to about
3.5 millimetres (¹⁄₈ inch) thick. The slim-line form is
ergonomic, durable and impenetrable. Turnstone
are also developing a programme to recycle, reuse
or refurbish the chair at the end of its lifespan.

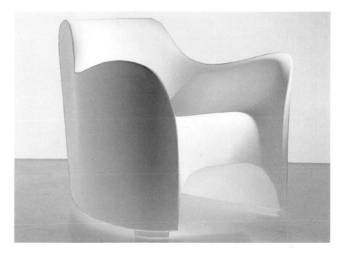

Armchair, Tokyo Pop
Tokujin Yoshioka
Polyethylene
H: 75.5cm (29 ³⁄₄in)
W: 86cm (33 ⁷⁄₈in)
D: 78cm (30 ³⁄₄in)
Driade SpA, Italy
www.driade.com

Armchair, T1
Tim Power
Plywood, metal
H: 94cm (37in)
H (seat): 44cm (17 ³/₈in)
W: 75cm (29 ¹/₂in)
D: 64cm (25 ¹/₄in)
Montina srl, Italy
www.montina.it

Lounge chair, FU 09
For Use Design
Lacquered fibreglass,
steel
H: 92cm (36in)
W: 47cm (18 ¹/₂in)
D: 65cm (25 ⁵/₈in)
MDF Italia srl, Italy
www.mdfitalia.it

**Easy chair and stool,
Omni**
Mårten Claesson and
Eero Koivisto
Wood, polyamide
Chair,
H: 97cm (38 ¹/₈in)
W: 62cm (24 ³/₈in)
D: 80cm (31 ¹/₂in);
Stool,
H: 42cm (16 ¹/₂in)
W: 62cm (24 ³/₈in)
D: 43in (17in)
Swedese Möbler AB,
Sweden
www.swedese.se

Chair, Catifa art 0207
Lievore, Altherr, Molina
Polypropylene
(one-piece, injection-
moulded shell)
H: 79cm (31in)
W: 77cm (30in)
D: 77cm (30in)
Arper SpA, Italy
www.arper.it

**Dining chair
indoor/outdoor,
Spiderman**
Louise Campbell
Steel, zinc, rubber
H: 81cm (32in)
W: 46cm (18 ⅛in)
D: 50cm (19 ⅝in)
Hay, Denmark
www.hay.dk

Chair, Nais
Alfredo Häberli
Chromium-plated or
colour-coated steel,
removable cover in
canvas, fabric or leather,
lightly quilted
H: 82cm (32 ¼in)
H (seat): 46cm (18 ⅛in)
W (with armrests):
56cm (22in)
W (without armrests):
46cm (18 ⅛in)
D: 53cm (20 ⅞in)
ClassiCon GmbH,
Germany
www.classicon.com

Chair, Nic
Werner Aisslinger
Polypropylene with
glass fibre, chromed
steel tube
H: 82.5cm (33in)
W: 51.4cm (20 ⅛in)
D: 53cm (20 ⅞in)
Magis SpA, Italy
www.magisdesign.com

Chair, Leaf
Lievore, Altherr, Molina
Metal
H: 82cm (32in)
W: 52cm (20 ½in)
D: 56cm (22in)
Arper SpA, Italy
www.arper.it

Chair, Carbon Chair
Bertjan Pot and
Marcel Wanders
Epoxy, carbon
H: 78cm (31in)
W: 48cm (18 ⁷/₈in)
D: 46cm (18 ¹/₈in)
Moooi, the Netherlands
www.moooi.nl

**Stacking chair,
Chair_One**
Konstantin Grcic
Die-cast aluminium
H: 80cm (31in)
W: 55.3cm (21 ⁵/₈in)
D: 63.5cm (25 ¹/₄in)
Magis SpA, Italy
www.magisdesign.com

Chair, Chair_One
Konstantin Grcic
Concrete, die-cast
aluminium
H: 80cm (31in)
W: 55.3cm (21 ⁵/₈in)
D: 59.1cm (23 ¹/₄in)
Magis SpA, Italy
www.magisdesign.com

Armchair, Roma
Ferruccio Laviani
Plywood
H: 72cm (28 ³/₈in)
W: 49cm (19 ¹/₄in)
D: 62cm (24 ³/₈in)
Emmemobili, Italy
www.emmemobili.it

Stacking chair, Air

Jasper Morrison
Air-moulded
polypropylene with
glass fibre
H: 77.5cm (31in)
W: 49cm (19 ¼in)
D: 51cm (20 ⅛in)
Magis SpA, Italy
www.magisdesign.com

Eugenio Perazza's company, **Magis**, was founded in the 1970s – a time when the market was flooded with 'tasteful' Italian design and when consumers were hungering for something different. Instead of ageless classic collections, there was a shift towards fashion – products that would represent a season and define individual styles. Magis is a Latin adverb meaning 'more' or 'additionally', and when placed in front of an adjective it intensifies its quality. A chair that is 'magis necessarius' is indispensable, and a bookcase that is 'magis elegans' is simply sublime. Magis also forms the basis of the word 'magisterial' – there to teach others. The products that Magis present are not based on market needs but rather on what, over the years, they have learned to do best and what they have become known for.

The company works mainly in plastics, and more recently in sheet metal (steel and aluminium), which is inexpensive, ecological and recyclable, as well as in die-cast aluminium, investing a lot of money on researching new methods of working with these materials. Perazza believes that while technology may be widely accessible – anybody with enough money can afford it – it is technique that allows the designer to turn technology into a good concept and ultimately an innovative design. The company develops ideas, and then commissions different designers to interpret them aesthetically. 'We want to use different vocabularies, languages and dialects,' explains Perazza. He believes that if an individual is chosen who can really relate to the subject he or she has been given, then you end up with a perfect product.

Chair, Universal chair

PearsonLloyd
PA66 injection-moulded
plastic, polypropylene
H: 79cm (31in)
W: 57cm (22 ½in)
D: 49cm (19 ¼in)
PearsonLloyd, UK
www.pearsonlloyd.co.uk

Armchair, Air

Jasper Morrison
Polypropylene,
glass fibre
H: 77.5cm (30 ¼in)
W: 49cm (19 ⅜in)
D: 50cm (19 ½in)
Magis SpA, Italy
www.magisdesign.com

Armchair, Hug

Anna Van Schewen
Solid bent beech,
steel tubing
H: 74cm (28 ⅛in)
W: 56cm (22in)
D: 51cm (20in)
Gärsnäs AB, Sweden
www.garsnas.se

Armchair, Cirene 03
Vico Magistretti
Solid ash, plywood
H: 76cm (29 ⁷/₈in)
W: 54cm (21 ¹/₄in)
D: 54cm (21 ¹/₄in)
De Padova srl, Italy
www.depadova.it

Chairs, NextMaruni 12 Chairs
From left: Alberto Meda, Shin + Tomoko Azumi, Harri Koskinen, Jasper Morrison, Kanji Ueki, Kazuyo Sejima + Ryue Nishizawa/SANAA, Masayuki Kurokawa,

Michele De Lucchi, Naoto Fukasawa, Shigeru Uchida, Tamotsu Yagi, Sean Yoo
Wood
Various dimensions
Maruni Wood Industry Inc., Japan
www.nextmaruni.com

Two shows were held during the Milan Furniture Fair 2005 that were the result of collaboration between East and West and craft and design. At the Triennale, Enzo Mari showcased the prototypes he designed in conjunction with the traditional manufacturing company Hida Sangyo. Unfortunately, these designs cannot be shown here, as they are not yet in production. However, the second exhibition in Milan, the 'NextMaruni Project', exhibited a series of twelve chairs that various Japanese and European designers had created in collaboration with one of the best-

known Japanese furniture companies, Maruni Wood Industry Inc., and which are all now readily available. Unlike the small company Hida Sangyo, Maruni has been famous since 1933 for mass-produced high-end wooden furniture. However, because of the problems of the Japanese economy and the threat from other Asian countries, Maruni now need to diversify to survive. Maruni consulted the architect Masayuki Kurokawa, who suggested that they approach international as well as national designers and ask them to come up with a range of small chairs that

could be produced easily and relatively cheaply using the company's expertise and resources. Kurokawa advertised the project with his Eight Manifestations (Bi, Hei, Ma, Fu, Hi, So, Ka, Ha) that basically emphasize the importance of detail, simplification, concealment, harmony and flowing, unrestrained lines (concepts he applies to life generally, and to design specifically). Jasper Morrison was attracted by the complexity of thought given in Japan to the subject of what makes a piece of furniture beautiful, and was so impressed when the document came to his attention that he visited the factory. Following his visit the NextMaruni Project was launched. Other collaborators include Alberto Meda, the Azumis, Harri Koskinen and Michele De Lucchi, as well as Japanese designers Kazuyo Sejima and Naoto Fukasawa and the US-born Sean Yoo. The competition is fierce, not only from the domestic Japanese market, but also from European manufacturing giants, but it is hoped that this initiative will allow Maruni to continue, and help craft to exist in an industrial world.

Chair, Torsio
Hanspeter Steiger
Natural or black oak, walnut, maple
H: 79cm (31in)
H (seat): 46cm (18 ¹/₈in)
W: 48cm (18 ⁷/₈in)
D: 58cm (22 ⁷/₈in)
Roethlisberger Kollektion, Switzerland
www.roethlisberger.ch

Chair, Couture
Philippe Starck
Chromed steel,
polypropylene
H: 78 cm (31in)
H (seat): 44 cm (17 3/8in)
W: 42cm (16 1/2in)
D: 42cm (16 1/2in)
XO, France
www.xo-design.com

Chair, Gubi
Boris Berlin and Poul
Christiansen, Komplot
Design
3D moulded plywood,
laminated veneer,
steel rod
H: 80cm (31in)
W: 51.5cm (20 1/2in)
D: 54.5cm (21 5/8in)
Gubi A/S, Denmark
www.gubi.dk

Chairs, Imprint
Johannes Foersom and
Peter Hiort-Lorenzen
Pressed plant-fibre material
H: 78cm (31in)
W: 55 or 53cm
(21 5/8 or 20 7/8in)
D: 62 or 58cm
(24 3/8 or 22 7/8in)
Lammhults Möbel AB,
Sweden
www.lammhults.se

It is not very often that a completely new material is developed, and certainly not one that is so obvious yet no one has thought of it before. In this age of increasing ecological responsibility, why is it only now that someone has come up with the idea of farming the basic structure of all plant-cell walls, cellulose, on an industrial scale? Readily available, recyclable and environmentally sound, '**Cellupress**' was developed by Foersom and Hiort-Lorenzen in collaboration with Lammhults and Dan-Web (a material manufacturer) for use in their new 'Imprint' chair. Soft cellulose mats are treated with non-carcinogenic glue, fed into a machine and compressed using very high temperatures and a lot of pressure. The result is as strong and hard as wood, but with the smoothness and versatility of a plastic. To give Cellupress varying textures and colours, spruce, coconut and oak have been added, enhancing the material from within. Imprinting the human form onto the square panels produces the chair. As Cellupress is absorbent, the surface is then treated with a non-toxic lacquer. The legs have been kept as minimal as possible to concentrate on the shape of the fibre shell.

Chair, Solid C2
Patrick Jouin
Stereolithography
using epoxy resin
H: 77cm (30in)
W: 42cm (16 1/2in)
D: 53cm (20 7/8in)
Materialise.MGX,
Belgium
www.materialise-
mgx.com

Patrick Jouin's '**Solid**' furniture carries on from experiments conducted by Ron Arad as early as 2000 in his series of limited batch vases 'Not Made by Hand, Not Made in China' (see page 197) and is a whole new way of looking at product manufacturing. Using the process of stereolithography (a technique originally invented by Chuck Hall in 1986 for rapid prototyping), Jouin is literally growing furniture in his studio. Sanjit Manku of Agence Patrick Jouin says, 'What's interesting is that we are able to develop objects structurally in the same sort of way that nature works.' Taking as his inspiration forms from the living world – cells, grass reeds, crystals – shapes are created using a CAD program. Jouin then uses a 3D layering system to build up successive sheets of 0.5-millimetre plastic, each one individually cut and photochemically hardened by laser before adding the next layer. Eventually the plan is to create bespoke furniture, with customers selecting from a range of colours, forms, textures and materials, which are then gestated in the laboratory into whatever item is desired, and delivered a week later.

Chair, Very Nice
François Azambourg
Birch wood
H: 82.5cm (33in)
W: 36cm (14 1/8in)
D: 48cm (18 7/8in)
Domeau & Peres, France
www.domeauperes.com

Armchair, Favela
Fernando and
Humberto Campana
Brazilian pinus wood
H: 73.7cm (29in)
W: 67cm (26 3/8in)
D: 61cm (24in)
Edra SpA, Italy
www.edra.com

Chair, MM

Jean Nouvel
Steel, coach hide
H: 84cm (33in)
H (seat): 45cm (17 ³⁄₄in)
W: 45cm (17 ³⁄₄in)
D: 51cm (20 ¹⁄₈in)
Matteograssi, Italy
www.matteograssi.it

Chair, Muku

Naoto Fukasawa
Mahogany solid wood
H: 81.5cm (32in)
H (seat): 45cm (17 ³⁄₄in)
W: 49cm (19 ¹⁄₄in)
D: 57.3cm (22 ¹⁄₂in)
Driade SpA, Italy
www.driade.com

Chair, Non

Komplot Design
PUR-rubber
H: 76cm (30in)
W: 44cm (17 ³⁄₄in)
D: 41cm (16 ¹⁄₈in)
Källemo AB, Sweden
www.kallemo.se

The success of a design
can lie in the readaptive
use of materials.
Komplot Design have
used PUR-rubber in
their 'Non' chair.
With simple, straight
geometric lines and
integral spring bands
for comfort, the product
is a piece of non-design
that is at home either
in or out of doors.

Stackable chair, Sonia

James Irvine
Laminated beech or
birch veneer
H: 79cm (31in)
W: 46cm (18 ¹⁄₈in)
D: 56cm (22in)
Swedese Möbler AB,
Sweden
www.swedese.se

Stacking chair, Taino
Jakob Gebert
Wood, aluminium
H: 82cm (32in)
W: 49cm (19 ¹/₈in)
D: 56cm (21 ⁷/₈in)
Vitra, Switzerland
www.vitra.com

Collaborating with Vitra, Jakob Gebert has produced 'Taino', a chair using two pressed wood sheets of fine layers, each sandwiched around the chair legs, rather than the typical two-layer shell mounted on top of the legs. 'Because it is a single unit', he says, 'it is a stronger chair. It's funny, but I found that the connection between wood and metal is better than that between wood and wood.'

Stackable chair, M1
Piergiorgio Cazzaniga
Co-injected moulded recycled plastic, matt stainless steel
H: 74cm (29 ¹/₈in)
W: 49cm (19 ¹/₄in)
D: 52cm (20 ¹/₂in)
MDF Italia srl, Italy
www.mdfitalia.it

Chair, Fold
Piergiorgio Cazzaniga
Lacquered wood, stainless steel
H: 78cm (30 ³/₄in)
W: 47cm (18 ¹/₂in)
D: 50cm (19 ⁵/₈in)
Tagliabue srl, Italy
www.tagliabuesrl.com

Chair, Clipt
Jeff Miller
Glass-reinforced injected nylon, steel
H: 75.5cm (29 ⁷/₈in)
W: 47.5cm (18 ⁷/₈in)
D: 52.5cm (20 ⁷/₈in)
Baleri Italia SpA, Italy
www.baleri-italia.com

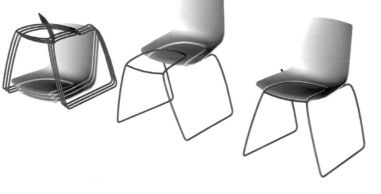

Chair, Jenette
Fernando and
Humberto Campana
Rigid structural
polyurethane, metal,
rigid PVC
H: 94cm (37in)
H (seat): 44cm (17 ³/₈in)
W: 41.2cm (16 ¹/₈in)
D: 50cm (19 ⁵/₈in)
Edra SpA, Italy
www.edra.com

Chair, Mummy
Peter Traag
Bent beech,
polyurethane foam,
polyester elastic ribbon
H: 84cm (33in)
H (seat): 48cm (18 ⁷/₈in)
W: 46cm (18 ¹/₈in)
D: 52cm (20 ¹/₂in)
Edra SpA, Italy
www.edra.com

**Stackable armchair,
Thin collection S15**
Karri Monni
Sandblasted stainless
steel, wood
H: 78cm (31in)
W: 56cm (22in)
D: 52cm (20 ¹/₂in)
Lapalma, Italy
www.lapalma.it

Chair, Supernatural
Ross Lovegrove
Polyamide reinforced
with fibreglass
H: 81cm (32in)
W: 53cm (20 ⁷/₈in)
D: 51cm (20 ¹/₈in)
Moroso SpA, Italy
www.moroso.it

Chairs, Kong
Philippe Starck
Aluminium
(brushed/anodized,
powder-coated or
hand-polished),
Lexan© foot caps
Various dimensions
Emeco, USA
www.emeco.net

Stacking chair, 1951
BMW Designworks USA
Aluminium, ABS,
polycarbonate
H: 77cm (30in)
W: 47cm (18 ½in)
D: 51cm (20 ⅛in)
Emeco, USA
www.emeco.net

The **Emeco aluminium chair** is an icon of 1950s
American furniture design. In 2000 the company was
approached by Philippe Starck, who asked if he could
be responsible for remodelling the chair. He has said,
'the Emeco chair is a timeless design but you can see
it comes from the 1940s or 50s. I wanted to keep the
heritage of the chair, but turn it into an almost future
classic.' He kept the main silhouette of the original
while making it stackable, lighter and better adapted
to today's needs. Such was the success of the
collaboration that Starck went on to produce his
signature 'Kong' chair for Emeco, and the company
made it a policy to approach other designers to
produce chairs for them. In 2004 Frank Gehry produced
his superlight chair, and in the following year BMW
Designworks brought out the colourful but highly
streamlined '1951' chair, which was based on the
long-lost Emeco chairs built for American navy
hospitals during the 1950s.

Chair, Superlight ™
Frank Gehry
Aluminium, plastic
H: 81cm (32in)
H (seat): 45.7cm (18 ⅛in)
W: 42cm (16 ½in)
D: 52cm (20 ½in)
Emeco, USA
www.emeco.net

Chair, Hudson
Philippe Starck
Highly polished
aluminium
H: 84cm (33 in)
W: 42cm (16 ⅝in)
D: 46cm (18 ¼in)
Emeco, USA
www.emeco.net

Chair, Alfa

Hannes Wettstein
SCM (polyester resin
compound reinforced
with glass fibre)
H: 80cm (31 1/4in)
W: 50cm (19 1/2in)
L: 49cm (19 1/8in)
Molteni & C. SpA, Italy
www.molteni.it

Chair, Iuta

Antonio Citterio
Die-cast aluminium,
mesh
H: 80cm (31 1/4in)
W: 61cm (23 3/8in)
B&B Italia SpA, Italy
www.bebitalia.it

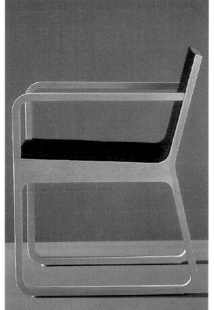

Armchair, Muu

Harri Koskinen
Oak
H: 72cm (28 3/8in)
W: 57cm (22 1/2in)
D: 62cm (24 3/8in)
Montina srl, Italy
www.montina.it

Chair, Muu

Harri Koskinen
Solid oak, oak plywood
H: 80cm (31 1/2in)
D: 50cm (19 3/4in)
Montina, Italy
www.montina.it

Stackable chair, Luna
Biagio Cisotti and
Sandra Laube
Metal, plywood
H: 83cm (33in)
W: 58cm (22 ⅞in)
D: 60cm (23 ⅝in)
Plank, Italy
www.plank.it

Plank have been
experimenting with a
totally new process of
curving plywood. A
single shell of plywood
is heat pressed in an
aluminium mould to
create a result that
would previously only
have been possible to
make in plastic. The
outcome is the 'Luna'
chair manufactured by
Cisotti-Laube.

Chair, Topcut
Philippe Starck
Polycarbonate
H: 84cm (33in)
H (seat): 46cm (18 ⅛in)
W: 47cm (18 ½in)
D: 43cm (16 ⅞in)
Kartell SpA, Italy
www.kartell.it

Stackable chair, Lac
Jasper Morrison
Polypropylene, leather
H: 77.5cm (31in)
W: 49cm (19 ¼in)
D: 51cm (20 ⅛in)
Cap Design SpA, Italy
www.cappellini.it

Chair, Segesta
Alfredo Häberli
Composite, multi-layer
techno-polymer body
with steel structure
H: 80cm (31in)
L: 59cm (23 ¹/₄in)
D: 56cm (22in)
Alias SpA, Italy
www.aliasdesign.it

Chair, Lago
Philippe Starck
Polyurethane
H: 80.5cm (32in)
H (seat): 45cm (17 ³/₄in)
W: 60cm (23 ⁵/₈in)
D: 57cm (22 ¹/₂in)
Driade SpA, Italy
www.driade.com

Chair, UNO
Bartoli Design and
Fauciglietti Engineering
R 606 'leather'
H: 79cm (31in)
H (seat): 44cm (17 ³/₈in)
W: 48cm (18 ⁷/₈in)
D: 45cm (17 ³/₄in)
Segis SpA, Italy
www.segis.it

Like the outline of a chair drawn by a child and produced
in primary colours, the form of 'UNO' is intentionally
elementary so that we focus our attention on the
innovative material in which it is manufactured. 'R606'
takes its inspiration from nature. Like the epidermis,
its outer skin protects the body within. Co-moulded in
a single production process, the chemically composed,
tight-celled skin is combined with the soft urethane-
foam padding inside, resulting in a sturdy and water-
resistant structure, hard on the surface yet soft to
the touch and with a flexibility never before achieved
by any manufacturing process.

Stacking chair, Tin
Konstantin Grcic
Metal
H: 77cm (30in)
W: 55cm (21 ⁵/₈in)
D: 50cm (19 ⁵/₈in)
Magis SpA, Italy
www.magisdesign.com

Stacking chair, Easy
Jerszy Seymour
Polypropylene,
glass fibre
H: 75cm (29 ¹/₂in)
W: 59cm (23 ¹/₄in)
D: 61cm (24in)
Magis SpA, Italy
www.magisdesign.com

Chair, FOL.D
Patrick Jouin
Polypropylene, chrome
tubular steel
H: 81cm (32in)
W: 43cm (16 ⁷/₈in)
D: 52cm (20 ¹/₂in)
XO, France
www.xo-design.com

**Folding chair,
Air-chair**
Jasper Morrison
Air-moulded
polypropylene with
glass fibre
H: 77.1cm (30 ³/₈in)
W: 46.5cm (18 ¹/₃in)
D: 49cm (19 ¹/₄in)
Magis SpA, Italy
www.magisdesign.com

Stackable chair, Bella Rifatta

William Sawaya
Polycarbonate
H: 85cm (33in)
W: 56cm (22in)
D: 56.5cm (22 ¹⁄₄in)
Sawaya & Moroni, Italy
www.sawayamoroni.com

Chair, Victoria Ghost

Philippe Starck
Polycarbonate
H: 90cm (35in)
H (seat): 47.5cm (18 ⁷⁄₈in)
W: 38cm (15in)
D: 40cm (15 ³⁄₄in)
Kartell SpA, Italy
www.kartell.it

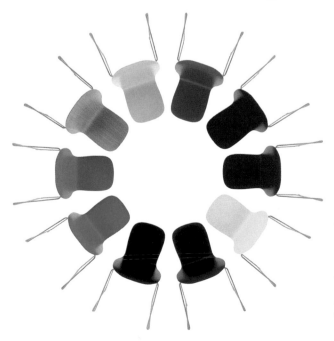

Stackable chair, Tate

Jasper Morrison
Beech plywood, oak,
polypropylene
H: 81cm (31 ⁷⁄₈in)
H (seat): 45cm (17 ³⁄₄in)
W: 53cm (20 ⁷⁄₈in)
D: 47.5cm (18 ³⁄₄in)
Cap Design SpA, Italy
www.cappellini.it

Folding chair, Elica
Gudmundur Ludvik
Plywood, sandblasted
stainless steel
H: 81cm (32in)
W: 48cm (18 ⁷⁄₈in)
D: 54cm (21 ¼in)
Lapalma, Italy
www.lapalma.it

Folding chair, Ori
Toshiyuki Kita
Aluminium,
polypropylene
H: 84cm (33in)
W: 46.5cm (18 ⅛in)
D: 52.5cm (20 ⁷⁄₈in)
Bonaldo SpA, Italy
www.bonaldo.it

Toshiyuki Kita's folding
chair, 'Ori', was
conceived to suit today's
restricted living spaces.
He has used extruded
aluminium, a particularly
lightweight material, and
when collapsed the chair
occupies only 5
centimetres (2 inches)
of space.

Armchair, Marcus
Jeffrey Bernett
Oak wood
H: 85cm (33in)
W: 51cm (20 ⅛in)
D: 57cm (22 ½in)
Montina srl, Italy
www.montina.it

James Irvine

Which of your designs to date would you like to be remembered by?
It is not important to me that I will be remembered but I would certainly be happy if people enjoyed things I have designed long after I am gone.

How do you think others view your work?
I never ask people because I am scared that they might say something nasty to me.

Which designer has influenced you the most and why?
I know who I admire as designers but I feel more influenced by places, materials and cultures than by individuals.

If you were not a designer, what would you like to be and why?
This changes every week. I have often thought I would like to be a writer but I am not very good at it. However, I am sure I could be a great motorcycle mechanic specializing in restoring old British bikes.

What role do you think the designer has in society today?
I often say that everything that is manufactured has been designed by somebody, even though they may not be called designers. If you look at designers in this way then they are essential to modern society.

Do you buy a lot of design pieces?
Well, let's say that I buy some interesting manufactured objects.

Is there a design in your home that you couldn't live without?
I would have a lot of trouble living without my toilet. It's a fantastic object that solves a difficult problem and I must say that the one in my home looks rather smart.

What do you consider to be the best piece of design since the millennium?
Seeing as the toilet was already invented it's a tough challenge. However, the Airbus A380, even though not exactly beautiful, is mind-blowing.

Where do you think design is heading? Is there someone we should be watching out for?
I just hope that in the future there is more to talk about than just very successful vacuum cleaner companies or wacky chair designs that seem to dominate the present popular perception of design. I would say watch out for the next generation, which might catch on to the idea that products could look normal. What a wonderful world that would be.

Is the cult of the personality taking over the design world?
I hope not.

Chair, Loop Chair
(A 660)
James Irvine
Bentwood, aluminium,
webbing
H (seat): 46cm (18 1/8in)
W: 51cm (20 1/8in)
D: 58cm (22 7/8in)
Thonet, Germany
www.thonet.de

Chair, Loop Chair
James Irvine
Bentwood
H: 87cm (34in)
H (seat): 46cm (18 1/8in)
W: 51cm (20 1/8in)
D: 58cm (22 7/8in)
Thonet, Germany
www.thonet.de

Chair, Lola
Jean Marie Massaud
Injection-moulded
plastic, aluminium
H: 80cm (31 1/2in)
W: 61cm (24in)
D: 52cm (20 1/2in)
Liv'it srl, Italy
www.livit.it

**Studio chair,
Hula Hoop**
Philippe Starck
Polypropylene
H: 77.4–90cm
(30 1/2–35 3/8in)
W: 67.7 cm (26 5/8in)
L: 67.2cm (26 3/8in)
Vitra, Switzerland
www.vitra.com

**Office swivel chair,
Oson S**
Antonio Citterio
Plastic or die-cast
polished aluminium
frame, fibreglass-
reinforced polyamide
backrest, fabric and
polyurethane foam
upholstery
H: 82–99.5cm (32–39in)
W: 54.3cm (21 1/in)
Vitra, Switzerland
www.vitra.com

Chair, Work
Vico Magistretti
Chromium-plated steel,
polyurethane foam,
fabric
H: 80–95cm (31–37in)
W: 62cm (24 3/8in)
D: 62cm (24 3/8in)
De Padova srl, Italy
www.depadova.it

Chair, Filo
EOOS (for Keilhauer)
Aluminium, polyester,
plastic-injection
moulding, hydraulic
moulding
Base with wheels,
H: 90–103cm (35–41in)
W: 65cm (25 ⅝in)
D: 66cm (26in);
Base without wheels,
H: 91cm (36in)
W: 67cm (26 ⅜in)
D: 67cm (26 ⅜in)
Bene AG, Austria
www.bene.com

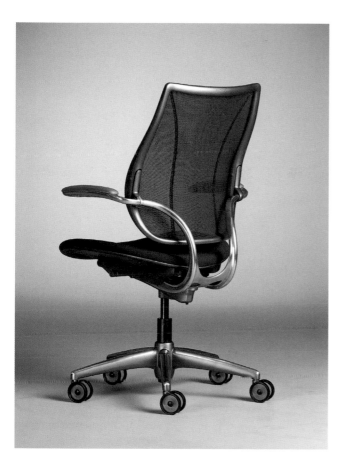

Chair, Liberty
Niels Diffrient
Aluminium, plastic,
non-stretch mesh
H (adjustable): 41–53cm
(16 ⅛–20 ⅞in)
W: 53cm (20 ⅞in)
D (adjustable):
42–48cm
(16 ½–18 ⅞in)
Humanscale, USA
www.humanscale.com

**Chair, Rolling Frame
Desk Chair**
Alberto Meda
Die-cast aluminium,
PVC-covered
polyester mesh
H: 99cm (39in)
W: 43cm (17in)
D: 75cm (29 ½in)
Alias SpA, Italy
www.aliasdesign.it

Sofas and Beds

Modular seating system, Tufty – Time
Patricia Urquiola
Plastic, fabric
Various dimensions
B&B Italia SpA, Italy
www.bebitalia.it

Patricia Urquiola was Designer of the Year in 2004, and she has since taken the design world by storm. She may be one of the very few women designers on the circuit today, but she is making up for this imbalance with her ubiquity, not to mention stamina, which is staggering. It is not surprising that she is nicknamed 'the Hurricane'. I cannot believe there are many major furniture manufacturers she has not worked with over the past couple of years – Driade, B&B Italia, Kartell, Agape, Molteni, Paola Lenti, Foscarini and Alessi are but a few of these companies. Add to this the fact that she frequently sits on illustrious design panels; was the Guest of Honour at the Stockholm Furniture Fair in 2004; designed her idea of the perfect domestic interior, along with Hella Jongerius, at the Ideal House Installation during the Cologne Furniture Fair in 2005; is developing stands and showrooms for Moroso, Knoll and Hansgrohe, as well as an interior for Valentino; and at last year's Milan Furniture Fair showcased a total of 21 products, and it is little wonder that her elegant yet unfussy, simple yet eye-catching pieces are collecting major design prizes internationally, as well as critical acclaim from the media and design peers alike.

Unlike many names that the fickle design press promotes one season and casts into obscurity the next, Urquiola's pedigree will ensure her a place among those set to stay. Her public image has been built up gradually; it is not dependent on press hype and as such will not be tied down to a period or nailed to a style. Contrary to belief, Urquiola has not appeared genie-like to take over the design world;

she has been around for some time and has earned her popularity through hard work and determination. Urquiola graduated from the Madrid Polytechnic, then moved to Italy and completed her education under Achille Castiglioni at the Milan Polytechnic. Until she set up her own Milan-based studio in 2001, she worked for Vico Magistretti, de Padova and Lissoni Associati, names associated less with the vagaries of fashion than with commercial and classical Italian design. From these experiences she has built up a strong head for business and a thorough knowledge of the manufacturing industry, while maintaining a personal style that is a blend of Spanish minimalism and Italian flamboyance.

Urquiola's relationship with Moroso dates from this time. She came to them just before Milan in 2001 with a model of a sofa. So impressed were they with the concept of the design that they decided to go ahead and produce it, even though they already had their new product list worked out. Patrizia Moroso saw in it what she later referred to as a perfect distillation of everything Italian: 'This Spanish girl coming from the outside could perhaps see more clearly than others the lessons of important Italian design.' The collaboration with Moroso is an important one because, early in her independent career, it gave Urquiola a chance to experiment, and in return she has produced many of the company's best-selling products, most notably the 'Fjord' chair and 'Lowland' sofa.

Her love of experimentation and an ability to turn classic ideas on their heads mean Urquiola has a lot in common with avant-garde designers. Among those

she admires she lists Konstantin Grcic, Jasper Morrison, Marcel Wanders and the Bouroullec Brothers, all of whom, like Urquiola, show sound commercial acumen while producing simple pieces with tiny details that have an emotional kick and provoke discussion. Her work is functional and unembellished – 'My designs don't need an explanation; they have to speak for themselves' – drawing inspiration from works of art, travel, fashion and everyday life. She strongly believes that every piece of furniture should have a context and not be produced in isolation. Recent products draw more and more from her own life and memories. The 'Bloomy' (see page 59), which follows the current trend for organic-shaped furniture, was inspired by a desert flower that Urquiola fell in love with on holiday, while her hammock for Moroso (see page 106) was a response to a distant recollection of her father napping in their summer house in Ibiza. An innocent memory turned into something risqué, when she designed the lounger in rubber. Although she admires the more conceptual designers so popular at the moment, she considers that a successful design should always bear the customer in mind. Her furniture is user-friendly, sensuous and accommodating, designed to mould to the body and fit in with surrounding architecture. 'I do want my work to be personal, but I'm not out to make an attention-getting statement.' Working as a woman in a man's world, Urquiola has had to fight hard to get to where she is today – a game she has managed to play successfully through a mixture of seduction, strength and a healthy dose of self-belief.

Sofa, Flap
Francesco Binfaré
Steel, polyurethane
H: 84cm (33in)
L: 355cm (139 3/4in)
D: 166cm (65 3/8in)
Edra SpA, Italy
www.edra.com

Sofa, Basket sofa
Ronan and Erwan
Bouroullec
Metal, fabric/leather
H: 82cm (32in)
W: 230cm (91in)
D: 90cm (35in)
Cap Design SpA, Italy
www.cappellini.it

Modular upholstery
system, Soft System
Tom Dixon
Multi-density foam,
wood
Various dimensions
Tom Dixon, UK
www.tomdixon.net

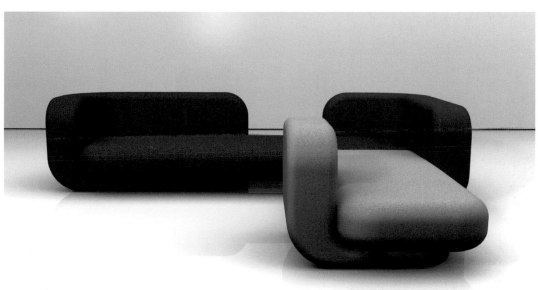

Modular seating
system, La Michetta
Gaetano Pesce
Wood, polyurethane,
Dacron, cotton
Various dimensions
Meritalia SpA, Italy
www.meritalia.it

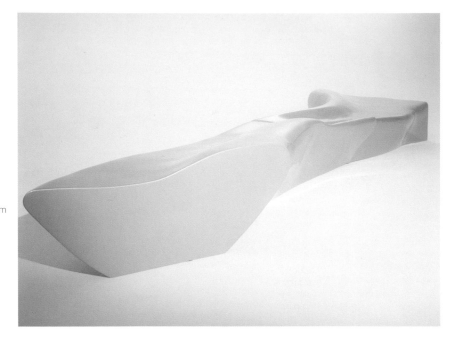

Sofa, Glacier
Zaha Hadid
Fire-varnished wood
H: 50cm (19 ³/₄in)
W: 125cm (49 ¹/₄in)
L: 500cm (197in)
Sawaya & Moroni, Italy
www.sawayamoroni.com

Sofa, Chester
Future Systems
Steel-sprung timber
frame, foam, felt
H: 85cm (33in)
W: 310cm (122in)
D: 150cm (59in)
Established & Sons, UK
www.established
andsons.com

**Furniture collection,
The Frank Gehry
Furniture Collection**
Frank Gehry
One-piece roto-
moulded polymer
Various dimensions
Heller, USA
www.helleronline.com

Cardboard sofa, Humble

Fernando and Humberto Campana
Corrugated cardboard and metal
H: 80cm (31 1/4in)
W: 180cm (70 1/4in)
L: 70cm (27 3/8in)
Campanas, Brazil
www.campanas.com.br

The muted, straight-lined 'Humble' folded cardboard furniture range comprising a table, screen and sofa is inspired by the cardboard collected for recycling by the poor of São Paulo in Brazil. Each day's booty of boxes is folded into striking patterns and then pulled through the streets on handcarts to the paper plant. The Campanas have borrowed these quasi-poetic forms, dyeing the cardboard and adding metal mesh to give strength to the pieces. According to Stephen Hamel, PR head of Edra in 2003, they have taken 'the richness of the poor and made a luxury out of it'.

Armchair, sofas, poufs, Oblong

Jasper Morrison
Polystyrene, fabric
Various dimensions
Cap Design SpA, Italy
www.cappellini.it

Sofa, Late Sofa

Ronan and Erwan Bouroullec
Cloth or leather for the upholstery, aluminium
H: 88.5cm (35in)
W: 254cm (100in)
D: 83cm (33in)
Vitra, Switzerland
www.vitra.com

Multi-sensory audiovisual sofa, Music Image Sofa System (M.I.S.S.)
Philippe Starck
Can be upholstered in fabric, feather or polyester filling, lacquered wood, special technical fabric permeable to sound and infrared rays of the remote control
L: 216–294cm (85–116in)
D: 107–123cm (42–48in)
Cassina SpA, Italy
www.cassina.it

Sofa, Elémentaire
Jean Nouvel
Solid wood, multi-layer wood, leather
H: 74cm (29 ⅛in)
H (seat): 38cm (15in)
W: 211cm (83in)
D: 91cm (36in)
Matteograssi, Italy
www.matteograssi.it

The 'Music Image Sofa System' ('M.I.S.S.') is the final outcome of years of research and collaboration between Starck and Cassina into developing new furniture typologies to suit the evolving patterns of the way we live and function within our home environments. It is always difficult to invent new ideas for comparatively uncomplicated forms such as beds and settees, yet Starck's concept is completely fresh, fusing as it does technology and furnishing. This is a sofa that houses a hi-fi integrated for home theatre and planned to function with any make of appliance. The external appearance is void of any reference to what is contained within – Starck refers to 'the minimum in the maximum'.

The system is made up of two parts: the sofa itself and a 'totem', which houses certain appliances and a screen. The sofa contains the speakers, two set in either end of the back, and a sub-woofer, hidden in the inner part of the larger arm. Sounds come from within the upholstery as if by magic. A projector can be included and is hidden in a compartment behind the back of the sofa. The divan and the screen have to be set a certain distance from each other, and to conceal the micro-cables and micro-connections between the two, Starck has developed an integral 'carpet'. To complement the design, Starck has also created 'M.I.S.T.E.R.', an accompanying settee in various measurements and arrangements but without the technical content.

**Sofa, Lorenzo
le magnifique**

Philippe Starck
Wood, polyurethane,
wool, aluminium
H: 82cm (32in)
W: 210cm (83in)
D: 82cm (32in)
Driade SpA, Italy
www.driade.com

**Sofa and armchair,
Ploof**

Philippe Starck
Polyethylene, adonized
drawn aluminium
Sofa,
H: 65cm (25 ⁵/₈in)
W: 180cm (70 ⁷/₈in)
D: 80cm (31 ¹/₂in);
Armchair,
H: 65cm (25 ⁵/₈in)
W: 86cm (33 ⁷/₈in)
D: 60cm (23 ⁵/₈in)
Kartell SpA, Italy
www.kartell.it

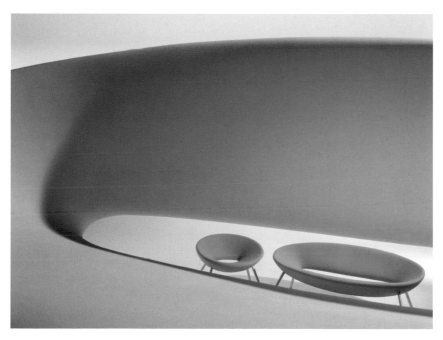

**Modular sofa system,
Orford**

Matthew Hilton
Beech, elasticized
webbing, foam,
aluminium
Various dimensions
SCP, UK
www.scp.co.uk

Seating, Sof Sof
Enzo Mari
Iron rods, polyurethane,
Dacron
H: 84cm (33in)
W: 57cm (22 ½in)
D: 46cm (18 ⅛in)
Robots SpA, Italy
www.robots.it

Massimo Iosa Ghini

Which of your designs to date would you like to be remembered by?
My next designs, and my earliest projects for Memphis.

How do you think others view your work?
Even without my name, my work and my designs are very recognizable. You can like them or not, but my designs are Iosa Ghini's.

Which designer has influenced you the most and why?
Frank Lloyd Wright, his shapes; Ettore Sottsass, his research into projects, beyond production and function.

If you were not a designer, what would you like to be and why?
Architect and designer, or painter.

Do you buy a lot of design pieces?
Not so many. I buy objects, pipes, cars that I like. I do not differentiate between 'design pieces' and 'not-design pieces'.

Is there a design in your home that you couldn't live without?
My personal chaise longue, designed for myself, and my LCD television.

Sofa and armchair, Moon
Massimo Iosa Ghini
Steel structure covered in cold-foamed polyurethane and acrylic fibre
Sofa,
H: 80cm (31in)
W: 250cm (98in)
D: 92cm (36in);
Armchair,
H: 80cm (31in)
W: 116in (46in)
D: 92cm (36in)
Cinova srl, Italy
www.cinova.it

Sofa, Folio HM
Francesco Bettoni
Steel frame cold-foamed with polyurethane rubbers, chromium-plated iron tube base
H: 90cm (35in)
L: from 134cm (53in)
D: 90cm (35in)
MDF Italia srl, Italy
www.mdfitalia.it

Seating, Barbarella
Ross Lovegrove
Plywood, beech,
springs, HR foam,
natural sheep skin
Sofa,
H: 57cm (22 ¹/₄in)
W: 270cm (106in)
D: 91cm (36in);
Footstool,
H: 35cm (13 ³/₄in)
W: 91cm (36in)
D: 97cm (38in)
Moooi, the Netherlands
www.moooi.com

**Furniture system,
Nido**
Vincent Van Duysen
Plywood structure,
expanded multi-density
polyurethane foam,
harmonic steel springs
Various dimensions
Cap Design SpA, Italy
www.cappellini.it

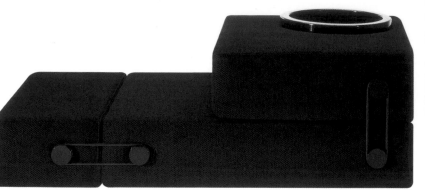

**Modular seating
system, Trix**
Piero Lissoni
Expanded polyurethane,
polyester fabric
Various dimensions
Kartell SpA, Italy
www.kartell.it

Sofa, Isobel
Michiel Van der Kley
Polyether, fabric and
chromed steel
H: 73cm (28 ³/₄in)
W: 190cm (75in)
D: 88cm (35in)
Artifort, the Netherlands
www.artifort.com

Garden furniture, Uno
Eckhoff+Kuebler+
Schurgacz
Injection-moulded
plastic
H: 120cm (47in)
W: 50cm (19 ⁵/₈in)
D: 35cm (13 ³/₄in)
Gandia Blasco, Spain
www.gandiablasco.com

Sofa, Horizon
Arik Lévy
Cold-processed flexible
polyurethane, fabric
H: 70cm (27 ½ in)
W: 226cm (89in)
D: 84cm (33in)
Baleri Italia SpA, Italy
www.baleri-italia.com

Sofa, Aspen
Jean Marie Massaud
Steel, nylon, fabric
or leather
H: 72cm (28 ³⁄₈ in)
W: 260cm (102in)
D: 90cm (35in)
Cassina SpA, Italy
www.cassina.it

Sofa, AU
Setsu and Shinobu Ito
Polyurethane foam,
lycra, leather
Small,
H: 70cm (27 ½ in)
W: 96cm (38in)
L: 106cm (42in);
Large,
H: 75cm (29 ½ in)
W: 151cm (59in)
L: 138cm (54in)
Edra SpA, Italy
www.edra.com

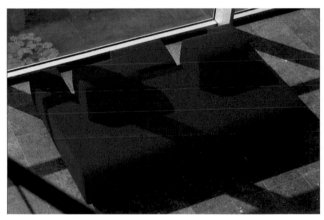

Modular seating system, Island
Fabiaan Van Severen
PUR, fabric
Various dimensions
Fabiaan Van Severen, Belgium
www.fabiaanvanseveren.com

Sofa, Odin

Konstantin Grcic
Synthetic resin,
polyurethane
H: 73.5cm (29 ⅛in)
H (seat): 45cm (17 ¾in)
W: 160cm (63in)
D: 69cm (27 ⅛in)
ClassiCon GmbH,
Germany
www.classicon.com

Armchair, Muff Daddy

Jerszy Seymour
Denim
H: 65cm (25 ⅝in)
W: 105cm (41 ⅜in)
L: 110cm (43 ¼in)
Covo srl, Italy
www.covo.it

Jerszy Seymour's 'Muff Daddy' is a twenty-first
century reinterpretation of the casual living concept
of the 1960s, of not taking the world too seriously.
Design should adapt to how we conduct our lives;
this armchair exemplifies 'cool' lounging. Seymour
predicts that, 'The future of design is going to be
fabulous, furry, furious and fun. It will be a tool of love,
a superhero ready to do battle for good and evil.
It will ask why it exists and what its purpose in life is.
It will stick its middle finger up, run through the
woods naked and save the world.'

Armchair/painting
cushion, Sofart

Lorenzo Damiani
Chromed steel, fabric
H: 40–70cm
(15 ¾–27 ½in)
W: 95cm (37in)
D: 95cm (37in)
Campeggi srl, Italy
www.campeggisrl.it

Sofa, Oxygen

Ann Tiukinhoy
Pamintuan
Welded metal washers
H: 78cm (31in)
W: 234cm (92in)
D: 104cm (41in)
The Gilded Expressions,
Philippines
gildex@mozcom.com

Rocking chair, Gunghult

James Irvine
Rattan, steel, lacquer
H: 73.5cm (29 1/8in)
W: 79cm (31in)
D: 106.5cm (42in)
IKEA, Sweden
www.ikea.com

Swedish design has always been very much tied to its history, political development and the physical exigencies of the country itself. A population that was until relatively recently isolated within its own boundaries and from the rest of the world has given rise to a 'do-it-yourself' mentality, while a Protestant tradition has resulted in a preference for simple, functional design. The harsh weather conditions make the home a refuge with a need to create a home environment that is at once beautiful and well planned. An affinity with the environment and the proliferation of natural products – pine, spruce, pure wools and linens – along with a light, muted palette and the use of the occasional strong flashes of colour have been used to brighten up drab winters. IKEA still flies the flag of modern functionalist furniture for all. Its product range is known throughout the world for modern but unpretentious, practical yet attractive, human-centred and child-friendly Swedish home-furnishing traditions.

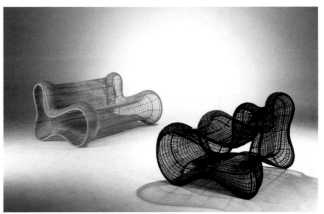

Armchair and sofa, Pigalle

Kenneth Cobonpue
Abaca (Manila hemp),
nylon, steel
Chair,
H: 79cm (31 1/8in)
W: 97cm (38 1/4in)
D: 94cm (37in);
Sofa,
H: 75cm (29 1/2in)
W: 158cm (62 1/4in)
D: 100cm (39 3/8in)
Interior Crafts of
the Islands, Inc,
the Philippines
www.kennethcobonpue.com

Seating system, Facett

Ronan and Erwan
Bouroullec
Foam, quilting,
stitching
Various dimensions
Ligne Roset, France
www.ligne-roset.com

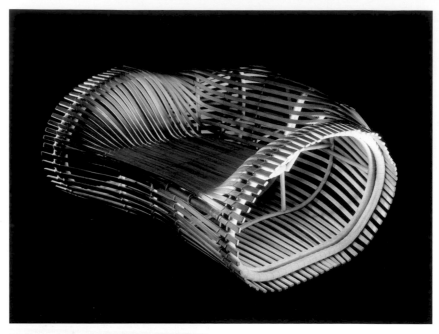

Lounge chair, Paloma
Kenneth Cobonpue
Rattan, nylon wire
H: 61cm (24in)
W: 130cm (51in)
D: 96.5cm (38in)
Interior Crafts of
the Islands, Inc,
the Philippines
www.kenneth
cobonpue.com

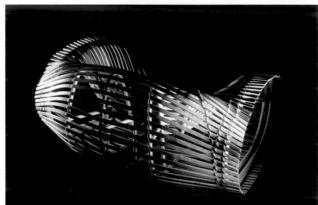

Kenneth Cobonpue first made his name at the Milan Furniture Fair 2001, when he showed his work alongside other designers from the Philippines in a joint show called Movement 8. Describing his design philosophy at that time, he told me that he looked at nature with the purity and innocence of a child, finding in it perfect visual qualities that were waiting to be transformed into modern man-made objects. Since then he has continued to use natural materials in unexpected and innovative ways, combining traditional skills with modern technology.

The 'Paloma' lounge chair uses thick rattan strips that have been steamed and bent over a structural rattan frame, each individually tied with nylon wire. This manufacturing process, developed by Cobonpue, is faster, easier and more cost efficient than the customary bentwood technique.

Departures from the majority of his products, which use bamboo and rattan indigenous to his country, are his new 'Dragnet' chair (see page 52), which is made from galvanized wire wrapped with 100 per cent outdoor acrylic fabric, and 'Kabuki' (see page 131). The latter is constructed from MDF. This fabricated material has been handcrafted: special tools are used to incise a pattern that imitates embedded bamboo stalks, and the surface is then hand-rubbed and polished four times with three different layers of colour. The name 'Kabuki' is the word for a traditional form of Japanese theatre.

Five leather elements,
Pools & Pouf!
Robert Stadler
Leather
Various dimensions
Galerie Dominique
Fiat, France
www.radidesigners.com

**Magnetic cushions,
Couines! Couines!**
Diego Fortunato
Technological fabric,
magnet
H: 15cm (5 ⁷/₈in)
W: 48cm (18 ⁷/₈in)
L: 48cm (18 ⁷/₈in)
Nani Marquina, Spain
www.nanimarquina.com

Lounger, Storvik
Carl Öjerstorm
Clear lacquered rattan
H: 77cm (30 ³/₈in)
W: 105cm (41 ³/₈in)
L: 130cm (51 ¹/₈in)
IKEA, Sweden
www.ikea.com

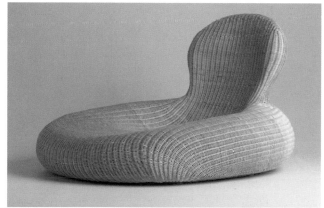

**Sofa covered with a
printed fabric, Print**
Marcel Wanders
Wooden structure,
polyurethane and
polyester fibre
H: 85cm (33in)
W: 270cm (106in)
D: 96cm (38in)
Moroso SpA, Italy
www.moroso.it

Sofa, Giubbe Rosse
Denis Santachiara
Plastic, fabric
H: 70cm (27 1/2in)
W: 192cm (75 1/2in)
D: 94cm (37in)
Styling srl, Italy
www.styling.it

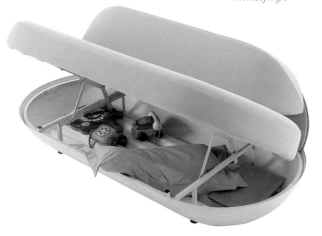

Seating, Leudo
Dodo Arslan
Stainless steel frame,
aluminium hinges,
W2 fabric, Zenith fabric
reinforcements
H (folded): 60cm (23 5/8)
H (unfolded): 68cm (26 3/4in)
W (folded): 13cm (5 1/8in)
W (unfolded): 120cm (47 1/4in)
Alias SpA, Italy
www.aliasdesign.it

Fernando and Humberto Campana

Which of your designs to date would you like to be remembered by?
The 'Vermelha' chair, Edra, 1998. The 'Banquete' chair, Estudio Campana, 2002.

How do you think others view your work?
Some look at it with a 'child's' smile and go for it. Others do not believe in it and look at it with a certain disbelief. We understand and respect both opinions.

Which designer has influenced you the most and why?
Humberto: Shiro Kuramata through his poetry and delicacy.
Fernando: Achille Castiglioni through his sense of humour and investigation in different fields of design.

If you were not a designer, what would you like to be and why?
Fernando: A bird or an aircraft, to fly.
Humberto: A gardener, for the silent act of planting.

What role do you think the designer has in society today?
To point to new ways for human beings to use and acquire objects whose functions or aesthetics are in accordance with the spirit, body and environment.

Do you buy a lot of design pieces?
Most of the design pieces are our own creations. Our homes are the experimentation field for them.

Is there a design in your home that you couldn't live without?
Fernando: My TV set (from Sony).
Humberto: The 'Vermelha' chair.

What do you consider to be the best piece of design since the millennium?
Fernando: The iBook, 'Snow'.
Humberto: The LAD glass projects by Ingo Maurer.

Is the cult of the personality taking over the design world?
The design must speak louder than the cult of personality.

Sofa, Boa
Fernando and Humberto Campana
Polyurethane foam, velvet
H: 80cm (31 ½in)
W: 150cm (59in)
L: 270cm (106 ¼in)
Edra SpA, Italy
www.edra.com

Bed, Hi-Ply
Luciano Marson
Beech
H: 23cm (9in)
W: 92, 122 or 184cm (36, 48 or 72in)
L: 210cm (83in)
Horm, Italy
www.horm.it

Sofa, Joe
De Pas, d'Urbino, Lomazzi
One-piece roto-moulded polymer
H: 86.5cm (34in)
W: 167cm (66in)
D: 112cm (44in)
Heller, USA
www.helleronline.com

Lounger, Pororoga
Flavia Alves de Souza
Stainless steel,
translucent/fluorescent
plastic film
H: 77cm (30in)
W: 51cm (20in)
L: 120cm (46 ⁷/₈in)
Edra SpA, Italy
www.edra.com

Chaise longue, Soft
Werner Aisslinger
Steel, aluminium alloy,
Technogel®
H: 85cm (33 ¹/₂in)
W: 60cm (23 ⁵/₈in)
L: 180cm (70 ⁷/₈in)
Zanotta SpA, Italy
www.zanotta.it

The '**Soft**' chaise longue for Zanotta demonstrates Aisslinger's love of technology and new materials – he believes that it is in these areas, rather than in artificial innovative forms, that new typologies will be developed. He says that he aims 'to work with 3D forms that are not minimalist and clean like the stuff that was being made in the 1990s'.

Armchair, Lazy
Patricia Urquiola
Steel frame,
polyester, PVC
H: 82cm (32 ¹/₄in)
W: 82cm (32 ¹/₄in)
D: 113cm (42 ¹/₄in)
B&B Italia SpA, Italy
www.bebitalia.it

Chaise longue, Fish
Thomas Sauvage
Aluminium, steel, mesh
polyester, PVC
H: 93cm (37in)
W: 76cm (29 ⁷/₈in)
D: 168cm (66in)
Ego, France
www.egoparis.com

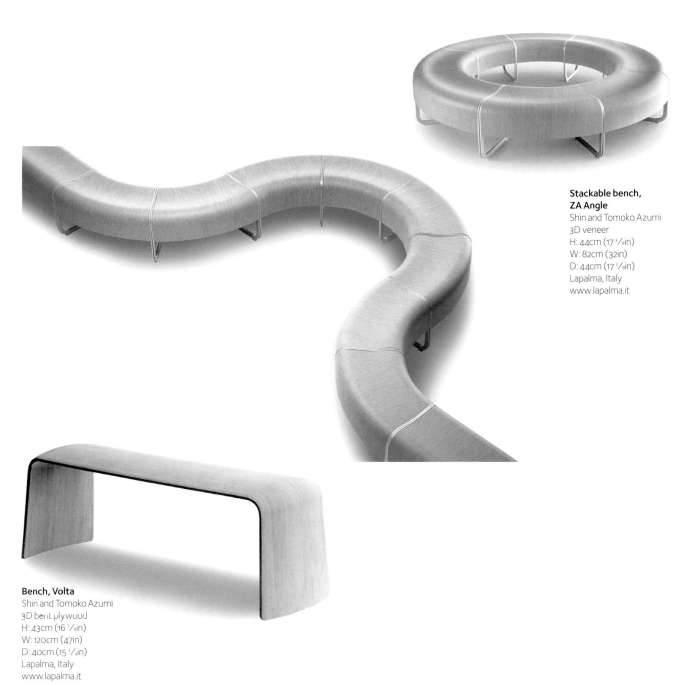

**Stackable bench,
ZA Angle**
Shin and Tomoko Azumi
3D veneer
H: 44cm (17 ³/₈in)
W: 82cm (32in)
D: 44cm (17 ³/₈in)
Lapalma, Italy
www.lapalma.it

Bench, Volta
Shin and Tomoko Azumi
3D bent plywood
H: 43cm (16 ⁷/₈in)
W: 120cm (47in)
D: 40cm (15 ³/₄in)
Lapalma, Italy
www.lapalma.it

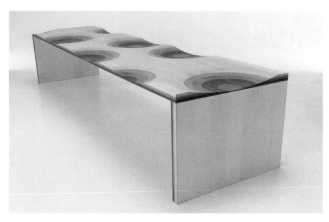

Bench, Ripples
Toyo Ito
Walnut, mahogany,
cherry, oak and beech
H: 40cm (15 ³/₄in)
W: 200cm (79in)
D: 50cm (19 ⁵/₈in)
Horm, Italy
www.horm.it

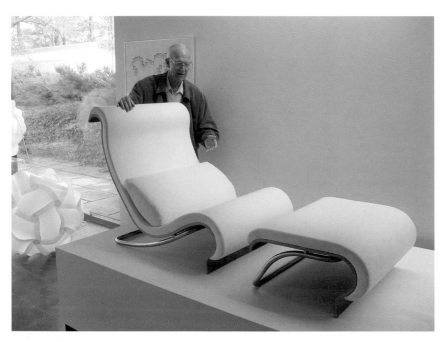

Jorn Utzon is without doubt one of the world's most famous living architects. Designer of the iconic wings of the Sydney Opera House, he has worked internationally and in many fields. His work embraces the lyrically curved ceilings of the church at Bagsvaerd, the monumentality of the Kuwait National Assembly Building and the sensuous tranquillity of the Can Feliz house in Mallorca. He draws inspiration from the mysteries of ancient civilizations (Mayan, Chinese, Japanese and Islamic), as well as the minimalism and clear lines of his native Scandinavia. The 'Aurora' chair was designed over forty years ago, in 1965, in connection with Utzon's work on the Sydney Opera House, but it is only today that the prototype is being produced by the Danish company Trio Line as part of the Bahnsen Collection. The profile of the chair owes much to the Opera House, in which Utzon employed large constructions in form-pressured wood, a technique he adopted for the pieces he later designed as furniture for the building. Utzon writes: 'When I sit in this chair: my friends seem more friendly, my view is more beautiful, my troubles seem smaller, my thoughts flow more freely and my life is more inspiring.'

Chair with cushion and footstool, Aurora
Jorn Utzon
Fabric or leather
Chair,
H: 80cm (31in)
W: 75cm (29 ¹⁄₂in)
D: 110cm (43in);
Footstool,
H: 35cm (13 ³⁄₄in)
W: 75cm (29 ¹⁄₂in)
D: 60cm (23 ⁵⁄₈in)
Trio Line A/S, Denmark
www.trioline.com

Chaise longue, Lofty
Piergiorgio Cazzaniga
Polished AISI304
stainless steel
H: 73cm (28 ³⁄₄in)
W: 79cm (31in)
L: 140cm (55in)
MDF Italia srl, Italy
www.mdfitalia.it

Lounger, Shadow
Christian Ghion
Thermoformed Corian®,
chrome-plated base
H: 70cm (27 ¹⁄₂in)
W: 72cm (28 ³⁄₈in)
L: 180cm (70 ⁷⁄₈in)
Cap Design SpA, Italy
www.cappellini.it

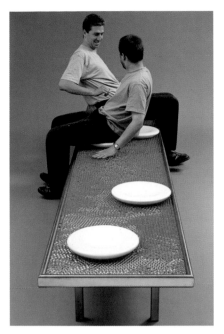

Bed, Lipla
Jean Marie Massaud
Wood, elastic textile
H: 70cm (27¹/₂in)
W: 243cm (96in)
L: 192 or 212cm
(76 or 83in)
Porro srl, Italy
www.porro.com

Bench, Come a little bit closer
Nina Farkache
Steel, glass, marbles
and MDF
H: 43cm (17in)
L: 460cm (181¹/₄in)
D: 68cm (26³/₄in)
Droog Design, the
Netherlands
www.droogdesign.nl

Always thought-provoking yet often tongue in cheek, Droog Design's collection for 2001 was entitled **Me, Myself and You** – a series of objects that either encourage or discourage participation. We have all experienced moments of being in the wrong place at the wrong time and wishing to fade into the background, or alternatively wishing we could introduce ourselves at a party but not having an opening gambit. Here, Nina Farkache's bench, 'Come a little bit closer', is an absolute joy. Users can just slide together discreetly and smoothly across a bed of marbles.

Maarten Van Severen died in 2005, and in his passing Belgium lost one of its best-known and most respected designers. His work was recognized internationally for its modernity, strict use of geometry, clarity, simplicity and individuality. Each piece was reduced to its absolute functionality in a constant process of elimination. He aimed to produce furniture that is, as he used to say, 'super real – as if it has always been there'. Son of abstract expressionist Dan Van Severen, Maarten was born in Antwerp in 1956, and studied architecture at Ghent Art Academy before deciding to work in product design, founding his studio in 1987. He came to worldwide attention through his collaboration with Vitra, where he was

exposed to new materials and production techniques. Although he has been associated with many other manufacturing companies – Bulo, Alessi, Edra and Kartell, to name just a few – it is with Vitra that he produced his most famous pieces, starting with the '03.chair' in 1996 and continuing until his death with work showcased during the Milan Furniture Fair 2005. As well as furniture design, Van Severen worked on many interior design projects, most prominently with Rem Koolhaas/OMA on the Villa dall'Ava in 1990 and the Maison à Florias in 1996, and more recently completing all the seating for OMA's concert hall in Porto, Portugal. He was working on a retrospective of his work for Ghent Design Museum when he died.

Seating, MVS chaise
Maarten Van Severen
Steel, polyurethane,
leather
H: 87cm (34in)
W: 46cm (18¹/₈in)
L: 154cm (61in)
Vitra, Switzerland
www.vitra.com

Chaise longue, Fly
Ora-Ïto
Plastic, fabric
H: 79.5cm (31in)
W: 162cm (64in)
D: 64cm (25¹/₂in)
B&B Italia SpA, Italy
www.bebitalia.it

Seating, Los bancos Suizos (The Swiss benches)
Alfredo Häberli
Steel
Various dimensions
Bd Ediciones de Diseño, Spain
www.bdbarcelona.com

Long chair, PI-Air
Harry & Camila
Fibreglass
H: 77cm (30in)
W: 65cm (25 ⅝in)
L: 147cm (58in)
Living Divani srl, Italy
www.livingdivani.it

Seating system, Light
Francesco Rota
Tubular galvanized steel, stress-resistant polyurethane foam, polyester fibre, fabric
Chair,
H: 76cm (29 ⅞in)
W: 76cm (29 ⅞in)
Pouf,
H: 30cm (11 ¾in)
W: 76cm (29 ⅞in)
Paola Lenti srl, Italy
www.paolalenti.com

Chaise longue
Ross Lovegrove
Loom membrane,
aluminium, steel/inox
H: 85cm (33 ¹/₂in)
W: 80cm (31 ¹/₂in)
L: 185cm (72 ⁷/₈in)
Loom GmbH, Germany
www.lloydloom.de

Ross Lovegrove's work for Loom is an example of a traditional manufacturer becoming involved with contemporary design to give its image a facelift. The managing director, Godobert Reisenthel, was impressed by the way Lovegrove mixed organic shapes with a modern technical expression of form. The designs were created on computer, and aluminium extrusions were added to the traditional paper and wire fabric.

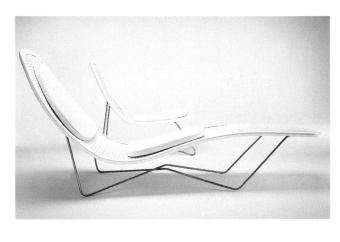

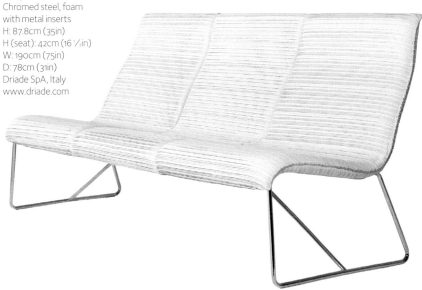

Chair, Tokyo Pop
Tokujin Yoshioka
Polyethylene
H: 178.5cm (70 ¹/₂in)
W: 74cm (29 ¹/₈in)
D: 157cm (61 ⁷/₈in)
Driade SpA, Italy
www.driade.com

Tokujin Yoshioka

Which of your designs to date would you like to be remembered by?
I'd like to be remembered for 'Honey-Pop'.

How do you think others view your work?
Perhaps they think of my design as design that is invisible.

Which designer has influenced you the most and why?
That would be Issey Miyake. His unconventional and innovative attitude towards creation has influenced me the most.

If you were not a designer, what would you like to be and why?
I'd have been a chef if I were not a designer. It is very similar in that we both create; I think there is a common ground.

Do you buy a lot of design pieces?
No, not really.

Is the cult of the personality taking over the design world?
I would not think so. A designer or any other creator should reflect his or her personality naturally. Performance is not necessary.

Sofa, Boing
Tokujin Yoshioka
Chromed steel, foam
with metal inserts
H: 87.8cm (35in)
H (seat): 42cm (16 ¹/₂in)
W: 190cm (75in)
D: 78cm (31in)
Driade SpA, Italy
www.driade.com

Fabio Novembre

Which of your designs to date would you like to be remembered by?
My sofa 'AND' reflects the DNA of a new generation that has embraced coexistence while denying tyranny. 'AND': it's time for conjunction!

How do you think others view your work?
Barock 'n' Roll!

Which designer has influenced you the most and why?
I think my design is situated somewhere between two opposites like Carlo Mollino and Shiro Kuramata.

If you were not a designer, what would you like to be and why?
I would like to be a movie director, but actually, thinking about it, I already make movies in 3D.

What role do you think the designer has in society today?
The task of a designer, of any human being, is to dream a better world and to work to make it true.

Do you buy a lot of design pieces?
Yes, I do. I love to sit on great ideas.

Is there a design in your home that you couldn't live without?
I want everything but need nothing.

Where do you think design is heading? Is there someone we should be watching out for?
Design is heading to a semiotic pollution followed by an overproduction of unnecessary needs. I believe we should do less and better.

Is the cult of the personality taking over the design world?
I think it's wrong to define it this way. I believe heroes have always existed. Having the capacity to inspire people is a big responsibility to be aware of.

Combinable seating system, AND
Fabio Novembre
Polyurethane,
wood, metal
H: 230cm (90 ¹/₂in)
W: 175cm (68 ⁷/₈in)
L: 160cm (63in)
Cap Design SpA, Italy
www.cappellini.it

Fabio Novembre's '**AND**' took pride of place at the entrance of Cap Design's exhibition at Superstudio Piu during Milan 2002. At once retro and organic, the multi-functional tunnel was inspired by a backwards interpretation of a string of DNA molecules. The structure both divides and defines a space. Once seated within the labyrinth, ambient sounds are muted, yet the gaps between elements allow communication with the surroundings.

Hammock, Amaca
Patricia Urquiola
Chromed steel, leather,
wool fabric
L (with rope holders):
320cm (126in)
L (without rope
holders): 200cm (79in)
D (max.): 120cm (47in)
Moroso SpA, Italy
www.moroso.it

El Ultimo Grito

Which of your designs to date would you like to be remembered by?
We would not like to be remembered ... at least not yet.

If you were not a designer, what would you like to be and why?
A butterfly, mainly because our daughter wants to grow up to be one and we don't want to miss her first flight.

What role do you think the designer has in society today?
Maybe not so much the designer as such, but design thinking, which is central to all our cultural and social activities.

Do you buy a lot of design pieces?
We don't think we have ever bought anything that has not been designed in one way or another.

Where do you think design is heading? Is there someone we should be watching out for?
Design is trying to set a new role for itself that is not defined by the materiality of the object and the industrial process.

Is the cult of the personality taking over the design world?
This has been a trend for quite a few years. It just serves to perpetuate the myth of the 'designed object'.

Leather-upholstered bench, Cowbenches (from left to right: Eileen, Belinda, Radia, Carla, Else)
Julia Lohmann
Italian cowhide, foam, wood
H: 60cm (23 ⅝in)
W: 80cm (31in)
D: 150cm (59in)
Julia Lohmann, UK in collaboration with Alma, UK
www.julialohmann.co.uk
www.almahome.co.uk

By making a light from tripe and a leather bench in the shape of a cow's torso, **Julia Lohmann** uses her work to explore our contradictory relationship with animals as sources of food and clothing.

Public seating and plant pot, Land Ho!
Rosario Hurtado and Robert Feo, El Ultimo Grito
Roto-moulded polypropylene
H: 80cm (31in)
Diam: 150cm (59in)
Nola Industrier AB, Sweden
www.nola.se

Bench, bdlove
Ross Lovegrove
Rotation-moulded polyethylene
H: 94cm (37in)
W: 130cm (51⅛in)
L: 265cm (104⅜in)
Bd Ediciones de Diseño, Spain
www.bdbarcelona.com

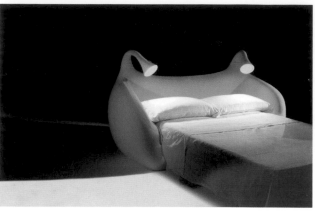

Sofa/bed, Morfeo
Stefano Giovannoni,
Rodrigo Torres
Flexible polyurethane,
elastic fabrics
H: 145cm (57in)
H (seat): 80cm (31in)
W: 200cm (79in)
D (sofa): 90cm (35in)
D (bed): 226cm (89in)
Modular srl, Italy
www.domodinamica.com

Double bed, Kalm
Karim Rashid
Emery-leather, metal
H: 40cm (15 ³/₄in)
W: 206, 212, 232 or
246cm (81, 83, 91 or 97in)
D: 220 or 225cm
(87 or 89in)
Bonaldo, Italy
www.bonaldo.it

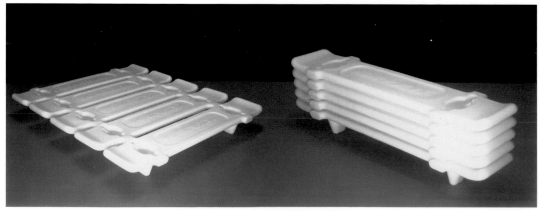

Furniture, Snoozy
Nick Crosbie and Paul
Crofts
Polyethylene
H: 26.5cm (10 ¹/₈in)
W: 170cm (66 ³/₈in)
L: 260cm (101 ³/₈in)
Inflate, UK
www.inflate.co.uk

Bed, Voyage
Kenneth Cobonpue
Rattan split, buri, abaca
and mild steel
H: 159cm (63in)
W: 165cm (65in)
D: 256cm (101in)
Interior Crafts of
the Islands, Inc,
the Philippines
www.kenneth
cobonpue.com

Sofa, Croissant
Kenneth Cobonpue
Rattan split, buri, abaca
and mild steel
H: 77.5cm (31in)
W: 257cm (101in)
D: 125cm (49in)
Interior Crafts of
the Islands, Inc,
the Philippines
www.kenneth
cobonpue.com

Bed, Edward II
Antonia Astori
Merbau solid wood,
stainless inox steel
H: 54cm (21¹⁄₄in)
H (frame): 250cm (98in)
W: 199cm (78in)
D: 219cm (86in)
Driade SpA, Italy
www.driade.com

Sofa bed, Menelikke
Vico Magistretti
Steel, polyurethane
H: 80cm (31¹⁄₂in)
W: 180cm (70⁷⁄₈in)
L: 108cm (42¹⁄₂in)
Campeggi srl, Italy
www.campeggisrl.it

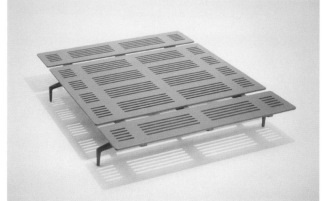

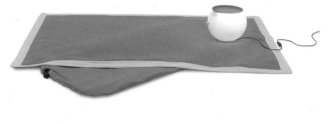

Carpet, lamp and airbed, Taplit
Denis Santachiara
100% cotton, PVC, lycra, polycarbonate, iron
Carpet,
W: 145cm (57in)
L: 200cm (79in);
Airbed,
H: 20cm (7 7/8in)
W: 83cm (33in)
L: 193cm (76in)
Campeggi srl, Italy
www.campeggisrl.it

'Taplit' is a carpet and lamp that transforms into an emergency airbed. The mattress is concealed within the rug and is inflated by the lamp, which acts as light source, pump and bedside table.

Bed, Legnoletto
Alfredo Häberli
Wood, aluminium
H: 37cm (14 1/2in)
W: 90, 140, 160 or 180cm (35 1/2, 55 1/8, 63 or 70 7/8in)
L: 212cm (83 1/2in)
Alias SpA, Italy
www.aliasdesign.it

Bed, La La Salama
Harry Allen
Walnut veneer, matt-lacquered MDF, satin chrome
H: 228.5cm (90in)
W: 223.5cm (88in)
D: 51.5cm (20 1/4in)
Dune, USA
www.dune-ny.com

'La La Salama' means 'peaceful sleep' in Swahili. Harry Allen's wall bed reminds me of those farcical scenes in old black-and-white movies, when a daffy peroxide blonde has to hastily transform her bedsit for an unexpected guest by throwing everything on to the bed and concealing it within the wall. This piece of Americana has been given a facelift. The walnut unit contains a pull-down, queen-size bed, and compartments hidden on one side by doors and on the other by a range of storage units, shelves and a mirror. A bedside table can also be lowered at night and pushed back into the unit during the day. As the bed is secured by legs to the floor and ceiling rather than to a wall, it is ideal for use as a room divider.

Bed, Scent
Piergiorgio Cazzaniga
Wood
H: 57cm (22 1/2in)
L: 240cm (94in)
W: 234cm (92in)
Porro srl, Italy
www.porro.com

Bed system, Dream
Marcel Wanders
Wood, Textile
H: 50cm (19 5/8in)
W: 200cm (79in)
D: 200cm (79in)
Poliform, Italy
www.poliform.it

Bed, Clip
Patricia Urquiola
Fabric or leather cover
H: 79cm (30in)
W: 194, 204 or 214cm
(76, 80 or 84in)
D: 228 or 253cm
(90 or 100in)
Molteni & C. SpA, Italy
www.molteni.it

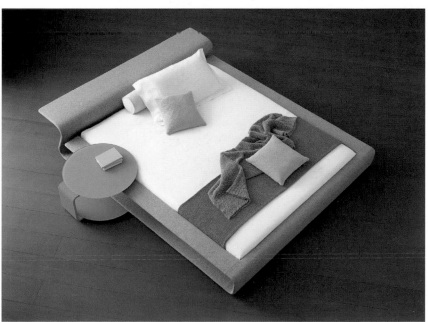

Double bed, Marilyn
Mario Bellini
Upholstery with cover
in fabric or leather
H: 102cm (40in)
W: 203, 213 or 223cm
(80, 84 or 88in)
D: 245cm (96in)
Flou SpA, Italy
www.flou.it

Bed, Highlands
Patricia Urquiola
Polyurethane fibre,
polyester fibre, steel
H: 70cm (27 ½in)
W: 183, 198 or 208cm
(71 , 78 or 82in)
D: 245cm (96in)
Moroso SpA, Italy
www.moroso.it

Bed, Nina Rota
Ron Arad
Fibreglass
H: 75cm (29 ½in)
W: 290cm (114in)
L: 250cm (98in)
Cap Design SpA, Italy
www.cappellini.it

Bed, Miss You
Philippe Starck
Fabric, wood
H: 112cm (44in)
W: 176 or 186cm
(69 or 73in)
D: 216cm (85in)
Cassina SpA, Italy
www.cassina.it

Bed, Grandlit
Hans Sandgren Jakobsen
Beech, steel
H: 78cm (30 ³/₄in)
W: 220cm (86 ⁵/₈in)
L: 200cm (78 ³/₄in)
Fredericia Furniture A/S,
Denmark
www.fredericia.com

Hans Sandgren
Jakobsen's '**Grandlit**' is
a new concept in bed
design. The table and
two back supports can
be placed anywhere
around the perimeter,
allowing for a variety
of uses.

Bed, Edward I
Antonia Astori
Merbau solid wood,
stainless inox steel
H: 54cm (21 ¹/₄in)
W: 187cm (74in)
D: 207cm (81in)
Driade SpA, Italy
www.driade.com

Storage

**Bookshelf, Hey, chair,
be a bookshelf!**
Maarten Baas
Objets trouvés with
a PU coating
H: 180cm (71in)
W: 60cm (23 ⁵/₈in)
D: 70cm (27 ¹/₂in)
Maarten Baas,
the Netherlands
www.maartenbaas.com

Dutch Design

Recently, *Frame* magazine published a polemic on
Dutch design by Ron Kaal. Considering Maarten
Baas's charred chandelier, table and armchair (the
'Smoke' series, variations of which appear on page
327, which Baas produced for Moooi in 2003), Kaal
asks what these items have to do with design. 'The
chair is not an original object, nor is it the result of a
new technique or method of construction. It is simply
the metamorphosis of an existing object, a product
based on a gimmick, one of many gimmicks churned
out by Dutch Design.' Kaal's piece is a critique not only
of Baas's work, but also of the value of the conceptual,
fresh and humorous products that we have come to
associate with Dutch design in general, and that have
enjoyed unprecedented exposure over the past ten
years. This association does not apply to Droog alone,
which has been seen by many as synonymous not
only with design from the Netherlands, but also with
the work of a range of individuals and companies that
are redefining a Dutch national style. What do we
mean when we say something is typically Dutch? And
why has the Netherlands engendered such a style?

If we can set aside the output of the long-
established Dutch commercial manufacturers – for
example Spectrum, Artifort and Leolux – then what
we are really talking about when we refer to Dutch
design is individuals and small practices producing their
work independently. These small-batch productions
are essentially but unorthodoxly plain, unpretentious,
eclectic, illustrating an original use of materials,
conceptually strong, often interdisciplinary, and
betraying a sense of humour and a concern for the
environment. How successful can this sort of design
be in the international marketplace? Marcel Wanders
considers that the essence of Dutch design has to
be distilled into something more commercial for its
influence to continue. Unsure whether one should, or
indeed can, define national styles, he told me that what
is generally considered to be Dutch design has had
such a great impact on design worldwide because of
'its brutal, direct and sensitive way of speaking, because
of the redefinition of imperfection and of material
qualities, as well as the notion that every industrial
process is developed in a craft environment'. The anti-
design nature of many of the products is a reaction to
design being too impersonal and a way of endeavouring
to create something more individual and warm.
However, this should not be at the expense of making
design too individual for the man in the street.

The Dutch have to move forward to survive.
Design is taught at Eindhoven in a very academic
manner, students being tutored into creating a
concept rather than coming up with a product that
functions in any realistic way. Although Wanders

believes that the Dutch approach has created a
'playing garden where beautiful and inspiring thoughts
can grow', he finds it a terrible shame that so few
products are designed for production and so do not
end up in the lives of regular people. The mentality of
the Dutch designer is still informed by the schoolroom,
and there is little connection with real industry or
interest in producing an article that functions well.

The Dutch 'style' both reflects and informs the
current zeitgeist. What we expect from design is
changing. There is a greater ideological freedom
combined with new insights, technology and materials,
which has given rise to unprecedented proposals in
design. Objects are becoming illustrations of intentions,
evoking experiences and establishing identities. There
is a growing demand for a synergy between high-
tech production methods and low-tech material –
natural fibres, recyclable substances, simple and
humane pieces – in other words stronger, more ethical
designs. Droog Design, and those that are following in
their footsteps, have flourished in this environment
and have in turn stimulated international discussion
on design and brought experimentation and a pre-
industrial arts-and-crafts design process back on the
agenda. If this energy can be harnessed into something
more commercial, then what we are seeing now could
be only the tip of what the Netherlands has to offer.

**Cabinet,
China Cabinet**
Frederik Roijé
Porcelain
H: 90cm (35in)
W: 90cm (35in)
D: 25cm (9 ⁷/₈in)
Studio Frederik Roijé,
the Netherlands
www.roije.com

**Cabinet,
Chrome Cabinet**
Scholten & Baijings
Lacquered MDF shelves
and back wall with
chrome steel
H: 108cm (43in)
W: 75cm (29 ½in)
Scholten & Baijings,
the Netherlands
www.scholtenbaijings.com

**Library, Bookcase-
wallpaper**
Tejo Remy and
Rene Veenhuizen
Plywood, birch
Various dimensions
Remy & Veenhuizen,
the Netherlands
www.remyveenhuizen.nl

**Magazine rack,
Oblique**
Marcel Wanders
Stained and lacquered
oak or solid beech base
with lacquered
veneer top
Small,
H: 210cm (83in)
W: 105cm (41in)
D: 6cm (2 ³⁄₈in);
Big,
H: 286cm (113in)
W: 105cm (41in)
D: 6cm (2 ³⁄₈in)
Moooi, the Netherlands
www.moooi.nl

**Straps, designed for
Mandarina Duck**
NL Architects
Rhodorsil Melange-
Maitre MF 345 U
W: 3cm (1 ¹⁄₈in)
D: 1cm (³⁄₈in)
L: 70cm (27 ⁵⁄₈in)
Droog Design, the
Netherlands
www.droogdesign.nl

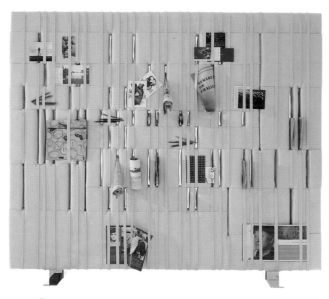

Soft Wall
Carsten Gerhards and
Andreas Glücker
Felt, chrome
H: 207cm (81 ½ in)
W: 20cm (7 ¾ in)
L: 250cm (98 ⅜ in)
B&B Italia SpA, Italy
www.bebitalia.it

Bookshelf, Three
Jakob + MacFarlane
Plexiglas
H: 199 or 255cm
(78 or 100in)
Diam: 145cm (57in)
Sawaya & Moroni, Italy
www.sawayamoroni.it

**Book tower for
paperbacks,
Buchstabler**
Tom Fischer
FU (birch plywood),
cement-cast, synthetic
fibre, flexible steel,
aluminium
H: 56.5–174cm (22–69in)
W: 33cm (13in)
D: 33cm (13in)
Nils Holger Moormann
GmbH, Germany
www.moormann.de

**Bookshelf,
Opus Incertum**
Sean Yoo
Expanded polypropylene
(EPP)
H: 100cm (39in)
W: 100cm (39in)
D: 35cm (13 ¾ in)
Casamania by Frezza,
Italy
www.casamania.it

Bookcase, Random
Neuland
MDF
H: 216.3cm (85in)
W: 81.6cm (32in)
D: 25cm (9 ⁷⁄₈in)
MDF Italia srl, Italy
www.mdfitalia.it

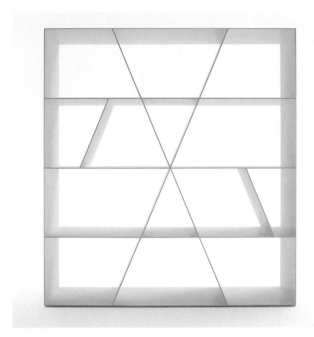

Bookcase, Shelf X
Naoto Fukasawa
Corian®
H: 145.5cm (57in)
W: 131cm (52in)
D: 37cm (14 ⁵⁄₈in)
B&B Italia SpA, Italy
www.bebitalia.it

Bookcase system, Loop
Biagio Cisotti and
Sandra Laube
Layered wood,
chromed steel
H: 50cm (19 ⁵⁄₈in)
L: 160cm (63in)
D: 30cm (11 ³⁄₄in)
BRF srl, Italy
www.brfcolors.com

A criticism that is often levelled at **Karim Rashid** is that his work is ephemeral; that it will not last the vagaries of time; that as his output increases, it is devalued by the sheer amount of products he has churned out, from perfume packaging and shoes, to commissioned pieces of furniture and DJ tables. I agree he is prolific – to date he has produced nearly 1000 items, examples of which you will find throughout the pages of this book. However, to condemn him in this way is to not fully appreciate what he wants to achieve. His aim is not only to produce objects that are available to all, but also to demystify design by making it more mainstream. 'Design must become more visible in a world of media so that design is of pedestrian interest and desire rather than a marginal subject.' Above all, he is concerned with the consumer. For Karim, a design should be de-stressing; it should add to the quality of life and if it does not then there is no place for it. It should be enjoyable, make life easier and appeal to our notions of beauty, as well as addressing specific problems. He believes that design should be disposable and biodegradable, with a built-in obsolescence of five years so that it is forced to continually reinvent itself and adapt to different social conditions as the century progresses.

Bookcase, Lotus
Karim Rashid
Acid, smoked and
tempered glass,
polished aluminium
H: 188cm (74in)
W: 107cm (42in)
D: 36cm (14 ¹/₈in)
Tonelli srl, Italy
www.tonellidesign.com

Karim has coined the expression 'Sensual Minimalism' to describe his style, which has an emotional appeal while staying minimal. Soft and tactile forms are more human, signifying comfort and pleasure. The blob is Karim's trademark. For him it is both the physical manifestation of his philosophy and a visual reaction to mechanization. Karim's organic style, unlike that of Ross Lovegrove, does not spring from observing natural artefacts. Rather it stems from the technical advances achieved by new computer

software, the shapes that have been liberated and the need for materials that can be moulded into these complicated soft forms. He creates natural configurations from digital processes. As a mediator between industry and the user, an 'artist of real issues' as he calls himself, Karim's work is a blend between professionally executed products, which result from a thorough understanding and appreciation of production methods, and today's more personalized, communicative and interactive design. He wants the items he creates – the interiors, graphics and products – to reflect the new digital age, which he sees as the third industrial revolution. He proposes new objects for new behaviours and produces work that suits the modern, cosmopolitan, casual, trendy, laid-back consumer of the computer society.

Karim describes himself as an intellectual and a cultural editor, and sees the ideas behind his work, or rather the importance he places on design as an instigator of social change, as in some ways more important than the products he creates. He is a man of missionary zeal and utopian ideals, who wants as many people as possible to hear his message, and for that message to change the way we perceive the world. Even his mobile phone voices the words of Gandhi – 'Be the change you want to see in the world.'

Modular shelving, Kurl
Karim Rashid
Curved glass
H: 150cm (59in)
W: 45cm (17 ³/₄in)
L: 150cm (59in)
Zeritalia/Curvet, Italy
www.zeritalia.it

Shelving system, Courier
Michael Marriott
Powder-coated steel, cherry wood, anodized extruded aluminium
H: 200cm (79in)
W: 120, 180 or 280cm (47, 71 or 110in)
D: 32cm (12 ⅝in)
Established & Sons, UK
www.established andsons.com

Modular shelving system, Boogie Woogie
Stefano Giovannoni
Standard injection-moulded ABS
One shelf unit,
H: 52cm (20 ½in)
W: 52cm (20 ½in)
Magis SpA, Italy
www.magisdesign.com

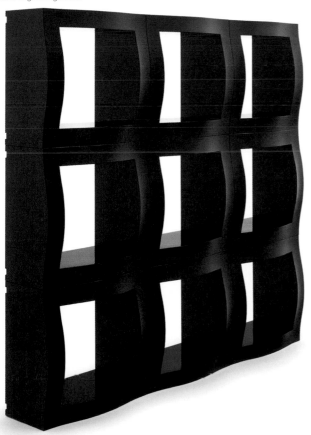

Shelves, Build and File
Thorsten Franck
Plywood, solid ash
H: 167cm (66in)
W: 70cm (27 ½in)
D: 32cm (12 ⅝in)
Möbelbau Kaether & Weise GmbH, Germany
www.kaetherundweise.de

Thorsten Franck's 'build-in-a-minute' range of furniture is just that. Each component is manufactured by a CDC-machine and is cut in a minute. Relying on the stabilizing effect of the tension between parts to keep it together, pieces are delivered as a flat pack and constructed without the need for tools. The range was designed with the nomadic urban citizen in mind.

Storage system/ bench/low table, Libre
Massimo Mariani
Wenge stained oak or bleached oak veneer, aluminium
H: 45cm (17 ¾in)
W: 120cm (47in)
D: 33cm (13in)
Targa Italia srl, Italy
www.targaitalia.it

**Bookshelf,
Anna Morph**
Matthew Sindall
Printed melamine,
stainless steel
H: 155cm (61in)
W: 115cm (45in)
D: 38cm (15in)
Sawaya & Moroni, Italy
www.sawayamoroni.com

Whether it is due to a 'devil may care' reaction to the depressing state of the world today, or a desire to get away from the past years of clean and severe minimalist designs, an emphasis on surface patterning is a trend that presented itself throughout 2004–5. In particular, a veritable bouquet of colourful floral motifs found its way on to objects and accessories.

Matthew Sindall, born in the UK but presently working in France, is not noted for flourishes of light-heartedness in his work. Chief designer in the architectural practices of MET Studios in London and then with Jean-Michel Wilmotte in Paris, his portfolio since going solo in 1995 consists more of heavy-duty industrial design – street lighting for Eclatec, UV transmission consoles for Guinot, seating for SNCF and publicity panels for Banque de Luxembourg. Yet for several years now he has been successfully collaborating with Sawaya & Moroni on a growing line of furniture.

Sindall has photographed flowers and geometric subjects and printed the images on to transparent melamine, which he has wrapped around wooden structures to form 'Anna Morph', a limited edition collection of bookshelves. Although at first glance these shelves may look like any other decorated piece, they are cleverly based on the sixteenth-century artifice 'anamorphosis', where an image was painted in a distorted way only to be understood when a mirrored cone or cylinder was placed in the centre of the painting. Similarly, the image on the 'Anna Morph' bookcase is broken down and becomes comprehensible from only three viewpoints (right, frontal and left).

Sindall told me that his work concentrates on perception, whether tactile, visual or latent: 'I try to imbue other values into a piece of furniture, offering the user different levels of interaction by working with materials and techniques.' He sees print as a modern type of marquetry and, with the advances made in printing processes, believes that personalized furniture will become more accessible, with owners able to select the images they want to decorate their surfaces.

**Wall and free-standing
modular shelving
system,
The interlocking
shelving system**
Dominic McCausland
Birch ply
Various dimensions
Wildercreative, UK
www.wildercreative.co.uk

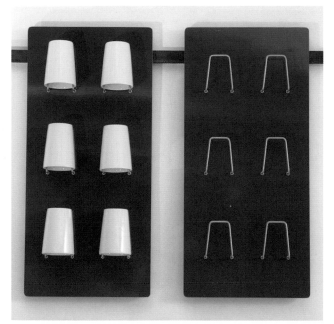

Coffee- and tea-kitchen on the wall, Erika
Storno
FU (birch plywood),
stainless steel,
sheet steel
Various dimensions
Nils Holger Moormann
GmbH, Germany
www.moormann.de

Bookshelf, Line
Blonder Yedidia
Aluminium,
stainless steel
Various dimensions
Blonder Yedidia, Israel
yblonder@bezeqint.net

Shelving unit, Paris
Barber Osgerby
American walnut veneer
or MDF, powder-coated
steel
H: 76 or 112cm
(29 $^7/_8$ or 44in)
W: 200cm (79in)
D: 35cm (13 $^3/_4$in)
ClassiCon GmbH,
Germany
www.classicon.com

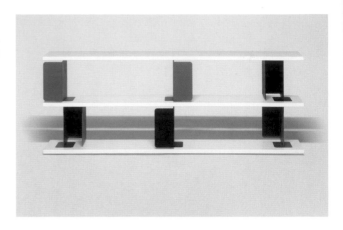

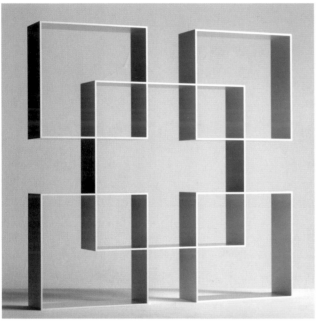

Storage, Quintet
Aziz Sariyer
Honeycomb anodized
aluminium
H: 196cm (77in)
W: 196cm (77in)
Moroso SpA, Italy
www.moroso.it

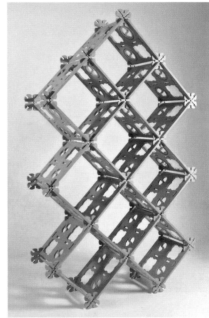

Bookcase, Jaju
Michael Lam,
Steve Choe
MDF
H: 203cm (80in)
W: 119.5cm (47in)
D: 39.5cm (15 $^1/_2$in)
Sasquatch, Canada
www.ssqtch.ca

**Articulated shelving
system, Graduate**
Jean Nouvel
Steel rods, plywood and
aluminium for shelves
H: 126.2, 164.6 or 203cm
(50, 65 or 80in)
L: 100, 200 or 300cm
(39, 79 or 118in)
D: 35cm (13 $^3/_4$in)
Molteni & C. SpA, Italy
www.molteni.it

Matali Crasset

Which of your designs to date would you like to be remembered by?
'When Jim comes to Paris', the hospitality column bed, my first piece of furniture.

How do you think others view your work?
Living, human and experimental.

Which designer has influenced you the most and why?
The work and the personalities of Oscar Niemeyer and Richard Buckminster Fuller are for me great examples.

If you were not a designer, what would you like to be and why?
An anthropologist looking at how people are living today.

What role do you think the designer has in society today?
To help people enter a more contemporary world.

Do you buy a lot of design pieces?
No. The house is full of prototypes.

Is there a design in your home that you couldn't live without?
No, I really feel free to change the structure around me whenever I want. I'm not design addicted.

Where do you think design is heading?
I hope to a less selfish and individual world.

Is the cult of the personality taking over the design world?
Yes, and it's a pity because the design schools are full of people who are there not for the good reasons.

Modular storage, Matalink
Matali Crasset
Extruded aluminium
H: 100cm (39in)
W: 95cm (37in)
D: 40cm (15 ³/₄in)
Duepuntosette by Erreti, Italy
www.erreti.com

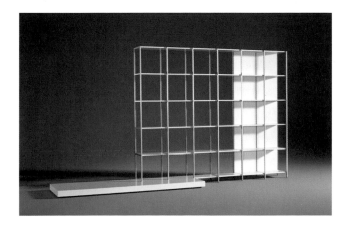

Modular cupboard system, Matrix System
Shigeru Uchida
Aluminium, lacquered wood
Various dimensions
Pastoe, the Netherlands
www.pastoe.nl

Wall panel with shelves and cabinets, Elevenfive
Bruno Fattorini
Available in various finishes: matt lacquered, matt veneered or covered with natural anodized aluminium
H: 216.3cm (85in)
L: 80, 100 or 120cm (31, 39 or 47in)
D: 3cm (1 ¹/₄in)
MDF Italia srl, Italy
www.mdfitalia.it

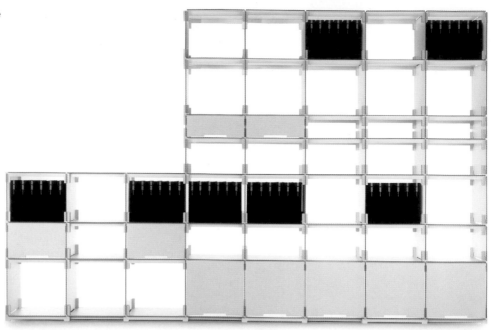

Shelves/assembly system, Platten-Bau
Florian Petri
4mm (¹/₈in) HPL boards
H: 15, 25, 35 or 40cm
(5 ⁷/₈, 9 ⁷/₈, 13 ³/₄ or
15 ³/₄in)
W: 40cm (15 ³/₄in)
D: 33cm (13in)
Möbelbau Kaether &
Weise GmbH, Germany
www.kaetherundweise.de

Bookshelf, Brick
Ronan and Erwan
Bouroullec
Polystyrene
H: 50cm (19 ¹/₂in)
W: 300cm (117in)
D: 35cm (13 ³/₄in)
Cap Design SpA, Italy
www.cappellini.it

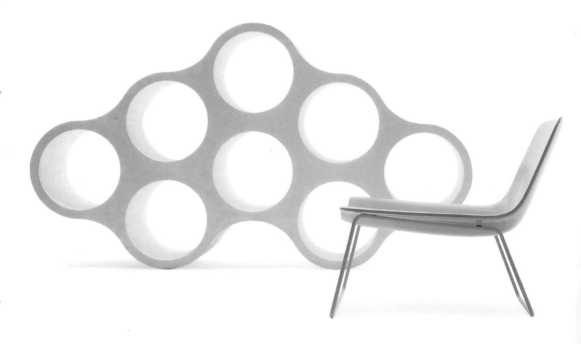

**Shelving modules,
Cloud**
Ronan and Erwan
Bouroullec
Polystyrene
H: 105cm (41in)
W: 187.5cm (74in)
D: 40cm (15 ³/₄in)
Cap Design SpA, Italy
www.cappellini.it

Storage system, Layout
Michele De Lucchi
Extruded aluminium, MDF
H: 199.5cm (79in)
W: 172cm (68in)
D: 79cm (31in)
Alias SpA, Italy
www.aliasdesign.it

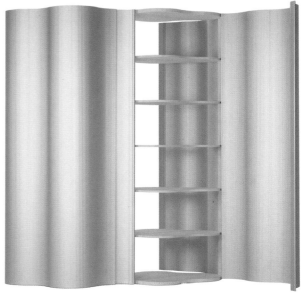

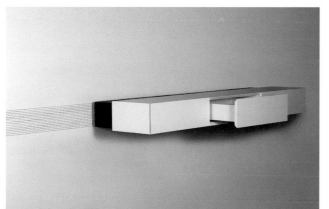

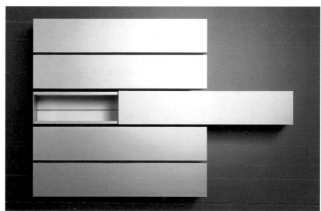

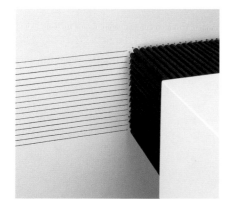

Shelf, HB Drawing Shelf
Fernando Brízio
Graphite pencils,
lacquered wood
H: 13cm (5 ¹/₈in)
W: 130cm (51in)
D: 47cm (18 ¹/₂in)
Fernando Brízio, Portugal
fernandobrizio@clix.pt

The backboard of the
'HB Drawing Shelf' is
covered with pencils.
Drawn lines extend
down the walls, making
it appear as if the shelf
has been carefully lifted
into position.

**Wall-mounted
aluminium objects
for CD or DVD,
Horizontals A-line**
Shigeru Uchida
Aluminium
H (for CDs): 17cm
(6 ³/₄in)
H (for DVDs): 26.3cm
(10 ¹/₄in)
W: 90cm (35in)
D: 18cm (7 ¹/₈in)
Pastoe, the Netherlands
www.pastoe.nl

Bookshelf, Sendai
Toyo Ito
Glass, wood
H: 194cm (76in)
W: 220cm (87in)
D: 38cm (15in)
Horm, Italy
www.horm.it

Wine rack, OLA
Hiroshi Tsunoda
Chromed or
painted metal
H: 51cm (20 ⅛in)
W: 91cm (36in)
D: 16cm (6 ¼in)
Hiroshi Tsunoda Design
Studio, Spain
www.hiroshitsunoda.com

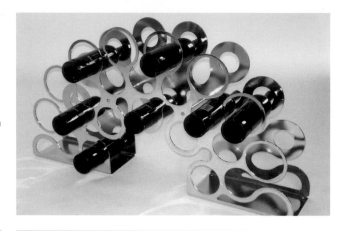

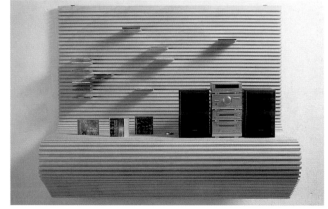

**Stereo and CD stand,
Flex**
Lorenzo Damiani
Wood, steel
H: 100cm (39in)
W: 150cm (59in)
D: 50cm (19 ⅝in)
Montina srl, Italy
www.montina.it

CD rack, CD-Snake
Peter Boy
ABS, POM
W: 15cm (5 ⅞in)
D: 2cm (¾in)
L: 100cm (39in)
Peter Boy Design,
Denmark
www.peterboy.dk

Storage, Breeze
Kazuhiro Yamanaka
MDF
H: 175cm (69in)
W: 35cm (13 ¾in)
D: 35cm (13 ¾in)
Pallucco Italia Spa, Italy
www.pallucco.com

Modular shelving system, Hang
Claudio Caramel
Extruded aluminium
Various dimensions
Desalto, Italy
www.desalto.it

CD rack, CD01 Slab
Poesis
European oak or walnut
H: 220cm (86 ⁵⁄₈in)
W: 17cm (6 ³⁄₄in)
D: 9cm (3 ¹⁄₂in)
e15 GmbH, Germany
www.e15.com

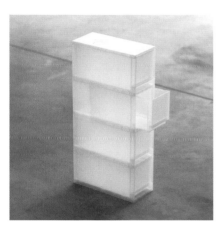

CD drawer unit
Polypropylene
H: 83cm (32 ³⁄₄in)
W: 18cm (7 ⁷⁄₈in)
D: 40cm (15 ³⁄₄in)
Muji, Japan
www.muji.net

Shelves, wardrobe, HP04 Kast Een
Hans De Pelsmacker
European oak, aluminium
H: 210cm (83in)
W: 45cm (17 ³⁄₄in)
L: 89cm (35in)
e15 GmbH, Germany
www.e15.com

What you see is almost certainly what you get with the modern and minimal, yet classic, furniture range from **e15**. Founded in London in 1995 and named after the postcode of their first studio, Florian Asche and Philipp Mainzer soon discovered that it made more business sense to move back to their native Germany, where cheaper production methods and a healthier attitude to the design industry would allow them to expand quicker and more cost effectively without sacrificing their own vision. Now based in Frankfurt, they have built up an international reputation based on quality and the care and attention they put into their product lines.

Each piece is determined by the look and feel of the material from which it is made. The shapes are contemporary while the craftsmanship is traditional. Although highly technical methods, such as computer-controlled table saws and milling machines, are used, every item is assembled by hand and polished up with oil in order to protect the surface and emphasize the aesthetic quality of the colour and grain of the woods. Various European timbers are specially selected from managed forestry plantations for their distinctive markings and warmth, while stainless steel, aluminium and leather are chosen for durability as well as strength, creating timeless, enduring and beautiful pieces. Their latest ranges include a collaboration with the bathroom manufacturer Duravit (see page 155) and a series of lamps (see page 263).

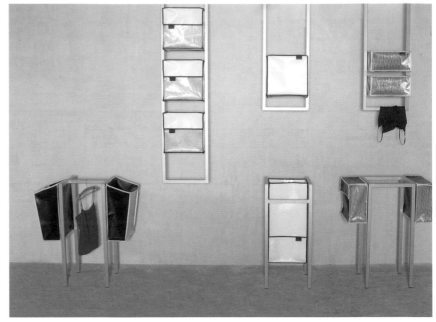

**Storage device,
Lastpak**
Meta & Renate
Powder-coated steel,
Bisonyl
Various dimensions
Meta & Renate,
the Netherlands
www.meta-renate.com

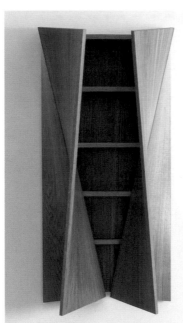

**Cabinet,
Twisted Cabinet**
Thomas Heatherwick
Solid oak
H: 111cm (44in)
W: 54cm (21 ¹/₄in)
D: 29cm (11 ³/₈in)
Benchmark Furniture,
UK
www.benchmark-
furniture.com

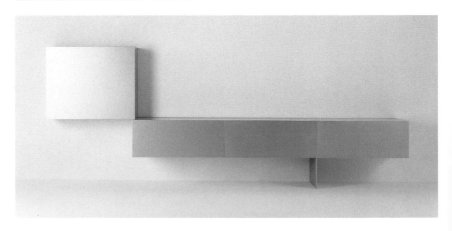

**Modular storage
system, Avio**
Piero Lissoni
Dolufolex aluminium
Various dimensions
Cap Design SpA, Italy
www.cappellini.it

**Storage system,
Wogg 20**
Benny Mosimann
PET, veneered beech,
aluminium
H: 96 or 184cm
(37 1/4 or 71 1/2 in)
W: 76cm (30 in)
D: 57cm (22 1/2 in)
Wogg AG, Switzerland
www.wogg.ch

'Wogg 20' is a development of Benny Mosimann's
range of sideboards and cupboards that share the
same sliding, transparent fronts. '20' is a larger
container with a more sophisticated and rounded
skinned form, coupled with a technologically innovative
casing. Because the container has a double PET
construction that has a smooth exterior joined to
a moulded inner base, vertically the storage system
is extremely still, but horizontally it is very flexible.
The striped pattern, however, makes it appear rigid,
while its transparency maintains the delicacy of
its appearance.

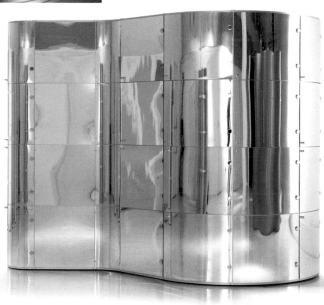

Case goods, Kabuki
Kenneth Cobonpue
MDF, stainless steel
H: 130cm (51in)
W: 70cm (27 1/2 in)
D: 40cm (15 3/4 in)
Interior Crafts of the Islands,
Inc, the Philippines
www.kennethcobonpue.com

**Storage system,
Paesaggi Italiani**
Massimo Morozzi
Lacquered melamine,
heat-moulded
acrylic doors
Various dimensions
Edra SpA, Italy
www.edra.com

**Cupboard, Eek
Dresser**
Piet Hein Eek
Steel
H: 100cm (39in)
W: 100cm (39in)
D: 50cm (19 ⅝in)
Moooi, the Netherlands
www.moooi.com

Sideboard, Crédence
Xavier Lust
Aluminium
H: 79cm (31in)
W: 140cm (55in)
D: 70cm (27 ½in)
De Padova srl, Italy
www.depadova.it

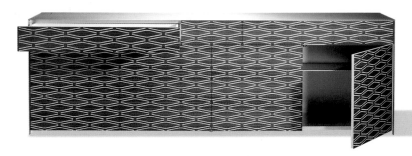

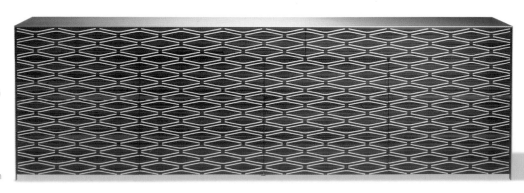

Sideboard, Baschenis
Tim Watson
Solid aluminium, Brazilian
walnut wood veneer,
beech wood
H: 76cm (29 ⅞in)
W: 241cm (95in)
D: 50cm (19 ⅝in)
Sawaya & Moroni, Italy
www.sawayamoroni.com

**Cabinets in 3 sizes,
Divine Glass**
Scholten & Baijings
Glass with stainless steel
Square module,
H: 49.5cm (19 ⁵/₈in)
W: 49.5cm (19 ⁵/₈in)
D: 22cm (8 ⁵/₈in)
Scholten & Baijings,
the Netherlands
www.scholtenbaijings.com

Container, Brosse
Inga Sempé
Lacquered alveolar
aluminium, propylene
industrial brushes
Various dimensions
Edra SpA, Italy
www.edra.com

Container, Optic
Patrick Jouin
PMMA
H: 40cm (15 ³/₄in)
W: 40cm (15 ³/₄in)
D: 40cm (15 ³/₄in)
Kartell SpA, Italy
www.kartell.it

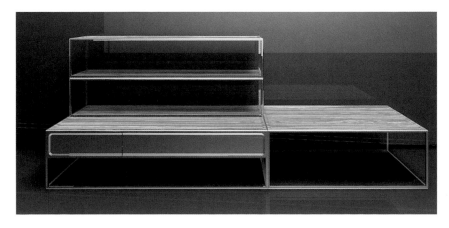

**Modular storage
system, Progetto
Tom Box**
Tom Dixon
Steel, plastic, MDF
Various dimensions
Pallucco Italia Spa, Italy
www.pallucco.com

System of modular containers, Sussex
Terence Woodgate
Oak
Floor version,
H: 74.3cm (29 1/8in)
W: 202.6cm (80in)
D: 48cm (18 7/8 in);
Wall version,
H: 51.3cm (20 1/8in)
W: 202.6cm (80in)
D: 28.5cm (11 3/8in)
Puntmobles s.l., Spain
www.puntmobles.es

Cabinet, Hub
Matthew Hilton
American oak veneer,
aluminium
H: 59cm (23 1/4in)
W: 180cm (71in)
D: 63cm (24 3/8in)
SCP, UK
www.scp.co.uk

Modular storage system, City
Marcel Wanders
Powder-coated steel
Various dimensions
Moooi, the Netherlands
www.moooi.nl

Sideboard, Simplon
Jasper Morrison
Honeycomb aluminium
and lacquered,
anodized aluminium
H: 72cm (28 ³/₈in)
W: 200cm (79in)
D: 90cm (35in)
Cap Design SpA, Italy
www.cappellini.it

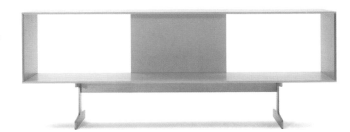

Cabinet, Multi LP
Michael Sodeau
Oak wood, aluminium
H: 42cm (16 ¹/₂in)
W: 180cm (71in)
D: 60cm (23 ⁵/₈in)
Modus, UK
www.modusfurniture.co.uk

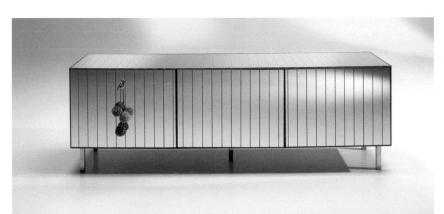

**Mirrored horizontal
container, The Other**
Studioilse
Patterned mirror
H: 60cm (23 ⁵/₈in)
W: 180cm (71in)
D: 40cm (15 ³/₄in)
Baleri Italia SpA, Italy
www.baleri-italia.com

Sideboard, Ludwig
Ludovico Acerbis
Wood, chrome-plated
metal, stainless steel,
glass
H: 63cm (24 ³/₄in)
W: 210 or 290cm
(83 or 114in)
D: 63cm (24 ³/₄in)
Acerbis International
SpA, Italy
www.acerbis
international.com

Small table on wheels, Magis Wagon
Michael Young
Sandblasted die-cast aluminium, injection-moulded ABS, polyurethane
H: 28.2cm (11in)
W: 66cm (26in)
D: 66cm (26in)
Magis SpA, Italy
www.magisdesign.com

Drawer unit on wheels, Groove
Christian Ghion
Rotation-moulded plastic
H: 50cm (19 ⅝in)
W: 180cm (71in)
D: 56.9cm (22 ¼in)
Driade SpA, Italy
www.driade.com

Sideboard, Alucobond sideboard Nr. 460
Kurt Thut
Stove-enamel-finished laminated panels
H: 61cm (24in)
W: 218cm (86in)
D: 55cm (21 ⅝in)
Thut Möbel, Switzerland
www.thut.ch

Low stools, Pebbles
Marcel Wanders
Plastics
H: 37cm (14 ½in)
W: 42cm (16 ½in)
D: 42cm (16 ½in)
Magis SpA, Italy
www.magisdesign.com

Werner Aisslinger

Which of your designs to date would you like to be remembered by?

Three projects were very important within my work:

1 'Juli' chair, 1996, armchair manufactured by Cappellini. This was the first seat shell produced in integral polyurethane foam and was selected for the permanent collection of the Museum of Modern Art in 1998 (first German chair design since Sapper and Zanuso chair of 1964 or Bauhaus pieces). It is also now in the permanent chair collection of the Vitra Design Museum and Die neue Sammlung, Pinakothek der Moderne, Munich.

2 Gel projects. The gel furniture was, together with Marcel Wanders's 'Knotted' chair and some other pieces, the first design object that identified itself through the use of new materials and production methods. Since then hype about new materials in design has increased rapidly. The first gel project was 'Soft cell', a limited edition of gel furniture that was the first project worldwide to use the translucent polyurethane technoGel as upholstery. Its presentation in Milan in 1999 was groundbreaking (it was selected for the permanent chair collection of the Vitra Design Museum). The second gel project was 'Soft', a chaise using technoGel manufactured by Zanotta (selected for the collection of Fonds National d'Art Contemporain, France, for the permanent collection of the Metropolitan Museum, New York, and for Die neue Sammlung, Pinakothek der Moderne, Munich). The third gel project was a chair family called 'Gel chairs' produced with Cappellini in 2002 with an inmoulded structure (selected for Die neue Sammlung, Pinakothek der Moderne, Munich).

3 'Loftcubo': the 'Loftcube' is a living vision, a 36 square-metre (387 square-foot) architectural module that can be helicoptered onto unused city rooftops. The worldwide response to it was overwhelming. It was included in the 2005 *International Design Yearbook* (and it was part of the German Pavilion of the 9th Architecture Biennale in Venice in 2004).

How do you think others view your work?

In terms of projects, others like design with an attitude of being visionary or futuristic. As some of my ideas fit into the sphere of creating ideas ahead of the mainstream this is seen quite positively. Formally my projects are related to basic and reduced shapes which underlie the concept of modularity and serial industrial production. In terms of background, even if my design socialization is international (Berlin/London/Milan) and I work with international clients, some people see a German affinity towards a technology-driven and conceptual and rational attitude to design in my work. This might be true – even if I see design as a global thing without strong local links from the design point of view.

Which designer has influenced you the most and why?

From the point of view of my personal work experience I like the mixture of: having been a student in Berlin of Professor Nick Roericht, a renowned German ULM designer with a preference for conceptual design; then having worked shortly at Ron Arad's workshop in London and being involved in doing one-offs; doing a stage at Jasper Morrison's office and being involved in utilitarian and minimalist design; and later working at Studio De Lucchi in Milan. It's a mixture of a post-Memphis design attitude with high professional industrial projects. From the point of view of design history my favourite designers are Joe Colombo (because of his living visions and modular projects), Hans Gugelot (because of his systematic and scientific/industrial approach), and the Eames (because of their homogenous and balanced work and life constellation).

If you were not a designer, what would you like to be and why?

A filmmaker, because the option of storytelling is partly missing from design.

What role do you think the designer has in society today?

I hope their influence rises to a position where designers are no longer seen mainly as a part in the chain of the industrial processes, but also in a role that is giving society a hint of the future of objects, forms of living, mobility ...

Do you buy a lot of design pieces?

Not really – just standards like an Apple laptop. I do not have a consumer type of character, and also, because of a lack of time, buying design stuff is rare. I am more interested in local things when I travel, like buying a fur somewhere or an old archetypal wooden bowl.

Is there a design in your home that you couldn't live without?

I am not an addict to a specific object. It's more the home itself, the composition with all items or architectural parts, that I would miss.

What do you consider to be the best piece of design since the millennium?

The Apple iPod.

Where do you think design is heading? Is there someone we should be watching out for?

Design is heading to becoming an overall presence and a global tool that is adapted by all brands. The effect might then be an inflation of design that will lead to a rediscovery of regional, local traditions and identity. We should watch all upcoming young designers, especially those from Asia and India.

Is the cult of the personality taking over the design world?

The group of personalities in the design world is a very small one and a declining one. Even if the magazines are full of pieces that are the results of personal design projects and if they like to promote single designers, most of those hundred designers worldwide are not the ones who do the big business. Most design projects worldwide are done by huge, anonymous studios, like the car-design studios.

It's also a declining situation because companies with owner-CEOs who have a personal interest in intense, long-term design cooperation with individual freelance designers are vanishing. Interesting design evolutions happen through people like Rolf Fehlbaum, Eugenio Perazza or Giulio Cappellini, whereas typical managers see design cooperation as a short-term tool that can be fulfilled by larger anonymous design studios and not necessarily by a single designer.

Modular drawer system, Plus Unit
Werner Aisslinger
Injection-moulded ABS, polished extruded aluminium
Various dimensions
Magis SpA, Italy
www.magisdesign.com

Coat stand, Corallo
Michael Sodeau
Cane
H: 190cm (74 ⅜in)
Diam: 75cm (29 ⅛in)
Gervasoni, Italy
www.gervasoni1882.it

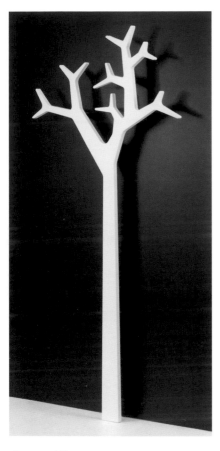

Coat stand, Tree
Michael Young and
Katrin Petursdottir
Lacquered MDF
H: 194cm (76in)
Swedese Möbler AB,
Sweden
www.swedese.se

Coat stand, Tri
Michele De Lucchi and
Philippe Nigro
Metal, leather
H: 172 cm (67 ⅜in)
W: 40cm (15 ¾in)
D: 40cm (15 ¾in)
Poltrona Frau srl, Italy
www.poltronafrau.it

**Coat rack,
Coathook#1**
Fredrikson Stallard
Coated steel
H: 22cm (8 ⅝in)
W: 32cm (12 ⅝in)
D: 17cm (6 ¾in)
Fredrikson Stallard, UK
www.fredrikson
stallard.com

Floor clothes stand, Dodici
James Irvine
Steel
H: 170cm (67in)
W (base): 40cm (15 ¾in)
L (base): 40cm (15 ¾in)
Pallucco Italia Spa, Italy
www.pallucco.com

Coat hanger, Gobble
Thomas Bernstrand
Chromed steel, elastic
cord, plastic hooks
H: 200cm (79in)
W: 100cm (39in)
D: 100cm (39in)
Cbi Design AB, Sweden
www.cbidesign.se

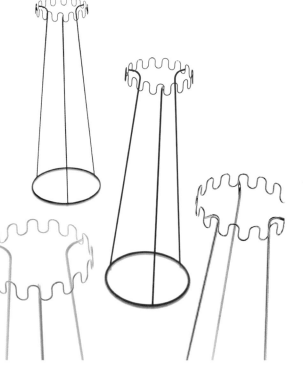

Coat rack, Crown
Stefan Schöning
Steel
H: 157cm (62in)
W: 60cm (23 ⅝in)
D: 38.5cm (15 ⅛in)
Desalto, Italy
www.desalto.it

**Containers, Fat-Fat
and Lady-Fat**
Patricia Urquiola
Lathe-turned metal,
nickelled or varnished
Fat-Fat,
H: 45cm (17 ¾in)
Diam: 66cm (26in);
Lady-Fat,
H: 30 or 35cm
(11 ⅞ or 13 ¼in)
Diam: 116 or 85cm
(45 ⅝ or 33 ½in)
B&B Italia SpA, Italy
www.bebitalia.it

Kitchens and Bathrooms

Kitchen, Spezie
Ludovica and Roberto
Palomba
Pine wood
Various dimensions
Schiffini, Italy
www.schiffini.it

Cabinet system, Cube
Werner Aisslinger
Fibreglass
Various dimensions
Interlübke, Germany
www.interluebke.com

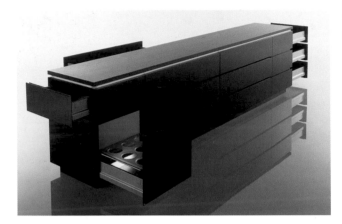

Mini-kitchen, Värde
Mikael Warnhammar
Solid birch, oil, clear
amino resin lacquer,
particleboard, birch
veneer, clear acrylic
lacquer, melamine foil,
stainless steel,
zinc, nickel-plated,
clear lacquer
H: 208cm (81 ⁷/₈in)
W: 140cm (55 ¹/₈in)
D: 69cm (27in)
IKEA, Sweden
www.ikea.com

Kitchen, K11
Norbert Wangen
Stainless steel
Various dimensions
Boffi SpA, Italy
www.boffi.com

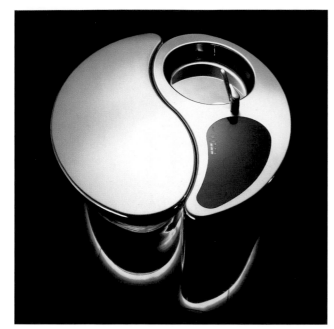

Kitchen, K12
Norbert Wangen
Melamine, stainless steel
H: 61.5 (24 ¹⁄₈in)
L: 400cm (158in)
D: 72.5cm (28 ³⁄₈in)
Boffi SpA, Italy
www.boffi.com

During 'Abitare il Tempo' 2004, **Setsu and Shinobu Ito** gathered many of their designs together in an exhibition that formed part of a series of workshops examining the evolution of the domestic space. I.E. Motion was concerned with the sensorial aspects of living, taking as its theme bonding, emotions and rhythm. The domestic interior produced combined Japanese and Western influences in a cross-cultural experience where handcrafted objects, conventional appliances and advanced technology harmoniously co-exist. Several of the objects exhibited are illustrated in this book. The 'Isola Bar' and 'Isola Cook' are kitchen blocks in stainless steel that couple freely together to become a dynamic centre around which rituals and relationships develop, while the 'Saturnia' (see page 152) is a hydro massage bath with a sinuous, soft form in the same material, which was designed to evoke sensations of luxury, relaxation and well-being. The 'Toki' glass side table (see page 19) has been crafted by bending a single sheet of glass to the limits of possibility. The conical base smoothly develops into a plane surface to store magazines, and ultimately folds upwards to form the table top.

Kitchen, Isola
Setsu and Shinobu Ito
Stainless steel
H: 90cm (35in)
W: 170cm (x 2) (67in)
D: 80cm (x 2) (31in)
Toyo Kitchen & Living, Japan
www.toyokitchen.co.jp

Compact kitchen, Single Kitchen
Alberto Colonello
Stainless steel
H: 80cm (31in)
W: 64cm (25 ¹⁄₄in)
D: 75cm (29 ¹⁄₂in)
Boffi SpA, Italy
www.boffi.com

**Kettle, Morrison
1.5L kettle (part of
Brunch set)**
Jasper Morrison
Polypropylene,
stainless steel
H: 25.5cm (10 ¹/₄in)
W: 18.5cm (7 ¹/₄in)
L: 22cm (8 ⁵/₈in)
Rowenta, UK
www.rowenta.co.uk

**Toaster, Morrison
toaster (part of
Brunch set)**
Jasper Morrison
Polypropylene,
stainless steel
H: 19.5cm (7 ⁷/₈in)
W: 11cm (4 ³/₈in)
L: 38.5cm (15 ³/₈in)
Rowenta, UK
www.rowenta.co.uk

When asked for a word to describe how his style is perceived, **Jasper Morrison** had no hesitation in replying 'simple'. The Brunch set for the French household appliance manufacturer Rowenta, which comprises toaster, kettle and coffee maker, is just that – pure in concept, with elegant, effortless lines and no gimmickry or superficial styling. At first glance the familiar white forms may even appear banal, yet closer inspection reveals a quiet intelligence, underlying subtlety and emotional creativity, qualities that have become synonymous with his work in general. Morrison believes that design should be a balance between the order demanded by a set of components and the creative inspiration that will lift an object from the workaday and appeal psychologically to the consumer. As he wrote in the introduction to the 1999 *International Design Yearbook*, 'Designers must give visual and conceptual order to an object, and at the same time provide something harder to define: "objectality". Nowadays even a power drill needs to send out a message to prospective customers. While a product is born for industry, it lives the rest of its life with the person who buys it, and it is the emotional response it elicits, or "objectality", that is the key to its success.' The Rowenta range is archetypal, yet unique in its interpretation of the everyday. Classical, with a lightness of touch and effortless practicality, the pieces are essential players in the modern kitchen.

Kitchen Scale
Stefano Giovannoni
18/10 stainless steel,
thermoplastic resin
H: 5cm (2in)
W: 11.5cm (4 ¹/₂in)
D: 38.5cm (15 ³/₈in)
Alessi SpA, Italy
www.alessi.com

**Coffee maker,
Morrison stainless-
steel thermo-jug
coffee maker
(part of Brunch set)**
Jasper Morrison
Polypropylene,
stainless steel
H: 15cm (6 ⁷/₈in)
W: 33cm (13in)
L: 29.5cm (11 ³/₄in)
Rowenta, UK
www.rowenta.co.uk

Espresso machine, XP5000
Konstantin Grcic
PP, stainless steel
H: 31.5cm (12 ⅝in)
W: 21.2cm (8 ⅜in)
D: 30.8cm (12 ⅛in)
Krups (Groupe SEB),
France
www.krups.com

Coffee maker, Senseo
WAACS/Philips
PP, stainless steel
H: 33cm (13in)
W: 22cm (8 ⅝in)
D: 32cm (12 ⅝in)
Philips, the Netherlands
www.senseo.com

The '**Senseo**' coffee system is taking on iconic proportions. It can be bought just about anywhere, including your local supermarket, and since its launch in 2001 over six million machines have been sold throughout the world. Its ubiquity, however, might well make you overlook the genius of its design. Based on the pressure-driven technology of the espresso machine, the 'Senseo' can brew one or two cups of coffee in a minute. Its anthropomorphic shape is intentional. Not only does the curve cut down on cost by keeping the distance between brewing chamber and cup short, but also it makes the machine appear to be bowing to the cups it is serving. The use of blue (a colour not normally associated with coffee makers) was to distinguish the 'Senseo' as something new and innovative on the market, while the uncomplicated, clean lines and simple operating buttons make this a product that will endure the vagaries of fashion.

Washing machine, Dyson Two-Drums Allergy
Dyson Research and Development Team
Tub: high-strength polymer containing 40% glass; outer door made from the same material as riot shields
H: 84.8cm (33in)
W: 59.5cm (23 ⅜in)
D: 57.5cm (22 ⅞in)
Dyson, UK
www.dyson.com

Dishwasher, IZZI
Roberto Pezzetta and Electrolux Zanussi Industrial Design Center
ABS, steel, stainless steel
H: 85cm (33in)
W: 60cm (23 ⅝in)
D: 60cm (23 ⅝in)
Electrolux Home Products, Italy
www.electrolux.it

According to **Dyson**'s research, 15 minutes of hand washing produces cleaner clothes than 67 minutes in the best washing machine. By replacing the traditional one drum with two aligned drums that rotate in opposite directions, the patented design replicates manual action. The long wash and soak programmes are replaced by a shorter, more rigorous process.

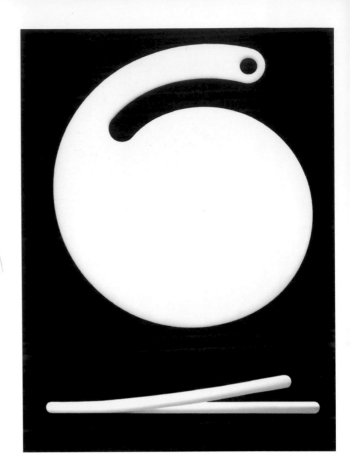

Samovar, Opera
Guido Metz &
Michael Kindler, Metz
und Kindler Design
Steel, silicon
H: 25.5cm (10in)
W: 20.5cm (8in)
D: 24cm (9 ½in)
WMF
Aktiengesellschaft,
Germany
www.wmf.com

Bowls, Hot Pot
Bodum Design Group
and Carsten Jørgensen
Porcelain, metal
Various dimensions
Bodum AG, Switzerland
www.bodum.com

**Espresso coffee
maker (from coffee
system series),
More Kult**
Guido Metz &
Michael Kindler, Metz
und Kindler Design
Steel, polypropylene
H: 14.2cm (5 ⅝in)
W: 10.4cm (4 ⅛in)
D: 14cm (5 ½in)
WMF
Aktiengesellschaft,
Germany
www.wmf.com

Bread board, Virgola
Paolo Ulian
Polyethylene
H: 3cm (1 ⅛in)
W: 30cm (11 ⅞in)
L: 35cm (13 ¾in)
Zani&Zani, Italy
zaniezani@tin.it

Bread bin, Gnam
Stefano Giovannoni
Thermoplastic resin
H: 16.5cm (6 ½in)
W: 30cm (11 ⅞in)
L: 46cm (18 ⅛in)
Alessi SpA, Italy
www.alessi.com

**Pressure cooker,
Mami**
Stefano Giovannoni
Steel and plastic
Various dimensions
Alessi SpA, Italy
www.alessi.com

The French kitchen appliances manufacturer **SEB** now
has nine prestigious brands under its umbrella, each
with clearly demarcated territories and styles. To
keep the resultant strategic advantage of this wide
coverage of all market segments, SEB have begun a
programme to reinforce the individual and well-defined
brands by approaching various internationally
renowned designers to add their personal touch to a
range of new products. Konstantin Grcic was asked to
design a coffee maker for Krups (see page 145) as SEB
believed his style suited the 'precise, professional and
structured' qualities of the marque, while Jasper
Morrison's Brunch series for Rowenta (see page 144)
shares the 'understated, refined and timeless quality'
long associated with the company. Most recently
RADI Designers have launched a range of electrical
appliances for Moulinex which offers 'simple, quick, and
accessible solutions to make everyday life easier'. Each
object is characterized by a smooth skin, with technical
elements hidden behind a user-friendly exterior.

**Kitchen appliances,
A new range for
Principio set**
RADI Designers
Polypropylene
Various dimensions
Moulinex, France.
www.moulinex.com

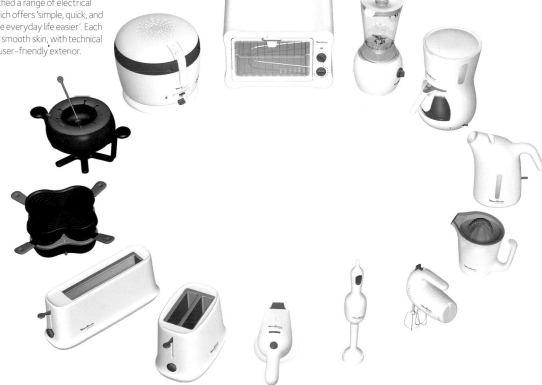

**Garlic press,
Inspired**
Claus Jensen & Henrik
Holbaek, Tools Design
Stainless steel, glass
Diam: 9.5cm (3 ³/₄in)
Eva Solo by Eva
Denmark A/S, Denmark
www.evasolo.com

**Bar product,
Chiringuito Shaker**
Ron Arad
18/10 stainless steel,
mirror polished
H: 25cm (9 ⁷/₈in)
W: 7.5cm (3in)
D: 7.5cm (3in)
Alessi SpA, Italy
www.alessi.com

**Set of knives, wooden
chopping boards and
block, Cinque Stelle**
Sottsass Associati
Stainless steel, wood
Various dimensions
Zani Serafino sas, Italy
www.serafinozani.it

Knife block, Throwzini
Adam + Harborth
Beech wood, magnets
H: 28cm (11in)
W: 22cm (8 5/8in)
D: 15cm (5 7/8in)
Konstantin Slawinski,
Germany
www.konstantin
slawinski.com

Shaped like a woman in a circus knife-throwing act, the clever 'Throwzini' wooden block artfully conceals magnets that can hold a set of kitchen knives.

Speciality cutlery, Style
Daniel Eltner
Cromargan
(18/10 stainless steel),
premium wood,
porcelain
Various dimensions
WMF
Aktiengesellschaft,
Germany
www.wmf.com

A quirky take on the post-modern dictum 'form follows function', each piece of Daniel Eltner's cutlery range 'Style' is created to be used only with certain food types. All share a thick and sculpturally simple chunky aesthetic, which makes them easy to use. Eltner considered not only the form of the human body, but also table ritual and cultural pointers before developing each ergonomically conceived item. The pasta server, for example, is an extension of the outstretched arm, with the head deliberately asymmetrical to mimic the human hand, and the pasta is gripped by widespread 'fingers'. The knife-spoon-fork was designed for the Oriental set. Observing that it is all but impossible to cut the meatball in wan-tang soup with the porcelain spoon usually provided, Eltner worked on a new material, which blends Cromargan and porcelain to produce a keener edge. The dumpling is dissected and can then either be skewered or cupped. The porcelain bowl is drop-formed to integrate the handle of the spoon-fork.

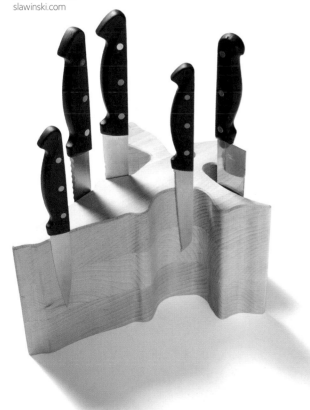

Cocktail shaker, Cosmo
Marc Newson
Crystal, PC
H: 18cm (7 1/8in)
D: 8cm (3 1/8in)
Alessi SpA, Italy
www.alessi.com

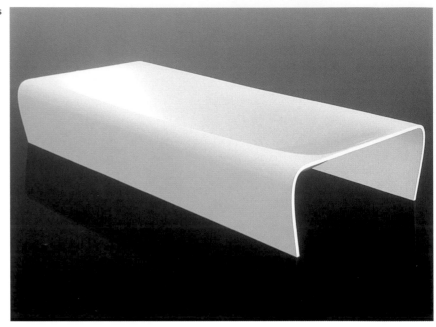

Bathtub, Strip
Michel Boucquillon
Corian®
W: 80 or 100cm
(31 or 39in)
L: 180 or 200cm
(71 or 79in)
Aquamass, Belgium
www.aquamass.com

**Freestanding bathtub,
Edition Andrée
Putman**
Andrée Putman
Sanitary acrylic
H: 62cm (24³⁄₈in)
W: 100cm (39in)
L: 190cm (75in)
Hoesch, Germany
www.hoesch.de

Bath, Navale
Xavier Lust
Anodized aluminium
W: 80cm (31in)
L: 180cm (71in)
Aquamass, Belgium
www.aquamass.com

Xavier Lust is one of the new wave of Belgian designers who are becoming increasingly important to the design scene. His products are minimal and sophisticated. An expert in working with metal, he prefers the material because it is at once pliable and totally solid. He is constantly searching for new techniques and methods of production. He told *Designboom* e-magazine 'the innovation is an essential data of the authenticity of any creation, as a specialist in the use of metals, I have developed expertise in the (de)formation of steel sheets'. The 'Navale' bath for Aquamass is a continuation of a theme. Because of its heat-conducting quality he has used aluminium instead of metal sheet, moulding it into what he considers to be the shape of a naval ship. The clip-on tray is for lotions, or maybe a glass of champagne.

Bath for two people, Paiova
EOOS Design Group
Sanitary acrylic
W: 130 or 140cm
(51 or 55in)
L: 170 or 180cm
(67 or 71in)
Duravit, Germany
www.duravit.com

Shower, Chiocciola
Benedini Associati
Exmar (composite material made from resin and quartz powder), Parapan
H: 202.5cm (80in)
W: 163cm (64in)
D: 136cm (54in)
Agape srl, Italy
www.agapedesign.it

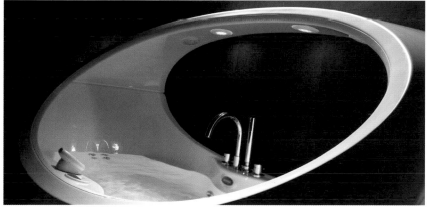

Whirlpool bath, Morphosis Alpha
Jacuzzi Design Team with Pininfarina Design Studio
High-gloss acrylic
H: 133cm (52in)
W: 107.5cm (43in)
L: 231cm (91in)
Jacuzzi Europe, Italy
www.jacuzzi.it

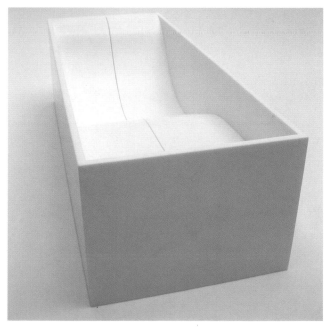

Bath, Well
Marike Andeweg
Corian®
H: 56.5cm (22 ½in)
W: 70cm (27 ½in)
L: 180cm (71in)
Marike Europe BV, the Netherlands
www.marike.net

Washbasin, Orca
Thomas Sandell
Corian®
W: 41cm (16 ¹/₈in)
D: 15cm (5 ⁷/₈in)
L: 65cm (25 ⁵/₈in)
Rapsel SpA, Italy
www.rapsel.it

Bathtub, Ufo
Benedini Associati
Stainless steel
H: 55cm (21 ⁵/₈in)
W: 204cm (80in)
Agape srl, Italy
www.agapedesign.it

Setsu and Shinobu Ito

Which of your designs to date would you like to be remembered by?
'AU' informal seats, 'Shiki' screen and 'How' series of stationery.

How do you think others view your work?
Interactive design as triggers of our actions in our life, and natural organic shapes.

Which designer has influenced you the most and why?
There are too many good and nice and friendly designers around us and they give us big energy, so it's difficult to be specific. Angelo Mangiarotti is great master to us; he is our matchmaker of marriage. Alessandro Mendini has great charisma, and is a most friendly counsellor to us.

If you were not a designer, what would you like to be and why?
Rock musicians or sports players because we would like to use our sensibility and body together.

What role do you think the designer has in society today?
A standard model of good and creative life actors.

Do you buy a lot of design pieces?
No, because we like to create each piece in our house by ourselves. But of course we buy some good samples for this.

Hydro massage bath, Saturnia
Setsu and Shinobu Ito
Stainless steel
H: 70cm (27 ¹/₂in)
W: 203.5cm (80in)
D: 148cm (58in)
Toyo Kitchen & Living, Japan
www.toyokitchen.co.jp

Bath and washbasin, Gobi
Marcel Wanders
Ecotec
Bath,
H: 50cm (19 ⁵⁄₈in)
W: 190cm (75in)
D: 85cm (33in);
Basin,
H: 16cm (6 ¹⁄₄in)
W: 50.6cm (20 ¹⁄₈in)
D: 37cm (14 ⁵⁄₈in)
Boffi SpA, Italy
www.boffi.com

Shower pipe with crane
Marcel Wanders
Stainless steel
H: 230cm (90 ⁵⁄₈in)
Diam: 9cm (3 ¹⁄₂in)
Boffi SpA, Italy
www.boffi.com

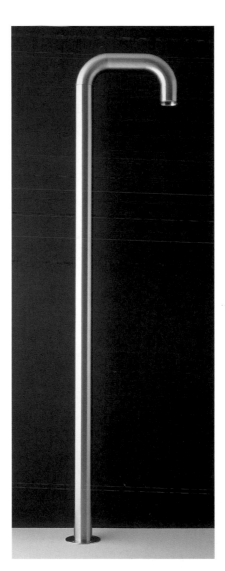

Marcel Wanders

Which of your designs to date would you like to be remembered by?
'Knotted' chair, 'Lace' table, 'Antilope', one-minute sculptures, 'Airborn snotty' vase, 'Can of gold', 'eo'.

How do you think others view your work?
My work speaks variously to the large variety of 'others', as do they about me.

Which designer has influenced you the most and why?
Starck, Castiglioni, Ponti, Sottsass, Branzi and many others. Why? Because I wanted to become as great a designer as them.

What role do you think the designer has in society today?
To inspire life to be better.

Where do you think design is heading? Is there someone we should be watching out for?
Design will find its place in the hearts of people, and yes, we have to start watching out for the people we touch.

Is the cult of the personality taking over the design world?
The only way to touch people is through people.

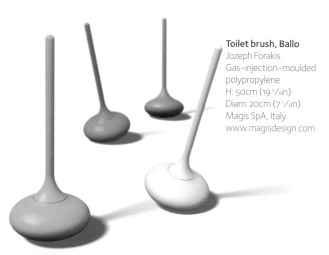

Toilet brush, Ballo
Jozeph Forakis
Gas-injection-moulded
polypropylene
H: 50cm (19 ⁵⁄₈in)
Diam: 20cm (7 ⁷⁄₈in)
Magis SpA, Italy
www.magisdesign.com

Sink,
Soap Stars
Marcel Wanders
Cristal plant
H: 16 or 19cm
(6 ¹⁄₄ or 7 ¹⁄₂in)
W: 55 or 92cm
(21 ⁵⁄₈ or 36in)
D: 40 or 46cm
(15 ³⁄₄ or 18 ¹⁄₈in)
Bisazza SpA, Italy
www.bisazza.com

Marcel Wanders has never been afraid of decoration. His latest works, and the collection he has art directed for Moooi, include pieces resplendent with surface patterning and heavy with eighteenth-century detailing. It is not surprising, then, that for Fuori Salone 2005 he collaborated with the glass tesserae company Bisazza in an exhibition that mixed his latest range of baths, sinks and toilets, 'Soap Series', with the most opulent of mosaics Bisazza could muster (one example sandwiched 24-carat gold between two layers of hand-cut Venetian glass). The result, 'Soap Stars', was a rich and luxurious installation designed by Marcel that combined different surroundings with diverse destinations – from the transitory 'motel' spaces (based on the design for the real hotel/apartments, the 'Lute Suites', Wanders has just completed outside Amsterdam) to the welcoming 'wellness' environment. His pure-white bathroom furniture, created for Bisazza, was shown alongside prototypes of neo-baroque consoles, set in front of beautifully patterned mosaics, mixing a decorative tradition with rigorous minimalism.

Bath,
Soap Stars
Marcel Wanders
Cristal plant
H: 58.6cm (23 ¹⁄₄in)
W: 200cm (79in)
D: 144cm (57in)
Bisazza SpA, Italy
www.bisazza.com

Shelf, HP04 KAST EEN
Hans de Pelsmacker
Powder-coated
aluminium
H: 210cm (83in)
W: 45cm (17¾in)
L: 210cm (83in)
e15 GmbH, Germany,
in collaboration with
Duravit, Germany
www.e15.com
www.duravit.de

**Washstand,
BA01 TOBA**
Philipp Mainzer
European oak, waxed
H: 75cm (29½in)
W: 92cm (36in)
L: 200cm (79in)
e15 GmbH, Germany,
in collaboration with
Duravit, Germany
www.e15.com
www.duravit.de

**Bath Tub, BA10
AOMORI**
Philipp Mainzer and
Johana Egenolf
European oak,
stainless steel
H: 90cm (35in)
W: 135cm (53in)
L: 135cm (53in)
e15 GmbH, Germany,
in collaboration with
Duravit, Germany
www.e15.com
www.duravit.de

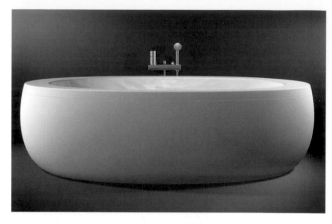

Floor-standing washbasin, Il Bagno Alessi
Stefano Giovannoni
Ceramic
H: 85cm (33 ½in)
W: 51.5cm (20 ¼in)
D: 53cm (20 ⅞in)
Laufen, Switzerland
www.laufen.com

Bathtub (wall version), Il Bagno Alessi
Stefano Giovannoni
Ceramic
H: 55cm (21 ⅝in)
W: 97.1cm (38 ⅛in)
L: 188cm (74in)
Laufen, Switzerland
www.laufen.com

Wall-hung bidet and toilet, Il Bagno Alessi
Stefano Giovannoni
Ceramic
W: 39cm (15 ⅜in)
D: 41.5cm (16 ⅛in)
L: 58.5cm (23 ¼in)
Laufen, Switzerland
www.laufen.com

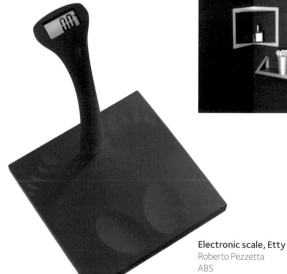

Bath accessories, Risma
Theo Williams
Diabond
Various dimensions
Merati srl, Italy
www.merati.com

Towel holder with storage trays, TWI
Theo Williams
Polyurethane, chrome
H: 88cm (35in)
W: 56cm (22in)
Dornbracht, Germany
www.dornbracht.com

Electronic scale, Etty
Roberto Pezzetta
ABS
H: 30.6cm (12 ¼in)
W: 30cm (11 ¾in)
L: 30cm (11 ¾in)
Fratelli Guzzini, Italy
www.fratelliguzzini.com

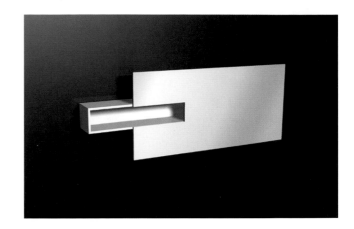

Bathroom cabinet, Lilliput
Theo Williams
Aluminium, mirror
H: 34cm (13 ³/₈in)
W: 58cm (22 ⁷/₈in)
D: 15cm (5 ⁷/₈in)
Merati srl, Italy
www.merati.com

Bathroom, The Newson Suite
Marc Newson
Vitreous china
Various dimensions
Ideal Standard, Italy
www.idealstandard.com

Single-lever basin mixer, Axor Starck X
Philippe Starck
Chrome
H: 28cm (11in)
W: 15cm (5 ⁷/₈in)
D: 13.5cm (5 ³/₈in)
Axor – Hansgrohe AG, Germany
www.axor-design.com

Floor-standing WC
Stefano Giovannoni
Ceramic
H: 46cm (18 ¹/₈in)
W: 58.5cm (23in)
L: 39cm (15 ³/₈in)
Alessi SpA, Italy
www.alessi.com

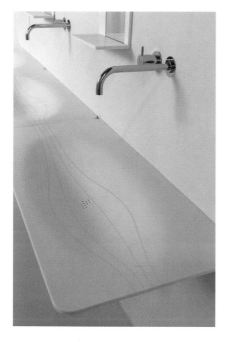

Washbasin, Tatoo
Elia Nedkov
Corian®
W: 100cm (39in)
D: 48cm (18 ⁷⁄₈in)
Rapsel SpA, Italy
www.rapsel.it

Washbasin, Bull
Carlo Colombo
Stone
Diam: 45cm (17 ³⁄₄in)
Antonio Lupi Design
SpA, Italy
www.antoniolupi.it

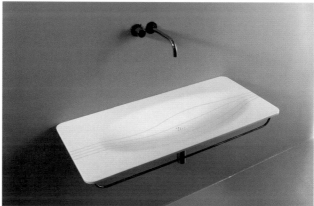

**Washbasin, Barcelona
Natural Stone**
Matteo Thun
Zimbabwe granite
H: 12.5cm (4 ⁷⁄₈in)
W: 40cm (15 ³⁄₄in)
D: 32cm (12 ⁵⁄₈in)
Rapsel SpA, Italy
www.rapsel.it

Washbasin, Bubble
Carlo Colombo
Crystal
Diam: 45cm (17 ³⁄₄in)
Antonio Lupi Design
SpA, Italy
www.antoniolupi.it

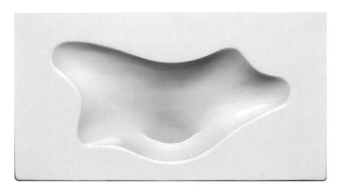

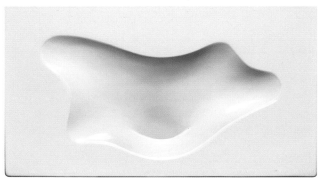

Washbasin, Thun
Matteo Thun
Fine fire clay
H: 15cm (5 ⁷/₈in)
W: 88cm (35in)
D: 48cm (18 ⁷/₈in)
Ceramica Catalano srl,
Italy
www.catalano.it

Lorenzo Damiani

Which of your designs to date would you like to be remembered by?
I would like to be remembered by the enthusiasm and the curiosity with which I designed all of my objects.

How do you think others view your work?
They appreciate my effort.

Which designer has influenced you the most and why?
I think a designer's work should be influenced by observation of what is going on in everyday life: the street, television, simple actions, new attitudes and anything that could make you guess how an object might be designed in a different way.

What role do you think the designer has in society today?
I think the role of the designer is very important: every project represents a very precise choice. Recently I've designed an object for an Italian supermarket chain (Coop): a cheap, well-designed, innovative product, good for everybody. I think this was a very specific choice.

Do you buy a lot of design pieces?
I usually buy cheap and functional objects, the designer of which is not as important as the object itself.

Is there a design in your home that you couldn't live without?
No, there isn't. I think that objects are replaceable material things. Sometimes they are even useless and are bought just for the sake of it, and not for a real need.

Where do you think design is heading? Is there someone we should be watching out for?
Maybe design will spread out more widely, even to those trade markets not yet taken into consideration, with the aim of finding more and more links between the object and the person it is aimed at. When I think about a designer we should be watching I always think about an eternal youth: Achille Castiglioni.

Is the cult of the personality taking over the design world?
Unfortunately the cult of the personality is becoming more and more predominant: I personally think that the objects I've designed should communicate something, not me.

Sink, H2O
Lorenzo Damiani
Plastic
H: 33cm (13in)
W: 34cm (13 ³/₈in)
D: 48cm (18 ⁷/₈in)
Lorenzo Damiani Studio,
Italy
lorenzo.damiani@tin.it

Washbasin, Foglio
Benedini Associati
Flexible opaque PVC
H: 15cm (5 7/8in)
W: 53cm (20 7/8in)
L: 69cm (27 1/8in)
Agape srl, Italy
www.agapedesign.it

Washbasin, Woodline
Benedini Associati
Birch plywood
H: 14cm (5 1/2in)
W: 100cm (39in)
D: 20cm (7 7/8in)
Agape srl, Italy
www.agapedesign.it

Tap, Carmensita
Aldo Cibic
Chrome brass
H: 15cm (5 7/8in)
D: 10cm (3 7/8in)
Rubinetteria Webert srl,
Italy
www.webert.it

Founder member of both Sottsass Associati and Memphis, **Aldo Cibic** may not enjoy the high profile of former co-partners Ettore Sottsass, Michele De Lucchi and Matteo Thun, yet his credentials are impeccable. Today, Cibic and Partners is one of the leading design studios in Italy. Active in the fields of architecture, interior design and industrial design, Cibic is probably best known for his public spaces – shops, restaurants, department stores, airports and hotels. Having moved away from the free forms and elite objects that we associate with Memphis, his product designs, while retaining post-modern creativity, have an eye for the commercial. Following Andrea Branzi's dictum, his aim is not only to 'design products for the home but to produce and sell them as well'. Blurring the boundaries between the artist and the industrialist, his designs combine clean, functional lines with an emotional warmth – he improves, softens and humanizes, taking inspiration from many sources and combining them into objects with universal appeal.

**Kitchen filter tap,
Cleartap Single Lever
Filter Mixer**
Ideal Standard
Cast brass construction
H: 18cm (7 1/8in)
Ideal Standard, UK
www.ideal-standard.co.uk

Tap, Seta
Marco Pisati
Unsealed brass,
stainless steel
H: 32.5cm (13in)
RB Rubinetterie Bandini,
Italy
www.rbandini.it

Bath tap
Christophe Pillet
Metal
Diam: 7.5cm (3in)
Zanetti Chini, Italy
www.zcg.it

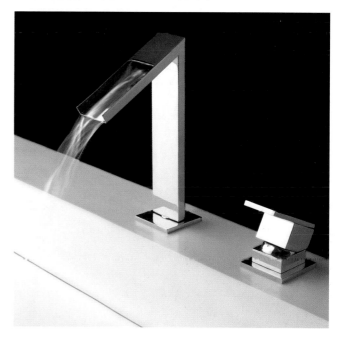

Tap, Dive
Marco Pisati
Unsealed brass,
stainless steel
H: 19.5cm (7 7/8in)
RB Rubinetterie Bandini,
Italy
www.rbandini.it

**Free-flowing mixer
tap, Hansamurano**
Bruno Sacco and
Reinhard Zetsche
Chromium-plated brass,
anti-calc treated
safety glass
Diam: 16 or 19cm
(6 1/4 or 7 1/2in)
Hansa Metallwerke AG,
Germany
www.hansa.de

Tableware

Cutlery
Jean Nouvel
Stainless steel
Knife, L: 22.7cm (9in);
Fork, L: 20.5cm (8¹/₄in);
Spoon, L: 20.6cm (8¹/₄in)
Georg Jensen, Denmark
www.georgjensen.com

These teaspoons by **Ed Annink** were designed as part of a series of gifts commissioned by the Prime Minister of the Netherlands. His aim was to present a collection of ordinary functional objects in a traditional Dutch design and using conventional materials but given an innovative and refreshing twist. The spoon below is cut away to accommodate a sugar lump, while the one above, a follow-up to the programme and produced by Droog Design, has a laser-cut decoration based on Delft Blue.

Teaspoon, DB (Delft Blue) Teaspoon
Ed Annink,
Ontwerpwerk
Polished stainless steel
W: 2.6cm (1in)
D: 1cm (³/₈in)
L: 11.5cm (4¹/₂in)
Droog Design, the Netherlands
www.droogdesign.nl

Teaspoon, MP (Prime Minister) Teaspoon
Ed Annink,
Ontwerpwerk
Polished stainless steel
W: 2.6cm (1in)
D: 1cm (³/₈in)
L: 11.5cm (4¹/₂in)
Ontwerpwerk, the Netherlands
www.ontwerpwerk.com

Cutlery, Knifeforkspoon
Jasper Morrison
18/10 stainless steel
Knife, L: 21cm (8¹/₄in);
Fork, L: 19.5cm (7⁷/₈in);
Spoon, L: 19.5cm (7⁷/₈in)
Alessi SpA, Italy
www.alessi.com

Knife and fork, Morode
Kazuhiko Tomita
Stainless steel
W: 1.9cm (¹/₄in)
L: 22.5cm (8⁷/₈in)
Covo srl, Italy
www.covo.it

Gijs Bakker is probably best known as the co-founder of Droog Design. More recently, however, he has mainly been involved in creating innovative products for leading international companies. His sense of observation and creative poetry has resulted in a range of table accessories called 'Flow'. Noting the shape and shading of a drop of falling water, he has translated his observations into a series of products in which the sensuously curved surfaces of the two constituent materials – glass and stainless steel – merge with one another into a harmonious whole. The range consists of a fruit bowl, salad bowl and serving set, cheese dome, carafe set and oil and vinegar bottles.

Tableware, Flow
Gijs Bakker
Stainless steel, glass
Various dimensions
Royal van Kempen &
Begeer, the Netherlands
www.kempen-begeer.nl

Cutlery, Minimal
David Mellor
Stainless steel
Knife,
W: 2.4cm (1in)
D: 0.6cm (¼in)
L: 21cm (8¼in)
David Mellor Design Ltd, UK
www.davidmellordesign.com

Set of cutlery, London
David Mellor
Stainless steel
Table knife,
W: 2.1cm (¾in)
D: 0.6cm (¼in)
L: 22cm (8⅝in)
David Mellor Design Ltd, UK
www.davidmellordesign.com

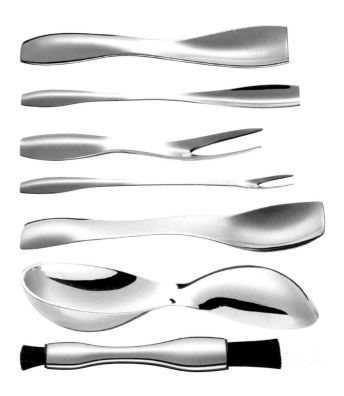

Cutlery, Columbia
Carsten Jørgensen
Stainless steel
Measuring spoon,
L: 15cm (5⅞in)
Bodum AG, Switzerland
www.bodum.com

Cutlery, Mango
Nanny Still
Matt, brushed
stainless steel
Table knife,
L: 22cm (8 ⅝in)
Iittala Oy Ab, Finland
www.iittala.fi

**Three-chambered
serving dish, Twist**
Scott Henderson
Chrome-electroplated,
injection-moulded ABS
H: 4.5cm (1 ¾in)
W: 21.5cm (10 ½in)
L: 44cm (17 ⅜in)
Wovo and Smart
Design Inc, USA
www.smartdesignusa.com

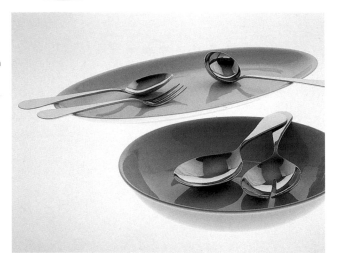

**Soup ladle and serving
spoon, Paloma**
Paola Navone
Stainless steel
Ladle,
H: 33.6cm (13 ¼in);
Spoon,
H: 22.7cm (9in)
Driade SpA, Italy
www.driade.com

Tableware collection
John Pawson
Crystal, ceramic,
porcelain, stainless steel,
polycarbonate
Various dimensions
When objects work,
Belgium
www.whenobjects
work.com

This refined yet sensuous
range of tableware was
originally designed for
use in **John Pawson**'s
Cistercian monastery
in Bohemia. Its elegant
minimalism offers just
what is necessary
for visual delight and
function without
anything extraneous
being added.

Cutlery, B.Y.
Bernard Yot
Silver plate and silver
Various dimensions
Christofle, France
www.christofle.com

Cutlery collection, Mami
Stefano Giovannoni
Satin steel/mirror-
polished steel
Table knife,
L: 23.5cm (9 ¹⁄₄in)
Alessi SpA, Italy
www.alessi.com

Set of knives, Mami
Stefano Giovannoni
Stainless steel/
mirror-polished steel
Steak knife,
L: 23.5cm (9 ¹⁄₄in)
Alessi SpA, Italy
www.alessi.com

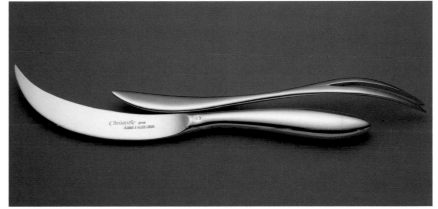

Knife and fork,
Couverts de la Terre
Alain Passard
Silver plate
Various dimensions
Christofle, France
www.christofle.com

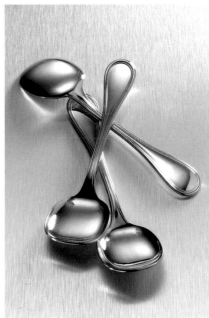

Cutlery set, Asta
Alessandro Mendini
18/10 stainless steel
Various dimensions
Alessi SpA, Italy
www.alessi.com

Ice-cream spoon, Albi
Christofle
Silver plate and silver
Various dimensions
Christofle, France
www.christofle.com

Tableware (diamond-scratched glass), Editor (5 versions)
Miguel Vieira Baptista
Glass
Various dimensions
Miguel Vieira Baptista,
Portugal
www.mvbfactory.com

'Editor' is a combination of a refined material (glass) and street graffiti. Pieces from the Ivama factory were commandeered and 'vandalized' with the edge of a diamond.

Portuguese design

Portugal today is at the centre of a cultural rebirth. Lisbon is one of the top weekend-break destinations, Oporto was named the European City of Culture in 1991 and in 1998 there was the Lisbon Expo. The Pritzker Prize was awarded to Avaro Siza and the Nobel Prize for literature to José Saramago. The football extravaganza of Euro 2004 resulted in a large-scale rebuilding programme, and international architects enthuse about their commissions to build in Portugal. Rem Koolhaus's 'Casa da Musica' was completed in spring 2005, and Frank Gehry's 'Parque Mayer' theatre complex is underway.

All this activity helps to focus international attention on a country that lies on the western border of Europe, its back to its dominant neighbour, Spain, and facing the Atlantic – a country that has until now been on the edge, looking out. This geographic isolation was compounded by the political isolation imposed on the country during the fascist Salazar regime, which only passed with the bloodless Sweet Revolution of 1974. Now, after becoming a member of the European Community in 1986, and due to the resultant substantial EC investment, Westernization has continued to help Portugal, which still has a culture of severe rural poverty, economic migration

and a dense population concentrated in a very small area between Lisbon in the south and Viana do Castelo in the north. Not surprisingly, therefore, the Portuguese design scene is in its infancy. Still based in the vernacular and craft orientated, the emergent style mixes a traditional Portuguese approach with influences gleaned from the rest of Europe. It is a discipline in transition, with new ideas being introduced as a younger generation travels more widely than its predecessors and is exposed to varying impressions.

Product design is slowly being liberated from the confines of dictatorship and political uncertainty. Today's young designers are the first generation to grow up in a land of freedom, making choices without fear of repression and breaking away from the restrictive conventions of their country's past dogmas. A design youth with an intellectual curiosity denied to

its ancestors is now keen and able to share ideas with the rest of the world. The Voyager Communication Project (an offshoot of Experimenta, the two-yearly arts and design fest) is a travelling showcase of contemporary Portuguese creativity and was the brainchild of the designer Miguel Vieira Baptista. Products on show demonstrate that there are two strands of contemporary Portuguese design. On the one hand there is a strong conceptually led anti-design movement evidenced in the works of collaboratives such as designwise (not illustrated), whose work calls upon characteristics such as simplicity and economy of production, recycling and reutilization. On the other hand there is a kind of Scandinavian coolness mixed with Portuguese inventiveness and sensitivity, as evidenced in the crisp works of Baptista and Fernando Brízio. Not unlike some of the more refined work of Droog Design, pieces such as 'Viagens' (Brízio) and 'Puzelaine' (Baptista) combine narrative and shared memory in items which function.

This second style trait is particularly evident in glassware. Glass manufacture has always been an important aspect of Portuguese culture, not to mention history. It was the rebellious workers of this industry who founded one of the most anarchistic groups of the mid-1930s, and who were honoured as the instigators of a movement that was eventually to lead to the 1974 revolution. The area of Marinha Grande is home to glass that has a long history of quality, technology and design, and is currently bringing glassblowers into the twenty-first century. It is collaborating with international designers such as Karim Rashid, as well as national personalities, on a range of highly stylized products that is attracting recognition around the world. Portuguese design is on the up and is set to continue as long as support for the emerging industry is forthcoming from both state subsidies and the design press.

Tableware, Viagens
Fernando Brízio
Porcelain
Various dimensions
Fernando Brízio,
Portugal
fernandobrizio@clix.pt

Pre-fired porcelain objects were taken for a drive in the back of a Land Rover over rough territory. During the trip the objects were deformed – once fired the memory of the journey is visible in each piece.

Tableware (glued pieces of porcelain), Puzelaine (3 versions)
Miguel Vieira Baptista
Porcelain
Various dimensions
Miguel Vieira Baptista, Portugal
www.mvbfactory.com

For 'Puzelaine', several rejects from the Vista Alegre factory were shattered and reformed; the aim was not to recreate the original but to find a new logic in a new form.

Series of vases, Stretch
Francisco Vieira Martins
Glass
H: 35cm (13 ³/₄in)
D: 17cm (6 ³/₄in)
Marinha Grande Mglass, Inc, USA
www.marinhagrande mglass.com

Series of vases, Fgo & Id
Karim Rashid
Glass
H: 36cm (14 ¹/₈in)
D: 28cm (11in)
Marinha Grande Mglass, Inc, USA
www.marinhagrande mglass.com

Cutlery range, mvb
Miguel Vieira Baptista
Stainless steel
Various dimensions
Miguel Vieira Baptista, Portugal
www.mvbfactory.com

Series of pots, Green
Isabel Cunha
Glass
H: 49cm (19 ¹/₄in)
D: 26cm (10 ¹/₄in)
Marinha Grande Mglass, Inc, USA
www.marinhagrande mglass.com

Alfredo Häberli

Which of your designs to date would you like to be remembered by?

I would like to be remembered for who I am and then maybe for a few projects like 'Kids' Stuff', 'Essence' for Iittala or 'SEC, Segesta' for Alias. But I am not the person who will decide that.

How do you think others view your work?

I have started to receive many compliments for my 'slow' work process. People and companies understand that there is a way of thinking behind it and not just a 'fast' shape language. If I have the opportunity to explain my ideas, then people say they can truly appreciate my products. On the other hand, if I see how much the product sells, then I know something was understood without any explanation.

Which designer has influenced you the most and why?

Giorgio Giugiaro (Ital Design) and Achille Castiglioni, because my curiosity for design started with their products and I ended up having my own design studio. Then I had the good luck to meet Bruno Munari, with his tremendous versatility and humour, and he taught me to take time and wait for the right moment. I also met Enzo Mari, who showed me the real cultural value of design.

If you were not a designer, what would you like to be and why?

A cartoonist, because you have to interpret what you see and what you observe by putting a few lines on paper – without words. This is very difficult. But I am very happy doing what I do. And in a way it is close to being a cartoonist; I use my observations for reflection.

What role do you think the designer has in society today?

Society today seems to want more celebrities, but to me it is more important to add something, to put more honesty into the ideas and to take care of our world, our future and not just the consumer aspect.

Do you buy a lot of design pieces?

Yes, more now than when I couldn't afford it! I believe in brand value, in companies doing research and in pioneer work, so I understand why some products have a higher price.

Is there a design in your home that you couldn't live without?

Not really. But if so, then my Caran d'Ache pencil and sketchbook (anonymous design). I also really love a vase I have from Shiro Kuramata and the puzzle '16 Animali' from Enzo Mari. And the sound and shape of my 1993 SAAB 900 convertible, which is stored in the garage when I can't drive it.

What do you consider to be the best piece of design since the millennium?

The work done by my friends Konstantin Grcic and Jasper Morrison.

Where do you think design is heading? Is there someone we should be watching?

We have a culture in Europe that is incomparable. We have to take care of it and we should not ruin hundreds of years of culture in just a short time. Designers should take their responsibility a little more seriously and with more respect. And the media should really watch for ideas, for geniality, for inventions – and not just look at ambitious individuals.

Is the cult of the personality taking over the design world?

Sometimes, yes, too much. I still believe in the product and its charisma. I follow that 'longer' way, but not to have a personal cult. Maybe that is a rather Swiss way to look at things; but I feel an integrity in it and I take the time for it.

Set of dishes for children, Kids' Stuff
Alfredo Häberli
Glass, wood, metal, plastic
Various dimensions
Iittala Oy Ab, Finland
www.iittala.com

Café latte spoon, Waterworks
Claus Jensen & Henrik Holbaek, Tools Design
Stainless steel
H: 18cm (7 $\frac{1}{8}$ in)
W: 2.8cm (1 $\frac{1}{8}$ in)
Eva Solo by Eva Denmark A/S, Denmark
www.evasolo.com

Fruit holder, Fruitscape
Stefano Giovannoni
Steel
H: 4cm (1 $\frac{1}{2}$ in)
L: 35.2cm (13 $\frac{7}{8}$ in)
Alessi SpA, Italy
www.alessi.com

Tea maker, Teashirt
Claus Jensen & Henrik Holbaek, Tools Design
Stainless steel, neoprene, glass, silicone
H: 19cm (7 $\frac{1}{2}$ in)
Diam: 14cm (5 $\frac{1}{2}$ in)
Eva Solo by Eva Denmark A/S, Denmark
www.evasolo.com

Magnetic pot stand, Magnifik
Sweedish Design studio (Henrik Kjellberg and Mattias Lindqvist)
Silicone, neodyme magnets
H: 0.5cm ($\frac{1}{4}$ in)
W: 18cm (7 $\frac{1}{8}$ in)
L: 24.5cm (9 $\frac{7}{8}$ in)
IKEA, Sweden
www.ikea.com

Tea set, Kult
Guido Metz & Michael
Kindler, Metz und
Kindler Design
High-grade steel,
borosilicate-glass, silicon
Various dimensions
WMF AG, Germany
www.wmf.de

**Tableware, coffee pot
and cups (Black Gold
Collection)**
Ineke Hans
Black porcelain
Coffee pot,
H: 22cm (8 5/8in)
Diam: 18.5cm (7 1/4in);
Cup,
H: 5cm (2in)
Diam: 13.5cm (5 3/8in)
Limited batch
production, Ineke Hans/
Arnhem, the Netherlands
www.inekehans.com

Tea thermos, Kult
Guido Metz & Michael
Kindler, Metz und
Kindler Design
High-grade steel,
porcelain, felt
H: 15cm (5 7/8in)
Diam: 14.5cm (5 3/4in)
WMF AG, Germany
www.wmf.de

**Double pitcher,
Mix drinks**
Guido Metz & Michael
Kindler, Metz und
Kindler Design
Glass
H: 19.5cm (7 7/8in)
W: 13.5cm (5 3/8in)
D: 21.3cm (8 1/4in)
WMF AG, Germany
www.wmf.de

**Table crockery, Black
Matt and White Matt
Porcelain Series**
Shin and Tomoko Azumi
Glazed porcelain
Various dimensions
Muji/Ryohin Keikaku Co,
Ltd, Japan
www.muji.net

**Coffee maker,
Geo Proust**
Alessandro Mendini
PP, PC, heat-resistant
glass
H: 45cm (17 ³/₄in)
W: 25.5cm (10 ¼in)
D: 18cm (7 ¹/₈in)
Alessi SpA, Italy
www.alessi.com

Container/vase, Flower
Scholten & Baijings
Porcelain
H: 9.5 (3 ³/₄in)
Diam: 12 cm (4 ³/₄in)
Produced within the
framework of the
European Ceramic Work
Centre project, 'Dutch
Souvenirs'
www.scholtenbaijings.com

Part of the 'Dutch Souvenirs' series produced by the
European Ceramic Work Centre, Scholten & Baijings'
'Flower' container/vase is filled with the old Dutch
liqueur 'Forget-Me-Not'. Distilled from flower buds,
blossoms, brandy and rum, this long-life elixir has a
distinctive floral aroma that evokes the bygone era
when the drink was given by womenfolk to their sailor
husbands or loved ones, to be opened only when they
reached their first port of call.

Salvation ceramics
Constantin and Laurene
Leon Boym
Styling and realization:
Rebecca Wijsbeek
Second-hand porcelain
Various dimensions
Moooi, the Netherlands
www.moooi.nl

**Tableware, Sets of
bowls and cups**
Alon Eliezer Meron
Porcelain, rubber
Bowls,
H: 10cm (3 ⁷⁄₈in)
Diam: 17cm (6 ³⁄₄in)
Alon Eliezer Meron,
Israel
www.promisedesign.info

**Espresso cup and
saucer, Infusion**
Ross Lovegrove
Acrylic, porcelain
Cup,
H: 5cm (2in)
Diam: 6cm (2 ³⁄₈in);
Saucer,
Diam: 12cm (4 ³⁄₄in)
Guzzini, Italy
www.fratelliguzzini.com

Dinner service, Mami
Stefano Giovannoni
Porcelain
Various dimensions
Alessi SpA, Italy
www.alessi.com

2003 saw **Alessi** exhibit a range of tea and coffee sets, 'Tea&Coffee Towers', at the Triennale during the Milan Furniture Fair. This was unremarkable, save for the fact that each of the twenty-two sets was designed by an architect. The concept of the show developed from an earlier exploration of cross-disciplinary collaboration. Alessandro Mendini curated the previous event, like the 'Towers', in the early 1980s. At a time when the glory days of 1960s and 70s Italian design were in decline, Mendini sought to open up a debate by inviting eleven architects from throughout Europe who had not previously worked in product design to create a set of expensive, limited-batch tea and coffee sets – a typological archetype – hoping to discover new talents capable of renewing the domestic landscape. From this experiment two of these designers, Michael Graves and Aldo Rossi, went on to enjoy a valuable partnership with Alessi, designing

serial products well into the 1990s. In much the same way Mendini again sought to refresh Alessi's product range by exploring the world of contemporary international architecture. The result was a series of incredibly beautiful architectonic objects by the likes of Zaha Hadid, Thom Mayne, Will Alsop and UN Studio, all of which demonstrated technological expertise and cultural reference. Once again the sets were mostly silver plated, and were only available in very limited batches and at great expense. Alessi were overwhelmed by positive feedback and to meet popular demand have now produced some of the original cups and saucers in porcelain. Denton Corker Marshall, Massimiliano and Doriana Fuksas, Toyo Ito and Wiel Arets were the architects selected to produce these re-editions.

Set of two mocha cups with saucers, Presto

John Denton, Bill Corker and Barrie Marshall
Bone china
Cup,
H: 5.3cm (2in)
W: 6.5cm (2 1/2in)
D: 5.3cm (2in);
Saucer,
W: 11cm (4 3/8in)
L: 13.5cm (5 3/8in)
Alessi SpA, Italy
www.alessi.com

Set of two mocha cups with saucers, E-LI-LI

Massimiliano and Doriana Fuksas
Bone china
Cup,
H: 6.5cm (2 1/2in)
W: 8cm (3 1/8in)
D: 4cm (1 5/8in);
Saucer,
W: 10cm (3 7/8in)
L: 14cm (5 1/2in)
Alessi SpA, Italy
www.alessi.com

Set of two mocha cups with saucers, Kaeru

Toyo Ito
Bone china
Cup,
H: 7cm (2 3/4in)
Diam: 4.5cm (1 3/4in);
Saucer,
Diam: 15cm (5 7/8in)
Alessi SpA, Italy
www.alessi.com

Set of two mocha cups with saucers, cup.it

Wiel Arets
Bone china
Cup,
H: 7cm (2 3/4in)
W: 5.5cm (2 1/8in)
D: 3cm (1 1/8in);
Saucer,
Diam: 14cm (5 1/2in)
Alessi SpA, Italy
www.alessi.com

Bowl, Blobdrop
Harry & Camila
Sterling silver, ceramic
H: 4cm (1 ⅝in)
W: 28cm (11cm)
D: 15.5cm (6 ⅛in)
De Vecchi, Italy
www.devecchi.com

Coffee cup, Espresso Riflesso
Johanna Grawunder
Sterling silver, ceramic
H: 5.5cm (2 ⅛in)
Diam: 14cm (5 ½in)
De Vecchi, Italy
www.devecchi.com

Tumbler, Barrique
Konstantin Grcic
Wood
H: 13.5cm (5 ⅜in)
W: 7cm (2 ¾in)
D: 7cm (2 ¾in)
Guzzini, Italy
www.fooddesign
guzzini.com

Tabletop collection, Morphescape
Karim Rashid
Glazed porcelain
Various dimensions
Gaia & Gino, Turkey
www.gaiaandgino.com

Soup Set
Hella Jongerius
Handmade faience
Large bowl,
H: 15cm (5 ⁷/₈ in)
Diam: 30cm (11 ⁷/₈ in);
Small bowl,
H: 9cm (3 ¹/₂ in)
Diam: 16.5cm (6 ¹/₂ in)
Koninklijke Tichelaar
Makkum,
the Netherlands
www.tichelaar.nl

Plates, Patchwork
Marcel Wanders
Handmade faience
Various dimensions
Koninklijke Tichelaar
Makkum,
the Netherlands
www.tichelaar.nl

Missoni Home coffee set, Pierrot
Rosita Missoni
Porcelain
Various dimensions
Missoni Home, Italy
www.missonihome.com

Blending old and new, the 400-year-old ceramic manufacturers **Koninklijke Tichelaar Makkum** invited three contemporary designers, Marcel Wanders, Hella Jongerius and Jurgen Bey, to work on a series of pottery. The results produced a perfect cross-fertilization of age-old techniques and modern design. Each designer decided to adapt the ancient craft of majolica. The products are fired twice, after which the typical character of this ancient method becomes visible. Majolica, which has its origins in the eleventh century, is the only way to produce the special feel associated with original Delftware. Jurgen Bey, however, went a step further. By using ingenious moulds and relief and printing techniques, he created a foundation that could then be hand-painted.

Coffee and tea set, 3035 minutes service
Jurgen Bey
Handmade faience
Various dimensions
Koninklijke Tichelaar
Makkum, the
Netherlands
www.tichelaar.nl

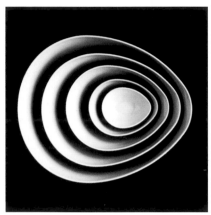

Tableware, Sunami
Lucia Kinghorn
Melamine
Various dimensions
Precidio Inc, Canada
www.precidioobjects.com

If you are of the generation born in the 1950s, as I am, then **melamine** conjures up childhood images of drinking E-ridden orange squash from plastic tumblers, or sitting in the wind-break of the family Morris Minor to eat an egg and tomato salad with Heinz Salad Cream off pastel-coloured unbreakable plates. What goes around comes around, and today chic 'retro' galleries celebrate pieces from melamine's heyday, while Ontario-based Precidio Objects are producing a line of tableware that investigates the potential of the material, moving it from picnic patio to the dining room. Melamine, developed in the 1930s and 40s and so popular throughout the 1950s and 60s, has always been well known for its clarity, stability in reaction to heat, light, chemicals and abrasion, and fire resistance, but not for its design possibilities. Precidio have invited three young designers to provide a modern take on an established material. Illustrated here are works by Jonathan Adler and Lucia Kinghorn.

Ceramics, Ryker
Lucy. D (Barbara Ambrosz)
Porcelain, platinum glaze
Various dimensions
Limited batch production, Lucy. D, Austria
www.lucyd.com

'Ryker' – recycled ceramic – developed from Karin Stiglmair and Barbara Ambrosz's desire to reuse odd pieces of crockery. By adding a unifying visual element to china of various sizes and shapes, they have created completely new dinner services. The rim of each plate is glazed with platinum and gives a square shape to the normally round plate.

Table set, The White Snow Rami
Antonia Astori and Vittorio Locatelli
Porcelain
Various dimensions
Driade SpA, Italy
www.driade.com

Ceramic bowl and cover, Pottery
Vincent Van Duysen
Ceramic, sandblasted oak
Diam: 30cm (11 ¾in)
When objects work, Belgium
www.whenobjects work.com

Adler Happy Home Tableware Collection, Stockholm Pots
Jonathan Adler
Melamine, acrylic
Various dimensions
Precidio Inc, Canada
www.precidioobjects.com

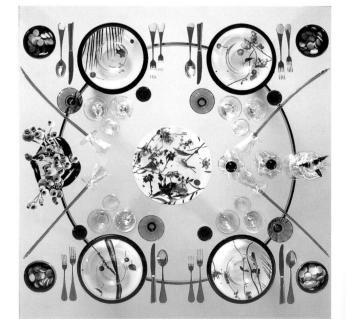

Hella Jongerius

Which of your designs to date would you like to be remembered by?
I don't know; I hope my products have an overall strong character based on one story, which allows it all to be read as one product.

How do you think others view your work?
Well, sometimes I read things so this is not a secret, but 'what do I think of it?' would be a better question.

Which designer has influenced you the most and why?
Not only designers, but the art world is even more interesting: Castiglioni, Ray Eames, William Morris, Bruno Munari, Jurgen Bey, Vermeer, Martin Margiela, Pipilotti Rist, Berlinde de Bruyckere, etc.

If you were not a designer, what would you like to be and why?
A farmer, but the romantic version.

What role do you think the designer has in society today?
To be honest, I think socially and politically not a big role, although a lot of people want to believe it is a mature role. Design just adds smartness and beauty to products or projects. As a design idealist I'm always trying to make my role as layered as possible, but in the end I'm always disappointed about how small the role of a designer is.

Do you buy a lot of design pieces?
No, I have more vintage pieces.

Is there a design in your home that you couldn't live without?
I can live without anything, that's also my survival strategy as a designer. Although I truly cry if my sweetheart breaks a nice piece.

What do you consider to be the best piece of design since the millennium?
My two girls.

Where do you think design is heading? Is there someone we should be watching out for?
Always looking and curious for the new generation, but for now they are very silent; can't wait to hear a new voice!

Is the cult of the personality taking over the design world?
True quality and talent will survive the media hype.

Plate, Wildlife
Hella Jongerius
European hard porcelain
Diam: 16cm (6 ¼in)
Nymphenburg Porcelain,
Germany
www.nymphenburg-porzellan.com

Bowl, Rabbit
Hella Jongerius
European hard porcelain
Diam: 35cm (13 ¾in)
Nymphenburg Porcelain,
Germany
www.nymphenburg-porzellan.com

Bowl
Massimo Micheluzzi
Murrina glass
H: 18cm (7in)
W: 10cm (4in)
Diam: 29cm (11 ³/₈in)
Massimo Micheluzzi,
Italy
T: +39 041 5282190

Italian designer
Massimo Micheluzzi's
pieces are graphic works
in three dimensions.
He was brought up in
Venice and collaborates
with traditional master
craftsmen, deriving his
inspiration from the city's
magical landscape and
in particular the play of
light on water, old stone
and salt-veined brick.

**Ceramics, Reinventing
Chinese Rituals**
Michelle Huang
Porcelain
Various dimensions
Droog Design,
the Netherlands
www.droogdesign.nl

Lazy Suzy, Piano
Francesca Bosa
Ceramic
H: 2cm (⅞in)
W: 66cm (26in)
D: 36cm (14⅛in)
Bosa Ceramiche, Italy
www.bosatrade.com

'Do Create' is a series of designs created for the 'do'
experimental brand, which was set up by the Dutch
publicity firm Kesselskramer. By asking for products
to fit a brand name rather than creating a brand from
existing items, Kesselskramer offered a clear canvas
for invention and improvisation. As the name suggests,
'do' is an ever-changing brand that depends on what
you do – a brand that is open to ideas from anyone
and anywhere. Droog have conceived objects with
which users interact emotionally and physically.
Users influence the design, and the design itself
becomes an indication of their character. By
scratching a message on Martí Guixé's light box
(see page 287), a personalized lamp, 'do scratch',
is created; while Frank Tjepkema and Peter van der
Jagt's vase 'do break' will never shatter, no matter
how many times it is hurled to the ground. Although
the exterior will show the vestiges of aggression,
the vase will remain intact because of the sticky
rubber interior.

Vase, do break
Frank Tjepkema,
Peter van der Jagt
Porcelain, rubber,
silicone
H: 34cm (13³⁄₈in)
Diam: 15cm (6in)
do + Droog Design,
the Netherlands
www.droogdesign.nl

Renny Ramekers,
Droog Design

How do you think others view your work?
They either love it or they hate it.

Do you buy a lot of design pieces?
If I buy things, I buy them with attention, but not
necessarily to their design.

**Is there a design in your home that you couldn't
live without?**
My bed.

**Where do you think design is heading? Is there
someone we should be watching out for?**
Too much design.

**Is the cult of the personality taking over the
design world?**
Unfortunately, yes.

**Bowls, Love/Big
Love/Super Love**
Miriam Mirri
PMMA, 18/10 stainless
steel
Various dimensions
Alessi SpA, Italy
www.alessi.com

**Drinking cup,
Liquid skin**
Lucy. D (Barbara
Ambrosz)
Crystal glass
H: 5.4cm (2 1/8in)
W: 13.4cm (5 3/8in)
D: 9.2cm (3 1/2in)
Fa. Lobmeyr, Austria
www.lobmeyr.at

**Goblet, Darkside
Collection**
Philippe Starck
Black crystal
H: 26cm (10 1/4in)
Baccarat, France
www.baccarat.fr

**Tumbler, Darkside
Collection**
Philippe Starck
Black crystal
H: 14cm (5 1/2in)
Baccarat, France
www.baccarat.fr

Decanters, Bohème
Fred Lambert
Left: Ceramic model
with brilliant white
enamel finish
(without stopper)
Right: Moulded mouth-
blown glass model,
with transparent
glass stopper
H (ceramic model):
25cm (9 7/8in)
H (glass model):
30cm (11 3/4in)
Diam: 14.5cm (5 3/4in)
Ligne Roset, France
www.ligne-roset.fr

Bowl, Mingle
Lena Bergström
Glass
Various dimensions
Orrefors Kosta Boda AB,
Sweden
www.orrefors.se

**Set of three plates,
Table stories**
Tord Boontje
Porcelain
Various dimensions
Authentics, Germany
www.authentics.de

**Plate, Table stories
'Deer in forest'**
Tord Boontje
Porcelain
Diam: 33cm (13in)
Authentics, Germany
www.authentics.de

**Glass, Table stories
'Birds Flower'**
Tord Boontje
Glass
H: 16cm (6 ¹⁄₄in)
Diam: 7cm (2 ³⁄₄in)
Authentics, Germany
www.authentics.de

A blend of craft, naturalism and technology, **Tord Boontje**'s work has become very popular over the last couple of years, not least on the London design scene. His affordable and successful 'Garland' lamp for Habitat can be found decorating many a light bulb across the land. He has collaborated with Alexander McQueen, creating a 6-metre (20-foot) high Christmas tree for the main hall of the Victoria and Albert Museum in 2003. Covered with 150,000 Swarovski crystals and mounted on a large turntable, the festive icon slowly revolved throughout the Christmas period to vibrant sparkling effect. The British Council brought Tord together with Paul Smith and Agent Provocateur. Along with Coopa-Roca, a women's handcrafts cooperative founded twenty years ago by Rio de Janeiro native Maria Teresa Leal, their designs were showcased in the Super Brands department of Selfridges as part of the London store's latest promotion, Brasil 40°. In addition, Boontje was asked to take part in the V&A's 'The Other Flower Show' exhibition during summer 2004, and created one of the ten garden-shed installations by contemporary artists and designers. The V&A also selected him as one of the international designers who, from February to April 2004, were chosen to take part in the museum's first exhibition of contemporary lighting. The National

Portrait Gallery, London, included a photograph of Tord in the 'Designer Faces' exhibition in 2003–4, *Blueprint* magazine nominated him as a finalist in their Product Designer of the Year, and in 2003 the Design Museum, London, selected him as their Designer of the Year.

Boontje's work is unashamedly decorative and appeals to the current zeitgeist away from the minimalism of the 1990s and towards surface patterning and ornamentation. With garlands and drapery, glitter and sparkle, the ostentatious appearance of many of his designs could be considered frivolous, yet what separates them from the merely decorative is his research into new manufacturing processes and innovative materials. He mixes motifs from nature with precision technology and industrial materials such as Tyvek and laser-cut, digitally printed fabrics, combining these most effectively to create contemporary versions of the romantic aesthetics and richness of the seventeenth and eighteenth centuries in an unrestrained installation for Moroso at the Milan Furniture Fair 2004, and a new range of furniture and lighting for their 2005 collection (see for instance his 'Witch' chair on page 52). Tord considers that his years at the Design Academy, Eindhoven, instilled in him the desire for experimentation, while his studies at the Royal College of Art in London gave

him an awareness of the larger context in which design operates. He would readily admit that his design studio resembles a classroom more than an industrial practice, yet he is one of the few Dutch designers who have made the crossover between the purely conceptual and the commercially successful. By harnessing technology, he is able to create objects with high production values, new industrial processes enabling him to explore the sensual qualities he so admires, while producing mass-market lines in a non-labour-intensive way.

Tabletop setting, Infinity Plate
Karim Rashid
Silk-screen-printed glass
H: 2.5cm (1in)
Diam: 36cm (14 ⅛in)
Egizia, Italy
www.egizia.it

Tumblers, Bamboo
Angelica Gustafsson
Handmade glass
H: 15cm (6in)
Diam: 6cm (2 ⅜in)
Skruf Glasbruk, Sweden
www.skrufs.com

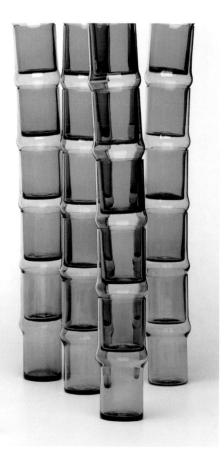

Glasses, Infinity Glassware
Karim Rashid
Silk-screen-printed glass
H: 10cm (3 ⅞in)
Diam: 9cm (3 ½in)
Egizia, Italy
www.egizia.it

Drinking glass, Caterpillar
Sean Yoo, Apt 5 Design
Handmade Bohemian crystal
H: 13cm (5 ⅛in)
Diam: 9.3cm (3 ⅝in)
Ars Temporis, Austria
www.arstemporis.at

Chalices
Aldo Cibic
Glass
H: 20, 22.5, 27 or 31 cm
(7⅞, 8¼, 8⅞ or 10½in)
Cibic & Partners, Italy
www.cibicpartners.com

Aldo Cibic

Which designer has influenced you the most and why?
I started as a designer with Ettore Sottsass when I was 22 and opened my own studio 12 years later at 34; the influence of Sottsass has basically always been considering our work as a research process.

If you were not a designer, what would you like to be and why?
A musician or a movie director.

What role do you think the designer has in society today?
In a world where industry focuses almost exclusively on familiar, standardizing mechanisms and approaches, producing ideas has become increasingly difficult. This leads to the desire to explore new spheres in which to inject creative energy. If we observe the things around us we notice some that don't work, some that no longer exist, and we realize that many things have yet to be invented, reinvented or simply combined in a new way. Everyday life can be seen as a complex or fragments of stories to be salvaged and reworked, a universe composed more of relations than of objects. The material of inspiration for many projects is all around us, and designers with their creative force can become the catalysts.

Do you buy a lot of design pieces?
Accessories like telephones, cameras, Apple items or cars.

What do you consider to be the best piece of design since the millennium?
The 'Aluminum Group' chairs of Charles Eames.

Where do you think design is heading? Is there someone we should be watching out for?
I see three different directions: a cynical one that just gives the market something tricky enough to sell; the design of beautiful objects – intelligent, with a soul – which show what the state of the art is; other areas of design like the design of new services, facilities, entertainments – interactive design that can open many new possibilities for the designs of the objects and for the relationships between them and the users.

Is the cult of the personality taking over the design world?
I think the cult of personality in the design world is pathetic because design does not have the visibility or the same amount of interest as football, music, fashion, cinema, etc.

Collection of drinking glasses, Shorties
James Irvine
Glass
Various dimensions
Covo srl, Italy
www.covo.it

Series of vases, Isabel Hamm for Blumenkraft
Isabel Hamm
Glass
H: 12.2–42cm
(4¾–16½in)
Diam: 7–22cm
(2¾–8⅝in)
Isabel Hamm Glas, Germany
www.isabel-hamm.de

Glassware, Campanella series
Enzo Mari
Barium crystal
Various dimensions
Arnolfo di Cambio –
Compagnia Italiana del
Cristallo SpA, Italy
www.arnolfodicambio.com

Glasses, Mami
Stefano Giovannoni
Glass
Various dimensions
Alessi SpA, Italy
www.alessi.com

Vases, Ken Kuts
Jerszy Seymour
Glass
H: 16–30cm (6 1/4–11 7/8in)
Diam: 13–17.5cm
(5 1/8–6 7/8in)
Covo srl, Italy
www. covo.com

In March 2001 Covo gave Emmanuel Babled the opportunity to invite designers from different disciplines to experiment with the traditional art of Murano glass-blowing, a plan he had entertained for some time. As art director of the **'Smash' collection** he invited Jeffrey Bernett, Stephen Burks, Stefano Giovannoni, Richard Hutten, James Irvine, Ritsue Mishima, Marre Moerel and Jerszy Seymour to produce designs that were then given form by a master Murano blower. The results mix tradition and modernity in a series of impressive and poetic pieces. Through the use of designers from other fields, new challenges have been imposed on glass, with the process of the blowing often adding to the end result. Many of the designers, especially those more used to industrial processes, were often surprised at the unpredictability of the material. At the same time, however, they found that this element of serendipity enhanced the final form. James Irvine commented: 'Like a typical industrial designer, I wanted to control the glass and design precise forms with precise shapes. But glass just doesn't work like that, so the surprise of the randomness of each form in fact became a pleasure for me. Every single one is slightly different.'

Vases, Cylinders
James Irvine
Glass
H: 38–40cm
(14 7/8–15 5/8in)
Diam: 10cm (4in)
Covo srl, Italy
www. covo.com

Vases, Serie Vegetali
Ritsue Mishima
Glass
H: 8–48cm (3 1/8–18 3/4in)
Covo srl, Italy
www. covo.com

Glass, Stream
Emmanuel Babled
Crystal
H: 22cm (8 ⁵⁄₈in)
Baccarat, France
www.baccarat.fr

Shot glasses, Nana, Gigi, Pepo
Toshiyuki Kita
Lead crystal with over 24% PbO
Various dimensions
Arnolfo di Cambio – Compagnia Italiana del Cristallo SpA, Italy
www.arnolfodicambio.com

Vase, Memore
Konstantin Grcic
Lead crystal with over 24% PbO
H: 31cm (12 ¹⁄₄in)
W: 10cm (3 ⁷⁄₈in)
D: 12.5cm (4 ⁷⁄₈in)
Arnolfo di Cambio – Compagnia Italiana del Cristallo SpA, Italy
www.arnolfodicambio.com

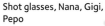

Candleholder, Punch
Karim Rashid
Lead crystal with over 24% PbO
H: 11.3cm (4 ³⁄₈in)
D: 17cm (6 ³⁄₄in)
Arnolfo di Cambio – Compagnia Italiana del Cristallo SpA, Italy
www.arnolfodicambio.com

Goblets, Laetitia
Michele De Lucchi with Alberto Nason
Lead crystal with over 24% PbO
Various dimensions
Arnolfo di Cambio – Compagnia Italiana del Cristallo SpA, Italy
www.arnolfodicambio.com

Paul Cocksedge's designs owe as much to science as to art. A modern-day Joseph Wright of Derby, the alchemy of his potions and reactions creates stunning light effects. Remember the way he shone a UV light on to a bulb full of gin and tonic, changing the liquid from crystal clear to an incredible glowing blue? In 'Bulb' he mixes three elements: electricity, water and a flower. An electrical charge is conducted through the water, along the sap in the flower stem, and illuminates a power source in the base of the vase. The water also acts as a lens and creates a patterned projection of the flower on to surrounding walls and ceilings, emphasizing the immaterial while distracting the attention from the designed object itself.

Light, Bulb
Paul Cocksedge
Glass, steel
Halogen UV-P,
BLV 12V 5W bulb
H: 26cm (10 ¹/₄in)
W: 13cm (5 ¹/₈in)
D: 13cm (5 ¹/₈in)
Paul Cocksedge, UK
www.paulcocksedge.co.uk

Drinking glass, Ro
Lucy. D
(Barbara Ambrosz)
Glass
Diam: 7.8 or 16.3cm
(3 ¹/₈ or 6 ¹/₄in)
Fa. Lobmeyr, Austria
www.lobmeyr.at

**Decanters,
Ilvino y laigua**
Javier Mariscal
Glass
Wine jug,
H: 18.5cm (7 ¹/₄in)
W: 12cm (4 ³/₄in)
D: 8.5cm (3 ³/₈in);
Water jug,
H: 24.5cm (9 ⁵/₈in)
W: 9.5cm (3 ³/₄in)
D: 8.5cm (3 ³/₈in)
Bd Ediciones de Diseño,
Spain
www.bdbarcelona.com

Decanter, Blob
Karim Rashid
Glass
H: 26cm (10 ¼in)
Diam: 18cm (7 ⅛in)
Leonardo, Germany
www.leonardo.de

Decanter, Spoo
Karim Rashid
Glass
H: 25cm (9 ⅞in)
Diam: 14.5cm (3 ⅛in)
Leonardo, Germany
www.leonardo.de

Decanter, Dive
Karim Rashid
Glass
H: 31cm (12 ¼in)
Diam: 13cm (5 ⅛in)
Leonardo, Germany
www.leonardo.de

Since the formula of mixing salt (sodium), bones (calcium) and sand (silica) to make **glass** was discovered over 4500 years ago, it has become a lasting source of inspiration for artisans and designers. It is an insulator, has an elastic quality, is transparent and – although it looks light – cubic metre for cubic metre its weight is equivalent to that of Portland stone. Glass has a life and the process of its manipulation for many designers is as important as the object created. Karim Rashid believes glass to be the most beautiful natural material in the contemporary environment. The sensual curves and ethereal quality of the graded colours of his 'Leonardo' series are intended to 'emphasize the need for beauty and material, through soft, solid, ergonomic, desirable forms'. However, it is Emmanuel Babled who has the greatest respect for the character, poetry and mysteries of glass. His hand-blown vases are all produced in Murano, Italy, by a master craftsman to Babled's design. For him it is the glass itself that determines the outcome of a piece, the designer and blower being merely servants to the wishes of the material. A large part of the end result cannot be predetermined, and it is this tension between the human desire and the moment of creation that he considers to be the most interesting aspect of working with glass. Changes can only be made at the last moment, in the furnace, while the glass is still malleable; the next second it crystallizes and becomes, as he puts it, 'fragile for the rest of eternity'. In his designs, he uses this instant to 'capture a fragment of emotion'.

Glassware, Primaire No. IX
Emmanuel Babled
Hand-blown glass
Diam (average):
45cm (17 ¾in)
Covo srl, Italy
www.covo.com

Bowl, Flip
Karim Rashid
Glass
H: 25cm (9 ⅞in)
Diam: 15cm (6in)
Leonardo, Germany
www.leonardo.de

Bowl, Loop low
Karim Rashid
Glass
H: 20cm (7 ⅞in)
Diam: 29cm (11 ⅜in)
Leonardo, Germany
www.leonardo.de

Bowl, Loop high
Karim Rashid
Glass
H: 25cm (9 ⅞in)
Diam: 23.5cm (9 ¼in)
Leonardo, Germany
www.leonardo.de

Vase, Spring Megalit
Emmanuel Babled
Hand-blown glass
H: 50cm (19 5/8in)
Diam: 40cm (15 3/4in)
Venini SpA, Italy
www.venini.com

Tableware, Akasma
Satyendra Pakhalé
Coloured, bent glass
H: 21.9cm (8 5/8in)
Diam: 36.5cm (14 3/8in)
Limited batch
production, RSVP, Italy
www.r–s–v–p.it

Bowl, Fresh Fat
Tom Dixon
Extruded woven plastic
H: 33cm (13in)
Diam: 66cm (26in)
Tom Dixon, UK
www.tomdixon.net

Vase, UFO
L'Anverre
Glass
H: 25cm (9 7/8in)
Diam: 50cm (19 3/4in)
L'Anverre, Belgium
www.lanverre.com

Hypnos range
Emmanuel Babled
Crystal and Corian®
Various dimensions
Baccarat, France
www.baccarat.fr

**Accessories,
containers, 01 02 03**
Tamar Ben David
Injection moulded in
structural techno-
polymer
H: 16, 20 or 24cm
(6 ³/₈, 7 ⁷/₈ or 9 ¹/₂in)
Diam: 59, 67 or 80cm
(23 ¹/₄, 26 ³/₈ or 31¹/₂in)
Alias SpA, Italy
www.aliasdesign.it

Vase, Medusa
Johanna Grawunder
Hand-modelled, blown
transparent glass
H: 25cm (9 ³/₄in)
W: 35cm (13 ⁵/₈in)
Salviati, Italy
www.salviati.com

Vases, Opal Rock
Kate Hume
Glass
H: 35cm (13 ³/₄in)
W: 37cm (14 ⁵/₈in)
D: 35cm (13 ³/₄in)
Kate Hume Glass,
the Netherlands
www.katehumeglass.com

Sculptural chair/vase, Chair – Please keep off the glass range
Thomas Heatherwick
Glass
H: 85cm (33in)
W: 60cm (23 ⅝in)
Vessel Gallery, UK
www.vesselgallery.com

Hand-blown glass vase, Sviluppo vase
Studio Dillon
Glass
H: 54cm (21 ¼in)
W: 36cm (14 ⅛in)
Vessel Gallery, UK
www.vesselgallery.com

Since his appointment as artistic director of the Venetian glass manufacturer **Salviati**, British glass designer Simon Moore has endeavoured to bring this traditional company into the twenty-first century by producing a series of glass pieces in collaboration with artists in different fields, from architecture, fashion, fine art to lighting design. Previous collections have seen work produced by Ingo Maurer (see page 195), Johanna Grawunder (see page 191), Ted Muehling, Nigel Coates, Tom Dixon, Tord Boontje and Anish Kapoor. Once again, the Vessel Gallery in London has teamed up with Salviati in an exhibition in 2005 entitled 'Salviati Meets London'. Future Systems, Studio Dillon, Ross Lovegrove and Thomas Heatherwick have all produced pieces in limited editions that adhere to Walter Gropius's maxim for good design – that an object should have beauty, quality and function.

Shown on the left are pieces from Jane Dillon's 'Muso' collection of vases and Thomas Heatherwick's chair/vase from his 'Please keep off the glass' collection. Heatherwick's studio combines architecture, art and design. Working in fields as varied as planning, infrastructures, urban development, sculpture and exhibitions, it has produced such attention-grabbing work as the Manchester Stadium monument and the Paddington Basin Bridge, which rolls up into a ball. With the Salviati piece, Heatherwick has been no less innovative. He writes: 'When you think of blown glass you automatically think of fine vases, bowls or vessels. As novices to the work of high glass-blowing craftsmanship, how could we compete with the amazing pieces that already exist? Rather than go down this route, we thought we would try to use the material and craftsmanship to do something it doesn't normally do. Could blown glass become structural? Could it be used to make furniture?' The result uses the largest glass elements the factory was able to produce, but does not yet meet EU safety regulations. For the time being the chair is a vase, but Heatherwick is working on realizing his dream.

Vase, Diamond
Helén Krantz
Glass
H: 26cm (10 ¼in)
W: 19.8cm (7 ⅞in)
Orrefors Kosta Boda AB, Sweden
www.orrefors.se

Glass decanter, Mickey

Takahide Sano
Blown borosilicate glass
H: 26cm (10 ¹/₈in)
L: 34cm (13 ¹/₄in)
Diam: 13cm (5 ¹/₈in)
Limited batch
production, Massimo
Lunardon & C. SNC, Italy
www.studiosano.it/
massimo.lunardon
@tiscali.it

Fully connected: all the
parts of the 'Mickey'
decanter are joined
together, allowing the
wine to move freely
between each.

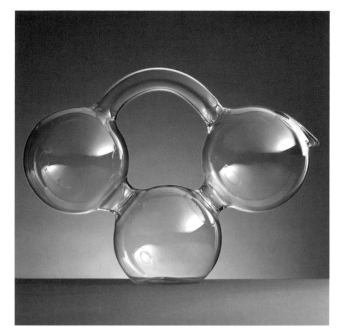

Crystal vase, Splinter

Marcel Wanders
Crystal
H: 15cm (5 ⁷/₈in)
W: 15cm (5 ⁷/₈in)
D: 15cm (5 ⁷/₈in)
Moooi, the Netherlands
www.moooi.com

Vases, Gem Group

Kate Hume
Glass
Various dimensions
Kate Hume Glass,
the Netherlands
www.katehumeglass.com

Vases, Ginza Boogey

Tomoko Mizu
Plexiglas
Various dimensions
Sawaya & Moroni, Italy
www.sawayamoroni.it

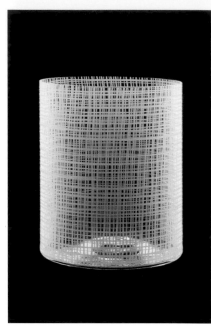

Vase, Swing vase
Britt Bonnesen
Glass
H: 20, 30 or 40cm
(7 $\frac{7}{8}$, 11 $\frac{3}{4}$ or 15 $\frac{3}{4}$in)
Normann Copenhagen,
Denmark
www.normann-
copenhagen.com

Vase, Slowfox
Ingegerd Råman
Crystal
H: 22.5cm (8 $\frac{7}{8}$in)
W: 20cm (7 $\frac{7}{8}$in)
Orrefors Kosta Boda AB,
Sweden
www.orrefors.se

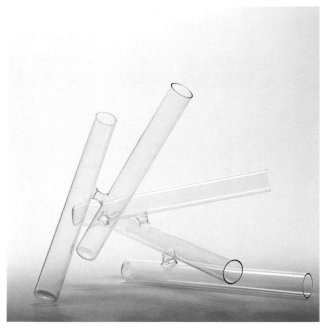

Vase, Bataque Vase
Fernando and Humberto
Campana
Glass
H: 47cm (18 $\frac{1}{2}$in)
W: 43cm (17in)
L: 50cm (19 $\frac{3}{4}$in)
Studio Campana, Brazil
www.campanas.com.br

Vase, Fish
Isabel Hamm
Hand-blown glass
H: 44cm (17 $\frac{1}{8}$in)
W: 13cm (15 $\frac{1}{8}$in)
Isabel Hamm Glas,
Germany
www.isabel-hamm.de

Vase, Blushing
Ingo Maurer
Transparent pierced
glass
H: 50cm (19 ³/₄in)
Diam: 23cm (9in)
Salviati, Italy
www.salviati.com

**Armature for flowers,
Twig 700 and
Twig 900**
Voon-Wong &
Bensonsaw
Metal
H: 70 or 90cm
(27 ¹/₂ or 35in)
Porro srl, Italy
www.porro.com

Vases, Twin wall
Olgoj Chorchoj
Simax (heat-resistant
glass)
Various dimensions
Libera, Czech Republic
www.olgojchorchoj.cz

One of **Ingo Maurer**'s earliest creations was a vase, but so long have we associated the designer with poetic, ethereal and theatrical lighting designs and installations that it comes as something of a surprise to find his name among the three people invited by Salviati to design hand-blown Murano glassware for their 2001 collection. (The other two are American Ted Muehling, who designs jewellery and decorative objects, and architect Johanna Grawunder.) Although Maurer was asked to reinterpret a medium with which he is relatively unfamiliar, he succeeded in producing a series of sculptural pieces of striking beauty. He 'enjoyed working with the old masters tremendously', although he found the process complicated and the glass unpredictable: 'Glass has a life of its own. I wanted to touch it and bend it, but of course I could not. I was creating in my mind and was entirely dependent on somebody else.'

Vase, Vanishing vase
Joris Sparenberg
PET recyclable plastic
H: 20.5cm (8 ¹/₈in)
W: 14cm (5 ¹/₂in)
Diam: 10cm (4in)
Counterpoint, USA
www.counterpoint1.com

Table canister series, Meta Lace
Talila Abraham
Stainless-steel foil
H: 18cm (7 ¹/₈in)
W: 30cm (11 ³/₄in)
L: 30cm (11 ³/₄in)
Talila Abraham, Israel
www.promisedesign.info

Vase, Bikini
Michal Pickel-Sagi
and Tami Pampanel
Ceramic, rubber,
stainless steel
H: 22.5cm (9in)
W: 15cm (5 ⁷/₈in)
L: 15cm (5 ⁷/₈in)
Pickel: Pampanel, Israel
www.promisedesign.info

Israeli Design

Like Dutch and Portuguese design, Israeli design draws heavily on national craft heritage and is in its infancy as far as design manufacturing is concerned. (The Netherlands has a long-standing manufacturing industry, but a quite separate movement has developed there that has little connection with real industry or producing an item that actually functions well – see page 116). As a reaction to the minimalist style of the 1990s, conceptual design is enjoying a vogue, as is decoration, baroque detailing and readymade, a natural correlation of which is the fact that a craft aesthetic is more likely to be accepted into the mainstream. What Holland, Portugal and Israel all have in common is a handmade style with a strong cultural identity, which encompasses not only an understanding of new technological manufacturing processes and an innovative use of materials, but also a wit and irony as well as a strong sense of self. Increased industrialization and globalization is not killing creativity, but is rather unleashing a backlash of national pride and individuality. Rather than having a homogenizing effect, it is apparent that technology is liberating designers to use and adapt shapes and materials from their native surroundings. Taking influences from local culture has often become the safest and best way to see beyond modernism without rejecting contemporaneity. The ability to create new adaptations of old forms and traditional fabrics and translate these through the medium of modern technology has, strangely enough, resulted in many ancient techniques being brought to the foreground, advanced materials often requiring the same amount of manipulations as more classical ones.

Mel Byars, author of *The Design Encyclopedia* published in 2004, declares that Israeli design is 'the world's best-kept secret'. During the 2005 Milan Furniture Fair, the Triennale hosted a group exhibition curated by Ely Rosenberg that gathered together over sixty Israelis' works. All of these reflected an experimental approach to design, examined characteristics of local identity and presented an interesting use of contemporary material. In his comprehensive catalogue to the 'Promisedesign' exhibition, Rosenberg offers several reasons for why he considers Israeli design to have developed as it has. He points out that it is impossible to subtract Israeli style from the geographical, cultural, industrial and economic factors that govern his country. Although Israel has a highly developed plastics industry that offers cutting-edge high-tech production facilities, designer furniture manufacturing has never developed. Add to this the large number of design schools to be found in the country, most notably the Bezalel Academy of Art and Design, and the result is a large number of people working in what can be described as a post-industrial craft sector, producing objects with a high level of creativity that would otherwise have been thwarted by the exigencies of mass manufacture. They create 'craft' pieces using advanced methods of production.

Talila Abraham uses photochemistry and computer scans to transfer patterns on to metal plates which are then cut out and moulded to form delicate items of tableware; while Ezri Tarazi's 'New Baghdad' table (see page 21) combines hundreds of different extruded aluminium profiles to form a futuristic aerial view of the city, with only the ancient

River Tigris left as a cultural and political reference point. In general Israeli design is not beautiful, a fact that Rosenberg attributes to the biblical ban on figurative representations and the rejection of Hellenism and the ancient Greek empire, which was regarded as an enemy of Judaism's spiritual and ethical values. What cannot be underestimated, however, in trying to isolate an Israeli design style, is the Jewish capacity to look at everything in a cynical and self-deprecating way. Jewish people have always been characterized by their sense of humour, which they have called upon throughout their troubled history. This trend has permeated Jewish film, literature and cinema, and can be seen in their design, which amuses and surprises. For example, Pickel: Pampanel's 'Bikini' vases expose flowers as they have never been seen before. Israeli design is, by and large, one-off or limited batch, post-industrial and not particularly aesthetically pleasing, but frequently surprising and self-mocking with a strong identity of place and culture. What worries me, however, is that unlike Dutch or Portuguese design, I do not think it is going anywhere. Although the show enjoyed a lot of success in Milan and when it travelled to Germany for Designmai, I cannot imagine it developing into an industry that can survive commercially. Maybe that is not its intention. However, Tarazi's 'New Baghdad' table was taken up by Edra last year, so maybe I am wrong. I hope I am, but I am also mindful that one swallow does not make a summer!

**Vase/Light,
Not Made by Hand,
Not Made in China**
Ron Arad
Polyamide
H: 5–34cm (2–13 ³/₈in)
Diam: 13cm (5 ¹/₈in)
Ron Arad Associates
www.ronarad.com

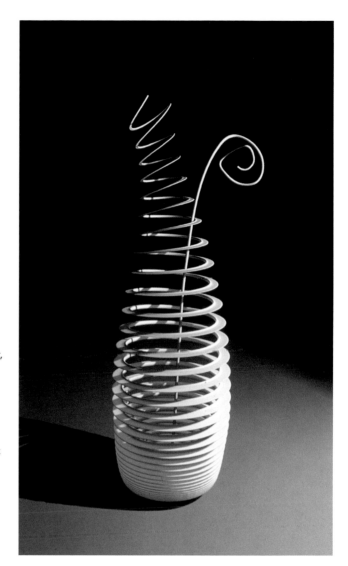

**Self-watering planter,
Evergreen**
Claus Jensen & Henrik
Holbaek, Tools Design
Glass, stainless steel,
metal, nylon
Diam: 11cm (4 ³/₈in)
Eva Solo by Eva
Denmark A/S, Denmark
www.evasolo.com

Four vases, Jonsberg
Hella Jongerius
Porcelain, stoneware,
terracotta, earthenware
H: 34cm (13 ³/₈in)
Diam: 30cm (11 ³/₄in)
IKEA, Sweden
www.ikea.com

**Blister for flowers,
YG 1203 (Blister
Collection)**
Andrea Branzi
Moulded and
sandblasted plastic
with magnetic closing,
enamelled metal,
blown glass
H: 47cm (18 ¹/₂in)
W: 49cm (19 ¹/₄in)
Design Gallery Milano,
Italy
www.designgallery
milano.com

Airborn Snotty Vases
Marcel Wanders
Polyamide ore in
non-pro terms nylon
H: 15cm (5 ⁷/₈in)
W: 15cm (5 ⁷/₈in)
L: 15cm (5 ⁷/₈in)
Cap Design SpA, Italy
www.cappellini.it

The vision behind the 'Airborn Snotty Vases' was to
make the unseen seen. Marcel Wanders wanted to
find a high-tech way of creating a series of objects
inspired by existent yet non-visual shapes. An individual
was invited to sneeze several times into a very
powerful scanner capable of recording microscopic
particles. The most 'beautiful' particle patterns were
selected and transferred to a computer, where they
were modified using specially created IFN software
to form CAD images. The results were sent to a SLS
machine which, using 3D drawing and a computer-
guided laser, built up unique models. Let us just hope
that Cap Design is not making us pay through the
nose for these enchanting little pieces.

**Flower vase,
Babyboop**
Ron Arad
18/10 stainless steel
H: 30cm (11 ⁷/₈in)
W: 11.4cm (4 ¹/₂in)
L: 22.5cm (8 ⁷/₈in)
Alessi SpA, Italy
www.alessi.com

Signature vase
Frank Tjepkema
Nylon
Various dimensions
Droog Design,
the Netherlands
www.droogdesign.nl

The ultimate
personalization of the
consumer in a product,
Frank Tjepkema's vases
for Droog Design's 'Your
Choice' collection are
produced by scanning
a signature and
transforming it into
a unique vase through
the process of
stereolithography.

Vase, Blossoms
Wieki Somers
Ceramic
H: 52cm (20 ¹/₂in)
W: 28cm (11in)
Cor Unum, the
Netherlands
www.corunum.nl

**'Architecture for
flowers', Golden Gate
(Blister Collection)**
Andrea Branzi
Golden brass, enamelled
metal, fine blown glass
H: 25cm (9 ⁷/₈in)
W: 18cm (7 ¹/₈in)
L: 72cm (28 ³/₈in)
Limited batch
production, Design
Gallery Milano, Italy
www.designgallery
milano.com

**Unique glass object,
Align, Clone and Grid**
Anu Penttinen
Hand-blown, wheel-
cut, engraved glass
H: 34cm (13 ³⁄₈in)
Anu Penttinen, Finland
www.anupenttinen.com

**Unique glass object,
Cityscope: Helsinki 1**
Anu Penttinen
Hand-blown, wheel-
cut, engraved glass
H: 25cm (9 ⁷⁄₈in)
Anu Penttinen, Finland
www.anupenttinen.com

**Unique glass object,
Map**
Anu Penttinen
Hand-blown, wheel-
cut, engraved glass
H: 22cm (8 ⁵⁄₈in)
Anu Penttinen, Finland
www.anupenttinen.com

Vase, Ming
Fredrikson Stallard
Porcelain, PVC
H: 40cm (15 ¾in)
Diam: 16cm (6 ¼in)
Fredrikson Stallard, UK
www.fredriksonstallard.com

Biscuit tin, Tin Tin
Marcel Wanders
Lacquered steel
H: 11.5cm (4 ½in)
Diam: 18cm (7 ⅛in)
Normann Copenhagen,
Denmark
www.normann-
copenhagen.com

Fruit bowl, 70cm fruit
Ed Annink,
Ontwerpwerk
Elm wood
H: 8cm (3 ⅛in)
W: 70cm (27 ½in)
D: 10cm (3 ⅞in)
Purple South,
New Zealand
www.purplesouth.com

Ed Annink's 'extruded'
wooden fruit bowl is
made from handcrafted
wych elm sourced from
a managed New Zealand
forest. The qualities of
the wood include its
resistance to fungi and
bacteria, which means
that the fruit stored
will not only look good
displayed on any one
of the four profiles
possible, but will also
last longer.

Flower vases, E–LI–LI
Massimiliano and
Doriana Fuksas
18/10 stainless steel
H: 30cm (11 ³/₄in)
W: 25cm (9 ⁷/₈in)
D: 8.2cm (3 ¹/₄in)
Alessi SpA, Italy
www.alessi.com

**Collection of vases
and candlesticks,
Black Out**
Iacchetti & Ragni
Sterling silver, ceramic
H: 14cm (5 ¹/₂in)
W: 12.5cm (4 ⁷/₈in)
D: 6.5cm (2 ¹/₂in)
De Vecchi, Italy
www.devecchi.com

Candlestick, Medusa
Roberto and Ludovica
Palomba
Silver
H: 53cm (20 ⁷/₈in)
W: 55cm (21 ⁵/₈in)
L: 7cm (2 ³/₄in)
De Vecchi, Italy
www.devecchi.com

Lighting, Flames
Chris Kabel
Metal construction with
standard gas cylinder
H: 55cm (21 ⁵/₈in)
W: 22cm (8 ⁵/₈in)
D: 10cm (3 ⁷/₈in)
Moooi, the Netherlands
www.moooi.nl

**Candle holder,
Matthew Boulton I**
Giuseppe Chigiotti
Aluminium,
polished nickel
H: 32.3cm (12 ⁵/₈in)
W: 25cm (9 ⁷/₈in)
D: 25cm (9 ⁷/₈in)
Driade SpA, Italy
www.driade.com

Vase
Ross Lovegrove
Glazed earthenware
H: 9cm (3 ¹/₂in)
W: 26cm (10 ¹/₄in)
L: 38cm (15in)
Cor Unum, the
Netherlands
www.corunum.com

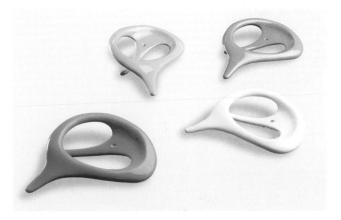

Textiles

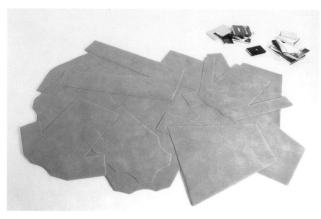

Rug, Dis-Order
Adrien Rovero
100% New Zealand wool
W: 175cm (69in)
L: 240cm (94in)
Tisca Tiara, Switzerland
www.tisca.com

**Rug/wall hanging,
Cityscape**
Monika Piatkowski
100% wool felt
W: 160cm (63in)
L: 220cm (87in)
HIVE, UK
www.hivespace.com

**Rugs, Red Rug,
Blue Rug**
Michael Sodeau
Wool
W: 100cm (39 ³/₈in)
L: various
Christopher Farr, UK
www.cfarr.co.uk

Carpet, Corale
Danskina
100% pure new wool
Various dimensions
Danskina,
the Netherlands
www.danskina.nl

**Hand-tufted
long-pile rug, Moss**
Gunilla Lagerhem-
Ullberg
Wool, flax
H (pile): 4cm (1 ⁵⁄₈in)
Various dimensions
Kasthall, Sweden
www.kasthall.com

Carpet, Puzzle Carpet
Satyendra Pakhalé
Soft expanded
polyethylene covered
with synthetic
stretch fabric
H: 1.5cm (⁵⁄₈in)
Diam: 36cm (14 ¹⁄₈in)
Magis SpA, Italy
www.magisdesign.com

Rug, Juliette
Nani Marquina
100% New Zealand wool
W: 170 or 200cm
(67 or 79in)
L: 240 or 300cm
(94 or 118in)
Nanimarquina, Spain
www.nanimarquina.com

Rug/nightlight, Baby Zoo/Good Night
Laurene Leon Boym
Injection-moulded polycarbonate; laminated cellulose with a chrome aluminium sheet; injection-moulded, self-extinguishing PA6 polyamide; pure virgin wool; LED Carpet,
W: 150cm (59in)
L: 150cm (59in);
Lamp,
H: 3.3cm (1 3⁄8in)
Diam: 18cm (7 1⁄8in)
Flos SpA, Italy
www.flos.it

The 'Baby Zoo' range of rugs is designed to interact with the Flos 'Good Night' light. The comforting colour-changing lamp sits on the spot indicated, changing night to day.

**Rugs,
above: Silence
left: John Deere**
Tore Vinje
Brustad/Permafrost
Designstudio
Virgin wool from
New Zealand
H: 3cm (1 1⁄8in)
Diam: 160cm (63in)
Permafrost, Norway
www.permafrost.no

Carpet, Kiki Carpet
Kiki van Eijk
100% wool
W: 300cm (118in)
D: 200cm (79in)
Moooi, the Netherlands
www.moooi.nl

**Hand-tufted carpet,
La Fontaine**
Linde Burkhardt
100% pure new wool
W: 200cm (79in)
L: 300cm (118in)
Driade SpA, Italy
www.driade.com

Rug, Cuks
Nani Marquina
100% wool
Various dimensions
Nanimarquina, Spain
www.nanimarquina.com

Carpet, Sconcigli
Mary-Ann Williams
Woolfelt 100%
new wool
Various dimensions
Illu Stration, Germany
www.illustration.de.tt

Patricia Urquiola

Which of your designs to date would you like to be remembered by?
I think that 'Fjord' armchair will represent me, even if I might desire that it would be something else!

Which designer has influenced you the most and why?
Achille Castiglioni. My formation and orientation are connected to him: vision for design process, curiosity, fun, method.

If you were not a designer, what would you like to be and why?
I am a designer and architect at the same time. If I hadn't come to Milan I would be an architect, as it's my other passion. I can add that in this period I'm also fascinated by the process of cinematographic narration, even in simple forms.

What role do you think the designer has in society today?
For sure that of a communicator – with different means. He or she won't change the world. It would be better, if it is possible, to be in synchrony with the world.

What do you consider to be the best piece of design since the millennium?
'Chair_One' from Konstantin Grcic for Magis. I see research for a new language, a forerunner; a kind of design language that corresponds with the vision of Olafur Eliasson in the art world or Toyo Ito in architecture.

Is the cult of the personality taking over the design world?
I think it's an issue. Communication has an ephemeral but strongly perceivable power – non-solid but spread. We should research ethical values and serenity. I think I'm part of a generation that is living the process, but not fully into it. Individualistic research should be contained within an equilibrated reality.

Hand-tufted carpet, Mildred II
Antonia Astori
100% pure new wool
W: 330cm (130in)
L: 330cm (130in)
Driade SpA, Italy
www.driade.com

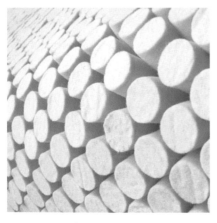

Textile, Circulation
Mark Dyson and Monika Piatkowski
Wool felt pellets
Various dimensions
HIVE, UK
www.hivespace.com

Rugs and tapestry, Crochet
Patricia Urquiola and Eliana Gerotto
Rope, modified polyolefin-based yarn for outdoors
Various dimensions
Paola Lenti srl, Italy
www.paolalenti.com

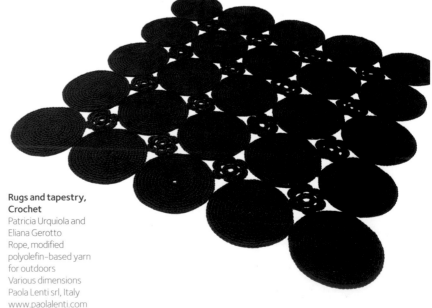

Rug, Fit
Oriol Guimerà
100% New Zealand wool
Diam: 76, 160 or 118cm
(29 $^{7}/_{8}$, 63 or 46in)
Nanimarquina, Spain
www.nanimarquina.com

**Rugs and cushions,
Zoom**
Nani Marquina
100% New Zealand wool
Rug,
W: 170cm (67in)
L: 240cm (94in)
Nanimarquina, Spain
www.nanimarquina.com

**Hand-tufted carpet,
Chambord**
Borek Sipek
100% pure new wool
W: 300cm (118in)
L: 300cm (118in)
Driade SpA, Italy
www.driade.com

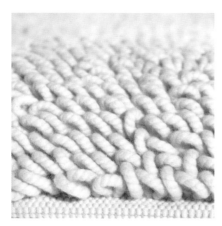

Rug, Salto
Christiane Müller and
Liset van der Scheer
Pure new wool
H: 4.5cm (1 ¾in)
Danskina, the
Netherlands
www.danskina.nl

Rug, Bicicleta
Nani Marquina and
Ariadna Miquel
100% recycled rubber
from bicycle inner
tyre tubes
W: 170cm (67in)
L: 240cm (94in)
Nanimarquina, Spain
www.nanimarquina.com

**Carpet, Soho e
Apostrophe**
Piero Lissoni
Pure wool
W: 170 or 200cm
(67 or 79in)
L: 240 or 300cm
(94 or 118in)
Porro srl, Italy
www.porro.com

Rug, Rajasthan
Nani Marquina
100% New Zealand wool
W: 170 or 200cm
(67 or 79in)
L: 240 or 300cm
(94 or 118in)
Nanimarquina, Spain
www.nanimarquina.com

Bedcover, Sunflower
Claudy Jongstra
Merino wool, Gotland
Pels, raw silk, silk
changeant organza
W: 220cm (85 ⅞in)
L: 350cm (136 ½in)
Not tom, dick & harry,
the Netherlands
www.claudyjongstra.com

Claudy Jongstra works entirely with natural material, primarily felt, to which she adds raw silk, linen, camel, cashmere and wool. The fabrics she creates are 'Beauty and the Beast' – they have the primeval look of the caveman touched with the delicacy and beauty of the gossamer wing. She has a repertoire of hundreds of designs. More sophisticated, smoother fabrics might be a combination of alpaca, merino and silk metallic organza, while hairier, wilder designs could be a mix of merino and raw linen. Jongstra says, 'Basically, felt is the oldest textile in the world and thus does not have a modern image. I wanted to find out more about how to develop some contemporary versions. I want to respect its original character, its strength, so that is why I work with raw, untreated materials.'

To be able to control the quality, colour and mix of wool she uses, Jongstra owns her own rare species of sheep. Currently she has a herd that consists largely of long-haired Drenthe Heath, whose shorn locks she often felts along with the straw and lanolin they accumulate. The industrial process of transforming the raw material into fabric is undertaken on machines which she has had specially made. Clients range from fashion designers Christian Lacroix, Donna Karan and John Galliano, to industrial designers Hella Jongerius, Ettore Sottsass, Jasper Morrison and, more recently, Maarten Baas (for whom she supplied the upholstery for the 'Smoke' series of furniture), as well as architects Will Bruder and Steven Holl. Her fabrics adorned the Jedi warriors in the 'Star Wars' movie *The Phantom Menace*, and she has created wall hangings for the ground-breaking Interpolis office scheme in Tilburg and blinds for the Lloyd Hotel in Amsterdam. She has worked on many interior design concepts and is currently collaborating with the Dutch architects Claus and Kaan on the interiors of the House of Culture and Government.

Carpet, Pappardelle
Mary-Ann Williams and
Alexander Pernitschka,
Illu Stration
100% wool felt on
cotton web
Various dimensions
Illu Stration, Germany
www.illustration.de.tt

**Hand-tufted carpet,
La Bruyere**
Linde Burkhardt
100% pure new wool
W: 300cm (118in)
L: 300cm (118in)
Driade SpA, Italy
www.driade.com

Carpet, Red skin rug
Claudy Jongstra
Merino wool, wild silk,
Drenthe Heath wool,
Wensleydale wool,
cotton
H: 400cm (158in)
W: 275cm (108in)
Prototype, Not tom dick
& harry, the Netherlands
www.claudyjongstra.com

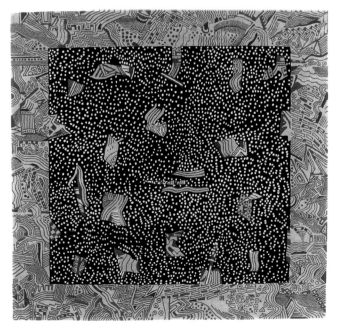

Hand-tufted carpet, Yaschilan
Vittorio Locatelli
100% pure new wool
W: 300cm (118in)
L: 336cm (132in)
Driade SpA, Italy
www.driade.com

Rug, Tarib
Alfredo Häberli
Wool felt
Various dimensions
Ruckstuhl AG,
Switzerland
www.ruckstuhl.com

Rug, Map (New York)
Harry Allen
Hand-tufted
New Zealand wool
Various dimensions
Dune, USA
www.dune-ny.com

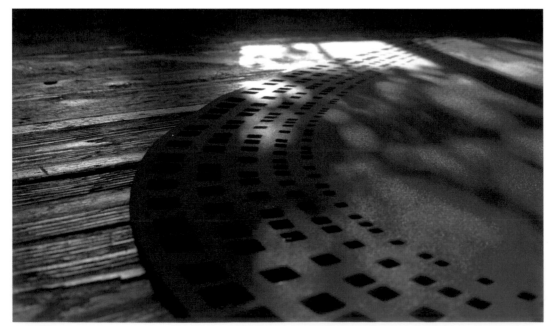

Rug, Salim
Alfredo Häberli
Wool felt
W: 160cm (63in)
L: 320cm (126in)
Ruckstuhl AG,
Switzerland
www.ruckstuhl.com

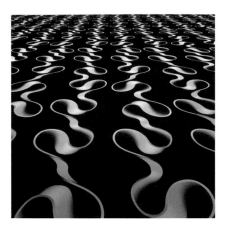

Left:
Carpet tile, No.5
Christian Ghion
Printed tile
W: 50cm (19 ⅝in)
L: 50cm (19 ⅝in)
Tarkett Sommer, France
www.tarkett.com

Right:
Rug, Line
Michael Sodeau
100% wool
W: 180cm (71in)
L: 240cm (94in)
Modus, UK
www.modusfurniture.co.uk

Rug, St Tropez
Eileen Gray
Pure wool
W: 204cm (80in)
L: 204cm (80in)
ClassiCon GmbH,
Germany
www.classicon.com

Rug, Wendingen
Eileen Gray
Pure wool
W: 200cm (79in)
L: 208cm (82in)
ClassiCon GmbH,
Germany
www.classicon.com

Three rugs
Verner Panton
Wool
W: 200cm (79in)
L: 200cm (79in)
Panton Carpets, Germany
www.designercarpets.com

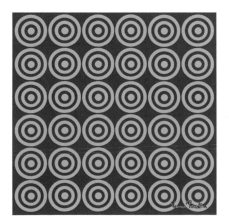

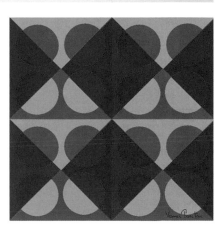

Missoni Home rug, Maracaibo
Rosita Missoni
Viscose wool
W: 170cm
L: 240cm
Missoni Home, Italy
www.missonihome.com

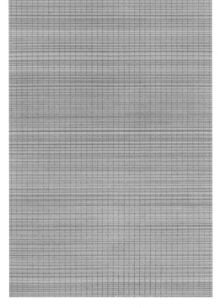

Tiles, Textura
Fabrizio Zanfi
Rectified porcelain stone
W: 40cm (15 ³/₄in)
L: 60cm (23 ⁵/₈in)
Viva srl, Italy
www.cerviva.it

Room divider/wall hanging/panel, Prism
Annemette Beck
100% paper yarn
W: 105cm (41in)
Somic, UK
www.somic.co.uk

Fabric (new environmentally friendly upholstery), Waterborn
Jean Nouvel
55% polyurethane, 22.5% polyester, 22.5% nylon
W: 120cm (47in)
Kvadrat A/S, Denmark
www.kvadrat.dk

Although often blamed for the uniformity of the machine age, technological advance can also liberate creativity. One of the most exciting shows during the Milan Furniture Fair 2003 was held by **Abet Laminati** at the Triennale. Digital print has developed since the turn of the last century and allows four-colour jet printing directly on to the computer base, thus liberating the design process from the cumbersome reliance on printing rollers and silk screens. Single sheets of unique patterns can now be produced and designs can be sent by e-mail, the quality allowing for very sophisticated and fine textures and minute stylistic nuances. Since the birth of Alchimia and Memphis, Paola Navone has enjoyed a long collaboration with Abet Laminati, and has creatively directed the exhibition that invited twenty young designers to produce a laminate using digital print and then conceive a piece of furniture covered in the pattern they had created. The result is a treasure trove of symbols, scribbles and textures inspired by nature, ornamental motifs, geometrical shapes, and floral and module elements, proving that surface design is far from dead.

Carpet tile,
Collection privées
Christian Ghion
Polyester
W: 50cm (19 ⁵/₈in)
L: 50cm (19 ⁵/₈in)
Tarkett Sommer, France
www.tarkett.com

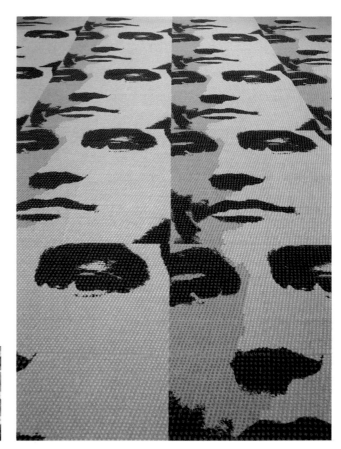

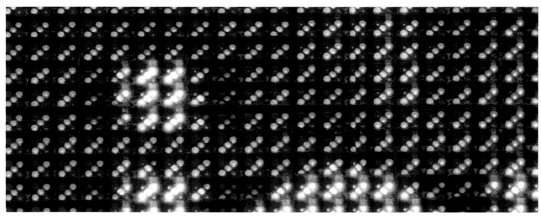

Digital print laminates
Abet Laminati, Italy
www.abet-laminati.it

Carpet Tile
Claudio Colucci
100% polymide solution
dyed yarn, chromatonic
printing system
W: 50cm (19 ³/₄in)
L: 50cm (19 ³/₄in)
Tarkett Sommer, France
www.tarkett.com

Rug, Hardwood Rug
Leon Ransmeier
Beech, rubber
W: 75.5cm (29 ⁷⁄₈in)
L: 150cm (59in)
Vlaemsch, Belgium
www.vlaemsch.be

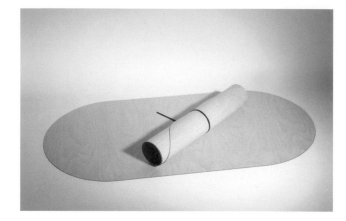

Wall tiling, insulating tiling, decorative surface, half fabricate for countless products, Hard Coated Foam Tiles
Tjeerd Veenhoven
Polystyrene,
polyester/cotton lace
(or metal mesh or any
other open fabric)
Various dimensions
Tjeerd Veenhoven,
the Netherlands
www.tjeerd
veenhoven.com

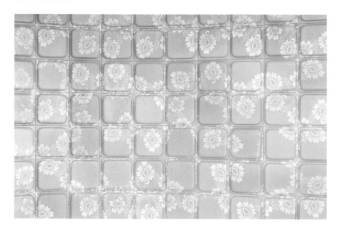

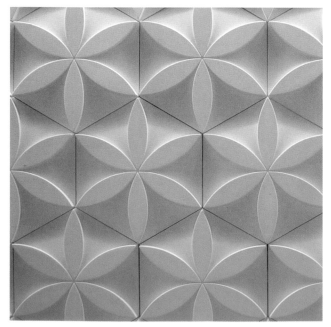

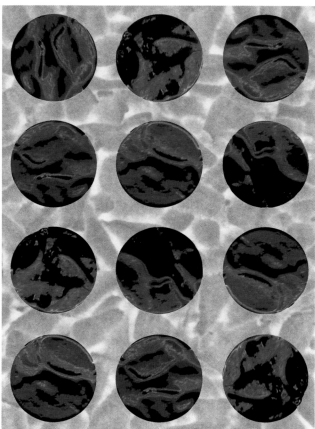

Laminate, Metalprint
Abet Laminati
Bubble muro finish
H: 305cm (120in)
W: 122 or 130cm
(48 or 51in)
Abet Laminati, Italy
www.abet-laminati.it

Tile
Barber Osgerby
Ceramic
Diam: 19.5cm (7 ⁷⁄₈in)
Teamwork srl, Italy
www.teamworkitaly.com

Flooring, PVC C.G.
Christian Ghion
PVC
L: 200cm (79in)
Tarkett Sommer, France
www.tarkett.com

Laminate, Silver
Abet Laminati
Silver finish
H: 305cm (120in)
W: 122cm (48in)
Abet Laminati, Italy
www.abet-laminati.it

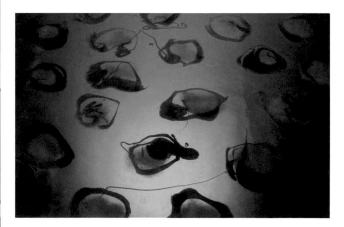

Transfer printed rib stitch
Yoshiki Hishinuma
100% polyester
Yoshiki Hishinuma Co.
Ltd, Japan
www.yoshiki
hishinuma.com

**Textile,
Underwater World**
Harry & Camila
Cotton, rubber silicone
W: 135cm (52 ⅝in)
L: 100cm (39in)
Harry & Camila, Spain
www.harrycamila.com

Carpet, Mat
Paola Lenti
'Rope' synthetic yarn
W (max.): 200cm (79in)
Paola Lenti srl, Italy
www.paolalenti.it

Rug, Mat
Paola Lenti
Synthetic rope
W (max.): 200cm (79in)
Paola Lenti srl, Italy
www.paolalenti.com

Blurring the distinction between interior and exterior, **Paola Lenti** has developed a textile that can be used both inside and out. The modified polyolefin-based yarn, which is twisted to create 'Rope', is reminiscent of the cords used by mountaineers and sailors. It is resistant to seawater, chlorine and sunlight, is non-permeable, non-allergenic and anti-mildew, and was engineered in collaboration with one of Italy's leading producers of high-performance yarns. 'Rope' can be woven and tufted to create different effects for various applications. Francesco Rota's series of furniture was designed specifically for this innovative material. The textile can also be hand-woven directly on to the structure of the furniture using a specialized traditional technique, and takes the form of the piece on to which it is applied. The end result brings the qualities of comfort and elegance associated with an interior collection to exterior environments.

Rug, Air
Paola Lenti
Synthetic rope
W (max.): 200cm (79in)
Paola Lenti srl, Italy
www.paolalenti.com

3D Airco systems fabric, Galaxy (part of the Cosmos Collection)
Aleksandra Gaça
100% Trevita CS
W: 140cm (55in)
Ferdinand Visser BV, the Netherlands
www.microcare.nl

Textile, Kirie 2004
Yoshiki Hishinuma
100% polyester
W: 50cm (19 ⅝in)
L: 50cm (19 ⅝in)
Yoshiki Hishinuma Co. Ltd, Japan
www.yoshiki
hishinuma.com

Rug, Royale
Liset van der Scheer (yarn design),
Christiane Müller (concept)
100% new wool
H (pile): 2.5cm (1in)
Various dimensions
Danskina, the Netherlands
www.danskina.nl

Rug, Bravoure
Danskina Design Team, Christiane Müller (concept)
100% new wool
H (pile): 6cm (2 ⅜in)
Various dimensions
Danskina, the Netherlands
www.danskina.nl

Throw, Flower throw
Persijn Broersen,
Margit Lukacs
Printed cotton
W: 160cm (63in)
L: 280cm (110in)
Moooi, the Netherlands
www.moooi.com

Throw,
Pantheon throw
Job Smeets,
Nynke Tynagel
Printed cotton
W: 160cm (63in)
L: 280cm (110in)
Moooi, the Netherlands
www.moooi.com

Throw, July throw
Marcel Wanders
Printed cotton
W: 160cm (63in)
L: 280cm (110in)
Moooi, the Netherlands
www.moooi.com

Mosaic mural, Blue Aloe
Maurizio Placuzzi
Waterglass, glimmer glass
H: 254cm (100in)
W: 122cm (48in)
Sicis, Italy
www.sicis.com

Recycled plastic sheet, Dapple
Colin Williamson
High molecular weight polyethylene
W: 100 or 150cm (39 or 59in)
L: 200 or 300cm (79 or 118in)
Smile Plastics Ltd, UK
www.smile-plastics.co.uk

Recycled plastic sheet, Mobiles
Colin Williamson
Mobile phone cases, pc/ABS alloy plastic
W: 80cm (31in)
L: 120cm (47in)
Smile Plastics Ltd, UK
www.smile-plastics.co.uk

To create 'Mobiles', discarded mobile phone shells and parts have been collected, melted and set into resin by Smile Plastics Ltd, with no other ingredients added.

Rug, Paper Cuts #1
Miguel Vieira Baptista
Wool
W: 200cm (79in)
L: 300cm (118in)
Miguel Vieira Baptista, Portugal
www.mvbfactory.com

A piece of paper was folded and cut, and the resultant pattern used as a template for 'Paper Cuts #1'. No refinements were made, maintaining the irregular edges and hand-cut shapes of each unique end-product.

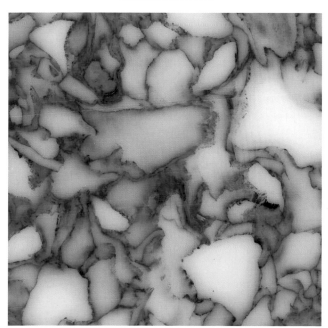

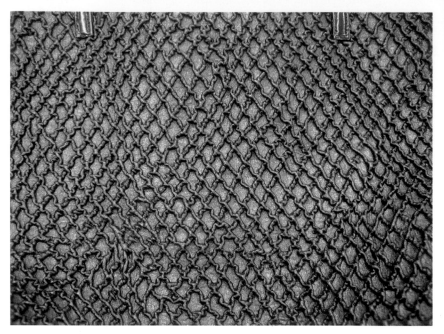

Yoshiki Hishinuma began his career as one of Issey Miyake's assistants, travelling extensively to research new, exotic fabrics, and then returning to experiment with ideas on how to translate these materials into fashion items. He expressed his opinions and ideas so freely that eventually a confrontation with Miyake resulted in his dismissal. Since then he has not collaborated with anyone and works only with the most progressive Japanese manufacturers, using modern artificial materials and the most up-to-date machinery. In his work textile design meets fashion and theatre. His clothes are body-conscious and distinctive in their form and construction, in which haute couture and handicraft are combined.

Hishinuma became famous in the 1980s for his huge, kite-like items of clothing that relied on wind to give them their final form, and over the years his personal approach to fabrics has resulted in highly dynamic and individual collections of textiles that are then transformed into structural, organic and colourful creations for the catwalk. He frequently uses the traditional methods of tie-dying and smocking, yet reinterprets these by the addition of high-tech materials or industrial processes. Interesting developments are the use of matt, coloured polyurethane paper bonded by heat to woven polyester or knitted cotton textiles; the application of collage consisting of woollen fabrics and knitwear; the use of bright, opaque lacquered colours over thin, supple art fibre; heat-cutting polyester film tape; the manufacture of metallic denim clothes; experimentation with shrinking and boiling, which resulted in a new material that shrank if treated but remained in its natural state if pre-heat-treated;

'wonder dye', a process whereby he could dye only those parts of a fabric he wanted to colour; and polyester laminates coated in polyurethane.

Hishinuma's collection, '3D Knit', sees him experimenting with knitwear. He has used a knitting machine that makes completely seamless, entire garments from beginning to end. This process has given rise to organic forms and patterns that are no longer constrained by the geometry of squares, circles and straight lines. The knitted dummy was made using a complicated process that began with a computer program to make the knitted shape. Then the knit was placed on a Styrofoam form and hardened with resin. The Styrofoam base was removed and the piece completed.

Textile, polyurethane-coated, synthetic leather crepe
Yoshiki Hishinuma
Nylon tricot
Various dimensions
Yoshiki Hishinuma Co.
Ltd, Japan
www.yoshiki
hishinuma.com

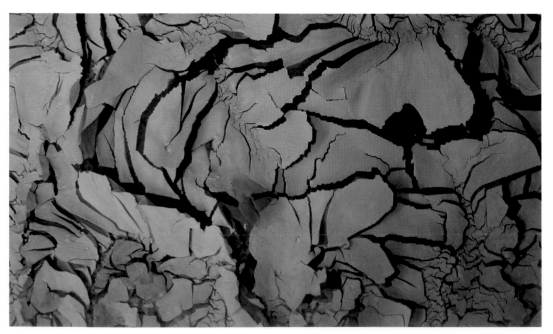

Polyurethane-laminated and sheer-dyed crepe
Yoshiki Hishinuma
Polyester
Various dimensions
Yoshiki Hishinuma Co.
Ltd, Japan
www.yoshiki
hishinuma.com

Seamless scarf, 3D crocodile scarf
Yoshiki Hishinuma
Wool 85%, nylon 15% (knit)
H: 87cm (34in)
W: 17cm (6 ³/₄in)
D: 2cm (³/₄in)
Yoshiki Hishinuma Co. Ltd, Japan
www.yoshiki hishinuma.com

Seamless dummy, 3D body
Yoshiki Hishinuma
Polyester 100% (knit), epoxy resin
H: 162cm (64in)
W: 45cm (17 ³/₄in)
D: 45cm (17 ³/₄in)
Yoshiki Hishinuma Co. Ltd, Japan
www.yoshiki hishinuma.com

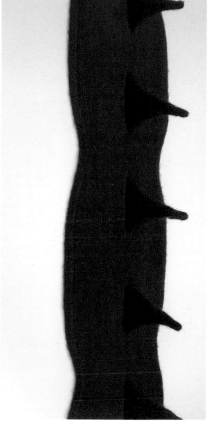

Seamless scarf, 3D antenna scarf
Yoshiki Hishinuma
Wool 85%, nylon 15% (knit)
H: 135cm (53in)
W: 15cm (5 ⁷/₈in)
D: 6cm (2 ³/₈in)
Yoshiki Hishinuma Co. Ltd, Japan
www.yoshiki hishinuma.com

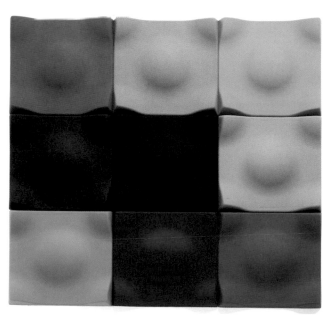

Lightweight sound absorbers and sound diffusers, Soundwave
Teppo Asikainen
Moulded polyester fibre (sound absorbers), PET material (sound diffusers)
H: 58.5cm (23 ¹/₄in)
W: 58.5cm (23 ¹/₄in)
D: 8cm (3 ¹/₈in)
OFFECCT, Sweden
www.offecct.se

Teppo Asikainen's 'Soundwave' wall panel is made from moulded polyester fibre, a material used in the interior panels of aircraft, cars and trains. This felt-like polyester is composed from recycled plastic bottles, and different fabrics can be added for varying finished and colour combinations. Each tile is joined to the next one with Velcro.

Ronan and Erwan Bouroullec

Which of your designs to date would you like to be remembered by?
We don't especially have an icon that would make people remember us. We have the impression that one of our values is the fact that we've been working in many different fields. Maybe people liked the fact that they could see our design from different points of view. This may be so – I'd like people to remember our book or an exhibition, with a kind of overall view though.

How do you think others view your work?
Well, it depends so much on who looks at it and how. Of course, we really listen to our friends, to people who are part of the development process, to those who attend our openings, and so on. But we've never been much in contact with the final user. And I would say, all of them have some reason to appreciate our work, and some others to dislike it, but usually all these reactions don't particularly match. This describes quite well the feeling we have that a good design is a strange alchemy of many factors.

Which designer has influenced you the most and why?
From my point of view, the question is not really about being influenced, but more about recognizing some languages that have been developed in the past and can't be ignored while working nowadays. In this respect, the American team of the Eames and Nelson, Saarinen, can't be ignored, particularly since they really settled a lot of the basis for industrial production today. Then the Italians have been this bridge between industry and research, a kind of bridge from ceramic to plastic. Then in more recent years, Jasper Morrison has certainly settled this new 'economic' way of designing things, and our work has been inspired a great deal by him. And I remember a really nice wooden bridge across a small river in Brittany, which I loved.

If you were not a designer, what would you like to be and why?
Erwan: Definitely a pop singer, for the incredible event that is a concert, with people shaking hands in rhythm.
Ronan: A surfer, for surfing.

What role do you think the designer has in society today?
To design all these things that are meant to be used.

Is there a design in your home that you couldn't live without?
No.

What do you consider to be the best piece of design since the millennium?
We'll answer that in ten years' time.

Where do you think design is heading? Is there someone we should be watching out for?
I have the impression that more and more of the things that surround us are kind of designed. In a way it means that they get more particular. Which means they are sometimes right, sometimes a bit over-designed. So this means there is more and more to look at, and sometimes less and less to consider. Is there someone to watch out for? Surely, but maybe they should come from India, or Africa or South America, which are countries I expect to develop and get a wider audience.

Is the cult of the personality taking over the design world?
Yes, but only in the design world. People don't mind when they buy a carpet.

Modular clipping system, Algue
Ronan and Erwan Bouroullec
Injected ABS
Module:
H: 27cm (10 ⁵/₈in)
W: 23 (9in)
D: 4cm (1 ⁵/₈in)
Vitra, Switzerland
www.vitra.com

Ronan and Erwan Bouroullec used the opportunity of the Ideal House Installation during the Cologne Furniture Fair 2004 to test a new product concept: a small, plastic, branched clipping device that can be 'knitted' together like a textile to act as a room divider or screen. Together with the Campana brothers, they were invited to come up with their concept for the perfect living space; the result was a series of basic components that could be easily adapted, snapping into place without tools, to create walls that could be constructed and deconstructed following the various life changes of the inhabitants.

The first prototype of the modular clipping system was produced for a French advertising agency, BETC, who used it to create a rooftop sun pavilion. At this stage the fastener was angular, resembling a clothes peg. For the Cologne installation, this had evolved into an organic module, each element creeping and joining the next like the spores of moss or algae. The system 'Algue' is now part of Vitra's launch of residential products, which includes other pieces by the brothers, and by Jasper Morrison. Commenting on the Bouroullecs, and the clip in particular, Rolf Fehlbaum, the chief executive of Vitra, wrote: 'Their work makes you wonder, "How did someone come up with that idea? It's so odd, why would you do that?" It's work that emerges not in the spirit of necessity, but which opens a new poetic possibility. It makes you think, "Yes, why not?"'

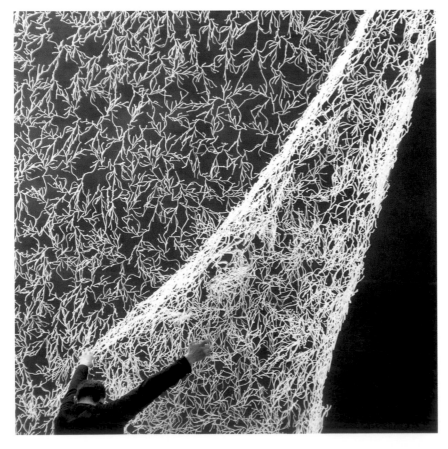

Pillows with prints in two different fabrics put together in pairs, Couples

Marcel Wanders
Exclusive B&B Italia linen and printed cotton fabric
W: 40 or 60cm
(15 ³/₄ or 23 ⁵/₈in)
L: 40 or 60cm
(15 ³/₄ or 23 ⁵/₈in)
B&B Italia SpA, Italy
www.bebitalia.it

Chair, Mademoiselle

Philippe Starck
Polycarbonate, fabric from the Missoni Home Collection
H: 73cm (28 ³/₄in)
H (seat): 47cm (18 ¹/₂in)
W: 50cm (19 ⁵/₈in)
D: 47cm (18 ¹/₂in)
Kartell SpA, Italy
www.kartell.it

Vase, The Big Vase

Kevin Walz
100% natural cork
H: 19cm (7 ³/₄in)
Diam: 14.5cm (5 ⁵/₈in)
KorQinc, USA
www.korqinc.com
www.walzworkinc.com

Floor/wall tile

Kevin Walz
100% natural cork
H: 30cm (11 ⁷/₈in)
W: 90cm (35 ¹/₂in)
KorQinc, USA
www.korqinc.com
www.walzworkinc.com

The 'ProntoKorQ' collection is 100 per cent environmentally friendly. Cork is the harvested bark of *Quercus sughero* – the Mediterranean oak. The material used here is recycled from the bottle-stopper industry and has been compressed to the greatest possible density. 'KorQinc' harnesses the natural properties of the cork – resilience and responsiveness – and combines these with new technologies to give the material structural capabilities.

Woven textile, Berq
Kendix Design Team
57% paper, 25% viscose,
17% polyester,
1% polyamide
W: 150cm (59in)
Kendix International
Textiles,
the Netherlands
www.kendix.nl

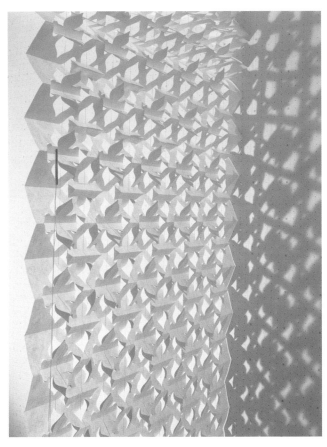

Curtain, Suncurtain
Froukje Kuiper
Paper with
fire-resistant coating
Various dimensions
Froukje Kuiper, UK
Froukje_kuiper@yahoo.co.uk

**Wall tile with digitally
manipulated
photograph, Lava**
Dominic Crinson
Printed ceramic wall tiles
H: 20cm (7 ⁷⁄₈in)
W: 20cm (7 ⁷⁄₈in)
Digitile Ltd: Dominic
Crinson, UK
www.crinson.com

**Fabric (curtain),
Dragon**
Ulf Moritz
100% polyester, plastic
embossed flowers
W: 160cm (63in)
Sahco, Germany
www.sahco-hesslein.com

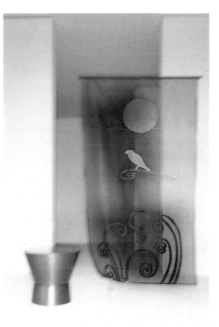

**Fabric (curtain panel),
Nightingale**
Ulf Moritz
57% silk, 43% acetate
W: 145cm (57in)
Sahco, Germany
www.sahco-hesslein.com

**Wallpaper,
Wall Invader**
RADI Designers with
Gilles and Vincent Turin
Kit contains posters, toy
arrow gun, arrows with
insect stamp and ink pad
H: 60cm (23 ⁵⁄₈in)
W: 40cm (15 ³⁄₄in)
RADI Designers, France
www.radidesigners.com

Fabric, London Toile
Timorous Beasties
Linen
H: 100cm (39in)
W: 135cm (53in)
Timorous Beasties, UK
www.timorous
beasties.com

**Printed furnishing
fabric, Glasgow Toile**
Paul Simmons
Linen
W: 136 cm (54in)
Timorous Beasties, UK
www.timorous
beasties.com

international acclaim and a nomination for Designer of the Year from the Design Museum in London. The toiles are a modern take on the 18th-century fabrics that were produced in the Jouy factory and traditionally depicted scenes of pastoral idyll set in magnificent vistas. The pattern on the modern-day versions may at first glance appear benign and bucolic, but closer examination reveals that something political is going on, something subversive. TB argue that the imagery of the eighteenth century was not actually that innocent. Concentrating as it did on scenes that were then contemporary, some wallpapers showed the Jouy factory itself, while others presented rural scenes of workers relaxing, dancing and womanizing.

Bringing the French countryside into inner-city Glasgow, the Beastie boys maintain that they have not changed much – 'a glass of wine became a can of super lager, a pipe a rollie, and an old man sitting on a stool in a rural scene became a tramp on a park bench'. Also borrowing from morality paintings of the time, graphic images take on symbolic meaning. A junkie

shoots up in a graveyard (the famous Glaswegian necropolis much favoured by drug abusers), the moral being that if you inject heroin then you are likely to end up in the graveyard – permanently; a young boy pisses against a tree while an old tramp takes a swig of lager – if you start misbehaving too early then you will end up homeless and drunk; Glasgow University towers above it all like an unobtainable fairytale castle, while Foster's Armadillo Building represents the changes happening along the Clyde. Similarly the 'London' toile depicts disaffected youths in hoodies, alienated office workers, pigeons, sellers of the *Big Issue* magazine, all going about their business in the shadows of East End tower blocks and London landmarks.

McAuley and Simmons have a love of traditional elements – academic drawings, use of complicated repeats and the hand-printed quality of inks – and call their work 'modern tradition'. 'We do love some of the traditional designs from the past, but it's great fun to give them a new angle, to make them speak to us in the present.'

There has been a long tradition of politicizing drawing rooms by the use of artfully designed wallpapers. As far back as the eighteenth century there were patterns depicting the Bastille being razed to the ground by French revolutionaries, a Britannia made to suffer at the hands of American patriots, Napoleon's campaigns and Hellenic Greeks battling against marauding Ottoman barbarians. Even in the White House, Jackie Kennedy hung revolutionary scenes that were covered over by the Clintons, only to be revealed once more by the Bushes. **Timorous Beasties** are returning to the tradition with their 'Glasgow' and 'London' toiles.

Alistair McAuley and Paul Simmons founded their own studio in 1990 and today are one of the few companies that both design and produce their own fabrics under one roof. Described as 'William Morris on Acid', their innovative patterns, depicting contemporary images that are silk-screen printed on to traditional textiles and wallpapers, have won them

Textile, No. 11
Yoshiki Hishinuma
70% cotton,
30% polyester
L: 90cm (35in)
W: 60cm (23 ⁵⁄₈in)
Yoshiki Hishinuma Co.
Ltd, Japan
www.yoshiki
hishinuma.com

Fabric, Cincinatti
Design-Team nya
nordiska
70% polyester,
30% lurex
W: 160cm (63in)
nya nordiska textiles
GmbH, Germany
www.nya.com

Printed fabric, Saskia
Manuel Canovas
100% cotton
W: 143cm (56in)
Manuel Canovas, France
www.manuelcanovas.com

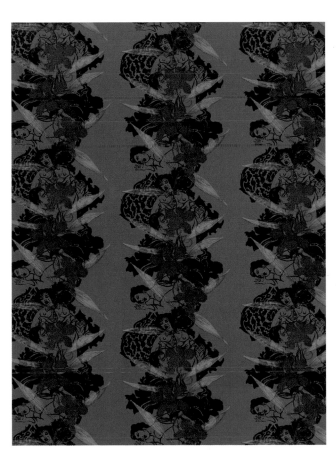

**Erotic wallpaper,
Oriental Orchid**
Paul Simmons
Ink, paper
W: 52cm (20 ½in)
Timorous Beasties, UK
www.timorous
beasties.com

Curtain fabric, Hagi
Anne Fabricius Møller
Trevira CS (polyester)
W: 140cm (55 ⅛in)
Kvadrat A/S, Denmark
www.kvadrat.dk

Fabric, Posey
William Wegman
Polyester, rayon
W: 137cm (54in)
Crypton, USA
www.cryptonfabric.com

Why can your pet not be design conscious too? Discovering a gap in the market, **Randy and Craig Rubin** founded their company in 1993, working with chemists and textile engineers to produce a textile for the healthcare industry that was stain and bacteria resistant yet soft and breathable – a departure from the hot and sticky vinyls and chemically treated fabrics much beloved of the hospital ward. They have now developed their line to include material for pets. Their new range includes a canine-pattern line created in collaboration with the photographer William Wegman, famous for his shots of posturing Weimaraners.

Wallpaper, Birds
Ed Annink,
Ontwerpwerk
Full-colour printed paper
Various dimensions
Designwall,
the Netherlands
www.designwall.nl

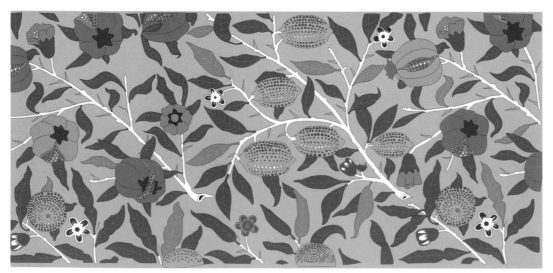

Wallpaper, William
Ed Annink,
Ontwerpwerk
Full-colour printed paper
Various dimensions
Designwall,
the Netherlands
www.designwall.nl

Ed Annink's wallpapers are based on works by William Morris and others of the Arts and Crafts school. Drawings in the public domain were scanned, digitized and then prepared for customized printing by order. This document can be altered to suit specific wall measurements, the pattern reduced or enlarged to fit around openings, and colour-ways changed, making every wall unique.

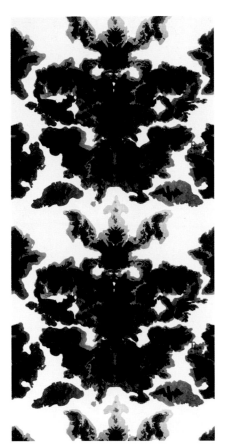

Hand-printed wallpaper, Euro Dam
Paul Simmons,
Timorous Beasties
Paper, ink
W: 52cm (20 ½in)
W (repeat):
51.5cm (20 ¼in)
Limited batch
production, Timorous
Beasties, UK
www.timorous
beasties.com

Wallpaper, Wallpaper made by Rats
Front Design
Paper
W: 50cm (19 ⅝in)
L: 1000cm (394in)
Front Design, Sweden
www.frontdesign.se

Four young women – Sofia Lagerkvist, Katja Pettersson, Anna Lindgren and Charlotte von der Lancken – forming the Swedish design group **Front** came up with an intriguing exhibition for the Salon Satellite show at the Milan Furniture Fair 2004. Part of the design of each of a series of objects was determined by an external factor or event that affected the design process at random. A hole created by a controlled explosion was turned into a cast for a soft chair; plastic heated and draped like a textile became a curtain-like screen; a UV-sensitive wallpaper changed pattern with the sunlight; and a vase was made with a built-in fall – its shape is repeated and stuck together throughout the path of its descent from shelf to floor.

A large part of the show, however, was given over to objects that had been influenced by the activities of animals. 'We asked animals to help us out. "Sure we'll help you out," they answered. "Make something nice," we told them. And so they did.' Ceramic vases were cast from dog tracks in the deep snow, and a lampshade was produced based on a fly's path around a light bulb, which was recorded by a motion-capture camera. The rat wallpaper, illustrated here, was created by allowing rodents to gnaw on rolls of pre-manufactured wallpaper, the holes created making a repetitive pattern that reveals the old wall covering to which the new wallpaper is glued.

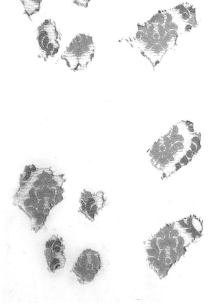

By taking silhouettes of various European countries, mutating them into traditional damask patterns and adding screens to resemble the mountain ranges on relief maps, **Timorous Beasties** have succeeded – fortuitously or not – in producing a designer version of the psychoanalytical Rorschach Ink Blot test. In this wallpaper, not only beauty but also comprehension is in the eye of the beholder.

Building cladding system (internal and external), Walled Paper
Eric Barrett
Cast concrete
Various dimensions
Concrete Blond, UK
www.concrete-blond.com

Textile, Repeat Dot Print
Hella Jongerius
Cotton, rayon, polyester
W: 140cm (55in)
Maharam, USA
www.maharam.com

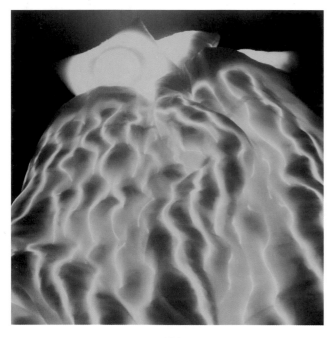

Reactive bedding/ alarm clock, Light Sleeper
Rachel Wingfield
Embroidered electro-luminescent wire and silk
Various dimensions
loop, UK
www.loop.ph

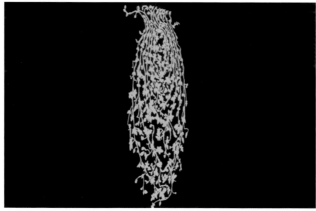

Reactive window blind/lamp, Digital Dawn
Rachel Wingfield
Printed electro-luminescent silk
H: 125cm (49in)
W: 65cm (25 ⁵/₁in)
Elumin8 Systems, UK
www.elumin8.com

Large and Small Dot Fabric
Charles and Ray Eames
Cotton, polyester, Teflon
W: 142.2cm (56in)
Maharam, USA
www.maharam.com

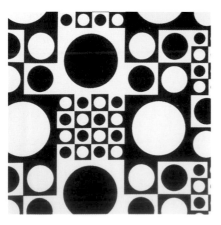

Textile, Geometri
Verner Panton
Cotton, polyester, Teflon
W: 139.7cm (55in)
Maharam, USA
www.maharam.com

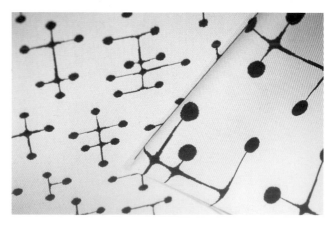

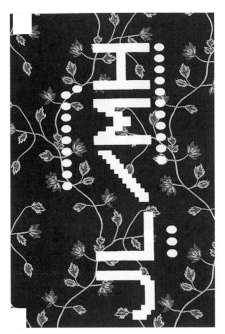

Tea towel, On the Shelf series, Vases
Jane Atfield and
Robert Shepherd
Cotton
H: 48cm (18 ⁷⁄₈in)
L: 76cm (29 ⁷⁄₈in)
Unity Peg, UK
www.unitypeg.co.uk

Textile, Repeat Classic Print
Hella Jongerius
Cotton, rayon, polyester
W: 140cm (55in)
Maharam, USA
www.maharam.com

Tea towel, On the Shelf series, Books
Jane Atfield and
Robert Shepherd
Cotton
H: 48cm (18 ⁷⁄₈in)
L: 76cm (29 ⁷⁄₈in)
Unity Peg, UK
www.unitypeg.co.uk

Tea towel, On the Shelf series, Crockery
Jane Atfield and
Robert Shepherd
Cotton
H: 48cm (18 ⁷⁄₈in)
L: 76cm (29 ⁷⁄₈in)
Unity Peg, UK
www.unitypeg.co.uk

Fabric, Digiweave
Karim Rashid
Wool, printed silk
Various dimensions
Edra SpA, Italy
www.edra.com

Lighting

**Range of lights,
Liquid_Light**
Hopf & Wortmann,
Büro für form
PE, glass
Bulbs, max. 100W/E27
Various dimensions
Next Design GmbH,
Germany
www.next.de

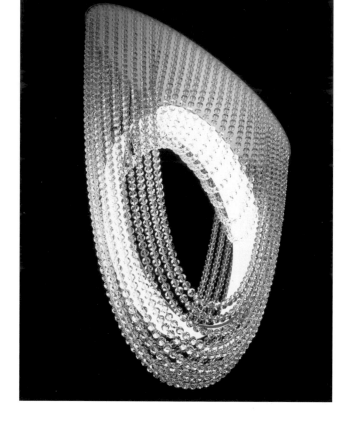

Chandelier, Nest
Yves Béhar with Pichaya
Puttorngul
Swarovski crystal
Electroluminescent light
H: 125cm (49in)
W: 100cm (39in)
Swarovski, Austria
www.swarovski.com

Floor lamp, Dandelion
Deepdesign
Aluminium, PMMA,
Hi-power LEDs
H: 200cm (79in)
Diam: 55cm (21 ⁵⁄₈in)
TecnoDelta, Italy
www.tecnodeltaitaly.com

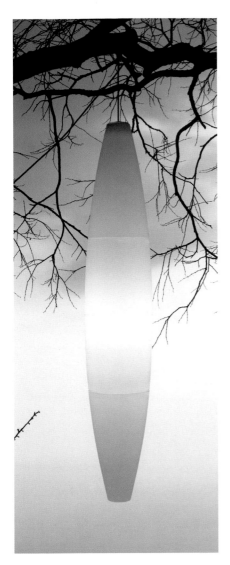

Ceiling lamp, Caboche
Patricia Urquiola and
Eliana Gerotto
Polymethylmethacrylate
balls
1 x 200W halogen bulb
Diam: 50cm (19 ⁵⁄₈in)
Foscarini, Italy
www.foscarini.com

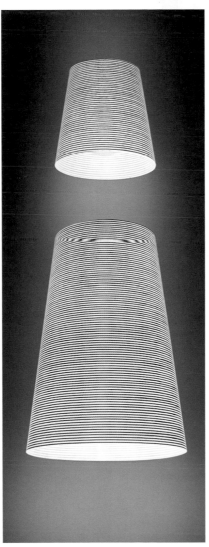

**Suspension lamp,
Havana Outdoor**
Jozeph Forakis
Polyethylene
1 x 60W incandescent
bulb; 1 x 23W
fluorescent bulb
H: 400cm (158in)
Diam: 23cm (9in)
Foscarini, Italy
www.foscarini.com

Wall lamps, Kite
Marc Sadler
Glass fabric, carbon–
thread application
1 x 40W incandescent
bulb; 1 x 11W
fluorescent bulb
Top,
H: 21cm (8 ¹⁄₄in)
W: 18cm (7 ¹⁄₈in)
D: 12cm (4 ³⁄₄in)
Below,
H: 42cm (16 ¹⁄₂in)
W: 27cm (10 ⁵⁄₈in)
D: 16cm (6 ¹⁄₄in)
Foscarini, Italy
www.foscarini.com

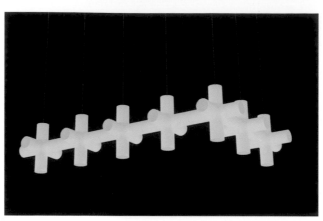

Table or pendant lamp, Crosslight
Jan Melis and
Ben Oostrum
Polyethylene
Each unit,
H: 38cm (15in)
W: 38cm (15in)
L: 38cm (15in)
MNO Design, the
Netherlands
www.mnodesign.nl

Mobile light, Aduki
Mathmos Design Studio
Polished die-cast zinc,
soft-touch thermoplastic,
silicone
LED
H: 9cm (3 ¹/₂in)
L: 13cm (5 ¹/₈in)
Mathmos, UK
www.mathmos.co.uk

Lamp, Shandy
Archirivolto
Metal, plastic
1 x 100W E27 or
1 x 15W E27 PL–EL/T
H: 33cm (13in)
Diam: 52cm (20 ¹/₂in)
Alt Lucialternative, Italy
www.altlucialternative.com

Lamp, Big Dish
Ingo Maurer and team
Fibreglass, metal, plastic
150W CDM-150 SA/R
H: 500cm (197in)
Diam: 230cm (91in)
Ingo Maurer GmbH,
Germany
www.ingo-maurer.com

Lighting, Cloud Series
Frank Gehry
Refined polyester
1 x 100–150W
incandescent lamp
Diam: 60cm (23 ⁵/₈in)
Belux, Switzerland
www.belux.com

**Chandelier,
Millennium Chandelier**
Stuart Haygarth
1000 exploded plastic
party poppers (from
01.01.2000), MDF
platform, fishing line,
split shot
1 x 60W yellow-toned
incandescent bulb
Diam: 90cm (35in)
Stuart Haygarth, UK
stu@haygarth.
abelgratis.co.uk

The 'Millennium
Chandelier' is
constructed from 1000
exploded Party Poppers
collected on 1 January
2000. Each popper is
suspended from a line
attached to a platform
above and the sculptural
shape sways and
undulates with each
breeze. This one-off
piece can be recreated
in self produced small
quantities.

Lighting, Jingzi
Herzog and de Meuron
Silicone
1 x 150W incandescent
lamp
H (head): 45cm (17 ³/₄in)
Diam: 30cm (12in)
Belux, Switzerland
www.belux.com

Lighting, Lantern
Ronan and Erwan
Bouroullec
Plastic
1 x 150W incandescent
lamp
H: 38cm (15in)
Diam: 38cm (15in)
Belux, Switzerland
www.belux.com

**Pendant globe light,
Copper Shade**
Tom Dixon
Plastic polycarbonate
with metalized copper
finish
Incandescent lamp
Diam: 45cm (17 ³/₄in)
Tom Dixon, UK
www.tomdixon.net

Tom Dixon

**Which of your designs to date would you like
to be remembered by?**
I'm still working on that one.

How do you think others view your work?
You really need to ask them, but I am always struck
by the variety of views.

**Which designer has influenced you the most
and why?**
Honestly? My inspiration has often come more from
sculpture and engineering, from people like Noguchi
and Brunel.

**If you were not a designer, what would you like
to be and why?**
Probably involved in the frontier of cyberspace, or
doing charity work, sculpture or civil engineering.

**What role do you think the designer has in
society today?**
To improve it.

Do you buy a lot of design pieces?
Everything you buy will have an element of design in it,
from your car to your airline ticket to your carton of milk.

**Is there a design in your home that you couldn't
live without?**
I think I could quite happily live without any of it.

**Where do you think design is heading? Is there
someone we should be watching out for?**
There are more and more fantastic, skilled and
innovative designers emerging and being trained in
the West, a lot of them chasing the same types of
design work. Bigger, more diverse industries need
their skills more and we will see a shift eastwards.

**Is the cult of the personality taking over the
design world?**
Not nearly as much as in music, television, royalty,
politics and sport. We have a long way to go before
Marc Newson is as well known as Kylie.

Light, Gé
Ferruccio Laviani
Polycarbonate
H: 30cm (11 ³/₄in)
Diam: 37cm (14 ⁵/₈in)
Kartell SpA, Italy
www.kartell.it

**Suspension lamp,
Supergiù**
Diego Rossi and
Raffaele Tedesco
Aluminium
150W incandescent
or halogen bulb,
42W fluorescent bulb,
70W metal halide bulb
H: 32.5cm (13in)
Diam: 37.5cm (15in)
Luceplan SpA, Italy
www.luceplan.com

Lighting, Garland
Tord Boontje
Brass
1 x max. 60W/E27 bulb
A3-size sheet
Habitat, UK
www.habitat.net

Chandelier, Bang
Tom Dixon
Swarovski crystals,
metal
Incandescent 10W
pilot bulbs
H: 115cm (45in)
W: 115cm (45in)
D: 70cm (27 ½in)
Swarovski, Austria
www.swarovski
sparkles.com

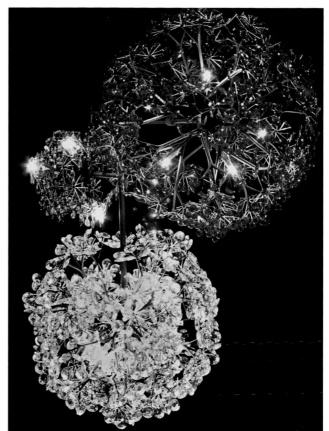

Lamps, Agave
Diego Rossi and
Raffaele Tedesco
Injection-moulded,
transparent
methacrylate
21, 26, 32 or 42W
fluorescent bulb
Diam: 17, 26 or 70cm
(6 ⅝, 10 ¼ or 27 ½in)
Luceplan SpA, Italy
www.luceplan.com

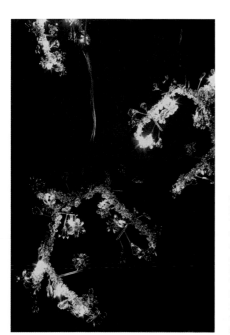

**Chandelier, Mini
Blossom**
Tord Boontje
Crystal
6 halogen bulbs (on two
separate circuits)
H: 53cm (20 ⅞in)
W: 15cm (5 ⅞in)
L: 54cm (21 ¼in)
Swarovski, Austria
www.swarovski
sparkles.com

Lamp, Dandelion
Richard Hutten
Laser-cut powder-
coated steel
1 x max. 100W/E27 bulb
H: 55cm (21⁵/₈in)
W: 80cm (31in)
Moooi, the Netherlands
www.moooi.com

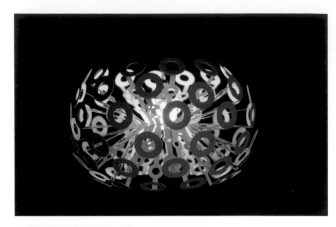

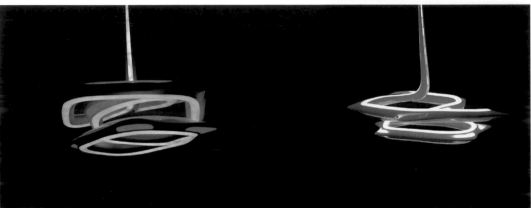

Chandelier, Vortexx
Zaha Hadid and
Patrick Schumacher
Moulded fibreglass,
thermo-shaped acrylic,
car paint
High-pressure LEDs
H: 160cm (63in)
Diam: 170cm (67in)
Sawaya & Moroni, Italy
www.sawayamoroni.com

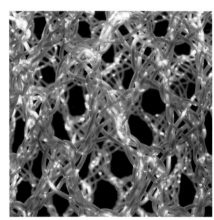

**Chandelier, Bobbin
lace lamp**
Niels van Eijk
Optic glass fibre
1 x 100W halogen bulb
L: 200 or 300cm
(78⁷/₈ or 118¹/₄in)
Diam: 40 or 80cm
(15³/₄ or 31¹/₂in)
Quasar, the Netherlands
www.quasar.nl

**Pendant lamp,
Zeppelin**
Marcel Wanders
Cocoon, powder-
coated steel, injection-
moulded PMMA
1 x 60W/E27 bulb (Size 1)
1 x 150W bulb (Size 2)
Diam: 55 or 110cm
(21 ⅝ or 43in)
Flos SpA, Italy
www.flos.com

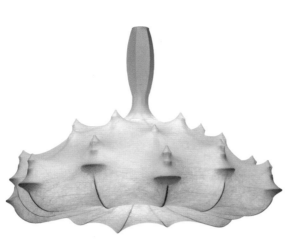

**Suspension lamp,
Fringe**
Edward Van Vliet
PVC/cotton laminate
on metal structure.
1 x max. 100W/E27 bulb
(per lamp)
H: 72cm (28 ³/₈in)
Diam: 106cm (42in)
Moooi, the Netherlands
www.moooi.nl

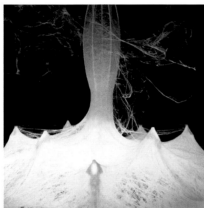

**Pendant lamp,
Taraxacum**
Achille and Pier Giacomo
Castiglioni
Cocoon
1 x 100W bulb
Diam: 68 or 87cm
(26 ³/₄ or 34in)
Flos SpA, Italy
www.flos.com

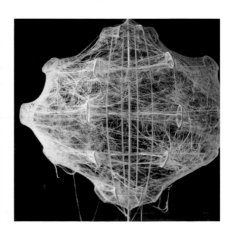

Suspension lamp, Magica
Andrea Bastianello
Iron, steel
3 x 100W 230V/E27 bulbs
H: 36cm (14 ^{1}/$_8$in)
Diam: 72cm (28 ^{3}/$_8$in)
Disegnoluce, Italy
www.disegnoluce.com

Lamp, C U–C ME
Kenneth Cobonpue
Hand-woven wire,
Salago fibre, fibreglass
Diam: 40cm (15 ^{3}/$_4$in)
Interior Crafts of
the Islands, Inc,
the Philippines
www.kenneth
cobonpue.com

Lampshade, Norm 69
Simon Karvov
Lampshade foil
Diam: 42, 51 or 60cm
(16 ^{1}/$_2$, 20 ^{1}/$_8$ or 23 ^{5}/$_8$in)
Normann Copenhagen,
Denmark
www.normann-
copenhagen.com

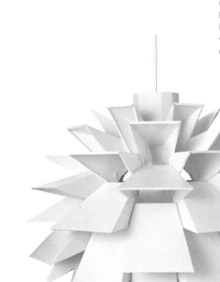

Pendant lamp, Blushing Zettel'z
Ingo Maurer
Stainless steel, heat-
resistant satin-frosted
glass, Japanese paper
Top bulb: 1 x halogen
Halolux Ceram clear,
250W; Bottom bulb: 1 x
halogen PAR 30, 75W, 30°
H (approx.): 120cm (47in)
Diam (approx.):
120cm (47in)
Ingo Maurer GmbH,
Germany
www.ingo-maurer.com

**Moulded resin-
drained yarn,
Random Light**
Monkey Boys
Epoxy and fibreglass
1 x max. 100W/E27 bulb
Diam: 50, 85 or 105cm
(19 ⁵/₈, 33 or 41in)
Moooi, the Netherlands
www.moooi.nl

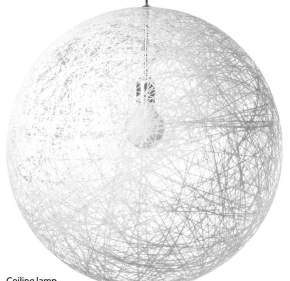

**Chandelier, Tide
Chandelier**
Stuart Haygarth
Clear and translucent
plastic collected from
one specific beach on
the Kent coast, fishing
line, split shot,
MDF platform
1 x 100W
incandescent bulb
Diam: 150cm (59in)
Stuart Haygarth, UK
stu@haygarth.
abelgratis.co.uk

**Ceiling lamp,
No Globe series**
Laura Agnoletto and
Marzio Rusconi Clerici
Acrylic, chromed metal
1 x 100W/E27 (E26 US)
bulb
Diam: 35, 50 or 60cm
(13 ³/₄, 19 ⁵/₈ or 23 ⁵/₈in)
Kundalini srl, Italy
www.kundalini.it

Chandelier, Mini Ball
Tom Dixon
Crystal
20 x LED
H: 106cm (42in)
Diam: 50cm (19 ⁵/₈in)
Swarovski, Austria
www.swarovski
sparkles.com

Moving jellyfish light, Aurelia
John Wischhusen
Non-woven polyester
fabric, rigid PVC,
blow-formed acrylic
1 x CFL bulb, powered
by 12V AC synchronous
motor via gears to peg
and slot mechanism
H: 91cm (36in)
Diam (dome): 58cm
(22 7/8in)
Original Solarplexus,
Germany
www.original-
solarplexus.com

Hanging light, Whoosh
Dumoffice
Hand-blown
frosted glass
2 x 40W bulbs
H: 20cm (7 7/8in)
W: 38cm (15in)
D: 7.5cm (3in)
Dumoffice, the
Netherlands
www.dumoffice.com

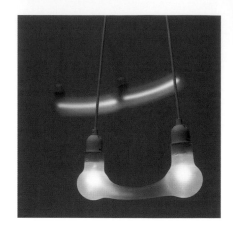

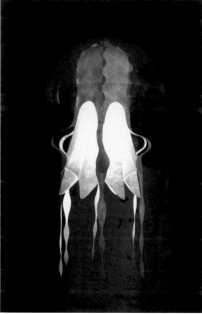

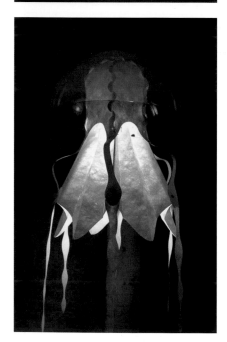

Pendant light, Nova Lamp
Barber Osgerby
Murano glass, crystal
1 x 250V, max. 100W bulb
H: 16cm (6 1/4in)
Diam: 50cm (19 5/8in)
Swarovski, Austria
www.swarovski
sparkles.com

Suspension light, Loom
Jacob de Baan
Anodized, polished
and/or painted
aluminium
50W, 200V hi spot
Small,
H: 10.5cm (4 1/8in)
Diam: 10cm (4in);
Large,
H: 30cm (11 7/8in)
Diam: 32.5cm (12 3/4in)
Jacob de Baan,
the Netherlands
www.jacobdebaan.com

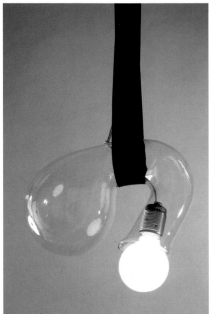

**Collection of lamps,
Liquid Lights – PX01,
PX02, PX04
left:**
Brunno Jahara (PX01 –
G-9 Hal, max. 3 x 60W)
right:
Masahiro Fukuyama
(PX02 – E27 G-95 Hal,
max. 100W)
above:
Rita João and
Pedro Ferreira (PX04 –
E27 G-95 Hal, max. 100W)
Pyrex
Various dimensions
Metalarte, Spain
www.metalarte.com

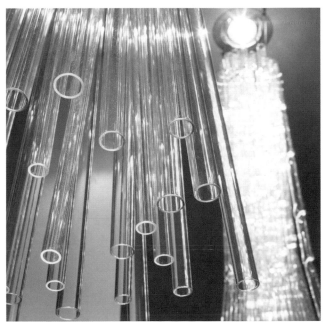

Chandelier, Munich
Isabel Hamm
Glass, stainless steel
Halogen reflectors,
halogen light
L (max.): 150cm (59in)
Diam (max.): 40cm (15 ³/₄in)
Isabel Hamm Gestaltung,
Germany
www.isabel-hamm.de

Suspension lamp, Electra
Christoph Steinemann
Solid aluminium casing
1 x 50W halogen bulb
L: 28 or 74cm
(11 or 29 ¹/₈in)
Belux, Switzerland
www.belux.com

Ceiling light, Light Big Light
Olivier Sidet
Polystyrene
Fluocompact bulb
H: 80cm (31 ¹/₂in)
Diam: 50cm (19 ³/₄in)
Tools Galerie, France
www.toolsgalerie.com

Chandelier, Darkside Collection
Philippe Starck
Black crystal
24 bulbs
H: 110cm (43in)
W: 105cm (41in)
Baccarat, France
www.baccarat.fr

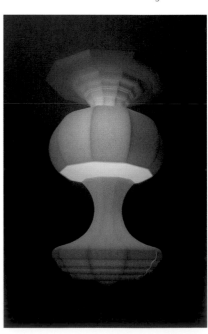

Pendant ceiling light, Flexlamp
Sam Hecht
Polyurethane
H: 11cm (4 ³/₈in)
Diam: 32.5cm (12 ³/₄in)
Droog Design,
the Netherlands
www.droogdesign.nl

'Flexlamp – 12 Light Years' is a lampshade made from a single polyurethane rubber moulding that slips over an ecologically sound bulb. The light will last for up to twelve years before needing to be changed.

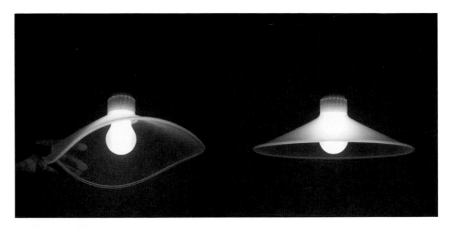

Ingo Maurer

Which of your designs to date would you like to be remembered by?
'Don Quixote'. Why? The way it was born, by chance and needs. It is a subversive design without pretension. 'Don Quixote' is mainly a success with high-end, superhuman beings. It has got guts. With TouchTronic, which is our development, it is very sensitive. It can be altered by the client and has almost all you want from a lamp.

How do you think others view your work?
If people told the truth I would rank very high in the area of creation and poetry. Fortunately, there are people who are sincere and I am grateful for that. I need critical feedback, provocation and risk. I am often insecure.

Which designer has influenced you the most and why?
My heroes are artists like Alexander Calder and Constantin Brancusi and designers like the Castiglioni brothers and Vico Magistretti. They also convinced me as human beings. I inhale their energy. Ray and Charles Eames, too. Calder's work is light, *naïve raffinée* and strong. It is obvious he influenced me. The Castiglioni brothers, Vico Magistretti and Enzo Mari – it sounds almost like a cliché – dared to take a big step ahead in their time. Most of all they had something that is getting rarer and rarer in the design world today: culture.

If you were not a designer, what would you like to be and why?
When I was young, for many years I wanted to be a tightrope dancer in a circus or above the streets. An architect – but that is a tedious business; it takes too long to see the results. Maybe a stage designer.

What role do you think the designer has in society today?
The role of the designer in today's world is even more important than it was twenty years ago. Why? With

the inflation of design and just as many designers, a domination of superficiality has taken place. An elegantly drawn line does not yet make a good design. In the process of creation, energy and intuitive intelligence are necessary, not thoughts about profit, marketing and publication. It is important that you can feel the persons involved in a design. The imperfect perfection! A product needs to leave room for the consumer's imagination to finish the work of designers and producers, not the cult of personality of a designer in all of its parts. The product should be honest and readable.

Do you buy a lot of design pieces?
I am not a good consumer of design. But I do have a few pieces. I am a big fan of anonymous objects.

Is there a design in your home that you couldn't live without?
I would miss some things. 'Taccia' by Castiglioni gives light but also energy. Ron Arad's spiral bookcase reminds me of intense moments we shared. But truly nothing is more stimulating than an empty room, with a mattress on the floor shared with the one you love.

Hanging Lamp, Lüster
Ingo Maurer
Imprinted moulded glass containing 287 white LEDs
H: 100cm (39in)
W: 65cm (25 ⁵/₈in)
Limited batch production, Ingo Maurer GmbH, Germany
www.ingo-maurer.com

Pendant lamp, Stardust
Ingo Maurer
LED, glass
Diam (approx.):
70cm (27 ¹/₂in)
Ingo Maurer GmbH, Germany
www.ingo-maurer.com

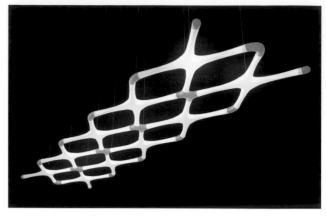

Lighting, K-Series
Shiro Kuramata
Acrylic
1 x 60W
incandescent lamp
H: 37, 58.5 or 82cm
(12 $\frac{1}{4}$, 23 $\frac{1}{4}$ or 32in)
Diam: 45, 70 or 85cm
(17 $\frac{3}{4}$, 27 $\frac{1}{2}$ or 33in)
Yamagiwa Corporation,
Japan
www.yamagiwa.co.jp

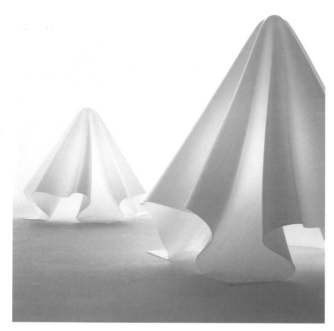

Since 1923 **Yamagiwa** have led the field as one of
Japan's major manufacturers of high-profile lifestyle
products from furniture to electronics and home
appliances, but it is probably in the field of lighting
that they are best known internationally, having
the worldwide distribution rights for the Frank
Lloyd Wright Collection. In collaboration with leading
architects and designers, they have been producing
their own lamps since the 1960s, and launched their
2005 range to critical acclaim during Euroluce. Ross
Lovegrove, Naoto Fukasawa, Tokujin Yoshioka and
Shiro Kuramata all created lamps that mixed high-end
technology with a timeless beauty. Fukasawa's 'Wan'
sits on the floor or a shelf giving off a subtle lighting
effect. The bowl can be positioned at any angle
by shifting its weight, which consists of sand-like
iron particles that are contained within its shell.
Lovegrove's 'Geon' desk light and modular 'System X'
ceiling light explore his fascination with organic
shapes and architectonic design respectively. The
former is an 'objet d'art' when not in use, but once a
button is pressed the arm swings up and the lamp
switches on automatically. The 'System X' has taken
many years to develop. A simple X module can be
configured to produce geometric systems from one
to an infinite number of units.

Lighting, SystemX
Ross Lovegrove
Plastic, aluminium
2 x T4 21W
fluorescent lamps
H: 6.8cm (2 $\frac{3}{4}$in)
W: 51.4cm (20 $\frac{1}{4}$in)
D: 83.4cm (33in)
Yamagiwa Corporation,
Japan
www.yamagiwa.co.jp

Lighting, Wan
Naoto Fukasawa
Polycarbonate,
aluminium
1 x 60W silver bowl lamp
H: 20.5cm (8 $\frac{1}{4}$in)
Diam: 33cm (13in)
Yamagiwa Corporation,
Japan
www.yamagiwa.co.jp

Lighting, ToFU
Tokujin Yoshioka
Methacrylate (PMMA),
aluminium
1 x 10W 12V-G4
halogen (35mm/MR11)
Various dimensions
Yamagiwa Corporation,
Japan
www.yamagiwa.co.jp

Pendant lamp, Airco
Willem van der Sluis and
Hugo Timmermans
Injection-moulded
PMMA
H: 4cm (1 ¹⁄₈in)
Diam: 100cm (39 ³⁄₈in)
Luceplan SpA, Italy
www.luceplan.com

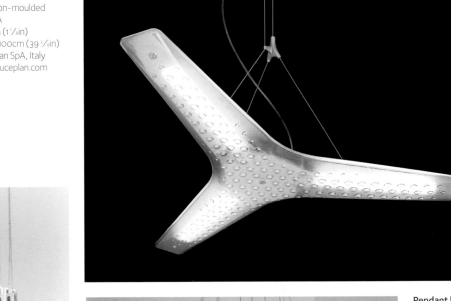

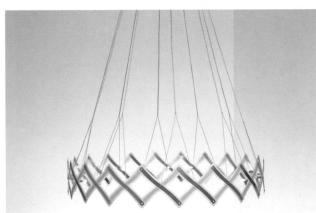

Pendant light, Zoom
Floyd Paxton
Flexible spring band
steel, translucent
fabric sheeting
20 x 10W low-voltage
tungsten halogen lamps
Diam: 20–130cm
(7 ⁷⁄₈–51 ¹⁄₄in)
Serien Raumleuchten
GmbH, Germany
www.serien.com

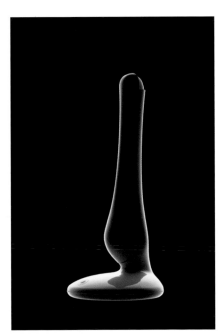

Lighting, Geon
Ross Lovegrove
Polycarbonate,
aluminium
1 x 50W halogen
12V-GY6.35
H: 47cm (18 ¹⁄₂in)
W: 20cm (7 ⁷⁄₈in)
D: 43cm (16 ⁷⁄₈in)
Yamagiwa Corporation,
Japan
www.yamagiwa.co.jp

Tom Dixon has gone through many incarnations since he first appeared on the design scene in the early 1980s: from rocker, biker and salvage artist, to internationally renowned designer and creative director of Habitat, probably the best-known furniture and accessories retailer in the UK. Most recently he has taken up the challenge of reinventing Artek (see page 50). He has gone from maverick to pillar of the community in less than twenty years. One of New Labour's gang of favoured British artists, he was even awarded an OBE in 2000 for services to British design. Yet he still remains something of a wild card, producing his own independent line of unconventional furniture and interiors.

It is Tom Dixon's eye for detail and innovation, technological know-how and the beauty of simplicity that make his own work so successful. His work today illustrates an increasing interest in what he refers to as 'reductionism'. Although excited by the eclectic nature of design today – the unusual shapes created by the computer and stereolithography machine; the necessary adoption of new materials to liberate the physical from the virtual; the 'revenge of ornamentation', as he likes to call it, which has produced a proliferation of patterns and surfaces; and the state-funded research into the conceptual object, which gives more weight to the idea than the product – he feels that the result of all these influences is a kind of giddy drunkenness. His latest collection is concerned with paring down an object to the essential, 'the removal of all artifice and extras, to find the substantial and explore the nitty gritty'. The felt shade explores the moulding possibilities of polyester felt and the copper light does nothing more than hold a light bulb and direct its glow.

Twisted lampshade, Twist Shade
Tom Dixon
Micro-pleated cotton
Incandescent bulb
H: 80cm (31in)
W: 40cm (15 ³/₄in)
Tom Dixon, UK
www.tomdixon.net

Lamps, Flow series
Tsutomu Kurokawa
Polycarbonate
Table lamp,
H: 43cm (17in)
W: 22.5cm (8 ⁷/₈in)
Daiko Electric Co. Ltd,
Japan
www.lighting-daiko.co.jp

Double layers of shades made from half mirrors shine refracted light on the wall and ceiling. The result is a transparent space, a light experience rather than a simple lamp.

Ceiling fan/lamp, Propeller
Yaacov Kaufman
Inox, white fabric
1 x 150W/E27
halogen lamp
H: 53cm (20 ⁷/₈in)
W: 92cm (36in)
D: 37cm (14 ⁵/₈in)
Serien Raumleuchten GmbH, Germany
www.serien.com

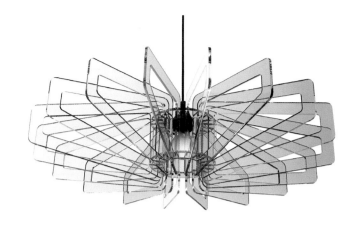

Pendant lamp, Light Frame
Stephen Burks
Acrylic
H: 17.4 or 30cm
(6 ⁷/₈ or 11 ⁷/₈in)
Diam: 72 or 100cm
(28 ³/₈ or 39 ³/₈in)
David design, Sweden
www.david.se

Ceiling lamp, Lampo
Michele De Lucchi
Brass
Max. 140W/E27
H (min.): 130cm (51in)
H (max.): 180cm (71in)
Produzione Privata, Italy
www.produzioneprivata.it

Stephen Burks

Which of your designs to date would you like to be remembered by?
Although I've had some mild success in my career and am very proud of the work I've done with many clients, I'm still working on my 'remember me by' piece.

How do you think others view your work?
I'd imagine it's considered formally diverse, eclectic and unconventional without a particular signature style. I hope the ideas speak louder than the form.

Which designer has influenced you the most and why?
I can't say that a particular designer has been very instrumental to my work, but more particular projects or concepts. I have great admiration for the Farnsworth house, for example, and the Bauhaus as an ideal, along with Duchamp's notion of the readymade in art.

If you were not a designer, what would you like to be and why?
I'd always be making things, if not designing them. Lately, I tend to be more interested in the physical process of making than designing.

What role do you think the designer has in society today?
We live in a world of unimaginable choice and options for every object that exists in every category, yet this small world of design that we all inhabit is still only recognized by an even smaller percentage of the population. Essentially, we are in the business of somehow expressing our age through even more formal choices for a very limited audience. I think the larger world of problem-solving in design that goes uncelebrated is much more fascinating and serves a greater number of people. But still we are all striving to make progress and hopefully communicate more than just beauty to how people interact with the physical world.

Do you buy a lot of design pieces?
Yes, a few, because I'm a bit of a collector at heart and there are a lot of pieces I wish I could own.

Is there a design in your home that you couldn't live without?
No. The things I can't live without are more like tools than anything else: my library, my sketchbook, a good pen, my music, my computer, etc.

What do you consider to be the best piece of design since the millennium?
I struggle to consider anything best, but there's been an explosion of amazing buildings since the end of the millennium and some beautiful objects. The first time I saw the Herzog & de Meuron Prada building in Tokyo I was breathless.

Where do you think design is heading? Is there someone we should be watching out for?
Design is now an integrated marketing tool for most of the world's multinational corporations. Are the products better? Sometimes. I think it's become clear that the more choice we are offered, the more choice we want, and neither mankind nor our manufacturing technology can sustain the pace we're setting for new products. I think this is dangerous, because there seems to be a lot less thinking about what we're making and why. Design has practically reached the level of entertainment for the consumer, and yet some of the best products are still not readily available internationally. I wonder about who the market will be for tomorrow's products, not who the designers will be.

Is the cult of the personality taking over the design world?
As we become a more entertainment-driven society and as the tools for personal expression become more and more accessible, personalities have been and will continue to be commodities. Unfortunately, in the personality-driven marketplace the consumption of design is no different from the consumption of music or film or any other entertainment industry.

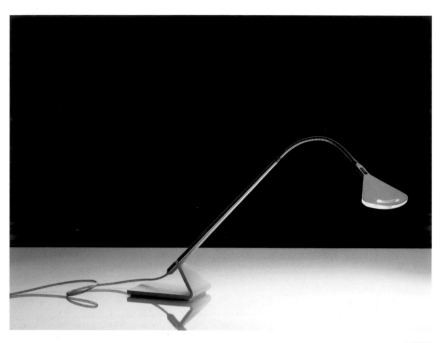

Spotlight, Solar II
Massimo Iosa Ghini
Die-cast aluminium
Superspot/spot/flood/
wide flood halogen lamps
(4 versions, 3 sizes)
Diam: 8.1–15.4cm
(3 $^1/_8$–5 $^7/_8$in)
Zumtobel Staff Lighting,
Austria
www.zumtobelstaff.com

Table lamp, Mix
Alberto Meda and
Paolo Rizzatto
Aluminium,
methacrylate
LED Chip On Board 5W
L: 72.5cm (28 $^3/_4$in)
Luceplan SpA, Italy
www.luceplan.com

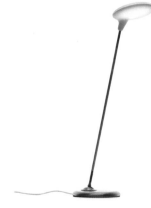

Desk lamp, Cloud
Jozeph Forakis
Aluminium,
polycarbonate
1 x 35W halogen bulb
H: 38–68cm
(15–26 $^3/_4$in)
Foscarini, Italy
www.foscarini.com

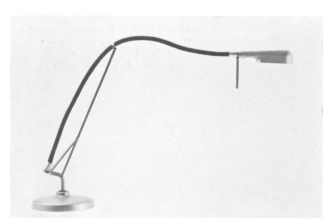

Task light, Arketto
Yaacov Kaufman
Flexible solid spring arm
covered with fabric
1 x 40W/G9 halogen bulb
L (max.): 95cm (37in)
Luxo Italiana SpA, Italy
www.luxit.it

It has been said of **Richard Sapper**, I think rather uncharitably, that he is a designer without a personal style. That is not the case. Like the man himself, his products, whether he is designing a pen for Lamy (see page 329) or, in this case, the 'Halley' lamp for Lucesco, all share a certain gravitas. They are solid, thoughtful, quiet and incredibly intelligent. Richard Sapper is old school. He does not need to be prolific, flamboyant or opinionated. His relatively small output of high-tech products (radios and televisions for Brionvega, cars for Mercedes-Benz, Fiat and Pirelli, tableware for Alessi, furniture for Castelli and Knoll and most famously the 'Tizio' lamp for Artemide) have had a profound effect on product design and he has influenced many, whether those he has taught or those he has inspired by example. Although outwardly severe, both the man and his work have something of the unexpected about them; they are at once serious and emotionally engaging. His work mixes Italian flamboyance with German precision, an elegant aesthetic with a self-effacing user-friendliness. Sapper was born in Munich in 1932 and although he lives in Milan, he has worked largely in his native Germany. His training was eclectic. Urged by his father, an artist, to learn something that would guarantee a good income, he studied business management, attending extra-curricular lectures in disciplines from philosophy, through anatomy, to engineering (his diploma was in the economic problems of industrial design), and only commenced his design career in the studio of Alberto Roselli and Gio Ponti in 1958. His polymath background has resulted in work that not only functions well and is aesthetically pleasing, but also reflects an understanding of why it looks as it does or is there in the first place. He often describes his methodological approach as 'giving form a meaning'.

Sapper's designs are all the result of many years of experimentation and development, but it is more his vocational morality and humanitarian concerns that will earn him a place in the annals of design history. When selecting for the *International Design Yearbook* in 1998, he emphasized over and over again that it is the designer's responsibility to produce only that which society actually needs and to avoid fashionable

styles and movements that he describes as being founded on superficial intellectual trends or 'marketing strategies connected to planned obsolescence – which is difficult to distinguish from common fraud ... As designers we see our responsibility as being to create things which improve life and the future for everyone.' In his introduction to the *Yearbook* he rather wittily quotes the *International Herald Tribune*, which compares the proliferation of a lot of impractical household products today with the cloning of sheep – 'Great – Just what we need! Sheep that look like more sheep.' Sapper points out that what is designed is what we live with, but is not necessarily what we want, and that today, *faute de mieux*, we buy a lot of useless junk. On the other hand, much of what we really should purchase to make our lives, and the future, better is not available because consumers, lulled into

a false security by the panacea of advertising, do not shout loudly enough for what they actually need. Design and consumerism have a joint responsibility towards society, and apathy is mankind's most deadly poison.

The lighting company Lucesco was founded in 2004 in Silicon Valley and the 'Halley' lamp is their first product. It was developed in just over a year using the latest LED technology and follows in the path of the iconic 'Tizio', which Sapper designed in 1972 for Artemide, and is likely to become an equal milestone in the lighting design industry. Sapper was familiar with LEDs through his work in computer design for IBM, but he had not heard of the new generation of new white lights that are now being manufactured to compete with the white incandescent light of halogen bulbs. He was further convinced of the benefits of using energy-saving LEDs (they have a lifespan of twenty years or 50,000 hours) when he realized that due to the small size of the LED head he could further refine the balancing act he had started over thirty years ago with Tizio. His fully articulated light for Artemide was conceived to shine a precise pool of halogen light on to a piece of paper while never getting in the way of the user. The 'Halley' lamp is even more flowing and responsive than 'Tizio' as a result of a specially patented joint that both connects and conducts electricity, and that is used at three junctures on the lamp, allowing 360 degrees of motion. Friction has been added to the joints so that the lamp does not act like a mobile, blowing freely in the breeze. The light source comprises sixteen miniature spotlights arranged in the head like soccer-stadium floodlights.

Lamp, Halley
Richard Sapper with
Nicole Sargenti
Aluminium, steel
LED (3 versions)
H: 40–128cm (16–51in)
Reach: 40–120cm
(16–48in)
Lucesco Lighting Inc,
USA
www.lucesco.com

Clamp lamp, Topolino
Bernhard Dessecker
Stainless steel, plastic,
silicone
1 x 20W halogen bulb
H (max.): 80cm (31in)
W (approx.): 80cm (31in)
Ingo Maurer GmbH,
Germany
www.ingo-maurer.com

To design for the sake of form or to suit the demands of the market are alien concepts for **Denis Santachiara**. He believes that all objects should be based on an ideology, or have a connotative language, without which they may be flat and superficial. Designs may be well executed, but they will never be expressive, or rise to the poetic. His work has consistently shown his obsession with invention and a desire for new experiences, and is always ahead of its time. In an interview for *Intramuros* magazine he writes that seventeen years ago he held a one-man show entitled 'Neo-Merchandise Design of Invention and Artificial Ecstasy' at the Milan Triennale. In an accompanying catalogue, Santachiara composed a glossary for the text he had written on the products shown, all of which had been designed with the latest ironic and 'performance' technologies. The glossary contained words such as 'interactive', 'virtual', 'high-performance', 'gadget', 'functionnoid', 'surprising', 'magical' and 'immaterial', all very forward looking and of much relevance today. To Santachiara, design is dying because too many are working without new visions, and because manufacturers are playing it safe. Inspiration should come not just from the design world, but also from other creative disciplines and forms of expression.

Santachiara's 2002 Milan show 'Sorry for the Plug' was dedicated to the nineteenth-century Croatian scientist Nikola Tesla, a pioneer in radiophonic experiments and inventor of the alternating current, the first cathode tube and the prototype of the electron microscope. Using luminescent tubes that produce X-rays, he photographed his own hands under wireless fluorescent lights. It is not the inventions themselves, however, that inspire Santachiara, but the visionary nature of the concepts and the amazement Tesla manifested in front of his own work. He described the effect of the microscope as being 'magnificent, a wonderful vision, a tremendous display, glorious, so marvellous that somebody might be scared to talk about it'. It is this enthusiasm and the allusion to the magical that captivates Santachiara, and that he wanted to recapture at the Galleria Post Design in 2001. The 'Mister Tesla' lamp installation consists of a small ceramic column upon which sits a glass jar containing neon lights, lit without the use of wiring. The tubes stay on even when the jar is being moved or handled. Added to this, a wall-fitted glass shelf switches on any neon light placed in its vicinity.

Lamp, Mister Tesla
Denis Santachiara
Tesla coil, fluorescent
tubes, glass, ceramic
W: 45cm (17 ³/₄in)
H: 90cm (35 ³/₈in)
Diam: 24cm (9 ³/₈in)
Memphis srl and
Galleria Post Design,
Italy
www.memphis-milano.it

**Table lamp,
Three Sixty**
Foster & Partners
Brass, zamac metal alloy,
resin parabola
1 x 50W halogen bulb
H: 54cm (21 ¹/₄in)
W: 93cm (37in)
Fontana Arte, Italy
www.fontanaarte.it

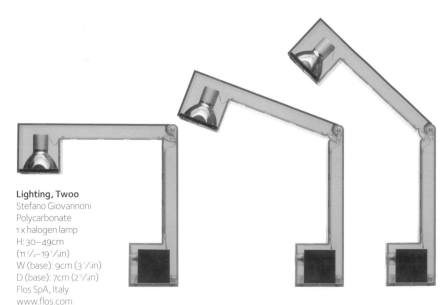

Lighting, Twoo
Stefano Giovannoni
Polycarbonate
1 x halogen lamp
H: 30–49cm
(11 ³/₄–19 ¹/₄in)
W (base): 9cm (3 ¹/₂in)
D (base): 7cm (2 ³/₄in)
Flos SpA, Italy
www.flos.com

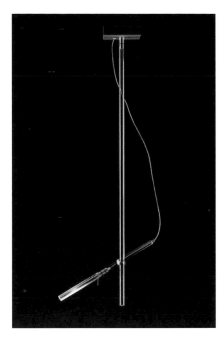

Hanging lamp, Cross
Giorgio and Max Pajetta
Metal, Pyrex glass
1 x 90W halogen bulb
H: 151cm (59in)
W: 60cm (23 ⁵/₈in)
Fontana Arte, Italy
www.fontanaarte.it

Table lamp, Cross
Giorgio and Max Pajetta
Metal, Pyrex glass
1 x 6W/T2 fluorescent bulb
H: 61cm (24in)
W: 60cm (23 ⁵/₈in)
Fontana Arte, Italy
www.fontanaarte.it

**Table lamp,
Miss K**
Philippe Starck
Injection-moulded
PMMA, injection-
moulded polycarbonate,
high-vacuum
aluminization process
1 x 100W/E27 bulb
H: 43.2cm (17in)
Diam: 23.6cm (9 ³/₈in)
Flos SpA, Italy
www.flos.com

Table lamp, Spacelab
Emmanuel Babled
Glass, metal
1 x max. 60W G9
halogen dimmer
H: 44cm (17 3/8in)
Diam: 33cm (13in)
Venini SpA, Italy
www.venini.com

Lighting, Flood
Cross/Mathias
Light bulbs, water
Various dimensions
Wokmedia, UK
www.wokmedia.com

Table lamp, Fluxus
Paolo Ulian
Aluminium, Pyrex
1 x 150W bulb
H: 60cm (23 1/2in)
Diam: 27cm (10 1/2in)
Luminara, Italy
www.luminara.it

Each of the forty transparent Pyrex tubes used in 'Fluxus' can rotate through 360 degrees, producing many different configurations from the same lamp. Since winning the Satellite prize at the 2000 Milan Furniture Fair, **Paolo Ulian** has been taken up by various leading manufacturers, who recognize in his work the right blend of technical expertise, experimentation and poetry. He is not interested in the merely elegant, but needs his designs to go that little bit further. He does not like to copy or reinterpret, preferring to find fresh means of arriving at a concept: 'It is precisely by following non-linear paths that you can achieve the definition of a good design.' He is very interested in materials, and often sits an example on his desk for weeks on end, looking, feeling, questioning: 'Many of my objects are born by observing and manipulating new or traditional materials, by understanding totally their individual qualities. Through this process I sometimes discover – often accidentally – hidden properties or unexpected applications.'

Table lamp, Kovac Lamp
Karim Rashid
Hand-blown Murano glass, chrome-plated steel
1 x 75W bulb
H: 45.7cm (18in)
W: 40.5cm (16in)
Karim Rashid Industrial Design, USA
www.karimrashid.com

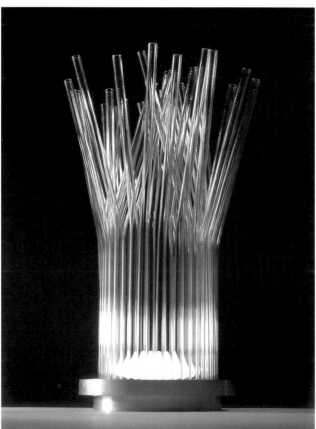

Portable light, Tumbler
Mathmos in-house design team
Glass, LEDs, recharger
H: 10cm (4in)
W: 6cm (3¼in)
L: 18cm (7½in)
Mathmos, UK
www.mathmos.co.uk

Lamp, LT02 Seam Two
Mark Holmes
Powder-coated aluminium
1 x max. 100W bulb
H: 30cm (11¾in)
W: 20cm (7⅞in)
L: 40cm (15¾in)
e15 GmbH, Germany
www.e15.com

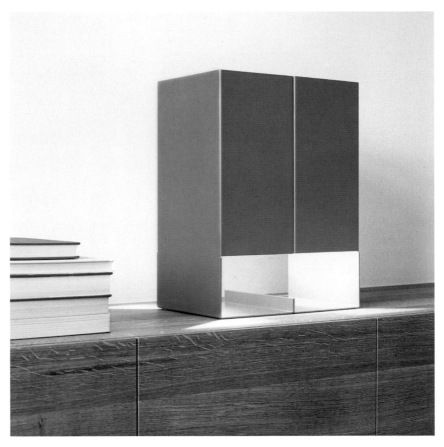

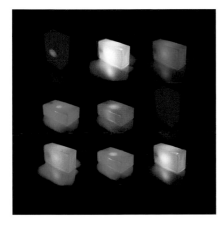

Charged like a mobile phone, 'Tumbler' can be used inside and out without the encumbrance of a lead or socket. The first variation can be set either to pulse or to be static in red, green or blue lights, while 'Tumbler Changing Colour' incorporates PIC chips and sensors to allow the lamp to glow in different hues depending on which of its fascias it is placed on. A variant phases through seemingly infinite colour combinations, the speed altering from gas to barely perceptible.

Lamp, Princess
Christophe Pillet
Polyethylene
l l: 100cm (39in)
Diam: 75cm (29½in)
P. Serralunga, Italy
www.serralunga.it

Lamp, Top-Pot
Ron Arad
Polyethylene
H: 100cm (39in)
Diam: 65cm (25⅝in)
P. Serralunga, Italy
www.serralunga.it

Lamp, Airswitch™ tc
Two create
Acid-etched mouth-
blown glass, plastic
1 x 40W bulb
H: 24cm (9 1/2in)
W: 13cm (5 1/8in)
Mathmos, UK
www.mathmos.co.uk

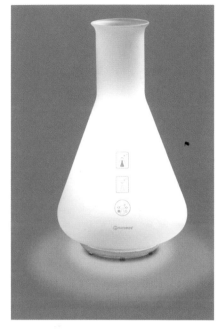

Lamp, Airswitch™ No.1
Mathmos Design Studio
Acid-etched mouth-
blown glass, plastic
1 x 40W bulb
H: 30cm (11 3/4in)
W: 17cm (6 3/4in)
D: 15cm (5 7/8in)
Mathmos, UK
www.mathmos.co.uk

With a patent pending, '**Airswitch**' is a range of innovative functional lights that share a unique switching/dimming technique achieved by means of an infrared beam that tracks the movement of an object above the lamp. Moving your hand in a horizontal direction activates or deactivates the light, while dimming and brightening is achieved by raising your hand up and down. 'Az' (see page 278) has a sandblasted finish with see-through dots; the glass can be rotated to turn the dots to the back. 'No.1' has a chemistry-flask look to emphasize the science of the mechanism. Simple graphics in red or white explain the functions. The latest version, 'tc', has a sleek acid-etched outer form and a glossy coloured insert.

Light and sound object, Tuba
Mathmos Design Studio
Pressed glass
LEDs
H: 32.5cm (13in)
W: 31cm (12 1/4in)
D: 26cm (10 1/4in)
Mathmos, UK
www.mathmos.co.uk

'**Tuba**' has two modes, faze and music. Placing the hand in what appears at first to be a solid-coloured light, but which in fact is a magically lit space, alters the function, producing either an ambient fazing light or an innovative reaction to sound.

Table lamp, Birzì
Carlo Forcolini and
Giancarlo Fassina
Silicon
1 x 60W incandescent
bulb
H: 26 cm (10 ¹/₄in)
Diam: 11.5 cm (4 ¹/₂in)
Luceplan SpA, Italy
www.luceplan.com

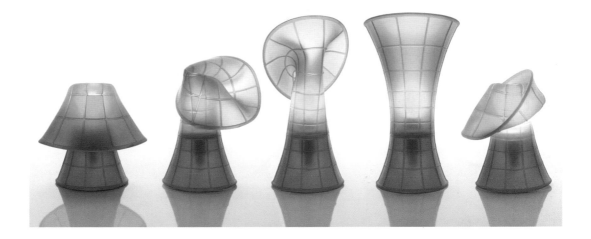

**Table lamp,
Circo di Lune**
Monica Guggisberg and
Philip Baldwin
Glass, metal
1 x max. Osram Dullux EL
Globe 20W/E27
H: 42cm (16 ¹/₂in)
Diam: 33cm (13in)
Venini SpA, Italy
www.venini.com

**Multi-faced light,
Snap**
Tom Dixon
Polypropylene Random
Copolymer
1 x incandescent bulb
Diam: 35cm (13 ³/₄in)
Tom Dixon, UK
www.tomdixon.net

Lighting, Ribbon Light
Claire Norcross
Chromed steel
1 x 60W/E27
H: 51cm (20 ⅛in)
W: 29cm (11 ⅜in)
D: 26cm (10 ¼in)
Habitat, UK
www.habitat.net

Lighting, Miss Pac
Habitat
Black glazed ceramic
1 x 60W/E27
H: 28cm (11in)
W: 28cm (11in)
Habitat, UK
www.habitat.net

Table lamp, Bokka
Karim Rashid
Triplex mouth-blown
water-jet cut glass,
chromed metal
1 x max. 150W/E27
(E26 US) Globolux
H: 60cm (23 ⅝in)
W: 38cm (15in)
Kundalini, Italy
www.kundalini.it

Table lamp, Gherkin
Norman Foster
Triplex mouth-blown
acid-etched glass,
chromed metal
1 x E27 (E26 US)
H: 32, 63 or 120cm
(12 5/8, 24 3/4 or 47in)
D: 13 or 37cm
(5 1/8 or 14 5/8in)
Kundalini, Italy
www.kundalini.it

Table lamp, Cand-led
Marta Laudani and
Marco Romanelli with
Marcello Pinzero
PMMA, aluminium
1 x max. 1W LED
H: 28cm (11in)
Diam: 17cm (6 3/4in)
Oluce srl, Italy
www.oluce.com

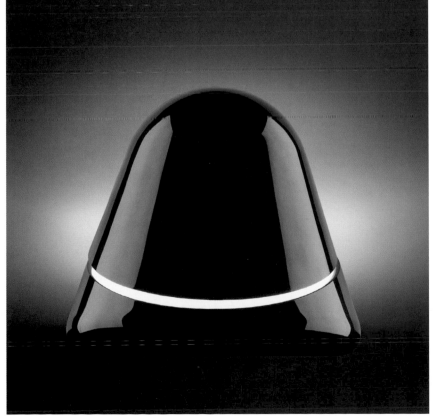

Table lamp, Tikal
Vico Magistretti
Die-cast aluminium
1 x 9W fluorescent bulb
H: 18cm (7 1/8in)
Diam: 20cm (7 7/8in)
Fontana Arte, Italy
www.fontanaarte.it

Lamps, 36-24-36 series
Studioilse
MDF, turned rubberwood, polyurethane lacquer, fabric
Various dimensions
Ferrious, UK
www.ferrious.com
www.studioilse.com

Table lamp, Orientalina
Michele De Lucchi
Murano glass, metal
1 x max. 60W/E14
H: 37cm (14 ⅝in)
Diam: 19cm (7 ½in)
Produzione Privata, Italy
www.produzione privata.it

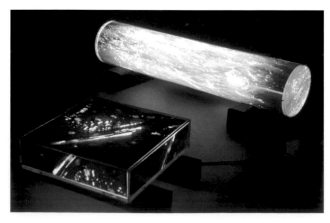

Bench, cube-tube and small table, Fonsino
Markus Benesch
Acrylic glass, lenticular/photopaper image, wood, silversurfer laminate
T5 dimmable neon light
Bench,
L: 140cm (55 ⅛in)
Diam: 30cm (11 ⅞in);
Table,
H: 15cm (5 ⅞in)
W: 60cm (23 ⅝in)
L: 60cm (23 ⅝in)
Benesch Project Design
www.moneyformilan.com

Markus Benesch's 'Fonsino' acts as a table, a stool, a lamp or all three simultaneously. When switched off, the components revert to silvery shining sculptures, an effect caused by the laminate he developed in 1997 especially for his designs.

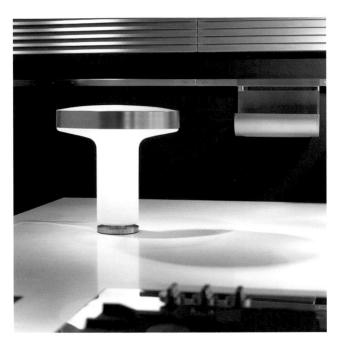

Table lamp, Boletus
Jorge Pensi
Spun brass
1 x 22W/E27 fluorescent
Duralux circular bulb
or 1 x 75W/E27
incandescent bulb
H: 57cm
Diam (base): 14cm (5 ¹/₂in)
Diam (top): 42cm (16 ¹/₂in)
Grupo Blux, Spain
www.grupoblux.com

**Table lamp,
Colonna di luce**
Ettore Sottsass
Glass, metal, marble
1 x max. 60W/E27
Globolux Opale, dimmer
H: 32cm (12 ⁵/₈in)
Diam: 42cm (16 ¹/₂in)
Venini SpA, Italy
www.venini.com

**Table lamp,
Abat-Jaour**
Ettore Sottsass
Ceramic, glass, chrome
4 x 40W/E14 bulbs
H: 60cm (23 ⁵/₈in)
D: 48cm (18 ⁷/₈in)
B&B Italia SpA, Italy
www.bebitalia.it

**Lamp made from
preserved cow
stomach,
Ruminant Bloom**
Julia Lohmann
Preserved cow
stomach, light fitting
1 x 7W/E14 pygmy bulb
H: 14cm (5 ¹/₂in)
W: 14cm (5 ¹/₂in)
D: 11cm (4 ³/₈in)
Julia Lohmann, UK
www.julialohmann.co.uk

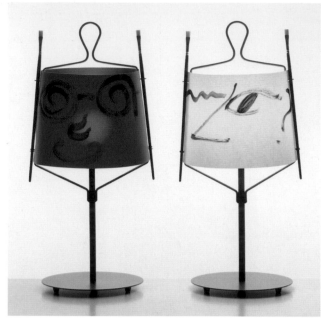

Family of lamps, Fold
Alexander Taylor
Powder-coated
aluminium
Bell lamp
H (max.): 23cm (9in)
W (max.): 12cm (4 ³/₄in)
L (max.): 12cm (4 ³/₄in)
Established & Sons, UK
www.established
andsons.com

Lamp, L'Artista
Michele De Lucchi
Paper
1 x max. 100W/E27
H: 52cm (20 ¹/₂in)
Diam: 25cm (9 ⁷/₈in)
Produzione Privata, Italy
www.produzione
privata.it

'L'Artista' light comes in
a gift box and contains
a stand, frame, two
paintbrushes and a
paper lampshade. The
motto of Produzione
Privata is to cultivate
experimentation and
encourage craftsmanship.
With this lamp the
customer can give
free reign to their innate
need for self-expression
and also create their
very own piece of
ready-made design.

**Outdoor lamp
(for swimming pools),
Waterproof**
Héctor Serrano
Rotation-moulded
polyethylene
1 x E10 4.8V 0.75A
(waterproof and
rechargeable) bulb
H: 53cm (20 ⁷/₈in)
W: 23cm (9in)
Metalarte, Spain
www.metalarte.com

Lamp, Flapflap
Büro für form
Iron, plastic
1 x 25-45W bulb
H: 50 or 80cm
(19 ⁵/₈ or 31 ⁷/₈in)
Next Design GmbH,
Germany
www.buerofuerform.de

Range of table and floor lamps, Collection Guns
Philippe Starck
Die-cast zamak, chrome-plated ABS stem
1 x 75W/E27 (Bedside)
1 x 150W/E27 (Table)
1 x 250W/E27 (Lounge)
Bedside,
H: 30cm (11 ¾in)
Table,
H: 75cm (29 ½in)
Lounge, H: 170cm (67in)
Flos SpA, Italy
www.flos.com

Lamp, B L O
Marcel Wanders
Plastics
H: 20cm (7 ⅞in)
W: 10cm (4in)
D: 10cm (4in)
Flos SpA, Italy
www.flos.com

Lamp, Bourgie
Ferruccio Laviani
Transparent polycarbonate
H: 73cm (28 ¾in)
Diam (shade): 37cm (14 ⅝in)
Kartell SpA, Italy
www.kartell.it

Philippe Starck certainly knows how to provoke a reaction; his latest collection of gold-plated floor, table and bedside lamps for Flos secured his place, once again, as the enfant terrible of the design world. You will either love them or hate them, but one thing is definite – you will not be indifferent (although Martí Guixé was quoted in *Domus* as saying 'It is just another lamp.'). I cannot make up my mind. I cannot decide whether Starck has gone too far in mixing opulence and murder – design is not art, the guns are not one off sculptures making a social comment, they are not decommissioned weapons transformed. These lights are objects that are going to be bought in their hundreds by the select group of people who will be able to afford them, and neither Flos nor Starck will have any power over what point the consumer will be making by their purchase or display. Should design get involved with politics? Should it have that function? If these lamps were not designed by Starck, would we feel the same about them? If they were by someone unknown would we say he or she has definitely transgressed the narrow borders of good taste? I can see it could be valid to make a comment on whether society is so complacent about guns today that it can be at ease to have a replica as a cosy night light, but in the end I think I am far more in accord with Hani Rashid who, again writing for *Domus*, states, 'When design privileges innovation, culture speeds along; when art drives forward relevant social commentary, culture flourishes. When one mixes the two, it is effectively the combination of salt and gasoline. The motor splutters to a deliberate and irreversible death.'

Lamp, Destructive Deco
Frank Tjepkema
Veneer, metal
1 x 40W bulb
H: 60cm (23 ⁵⁄₈in)
Droog, the Netherlands
www.droogdesign.nl

Whether or not as a reaction to the minimalist, high-tech designs of the 1990s, or as just part of the increasing pluralism we have seen in design since the turn of the century, recent years have witnessed a significant increase in the use of patterning and baroque elements in furniture, textiles, lighting and accessories. In the pages of this book there are examples from Urquiola, Starck, Wanders, Nani Marquina, Timorous Beasties and Ilse Crawford, to name but a few. Yet can this desire for lux and decoration go too far? **Frank Tjepkema**'s range of lights could be read as a critique – giving physical form to the destructive nature of sensory overload. The lamps are made of laser-etched veneer. The lasers are set to apply three independent overlapping patterns, the first based on a traditional baroque wallpaper, the second on a 1960s motif, while the third is an illustrative butterfly decoration. As the laser operates, it goes deeper and deeper into the material, from engraving to cutting, until a point is reached where it is actually destroying what it is creating. The question Tjepkema is asking is, 'When should the laser stop? Until when does it add to the beauty of the object?' The lamps were designed for the 2005 Droog Design 'Value for Money' exhibition, which questioned what determines the price of a product. The amount of raw material? The value of the material? Production time? Labour costs? Edition? Uniqueness? The name and reputation of the designer or brand? In this instance the most expensive lamp is the one that has been 'treated' the longest – the most 'destroyed' one has the greatest value.

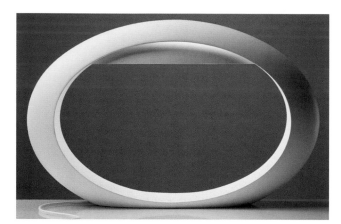

Lamp, Ellipsis
Bernard Brousse
Polyurethane,
technopolymer
1 x max. 20W/E 27, Fluo E1
H: 29.5cm (11 ⁵⁄₈in)
W: 48cm (18 ³⁄₄in)
Baleri Italia SpA, Italy
www.baleri-italia.com

Light, Bellissima Brutta
Ingo Maurer
Printed circuit board,
LED, steel
1 x 40W bulb
H: 50cm (18 ⁷⁄₈in)
Ingo Maurer GmbH,
Germany
www.ingo-maurer.com

Ingo Maurer's hauntingly beautiful 'vase of flowers', '**Bellissima Brutta**', creates poetry from cutting-edge technology. Red and green LEDs have been combined with blue to produce a soft white light.

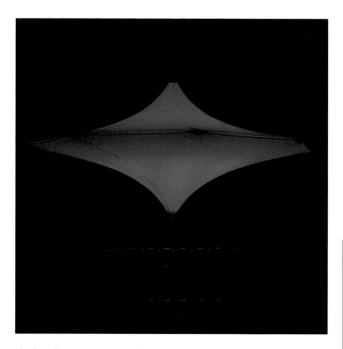

Shade maker, Juri G
Studio Vertijet
LED lighted fabric,
stainless steel
H: 225–300cm
(89–118in)
Diam: 310cm (122in)
Skia GmbH, Germany
www.skia.de

LED lights constantly
change colour within
the shade of the 'Juri G'
parasol. For those who
prefer a more static
ambiance, a favourite
colour can be made to
glow constantly. For now
the base is unmoveable,
but a transportable
version is in the pipeline.

**Suspension and floor
light, Roundlight**
Perry King and
Santiago Miranda
Steel sheet and turned
aluminium
2 fluorescent circlines:
1 x 40W, 1 x 22W, T-5
Various dimensions
Luxo Italiana SpA, Italy
www.luxo.it

**Outdoor floor lamp
with speakers, Ibiza**
Francesco Rota
Polyethylene,
stainless steel
1 x 20W/E27, Fluo
H: 70 or 120cm
(27 ¹/₂ or 47in)
Diam: 12cm (4 ³/₄in)
Oluce srl, Italy
www.oluce.com

Floor lamp, Camp
Jakob Timpe
Polypropylene
1 x E27 bulb
H: 143.5cm (50in)
H (upright):
184.5cm (73in)
Diam (base):
30cm (8 ³/₄in)
Marset, Spain
www.marset.com

**Lamps for interior and
exterior use, Inout
series**
Ramón Ubeda and
Otto Canalda
Waterproof plastic
Bulb
H: 66.5, 166 or 215.8cm
(26 ³/₈, 65 or 85in)
Metalarte, Spain
www.metalarte.com

Floor lamp, Shakti
Marzio Rusconi
Tubular, laser-cut
Plexiglas diffuser, steel
base with satin or
chrome-plated finish
2 x E27 bulbs
Various dimensions,
up to:
H: 400cm (158in)
Diam: 25cm (9 ⁷/₈in)
Kundalini srl, Italy
www.kundalini.it

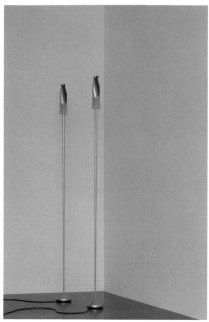

Floor lamp, Cool Magic
Beckert, Soanca-Pollak,
Thammer
Bi-metal, fibreglass
1 x 150W/E27
halogen lamp
H (adjustable):
110–183cm (43in–72in)
W (closed):
7cm (2 ³⁄₄in)
W (fully open):
25cm (9 ⁷⁄₈in)
Serien Raumleuchten
GmbH, Germany
www.serien.com

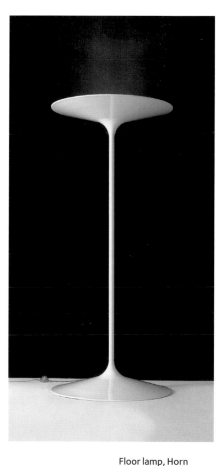

**Lamp/stool,
Ufosausoo**
Patrick Chia
Opalescent Plexiglas,
chromed metal,
fluorescent bulb
Lamp,
H: 79cm (31in)
W: 38cm (15in)
D: 40cm (15 ³⁄₄in);
Stool,
H: 115cm (45 ¹⁄₄in)
W: 48cm (18 ⁷⁄₈in)
D: 40cm (15 ³⁄₄in)
BRF srl, Italy
www.brfcolors.com

Lamps, Venti
Alessandro Mendini
Opalflex®
100W bulb
Various dimensions,
up to:
H: 160cm (63in)
W: 21cm (8 ¹⁄₄in)
D: 37cm (14 ⁵⁄₈in)
Slamp, Italy
www.slamp.it

Floor lamp, Horn
Carlo Colombo
Aluminium,
polyurethane and glass
1 x 40W/E14 halogen bulb
H: 100cm (39in)
Diam: 80cm (31in)
Solzi Luce, Italy
www.solziluce.com

Lamp, Squeeze
Claudio Colucci
Corian®
H: 178cm (70in)
Diam: 47cm (18 ¹/₂in)
Créa Diffusion, France
www.crea-diffusion.com

Floor lamp, Satel.light
Ingo Maurer
Fibreglass, metal,
plastic, glass
Halogen, 150W, B 15d
H: 240cm (94in)
Diam (shade):
80cm (31in)
Diam (base):
37cm (14 ⁵/₈in)
Ingo Maurer GmbH,
Germany
www.ingo-maurer.com

Light, Stem
Michael Sodeau
Rotationally moulded
polyethylene
High spot 50W bulb
H: 190cm (75in)
W: 67.8cm (26 ³/₄in)
Modus, UK
www.modusfurniture.co.uk

Floor lamp, Gilda
Enrico Franzolini
Synthetic paper,
die-cast aluminium
1 x 250W halogen bulb or
1 x 200W incandescent
bulb
Diam: 60cm (23 ⁵/₈in)
Pallucco Italia Spa, Italy
www.pallucco.com

**Lighting, Set up
shades 5, 6, 7**
Marcel Wanders
PVC/cotton laminate,
metal
1 x max. 60W/E27
H: 60, 116 or 180cm
(23 ⁵/₈, 45 ⁵/₈ or 70 ⁷/₈in)
Diam: 20, 30 or 40cm
(7 ⁷/₈, 11 ³/₄ or 15 ³/₄in)
Moooi, the Netherlands
www.moooi.com

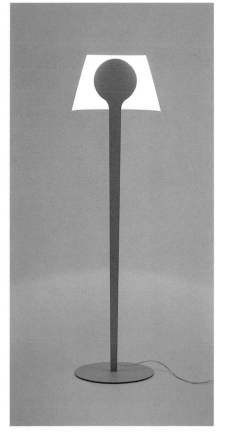

Standard lamp, Asa
Laura Agnoletto and
Marzio Rusconi Clerici
Steel, epoxy powders,
steel plate
Incandescent bulb
H: 138 or 168cm
(54 ³/₈ or 66 ¹/₈in)
Pallucco Italia Spa, Italy
www.pallucco.com

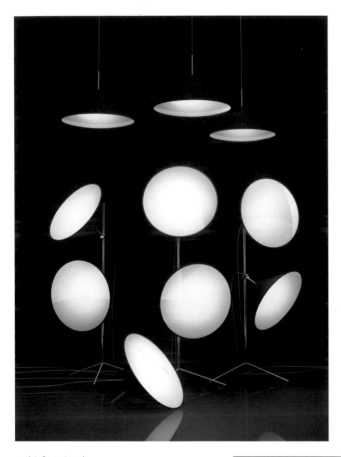

Lighting, l'uovo
Shigeru Uchida
Polyethylene
Incandescent lamp
1 x 150W (large lamp),
1 x 60W (small lamp)
H: 45 or 88.5cm
(17 ³/₄ or 35in)
Diam: 33 or 64.5cm
(13 or 25 ⁵/₈in)
Yamagiwa Corporation,
Japan
www.yamagiwa.co.jp

**Multi-functional
lamp, Cone Light**
Tom Dixon
Aluminium, acrylic
1 x incandescent
100W bulb
H: 42cm (16 ¹/₂in)
W: 22 or 74cm
(8 ⁵/₈ or 29 ¹/₈in)
Tom Dixon, UK
www.tomdixon.net

Lamp, Airswitch™ Az
Shin and Tomoko Azumi
Sandblasted mouth-
blown glass, metal
2 x 60W bulbs
H: 50cm (19 ⁵/₈in)
W: 25.5cm (10 ¹/₈in)
Mathmos Ltd, UK
www.mathmos.co.uk

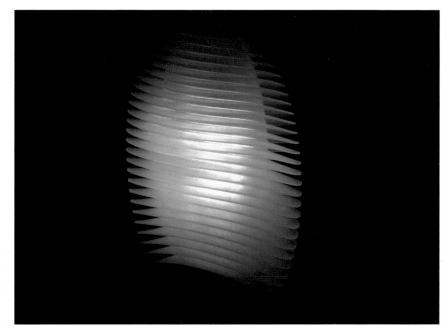

Pendant lamp, Palea
Dan Yeffet
Epoxy
Halogen max. 50W
Various dimensions
Materialise.MGX,
Belgium
www.materialise-
mgx.com

Materialise's lampshades
are produced through
prototyping techniques
(stereolithography and
selective laser sintering)
that offer almost
unlimited freedom of
design – a mass
customized design.

Table lamp, Globolus
Watanabe & Tanaka
PMMA, chrome
1 x max. 22W and
3 x max. 1W LED
H: 27.5cm (11in)
Diam: 31cm (12 ¼in)
Oluce srl, Italy
www.oluce.com

**Desk/floor lamp,
Dione**
PearsonLloyd
Satinated and lacquered
nickel, mouth-blown
glass
1 x 75W bulb
H: 20cm (7 ⅞in)
Diam: 40cm (15 ¾in)
ClassiCon GmbH,
Germany
www.classicon.com

Lamp, Everywhere
Ora-Ïto
Artemide Design, Italy
www.artemide.it

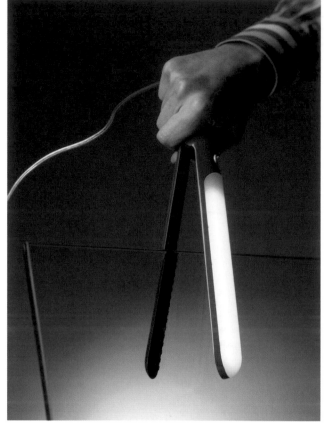

**Illuminator Wind-Up
Flashlight**
ABS plastic
Three LEDs
H: 5cm (2in)
W: 5cm (2in)
L: 14cm (5 ½in)
MoMA store, USA
www.momastore.org

This **LED flashlight**
never needs replacement
batteries or bulbs. It is
wound up by way of a
built-in handle and
provides one hour of
continuous light. Two
levels of brightness can
be selected with a touch
of a button.

There is nothing poor about this little rich boy. Born with a silver spoon in his mouth, **Ora-Ïto**'s father is a well-known designer of luxury items with a shop in the Place Vendôme in Paris and his uncle, Yves Bayard, is one of the architects of the Museum of Modern Art in Nice. Ïto was brought up in Paris and St Tropez, and has a high-school degree from an American college in Paris, but flunked design college, preferring instead to play tennis to championship level and mix, as a youngster, with the likes of Helmut Newton, Keith Haring and Vaserely. Maybe this privileged upbringing gave him the self-assurance, intuition and daring (or is it just plain old chutzpah?) to launch himself on the path to superstardom by designing his own website advertising his non-existent studio and creating a line of virtual brand products that were launched into the ether in 1998, when he was only 21 years of age. His motto is the famous Nike quote 'Make it Happen', and he certainly did. His 'designs' were exhibited in museums and art galleries and taken up by the design media worldwide. Vuitton, Nike, Bic, Cartier, Apple and others admired his cunning, not to mention his talent, with the result that many of his 'victims' approached him to design actual products for their ranges. Today he heads a studio with a turnover of over 5 million Euros. His work covers all manner of consumer items, most notably the now famous aluminium Heineken bottle, a laptop for Toshiba, a mobile phone for Sagem, the entire L'Oréal Studio Line, furniture for Cappellini and B&B Italia and lamps for Artemide, as well as interiors for Nike, a large car showroom and the Cab Club on the Place du Palais Royal in Paris. His designs are inspired, unpredictable and, although often pure in line, nonetheless attention grabbing. His fascination with brands continues. His visionary idea for Paris 2010 is of a city devoted to labels, bought up by mega corporations, the Arc de Triomphe becoming a giant billboard for Nike, and the Eiffel Tower an Yves St Laurent possession. For Ïto a brand is a person who has a dream and manages to realize it. Maybe Ïto is turning himself into a brand. He is a fabrication, a Frenchman with a Japanese/Italian-sounding name (Morabito became Ora, which is Italian for Pray, Ïto) all adding to the mystique, which makes you ask, 'Who is this man, can we pin him down and where's he heading?'

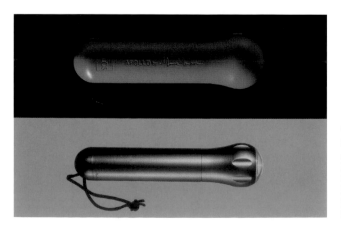

Torch, Apollo
Marc Newson
Aluminium, plastic,
leather
L: 5.6cm (2 ¼in)
Diam: 2.4cm (1in)
Flos SpA, Italy
www.flos.com

Lamp, Bubble Light
Aaron Rincover,
Mathmos Design Team
Silicone, 4 LEDs and
rechargeable battery
Diam: 8cm (3 ⅛in)
Mathmos Ltd, UK
www.mathmos.co.uk

With its squeeze on/
squeeze off bubble light,
Mathmos has produced
the ultimate anti-stress
device. The lamp is
charged through a long
white cable, from which
it can be suspended or
draped across the floor.
The '**Bubble**' light
contains blue, green or
orange LEDs; the light is
diffused through
silicone, creating a richly
coloured glow.

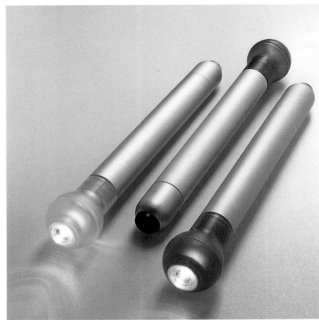

Torch, Handy Light
Theo Williams
ABS, aluminium
L: 14.8cm (5 ³⁄₄in)
Diam: 1.6cm (⅝in)
Lexon, France
www.lexon-design.com

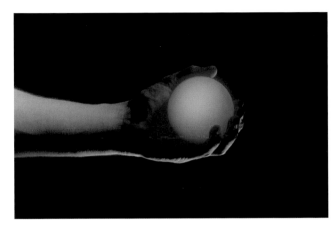

Lamp, Agaricon
Ross Lovegrove
Polycarbonate with silk
opaque treatment
1 x 150W bulb
H: 28cm (11in)
Diam: 40cm (15 ³⁄₄in)
Base: 8.5cm (3 ⅜in)
Luceplan SpA, Italy
www.luceplan.com

Light, Pigeon Light
Ed Carpenter
Perspex
1 x 25W bulb
H: 23cm (9in)
W: 21cm (8 ¼in)
D: 10.5cm (4 ⅛in)
Thorsten van Elten, UK
www.thorsten
vanelten.com

System to create illuminated room dividers and lights, Net
Isabel Hamm
Glass, stainless steel
Halogen reflectors
H: 10cm (3 ⁷/₈in)
W: 12cm (4 ³/₄in)
D: 1.2cm (³/₈in)
Isabel Hamm
Gestaltung, Germany
www.isabel-hamm.de

Wall lamp, Ipy parete
Michele De Lucchi with
Nora De Cicco
Pyrex
1 x max. 60W/E14 bulb
H: 13cm (5 ¹/₈in)
Diam: 13cm (5 ¹/₈in)
Produzione Privata, Italy
www.produzioneprivata.it

**Right:
Chandeliers,
Cicatrices des Lux
3, 5 and 8**
Philippe Starck
Hand-ground crystal,
polished crystal sheets,
conductive varnish
Various dimensions
Flos SpA, Italy
www.flos.com

**Left:
Wall/ceiling lamp,
Diamond**
Oluce
Sandblasted moulded
glass, stainless steel
1 x max. 40W/G9
H: 13.5cm (5 ³/₈in)
W: 13.5cm (5 ³/₈in)
D: 7.5cm (3in)
Oluce srl, Italy
www.oluce.com

Martí Guixé

Which of your designs to date would you like to be remembered by?
'HIBYE'.

How do you think others view your work?
Depending on who the others are – variously.

Which designer has influenced you the most and why?
I have no references.

If you were not a designer, what would you like to be and why?
I am already an ex-designer. I don't like to be into the borders of the profession.

What role do you think the designer has in society today?
To search and develop the limits of decadence.

Do you buy a lot of design pieces?
Only wearable ones.

Is there a design in your home that you couldn't live without?
Google.

What do you consider to be the best piece of design since the millennium?
Google.

Where do you think design is heading? Is there someone we should be watching out for?
Very Lustre.

Is the cult of the personality taking over the design world?
It is because of the media-ization of it. It happens with everything.

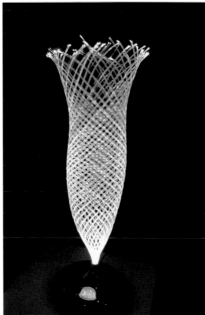

Lamp, do scratch
Martí Guixé
Light box, black coating
H: 9cm (3 ¹/₂in)
W: 65cm (25 ³/₄in)
D: 9cm (3 ¹/₂in)
do + Droog Design,
the Netherlands
www.droogdesign.nl

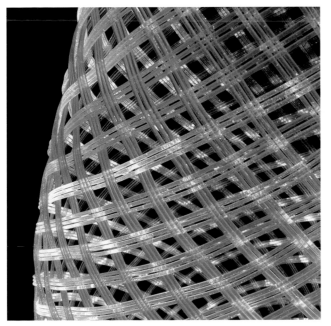

Lamp, Yvette
François Azambourg
PMMA optic fibre, metal
H: 150cm (59in)
Diam: 35cm (13 ³/₄in)
Galerie Kreo, France
www.galeriekreo.com

Azambourg uses fibre optics with lateral emission, which he braids together into a tube that can then be formed into a variety of shapes.

Electronics

Mobile phone accessory, Aliph Jawbone headset
Yves Béhar with Geoffrey Petrizzi, Youjin Nam and Johan Liden
Elastomeric rubber, brushed steel
L: 5cm (2in)
Aliph, USA
www.aliph.com

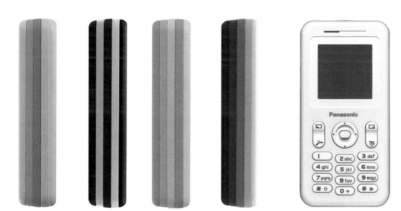

GSM mobile phone (for Japanese market), EB-A 200
Metal, plastics
H: 9cm (3 ½in)
W: 4.4cm (1 ¾in)
D: 1.8cm (¾in)
Panasonic Mobile Communications Co., Ltd, Japan
www.panasonic.co.jp

The Plantronics 'Discovery 640' (code named Tahiti) is an extremely discreet, light-weight Bluetooth headset. It employs an innovative AAA battery charging system that continuously recharges the set while not in use, providing 15 hours of talk time.

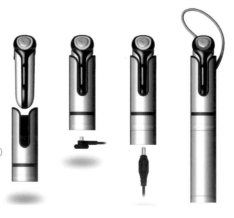

Bluetooth headset, Discovery 640
Soohyan Ham
Painted ABS/PC, TPE
H: 5.5cm (2 ⅛in)
W: 1.91cm (¾in)
D: 1.71cm (⅝in)
Plantronics, USA
www.plantronics.com

Sam Hecht

Do you buy a lot of design pieces?
I have a collection called 'Under a Fiver' that I've been doing for many years. They are well-considered and inspiring pieces from around the world, which influence the studio in many ways. Many of them are good examples of what design can do, but your question is whether I buy 'designer' pieces – something the collection is not.

Which designer has influenced you the most and why?
For me, the writings of Otl Aicher are very profound – not because they are necessarily contemporary, but because his thoughts are so thorough and insightful that they cut through much of the bullshit of the 1980s and 90s. It's also so much more interesting to read what he has to say, rather than view images, because the interpretations allow a freedom of influence. I wouldn't regard myself as a rationalist because of Aicher, but as a realist, and that's important for any style or approach to design.

What role do you think the designer has in society today?
Firstly, there is no single role that a designer has. It is now indefinable, for several reasons. The world is overwhelmed with possibility. And economic reality means that where you study is not necessarily where the job at hand can be performed. Thousands of designers graduate in the UK each year, yet there is no local industry to support them. So they try other things, building their own contexts and destinies. The result is that they might remain designers, but not in the traditional roles we have relied upon in the past. Your book is a perfect example. You used to separate the fields of design into chapters of product, furniture and so on. But now, the chapters are more difficult – designers are protagonists, theorists, educators, commentators and conceptualists. What role, then, does a designer have in society? To produce quality – absolute quality in whatever they do.

Is there a design in your home that you couldn't live without?
I live with very little, which means that everything I have is there because it has avoided the wastepaper bin or eBay. For some reason, Ricardo Blumer's light chairs continue to live well. They are comfortable and warm, and my three-year-old boy can now pick them up and move them around, giving him his own responsibility.

Where do you think design is heading? Is there someone we should be watching?
I would want to believe that there will be a greater sense of the designer making connections with the environment that we inhabit. Not just in the hardware sense, but also in the software sense. The young designer Martino Gamper is doing some interesting interjections, and also the works of Takeshi Ishiguro have always given me a sense of jealousy because of their absolute wonderment.

Is the cult of the personality taking over the design world?
For many people, personality equals value. As long as people believe that the importance of the creator behind the work adds a level of value to the object, it will exist. But whether this improves the design, I am not sure. Some of my most satisfying projects are the ones that people are not aware I have designed. I like that.

Telephone, 2nd Phone
Sam Hecht
Electronic components, metals, plastics, rubber flex
H: 13.4cm (5 ¹⁄₈in)
W: 6.2cm (2 ³⁄₈in)
D: 3.4cm (1 ³⁄₈in)
Muji, Japan
www.muji.net

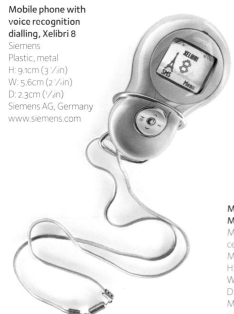

Mobile phone with voice recognition dialling, Xelibri 8
Siemens
Plastic, metal
H: 9.1cm (3 ¹⁄₂in)
W: 5.6cm (2 ¹⁄₈in)
D: 2.3cm (³⁄₄in)
Siemens AG, Germany
www.siemens.com

Mobile phone, Motorola Pebl V6
Motorola's design centres
Metal
H: 8.7cm (3 ¹⁄₂in)
W: 4.9cm (2in)
D: 2cm (³⁄₄in)
Motorola, USA
www.motorola.com

Mobile phone, V601T
Hiroko Nakano,
Taihei Miyaji,
Nobuhiro Yamane
and Tadatsugu Kotani
Polycarbonate, acrylic
H: 9.4cm (3 ½in)
W: 4.9cm (2in)
D: 2.4cm (¾in)
Toshiba Corporation,
Mobile Communications
Company, Japan
www.toshiba.co.jp

Mobile phone, Samsung 5 Megapixel Camera Phone (SCH-S250)
Nam Mi Kim
Polycarbonate,
SUS, iron, urethane,
transparent acrylic
H: 11.48cm (4 ½in)
W: 4.96cm (2in)
D: 2.06cm (¾in)
Samsung Electronics,
Korea
www.samsung.com

The **Samsung 'SCH-S250'** is the world's first mobile phone to incorporate a 5-megapixel camera that takes photos of the same quality as a high-end digital camera.

Multimedia mobile phone, Nokia N92
Nokia Design Team
Stainless steel, plastic,
glass
H: 2.5cm (1 in)
L: 19.7cm (7 ¾in)
D: 5.8cm (2 ¼in)
Nokia, Finland
www.nokia.com

The 'N92' has all the features we expect from a top-end Nokia model: integrated Wi-Fi, web browsing and music playback, but over and above all this it includes a DVB-H decoder, which means it is now possible to watch a package of Sky TV channels, including Sky One and MTV, in a resolution equivalent to VHS. The style of the phone may be a bit heavy and clumsy, yet is ingenious in the way the 16 M colour screen can flip round to resemble a tiny DVD player, ideal for those long car journeys.

BlackBerry, 7100 series
RIM (Research in Motion)
Various materials
H: 11.7cm (4 ¾in)
W: 5.9cm (2 ⅜in)
D: 2.1cm (¾in)
RIM (Research in Motion), Canada
www.rim.com

Mobile phone, MYX 8
Ora-Ïto
Aluminium, plastic
H: 11.5cm (4 1/2in)
W: 4.7cm (2in)
D: 2cm (3/4in)
Sagem, France
www.sagem.com

**Mobile Walkman
phone, W800**
Henrik Jensfelt with
Charlotta Franzen
and Rui Yamagami
Plastics and metal
H: 10cm (3 7/8in)
W: 4.6cm (1 3/4in)
D: 2.05cm (3/4in)
Sony Ericsson Mobile
Communications,
Sweden
www.sonyericsson.com

The **Sony Ericsson 'W800'** is the first mobile phone that can store up to a dozen CDs. Branded as the 'Walkman phone', users copy CDs to a memory card or download music directly from the Internet. The editor of the gadget magazine *Stuff*, Adam Vaughan, sees this as the death knell for the iPod. 'Who needs an MP3 player when you can run out of the house with just your keys, wallet and phone and still have music wherever you go? Every mobile phone manufacturer is making a version and it will not be long before the iPod is redundant.' Apple itself has been collaborating with Motorola on the production of music phones that include its iTunes software.

**Mobile phone,
Nokia 8800**
Ora-Ïto
Lead Designer: Pekka
Majanen; 8800 Design
Team: Todd Wood, Tanja
Fisher, Grace Boicel
Stainless steel, sapphire-
coated glass
H: 10.7cm (4 1/8in)
W: 4.5cm (1 3/4in)
D: 1.5cm (5/8in)
Nokia, Finland
www.nokia.com

Another mobile phone for the fashion conscious, the sleek stainless steel **Nokia '8800'** also contains the latest technology: a digital music player, video streaming and integrated SVGA camera. The ring tones are by award-winning composer Ryuichi Sakamoto.

**Mobile phone,
Nokia 7280**
Lead designer:
Nokia Design Team
with Tej Chauhan,
Grace Boicel and
Tanja Fisher
Injection-moulded PC
ABS, metal and suede
detailing
H: 11.5cm (4 ½in)
W: 3cm (1 ⅛in)
D: 1.5cm (⅝in)
Nokia, Finland
www.nokia.com

**Mobile phone,
Motorola V80**
Motorola's design
centres
Metal alloys
H: 9.9cm (3 ⅞in)
W: 4.5cm (1 ¾in)
D: 2.3cm (⅞in)
Motorola, USA
www.motorola.com

At first glance you would be forgiven for not knowing
what the **Nokia '7280'** is, let alone how it functions.
The mobile phone's pen-shaped art deco design is by
far one of most outrageous Nokia has yet conceived.
The display is used horizontally with the screen (which
doubles up as a mirror when not in use) to the left and
the Navi Spinner to the right. There is no keypad, and
the only buttons are the upper and lower soft keys,
the 'call' and 'end' keys and the middle selection pad.
The spinner, which can be moved clockwise or counter-
clockwise, is the only way to dial a number, type an
SMS or navigate through the menus. The earpiece
is located above the screen and is lined in suede.

Telephone handset for mobile phones, P*Phone

Hulger (Nicolas Roope)
Plastic, electrical components
H: 21.5cm (8 ⁵/₈in)
W: 6.6cm (2 ⅛in)
D: 6cm (2 ³/₈in)
Hulger Ltd, UK
www.hulger.com

Answering the question 'Why does design always have to look forward rather than back?' the 'Hulger P*Phone' was initially produced in Bakelite with a soldered on hands-free kit, and sold in its hundreds over the Internet as the 'Pokia' phone until Nokia blocked the trademark application. Developing the limited batch prototype, Hulger have now launched a much more useable version. With adapters to suit all brands of mobile phone, the Hulger is available in a variety of colours. It is a playful antidote to often-soulless technology.

Cordless DECT telephone, Il Telefono Alessi

Stefano Giovannoni with Siemens
Double-injected transparent PMMA plastic, opaque ABS plastic interior
H: 7.1cm (2 ³/₄in)
W: 13.8cm (5 ¼in)
L: 20.2cm (8in)
Siemens AG, Germany
www.siemens.com

'Il Telefono Alessi' by Stefano Giovannoni is the first collaboration between Alessi and an industrial design manufacturer. Alberto Alessi believes that artistic creativity is too often sacrificed to the huge technological advances that have been made over the last decade. Appliances are becoming ever more homogenous and make little allowance for man's poetic capacity. Alessi was founded in 1921 by Alberto's grandfather, Giovanni. A skilled craftsman, he produced small metal objects for the house and kitchen. Alberto's father, Carlo, who trained as an industrial designer, brought the concept of contemporary design to the small artisanal company, working with international designers to create pieces such as the '870' cocktail shaker, which is still part of their catalogue today. Throughout the last thirty years, Alessi has become a research laboratory in the applied arts field, working with some of the major names in the design world. With the help of these designers the company has developed in a highly personal way, referring to itself as the 'dream factory', combining as it does creativity, culture, vision, modernity and design excellence with eccentricity, irony and humour. The chance to work with Siemens gave Alberto the opportunity to redress the balance between the vision of Alessi and the more prosaic concerns of a major industrial manufacturer.

Stefano Giovannoni has reinvented the cordless phone; no longer macho and phallic, the handset does not stand upright from the base but forms the top half of an interlocking horizontal and curvaceously female unit, as sensuous to look at as it is to touch. The base and the back of the handset are enveloped in an injected, transparent crystal-clear layer, giving an appearance of depth and adding a smooth and aesthetic finish to the surface. According to Alberto Alessi, 'The gigantic size of Siemens and the tiny one of Alessi, the technological dimension of the German industry and the poetic approach of the Italian factory might provide an effective new paradigm for the next phase in our consumer society.'

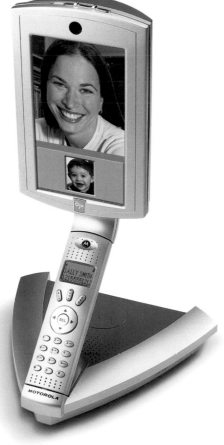

Personal video phone, Ojo™

WorldGate Communications, Inc
Injection-moulded plastic
H: 39cm (15 ³/₈in)
W: 23cm (9in)
D: 20cm (7 ⅞in)
WorldGate Communications Inc, USA
www.wgate.com

The 'Ojo ™' is the first videophone to work through a cable modem. It delivers video at an almost life-like thirty frames per second.

The Japanese love their gizmos and the young and trendy design-conscious Japanese youth also like those gizmos to be beautiful. **KDDI** have tapped into this market by producing a range of mobile phones through their sub-division 'au', which are both technologically advanced and fashion status symbols. The range includes the 'Infobar' by Naoto Fukasawa, the in-house 'CDMA 1X WIN W11K', and the latest, Makoto Saito's 'Penck'. All have a completely different aesthetic, but each shares an experimentation with form that turns the humble mobile phone into a perfectly designed object. Fukasawa wanted to personalize his phone, so the colours of the tile-like keys can be individually selected. He says, 'Mobiles are not just a communication tool, but a tool that expresses an individual's identity, and can be viewed as a fashion.'

The 'W11K' has broadband power with CDMA 1x WIN compatibility, advertised 'as the world in your hand', but it was designed more for its tactile quality than its function. Nowadays we are all so attached to our mobiles that we do not really like to have them out of our hands. We play with them, flip them open and closed, caress them and use them as a modern form of the worry bead. It is a relationship built up on touch and this is why the 'W11K' has been cut with such inviting facetted surfaces. However, the award for sensuousness must go to the 'Penck'. Its body is so soft and curved that you cannot resist running your fingers over it. It has an internal antenna and no visible display. It comes in three variations, and the most eye-catching one has its entire surface coated in metal plating. It is an item of luxury, a jewel. Conceived by the graphic designer Saito, it takes its influence from the drawings of the German artist A.R. Penck, after whom it is named. Functions include a high-quality screen and 3D surround stereo speakers, and a street-navigation system that works like the in-car version. These phones are only available in Japan but are well worth the trip to experience them.

Mobile phone, W11K
Naoto Fukasawa
Plastic
H: 10cm (3⁷⁄₈in)
W: 5cm (2in)
D: 3cm (1¹⁄₈in)
KDDI Corporation,
Casio Hitachi Mobile
Communications
Co. Ltd, Japan
www.au.kddi.com

Mobile phone, Penck
Makoto Saito
Plastic
H: 9.8cm (3⁷⁄₈in)
W: 5.7cm (2³⁄₈in)
D: 2.8cm (1¹⁄₈in)
KDDI Corporation,
Casio Hitachi Mobile
Communications
Co. Ltd, Japan
www.au.kddi.com

Mobile phone, Infobar
Naoto Fukasawa
Magnesium alloy,
polycarbonate,
ABS, acrylic
H: 13.8cm (5¹⁄₂in)
W: 4.2cm (1⁵⁄₈in)
D: 1.1cm (³⁄₈in)
KDDI Corporation,
Casio Hitachi Mobile
Communications
Co. Ltd, Japan
www.au.kddi.com

**USB device,
USB Bracelet**
Michael Young
Plasmocylene matter
Diam: 8cm (3 ¹/₈in)
Dem Inc, Taiwan
www.dem.com.tw

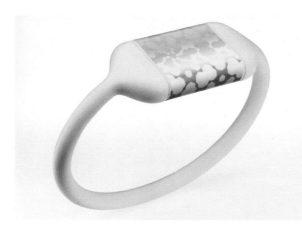

Michael Young is not afraid to take a chance. When he tired of the London design scene he moved to Iceland, where he said he could concentrate on his work in a more academic way; then he decided to open a second studio/home in Brussels, a more convenient location from which to work on the increasing number of projects he has been offered in Europe. Now that China is set to dominate design manufacturing, he has upped sticks and decamped to Taipei, where he has founded a new industrial design studio in collaboration with a young Taiwanese designer and entrepreneur, Yo-Bu-Chiang (who incidentally, but not terribly relevantly, is the grandson of Chiang Kai-Shek, famous nationalist opponent of Mao Tse Tung). Yo-Bu-Chiang's original company was called Spots, a division of which became MY-Spots after Michael joined, and is now known as DEM. Although in Chinese MY-Spots is considered a very cool name, Michael couldn't live with it any longer. The change of name has helped Michael create a new identity for the company, moulding it in the direction he wants it to go.

Michael Young's work has a retro-pop look about it. Using bold shapes and colours and interesting mixes of materials, his designs are at once aesthetically simple yet technically involved, and guaranteed to amuse without being silly or gimmicky. Since his move to China he has become increasingly involved in industrial and interior design. His new range of consumer electronics for DEM is intended for the 25- to 35-year-old market. It consists of objects that include a USB Bracelet, MP3 player and trendy watch, as well as pens, handbags, cigarette lighters, bottle-openers and even a baby's dummy. Again, the style is a perfect blend of retro and futuro, the lines being clean, fluid and modern. Already the products have created huge interest, 'quite massive' according to Michael. The young company is working on many things. 'The future is facing me now and I need to grab things while I can. At the moment we are working on bicycles and motorbikes.' I asked him where he thought the company was going. 'Well, as long as I can enjoy China it will be OK. It is very hard work living out here … bugs, dirt and heat, but in many ways it is a nice contrast to Europe. It is good to have the opportunity of working on serious industrial things which are not influenced by fashion, etc. … but I do miss a bit of glam …'.

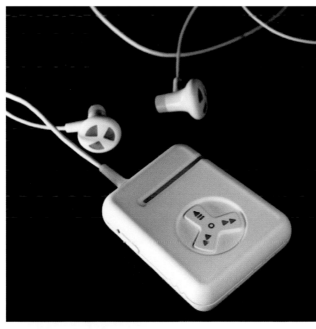

MP3 player, Qwark
Michael Young
Double-injection
moulded ABS with TPE
(thermoplastic
elastomer)
H: 1.65cm (³/₄in)
W: 5.2cm (2in)
L: 6.2cm (2 ³/₈in)
Dem Inc, Taiwan
www.dem.com.tw

**Network Walkman,
NW-E403/E405/E407**
Takayuki Kobayashi
Zinc die-cast, acrylic
H: 2.9cm (1¹/₈in)
W: 8.5cm (3 ³/₈in)
D: 1.6cm (⁵/₈in)
Sony Corporation, Japan
www.sony.net

Personal music player, iPod, 4th Generation
Apple Design Team
Polycarbonate/ABS
and stainless steel
H: 10.4cm (4 ¹/₈in)
W: 6.1cm (2 ³/₈in)
D (20 GB model):
1.6cm (⁵/₈in)
D (60 GB model):
1.9cm (³/₄in)
Apple Computer, Inc.,
USA
www.apple.com

Personal music player, iPod nano
Apple Design Team
Polycarbonate/ABS and
stainless steel
H: 8.9cm (3 ¹/₂in)
W: 4.1cm (1 ⁵/₈in)
D: 0.7cm (¹/₄in)
Apple Computer, Inc.,
USA
www.apple.com

MP3 player, Play
Norway Says
Plastic
H: 4.7cm (2in)
W: 3.7cm (1 ⁵/₈in)
D: 1.6cm (⁵/₈in)
Asono, Norway
www.asono.com

Personal music player, iPod mini
Apple Design Team
Aluminium
H: 9.1cm (3 ¹/₂in)
W: 5.1cm (2in)
D: 1.3cm (³/₈in)
Apple Computer, Inc.,
USA
www.apple.com

Is it correct to lump all Scandinavian design together? Espen Voll, Andreas Engesvik and Torbjørn Anderssen certainly do not think so. The group have worked together since 2000, when they impressed Milan with a range of furniture under the label **Norway Says**. They have now built up their product range to include textiles, glassware, lighting and porcelain. The company was incorporated in 2003, and quickly became a collaborative of firms and individuals from Norway as well as ex-pats (see page 206 for the 'Cityscape' rug designed by HIVE, who are based in London). The enterprising gang have now expanded into electronics, with the founders creating an ultra-light, slimline MP3 player for Asono. Wanting to stay clear of any comparison with the iconic iPod, while still staying true to a reductionist Norwegian aesthetic, they have produced an electrical product that has more to do with clothing or jewellery than with gadgetry. The player is no bigger than a matchbox (the team worked closely with a Korean factory specializing in electronic parts in order to keep all the working parts as tiny as possible), and can be worn around the neck like a locket. There are no graphics to describe the control buttons, and the profile of the player tapers neatly towards the display end, where an LCD screen can be programmed in eight different colours according to mood or preference. The front has one centrally placed joystick to easily navigate power, volume and selection, while the back houses three further buttons: one for recording, one for mode locking and the third for mode selection. Everything has been kept minimal and simple to emphasize the design rather than the function of the mini-player. For now it comes in white, grey and red, with Levi's running a special-edition programme in black. The product will also be sold under the Sharp label in Asia.

**Network Walkman,
NW–HD3**
Takatoshi Nakamura
Aluminium
H: 6.2cm (2 ³/₈in)
W: 9cm (3 ¹/₂in)
D: 1.5cm (⁵/₈in)
Sony Corporation, Japan
www.sony.net

Reproducing both MP3-
coded and Altrac3plus
files, the latest Sony MP3
player, the 'NW–HD3',
can store the equivalent
of 13,000 tracks or
900 CDs.

**Speakers and sound
diffusion systems,
Oh by tutondo**
Valentina Lollio and
José Merla Laguna
Aluminium, fabric
Diam: 14.9cm (5 ⁷/₈in)
ATEC srl, Italy
www.ohbytutondo.com

The 'Oh by tutondo'
speakers come in a range
of interchangeable
colours and are suitable
for outdoor use.

**Transistor radio,
Bush TR130
(relaunched)**
Tom Karen
Leather-effect plastic,
metal
H: 18cm (7in)
W: 32cm (12 ¹/₂in)
D: 9cm (3 ¹/₂in)
Bush, UK
www.bush-radio.co.uk

The 'TR130' was the UK's
best-selling radio in the
1960s. Bush relaunched
this model in time for the
2002 World Cup.

Powered speaker system for iPod, Bose SoundDock™ digital music system
Bose Design Center
Injection-moulded polycarbonate, metal
H: 16.9cm (6 ³⁄₄in)
W: 30.3cm (11 ³⁄₄in)
D: 16.46cm (6 ¹⁄₄in)
Bose Corporation, USA
www.bose.com

The Bose 'SoundDock™' was engineered specifically for Apple. Simply insert the iPod and listen to your favourite songs in Bose quality sound. The docking cradle recharges the iPod while it is playing. There are no cables or adapters.

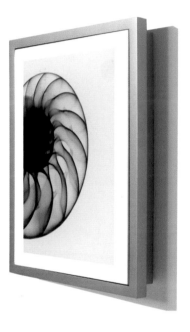

Flat wall-hanging loudspeakers with interchangeable screen of your choice, Artcoustic Loudspeaker DF65-50
Kim Donvig
MDF, fabric, drive units
H: 65cm (25 ⁵⁄₈in)
W: 50cm (19 ⁵⁄₈in)
D: 7.2cm (2 ³⁄₄in)
Artcoustic Loudspeakers, Denmark
www.artcoustic.com

The Danish company Artcoustic's **DF series** of flat speakers looks more like pieces of art than audio equipment. The speakers are customized by covering the front screen in a variety of fabrics and designs. An exclusive contract with the Getty image gallery at the Hulton Picture Library allows the company access to over 350,000 prints. Alternatively, for a fully personalized system, you can nominate your favourite reproduction or digital photograph from your own archives. The audio quality of the speakers is such that they are often used in cinemas and studios.

Wireless speaker
Kyoko Inoda + Nils Sveje Architecture and Design Studio
Resin-reinforced chalk
W: 20cm (7 ⁷⁄₈in)
D: 14.3cm (5in)
L: 20cm (7 ⁷⁄₈in),
Limited batch production,
One Off, Italy
www.oneoff.it

The Japanese/Danish duo Kyoko Inoda and Nils Sveje have updated 'His Master's Voice'. Their **wireless speaker** may look like a tennis ball but it can play the tones of any musical device, from stereo to computer, wherever and whenever needed.

Console, satellites, Acoustimass® module, remote control, Bose Lifestyle® 48 DVD Home Entertainment System
Bose Design Center
Injection-moulded ABS, metal, vinyl, MDF
Various dimensions
Bose Corporation, USA
www.bose.com

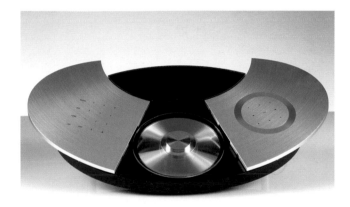

The 'Lifestyle® 48' digitally stores and organizes up to 340 hours of music in the media centre. The ADAPTiQ audio calibration system analyses your room and adjusts the system's sound according to size, shape, textures and other elements that affect the sound you hear. A Bose link allows connections for compatible products in as many as fourteen additional rooms. The uMusic intelligent playback system actually listens to and learns your preferences, and automatically makes selections based on what you like.

CD, radio and DVD player (master unit), BeoCenter 2
David Lewis
Brushed aluminium
H: 5cm (2in)
W: 37.2cm (14 ⁵⁄₈in)
D: 24.3cm (9 ¹⁄₂in)
Bang & Olufsen, Denmark
www.bang-olufsen.com

Looking like a robotic insect from the set of *Alien*, a gentle touch opens up the metallic wings of the 'BeoCenter' to reveal an integrated CD-DVD player. The wings close again automatically as soon as the player starts, returning this state-of-the-art piece of equipment to its elegant elliptical form. The single remote control operates all Bang & Olufsen's products. Cabling is rolled up into a separate unit that is easily hidden away, allowing uncluttered display of the BeoCenter on a wall, table top or pedestal.

CD player
Naoto Fukasawa
Plastic
H: 17cm (6 ⁵⁄₈in)
W: 17cm (6 ⁵⁄₈in)
D: 4cm (1 ⁵⁄₈in)
Muji, Japan
www.muji.net

Marcel Wanders has turned his hand to electronics. His line of home entertainment products for **Holland Electro**, 'HE', a Dutch brand made famous by its vacuum cleaners, was launched at IFA Berlin in September 2005. Never one to design the obvious, each item hides cutting-edge technology behind a patterned domestic aesthetic. Speakers, home cinema, music centres and transmitters are cunningly disguised as wooden side tables and objets d'art.

'Theatre': a side table with integrated home cinema. A DVD and central speaker are built into the left side, and a subwoofer on the right. It comes with four highly decorated satellite speakers, 'Egg'.

'Pandora': a side table with integrated woofer and two wireless speakers. It generates a 2.1 stereo sound for music on a laptop or MP3 player.

'Merlin' and 'Mathilda': two transmitters receiving wireless audio signals which can send music from a laptop or MP3 player to speakers 'Egg' or 'Domino'. The former has a USB connector and the latter a 3.5mm plug using batteries.

'Wave TV': a microwave that has an integrated TV screen in the door as well as a DVD player.

Multi-media system, Pandora
Marcel Wanders
Wood
H: 17.5cm (6 ⁷/₈in)
W: 35cm (13 ³/₄in)
L: 35cm (13 ³/₄in)
HE Electronics –
Boxford Holland BV,
the Netherlands
www.he-marcel
wanders.com

USB wireless personal sound system transmitter, Merlin
Marcel Wanders
Plastic
H: 1.3cm (³/₈in)
W: 8.8cm (3 ¹/₂in)
L: 2.5cm (1in)
HE Electronics –
Boxford Holland BV,
the Netherlands
www.he-marcel
wanders.com

Wireless sound transmitter, Mathilda
Marcel Wanders
Plastic
H: 3cm (1 ¹/₈in)
W: 5.4cm (2 ¹/₈in)
L: 7cm (2 ³/₄in)
HE Electronics –
Boxford Holland BV,
the Netherlands
www.he-marcel
wanders.com

Speaker system, Domino
Marcel Wanders
Wood
H: 24cm (9 ¹/₂in)
W: 6.5cm (2 ¹/₂in)
L: 22.5 or 15.5cm (9 or 6 ¹/₈in)
HE Electronics –
Boxford Holland BV,
the Netherlands
www.he-marcel
wanders.com

Speaker, Egg
Marcel Wanders
Plastic
H: 6.2cm (2 ³/₈in)
Diam: 12.4cm (4 ⁷/₈in)
HE Electronics –
Boxford Holland BV,
the Netherlands
www.he-marcel
wanders.com

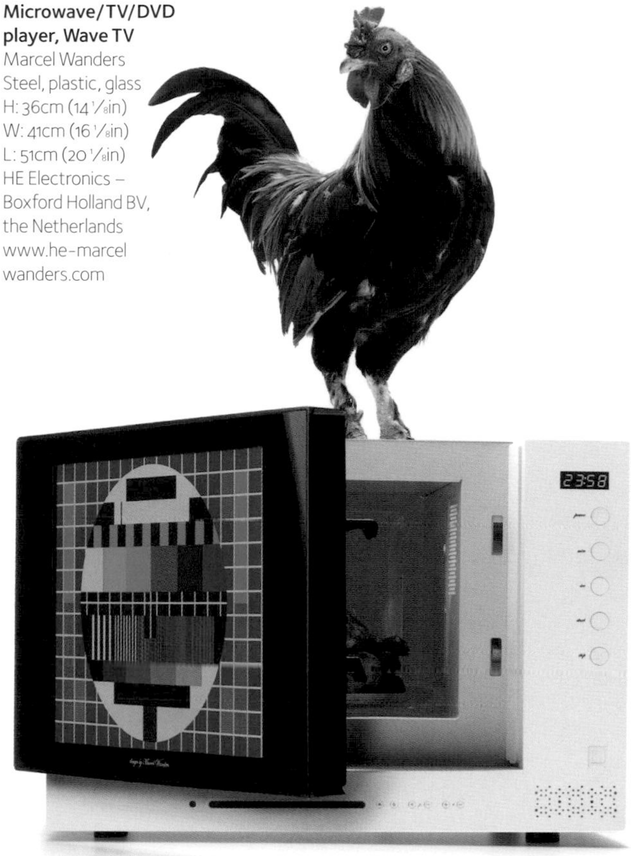

Microwave/TV/DVD player, Wave TV
Marcel Wanders
Steel, plastic, glass
H: 36cm (14 1/8in)
W: 41cm (16 1/8in)
L: 51cm (20 1/8in)
HE Electronics – Boxford Holland BV, the Netherlands
www.he-marcelwanders.com

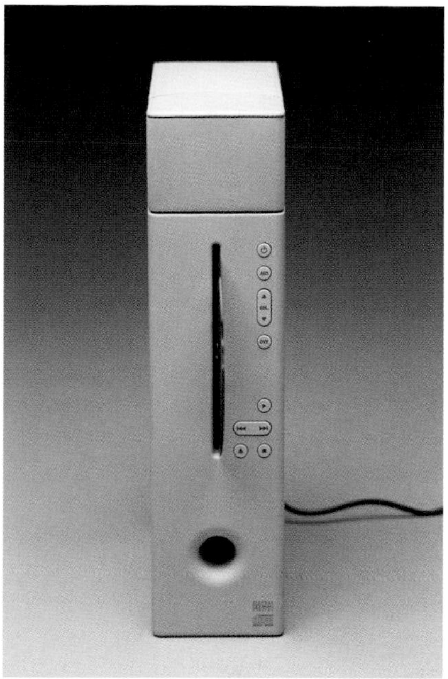

CD player, Bookshelf
Muji Design Team
Plastics, electronics
H: 31.5cm (12 5/8in)
W: 7.8cm (3 1/8in)
D: 20.4cm (7 7/8in)
Muji, Japan
www.muji.net

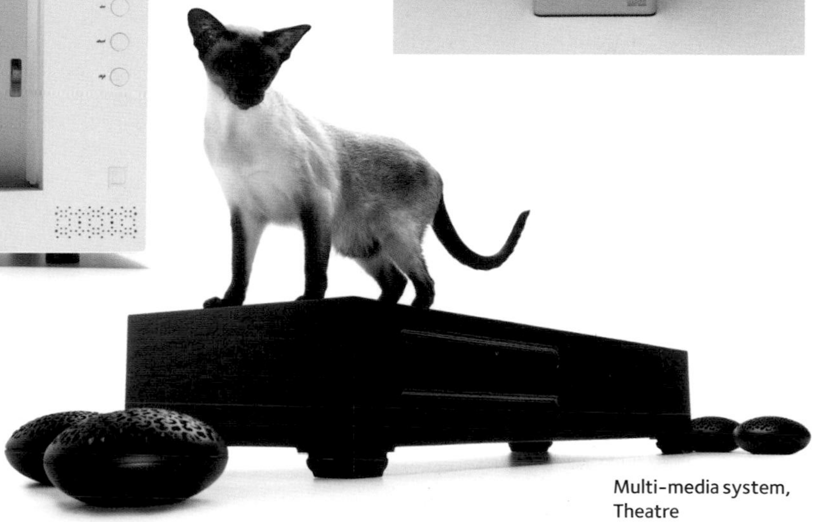

Multi-media system, Theatre
Marcel Wanders
Wood
H: 17.5cm (6 7/8in)
W: 32cm (12 5/8in)
L: 100cm (39in)
HE Electronics – Boxford Holland BV, the Netherlands
www.he-marcelwanders.com

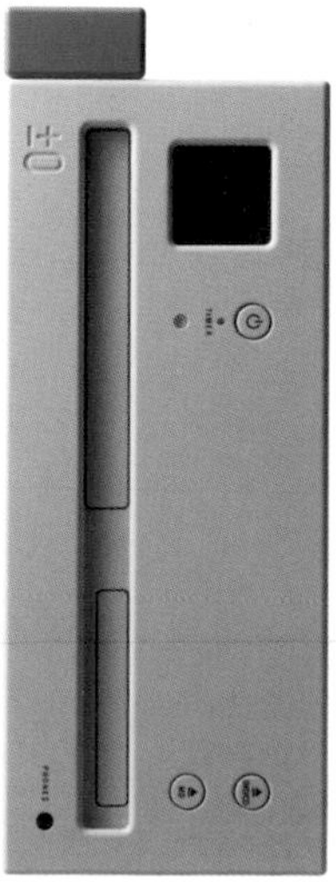

DVD/MD Stereo Component
Naoto Fukasawa
Polycarbonate, ABS
H: 27.5cm (11in)
W: 11.2cm (4 3/8in)
D: 26.3cm (10 1/4in)
Plusminuszero Co. Ltd, Japan
www.plusminuszero.jp

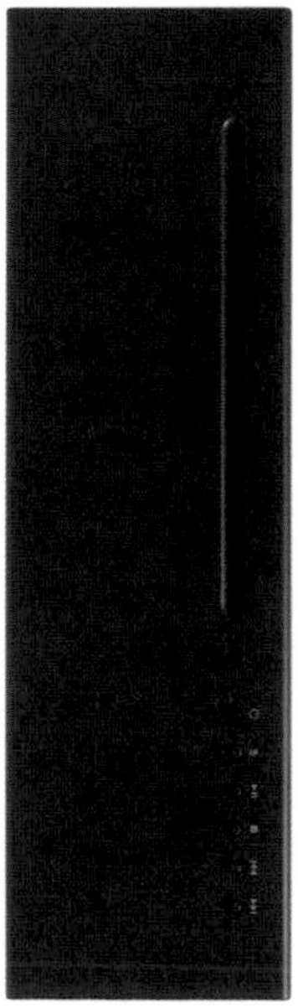

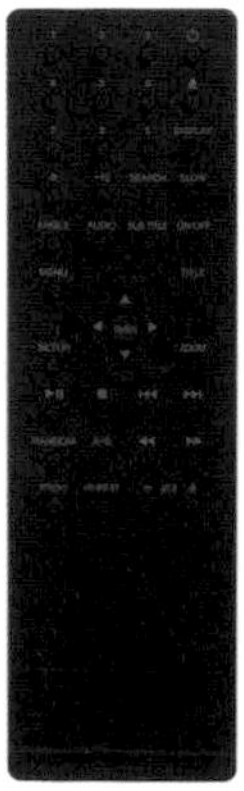

DVD player
Muji Design Team
Metal, plastic
H: 25.7cm (10 1/4in)
W: 7.5cm (3in)
D: 18.2cm (7 1/8in)
Muji, Japan
www.muji.net

Wall-mounted home server with socket, Com Station Internal Double

Toshihiko Sakai
ABS, aluminium
H: 12cm (4 ³/₄in)
W: 11.6cm (4 ¹/₂in)
D: 0.5cm (¹/₄in)
Comfortable
Communications Co.,
Ltd, Japan
www.com2.jp

Toshihiko Sakai is one of a handful of Japanese industrial designers who work independently but are called in by big companies looking for fresh ideas. The 125mm 'Com Projector' is one of the twenty-two micro appliances he developed for ComCom (Comfortable Communications), which are controlled by one remote. All are technically complicated but have been given a clean, white, simple aesthetic. The light switches and plug sockets belong to the audio-visual line Sakai also developed for ComCom. They include a hard disk and USB port, and can store music and movies or send them to other products. In addition, the double socket incorporates a built-in extension lead.

Home entertainment device, Moviebeam receiver and remote

Yves Béhar, Fuseproject
Injection-moulded ABS
H: 11.4cm (4 ¹/₂in)
W: 30.5cm (12in)
L: 30.5cm (12in)
Buenavista Datacasting,
USA
www.fuseproject.com

The 'Moviebeam' receiver and remote by Yves Béhar for Buenavista uses conventional FM signals to download, store and then play movies for a negligible monthly fee. Although John R. Hoke III, Nike's vice president and global creative director of footwear design, recently referred to Yves Béhar as 'a fantastic design force … [who's] about to explode on to the world scene', Béhar has actually been making his mark since the late 1990s, when he designed the distinctive and well-publicized accessories that surrounded the launch of the new Mini Cooper. Unlike most automobile logo-based items, 'Mini-Motion' concentrated instead on products that could be owned by people with or without the car itself. Recently, however, Béhar's profile has risen to such an extent that in 2004 he was honoured with a solo show at the San Francisco Museum of Modern Art, which he referred to as a 'futurspective' rather than a 'retrospective' (and for which, incidentally, he designed a smart shoe, complete with a chip that collected data on the wearer during their visit to the exhibition).

Yves Béhar, design principal and founder of Fuseproject, is a multi-disciplinary industrial designer whose clients include Herman Miller, Nike, Birkenstock and Microsoft. He believes that his products should influence how design permeates culture; they should not only have lasting impact and be technologically sound, but should also communicate on a personal level with users, making them question the functioning of an object or why and how an item of clothing should be worn. If this connection is made, Béhar argues, it can only be good for business, because the stronger and more complex the link with the consumer, the longer lasting customer loyalty will be. The opening message on Béhar's website is 'Design Brings Stories to Life', and his work is dedicated to creating narratives to develop our emotional experience of well-known brands. His most recent research is a non-product-based investigation into consumers' perception of brands.

Projector, Com Projector

Toshihiko Sakai
ABS, aluminium
H: 12.5cm (4 ⁷/₈in)
W: 5.6cm (2 ¹/₈in)
D: 5.8cm (2 ³/₈in)
Comfortable
Communications Co.,
Ltd, Japan
www.com2.jp

Digital projector, PX3
3M Design
Metal
H: 3.5cm (1 3/8in)
3M, USA
www.mmm.com

DVD player, DVD Tablet
DB-Line
LCD screen
H: 15.5cm (6 1/8in)
W: 20cm (7 7/8in)
D: 2.5cm (1in)
Joytech, USA
www.joytech.net

The tiny 'DVD Tablet' incorporates an LCD screen (which contains a hidden slot for the DVDs), and high-quality integral Dolby Digital stereo speakers, guaranteeing crystal-clear images and perfect sound.

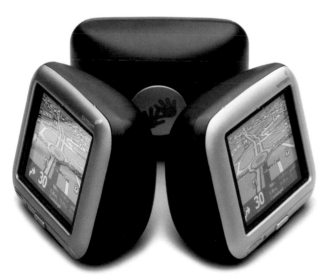

Navigation solution (GPS), TomTom GO 700
Therefore
PC, ABS
H: 8.8cm (3 1/2in)
W: 14.4cm (5 1/2in)
D: 5.7cm (2 3/8in)
TomTom International BV, the Netherlands
www.tomtom.com

**Air conditioner,
Cool Curtain**
Jozeph Forakis
Textile, satin-aluminium
H: 180cm (71in)
W: 80cm (31in)
D: 15cm (5 7/8in)
LG Electronics, Korea
www.lge.com

While internationally recognized as a producer of innovative electronics, **Philips** believes in 'humanware' not 'hardware'. When the company first became involved in the mass production of consumer goods in the 1920s, its then managing director Louis Kalff carried out market research to discover the differences in consumers' tastes worldwide so that these considerations could be added to Philips's already revolutionary designs. Not until 1980, when Robert Blaich was made director of Philips Industrial Design Bureau, was a policy developed whereby design of any product was not only to be utilitarian and pragmatic, but also to address the more private and personal demands of the modern consumer.

Stefano Marzano (managing director of Philips Design since 1991) is the creator of 'High Design', which takes this concept one step further. 'High Design' is a philosophy that is propagated throughout the whole company. Marzano believes that many human values have been lost from the world. Industrial design has become preoccupied with flashy gimmickry and less concerned with the needs of the consumer. He quotes Ezio Manzini of the Domus Academy: 'We have forgotten that objects are creatures produced by our spiritual sensibilities and by our practical abilities.' Marzano considers that generally people are scared of technology, and that as MD of Philips Design he is responsible for allaying that fear. By using more traditional shapes and working with a research team of sociologists, anthropologists and psychologists to maintain a human focus, Philips has bridged the gap between technology and 'the man in the street'. His aim is to create a corporate identity that 'fathers meaningful objects that support people in their daily tasks, express the values they believe in, and stimulate their emotions and creativity'.

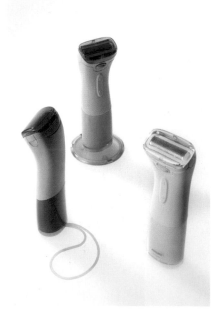

**Ladyshave, Philips
Ladyshave HP6317-19**
Philips Design
ABS, SEBS
H: 15cm (5 7/8in)
W: 4cm (1 5/8in)
D: 3cm (1 1/8in)
Royal Philips Electronics,
the Netherlands
www.philips.com

Who is **Naoto Fukasawa** and where did he come from? A couple of years ago there was hardly a trace of him, yet today it is impossible to open a design magazine without reading about him – which cannot be making him very happy. Interviewed by the e-magazine *Designboom* he has been quoted as saying, 'I like when a project doesn't sell my name or my characteristic, when it is just an object that happens to be there.' Throughout the 1990s he was in-house designer for IDEO, setting up their Japanese branch in 1997 and anonymously working away to change the way we think about Japanese electronic products. Similarly, he built up an exciting range for Muji when he joined their advisory board in 1999, from which time dates his now-famous wall-hanging CD player (see page 301). In 2003 he founded his own electronics company, Plusminuszero, which was such a hit during Tokyo Designers Block in 2004.

Fukasawa's collection of simple, accessible but extremely beautiful designs liberates electronics from impenetrable technicality without resorting to patronizing over-simplification. 'Good design means not leaving traces of the designer and not overworking the design,' he writes. His work employs what the head of IDEO refers to as 'New Rationalism', whereby an object may look 'elegant and laid back but has that something extra – an engagement, an entertainment value or something exciting happening inside'. Fukasawa takes his inspiration from experience. As lecturer in the product department of the Tama Art University in Tokyo, his workshops often have the title 'Without Thought'. His premise is that as design is informed by our subconscious movements and the environment, the process takes time to be thought through clearly. Often we react emotively to something, thinking it is what we need, but it is only when the object is tested that the realization dawns that there is something missing. That something is the very essence of the product itself. It has been designed 'without thought'. His creations all share the same characteristic – a relationship between technology and human behaviour, 'design dissolving in behaviour' as he likes to call it.

The Plusminuszero range that Fukasawa developed with Keita Satoh of Takaram (the Japanese toy manufacturer that brought us 'Bowlingual', a box which translates dog barks into Japanese) consists of products that are fun without being gimmicky, with stripped bare aesthetics. They have a playful element that never slips into parody – an LCD TV in the shape of a cathode ray tube, a DVD player that is encased in lacquered wood instead of the normal metallic finish we associate with such products and a humidifier that recalls a large drop of water. On the back of this success, Fukasawa is branching out with a range of furniture for B&B Italia, and in the pipeline are designs for cars and motorcycles.

LCD projector, NEC VT70 Series VT470
Naoto Fukasawa
Polycarbonate, ABS
H: 11cm (4 ³/₈in)
W: 29.4cm (11 ³/₈in)
D: 28cm (11in)
NEC Viewtechnology, Ltd, Japan
www.nevt.co.jp

Humidifier
Naoto Fukasawa
Polycarbonate, polypropylene
H: 15cm (5 ⁷/₈in)
Diam: 29.5cm (11 ³/₄in)
Plusminuszero Co. Ltd, Japan
www.plusminuszero.jp

8-inch LCD TV
Naoto Fukasawa
Polycarbonate, ABS
H: 17.3cm (6 ³/₄in)
W: 21.4cm (8 ¹/₄in)
D: 17.1cm (6 ³/₄in)
Plusminuszero Co. Ltd, Japan
www.plusminuszero.jp

LCD TV, Spheros 37
Phoenix Design
Varnished plastic,
varnished metal, glass,
brushed aluminium
H: 67cm (26 ³/₈in)
W: 99cm (39in)
D: 9cm (3 ¹/₂in)
Loewe Opta GmbH,
Germany
www.loewe.de

DLP projection TV,
DLP Profile Scenium 5
Tim Thom
Polystyrene
H: 122cm (48in)
L: 158cm (62in)
D: 17.4cm (6 ⁷/₈in)
Thomson, France
www.thomson.fr

Flat TV, Philips
Ambilight FTV
Top 42PF9966
Philips Design
Polycarbonate, ABS
H: 75.5cm (29 ⁷/₈in)
W: 124.5cm (49in)
D: 96 cm (38in)
Royal Philips Electronics,
the Netherlands
www.philips.com

**Wall panel,
LCD/Plasma TV Panel**
Bruno Fattorini
Polished aluminium
H: 189cm (74in)
L: 80, 100 or 120cm
(31, 39 or 47in)
MDF Italia srl, Italy
www.mdfitalia.it

This is a stylish way to
store your latest
plasma TV. **MDF** have
developed a self-
supporting polished
aluminium panel with
CD, DVD and computer
sockets. All the cables
are invisible, housed
behind the panel, and
require no wall ducts.

**LCD monitor, Philips
190B4 LCD**
Philips Design
ABS, paint
H: 37.7cm (15in)
W: 42.5cm (16 ⁷/₈in)
D: 6.5cm (2 ¹/₂in)
Royal Philips Electronics,
the Netherlands
www.philips.com

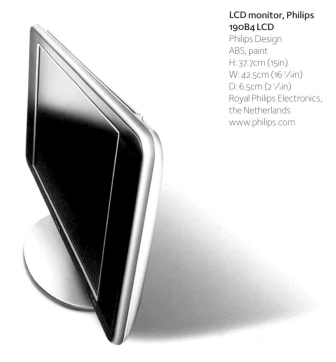

LCD TV, LC-32GD1E
Toshiyuki Kita
Plastic, stainless steel
H: 63.8cm (25 ¹/₄in)
W: 79.5cm (31in)
D: 30.7cm (12 ¹/₄in)
Sharp Corporation, Japan
www.sharp-world.com
www.sharp.co.jp

**Laptop, Averatec
1000 series**
Averatec design team
ABS, magnesium
W: 20.2cm (7 ⁷/₈in)
D: 2.9cm (1 ¹/₈in)
L: 26.6cm (10 ⁵/₈in)
Averatec, Taiwan
www.averatec.com

**Desktop computer,
iMac G5**
Apple Design Team
Injection-moulded
polycarbonate/ABS
H: 43cm (16 ⁷/₈in)
W: 42.6cm (16 ⁷/₈in)
D: 17.3cm (6 ³/₄in)
Apple Computer, Inc.,
USA
www.apple.com

**Notebook PC,
Portege M200**
Satoshi Araki
Magnesium alloy
H: 3.84cm (1 ⁵/₈in)
W: 32.8cm (13in)
D: 28.97cm (11 ³/₈in)
Toshiba Corporation,
Personal Computer &
Network Company,
Japan
www.toshiba.co.jp

**High-definition LCD
PC/TV displays,
MFM-HT95**
Hiroaki Yokota
ABS resin, aluminium
H: 43.7cm (17 ³/₈in)
W: 46.66cm (18 ¹/₄in)
D: 18.5cm (7 ¹/₄in)
Sony Corporation, Japan
www.sony.net

Computer peripherals/ networking box (for the home), Netgear Platinum II
Newdealdesign LLC (Gadi Amit, Yoshi Hoshino, Bryan Grziwok, Mike Massucco)
Injection-moulded ABS, Mylar label
H: 17.2cm (6 ³⁄₄in)
W: 11.4cm (4 ¹⁄₂in)
D: 2.7cm (1in)
Netgear Inc, USA
www.newdealdesign.com

Computer accessories are often boring and utilitarian in design. The 'Netgear Platinum II' communication box, which houses a Wi-Fi board, is anything but. Sitting alongside the home PC or entertainment system, it is understated but, unlike the usual bland boxes, draws attention to itself by a clever use of light and material. The exterior band has two layers: the inner one of a mirror material and the outer one made from clear plastic in the shape of a lens. The combination of these two layers creates an optical effect. The housing reflects the colour and textures of the surroundings, while the mirror projects a band of light around the perimeter of the product, an effect that contrasts with the generic shadow found around similar products. The stand, which enables the box to be used vertically as well as horizontally, lends a quirky, almost cartoon effect to this little box.

Computer display, Cinema Display
Apple Design Team
Aluminium
Various dimensions (3 sizes)
Apple Computer, Inc., USA
www.apple.com

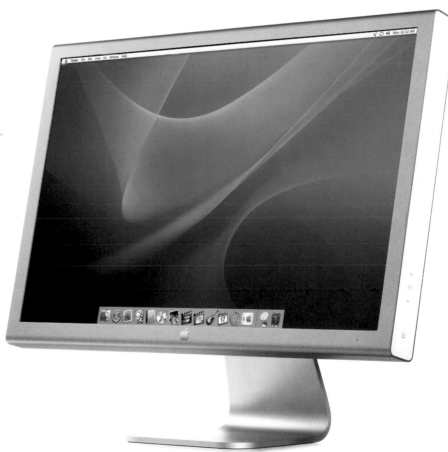

Desktop computer, Mac mini
Apple Design Team
Aluminium, polycarbonate
H: 5.08cm (2 ³⁄₈in)
W: 16.5cm (6 ¹⁄₂in)
D: 16.5cm (6 ¹⁄₂in)
Apple Computer, Inc., USA
www.apple.com

Notebook PC, Qosmio G10
Tadashi Kurokawa and Manabu Tago
Polycarbonate, ABS
H: 4.1cm (1 ⁵/₈in)
W: 40.6cm (16 ¹/₈in)
D: 28.5cm (11 ³/₈in)
Toshiba Corporation, Personal Computer & Network Company, Japan
www.toshiba.co.jp

VAIO notebook computer, PCG-X505
Yujin Morisawa
Carbon fibre, magnesium
H: 9.7cm (3 ³/₄in)
W: 25.9cm (10 ¹/₄in)
D: 20.8cm (8 ¹/₄in)
Sony Corporation, Japan
www.sony.co.jp

LCD monitor, FP785
BenQ
LCD flat panel with metal and plastic body and stand
H: 50cm (19 ⁵/₈in)
W: 38cm (15in)
D: 5.5cm (2 ¹/₈in)
BenQ, UK
www.benq.co.uk

Winner of the communication-entertainment section of the IF Design Award, the 'BenQ FP785' LCD monitor has a unique grip that swivels through 180 degrees to act as a stand. At 3.5 centimetres (1½ inches) the screen is half the normal thickness.

**Flatbed scanner,
Canon CanoScan
LiDE 500F**
Naofumi Sekine,
Yoshinori Inukai, Design
Center, Canon Inc
ABS, PC, glass, metal
H: 3.5cm (1 ³⁄₈in)
W: 28cm (11in)
D: 39.7cm (15 ³⁄₄in)
Canon Inc, Japan
www.canon.jp

**Laptop, Toshiba
transformer laptop**
Yves Béhar with
Geoffrey Petrizzi,
Shawn Sinyork and
Pichaya Puttorngul
Injection-moulded ABS
H: 4cm (1 ⁵⁄₈in)
W: 41cm (16 ¹⁄₈in)
D: 25cm (9 ⁷⁄₈in)
Toshiba, Japan
www.toshiba.co.jp

Yves Béhar

**Which of your designs to date would you like
to be remembered by?**
'Inner Light', a project about love that I did for UNESCO
and the San Francisco Museum of Modern Art.

How do you think others view your work?
I am not sure ... hopefully as eclectic and poetic, but
at the end of the day, one cannot control others'
perceptions, so it is best to simply put my best foot
forward with sincerity.

**Which designer has influenced you the most
and why?**
Achille Castiglioni, a man of humour and wit. He was
not a slave to style, but rather a man of ideas ...
beautiful and free ideas.

**If you were not a designer, what would you like
to be and why?**
I would love to be telling stories in a different medium in
the tradition of the 'raconteur', as a writer or filmmaker.

**What role do you think the designer has in
society today?**
I feel that it is a designer's responsibility to show what
the future could be, rather than wait for the way
industry wants it to be. When done with sincerity and
integrity, experimental projects often lead to real
products. Experimental projects are first and foremost
ways to envision possibilities, to create a direction for
the present to follow. Usefulness can be about function
... but inspiring, resting the soul, creating a sense of
wonder and intelligence around one's life is a form of
usefulness that goes beyond function.

Do you buy a lot of design pieces?
Sometimes ... today I mostly like odd pieces and
prototypes.

**Is there a design in your home that you couldn't
live without?**
My large and very comfortable bean bag.

**What do you consider to be the best piece of
design since the millennium?**
Ron Arad's latest Swarovski 'Crystal Palace' chandelier.

**Where do you think design is heading? Is there
someone we should be watching out for?**
My fear is that companies will jump onto the 'design'
bandwagon and bring a lot of resurfaced, shiny
objects to the market, an effort that will inevitably fail
if these products neglect to deliver great ideas. This
undoubtedly would give design a bad name. What I
look for is a sense of wonder, a pause from the
commercialization of everything ... I also stay away
from a visual style, a clear signature, as I believe that
in order to be relevant today, one needs to constantly
evolve: style is commercial, ideas are not.

**Is the cult of the personality taking over the
design world?**
Personalities have always been a big part of the design,
architecture and art world ... as long as personalities
produce ethical work, I salute the effort: if it is not
ethical, it cannot be beautiful.

Inkjet printer, Canon PIXMA iP5000
Naoki Tashiro, Design Center, Canon Inc
ABS, PS
H: 17cm (6 ³/₄in)
W: 41.8cm (16 ¹/₂in)
D: 28.6cm (11 ³/₈in)
Canon Inc, Japan
www.canon.jp

Digital camera, Canon Digital IXUS 700
Hisakazu Shimizu, Design Center, Canon Inc
Stainless steel, plastic
H: 5.7cm (2 ³/₈in)
W: 8.9cm (3 ¹/₂in)
D: 2.7cm (1 ¹/₈in)
Canon Inc, Japan
www.canon.jp

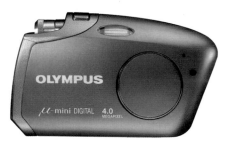

Digital camera, Olympus μ-mini DIGITAL S
Olympus Design Team
Weatherproof metal
H: 5.6cm (2 ¹/₈in)
W: 2.8cm (1 ¹/₈in)
L: 9.5cm (3 ¹/₂in)
Olympus, Japan
www.olympus.com

A single sheet of liquid metal is transformed into the sleek form of this Olympus camera. Cutting-edge technology includes a new zoom with three lenses and thirteen programs, one that deals with problem situations such as candlelight, sunsets and fireworks.

Printer, Kodak EasyShare Printer Dock Plus
Eastman Kodak Company
Metal, plastic
H: 18.8cm (7 ¹/₂in)
W: 33.4cm (13in)
D: 8.3 cm (3 ¹/₈in)
Eastman Kodak Company, USA
www.kodak.com

Digital compact camera, Pentax Optio WP
Pentax Corporation
Glass lenses, plastic
H: 5.1cm (2in)
W: 10.2cm (3 ⁷/₈in)
D: 2.2cm (¹/₄in)
Pentax Corporation, Japan
www.pentax.co.jp

**Digital camera,
Leica D-Lux**
Achim Heine
Anodized aluminium
H: 5.2cm (2in)
W: 12.1cm (4³/₄in)
D: 3.4cm (1¹/₈in)
Leica Camera AG,
Germany
www.leica-camera.com

**Wearable digital
camera, Philips
KEY007**
Philips Design
Plastic, stainless steel,
chrome plating
H: 8.6cm (3¹/₂in)
W: 2.8cm (1¹/₈in)
D: 1.6cm (³/₄in)
Royal Philips Electronics,
the Netherlands
www.philips.com

The **Philips 'KEY007'**
digital camera can take
up to 200 photos of
2-megapixel quality
and record 25 minutes
of continuous video.
The USB plug and play
connection downloads
to a PC in just a few
seconds so that it can
also be used as an
external memory for
transferring data and
documents from one
PC to another.

**Camcorder,
D SNAP SV–AV50**
Panasonic
Metal
H: 10cm (3⁷/₈in)
W: 4.9cm (2in)
D. 2cm (³/₄in)
Panasonic, UK
www.panasonic.co.uk

**Digital SLR camera,
Canon EOS 350D
DIGITAL**
Seiichi Omino, Design
Center, Canon Inc
Engineering plastics,
metals
H: 9.4cm (3¹/₂in)
W: 12.7cm (5¹/₈in)
D: 6.4cm (2³/₈in)
Canon Inc, Japan
www.canon.jp

Miscellaneous

Michael Young

Which of your designs to date would you like to be remembered by?
Most of them mean a lot to me, but I guess the 'PXR-5' watch would be a good one since it is perpetually functional, it's not a function that can date as such.

How do you think others view your work?
Love and hate has always been the response to my work, which is good for me as the people whom I care about normally like it and it gives me pleasure that it irritates others.

Which designer has influenced you the most and why?
Hitting the nail on a head I would say that Starck has been inspirational because he has opened up the vision between industry and thinkers; he made me, and millions of others, realize anything is possible.

If you were not a designer, what would you like to be and why?
Other than design I can only lounge by a pool and drink champagne. I am not cut out for anything more than that; I can't lift a finger but I can walk a dog.

What role do you think the designer has in society today?
To create purposeful objects that generate economy, or inspire others to do so.

Do you buy a lot of design pieces?
Not really. I have them but mainly from companies I work with. I did buy an Eames lounger recently which will be my retirement chair, but on the whole, since I'm living all over the world, I like to buy non-design things, which are often more inspiring.

Is there a design in your home that you couldn't live without?
Like many people, the one thing that holds everything in my life is my little Apple PowerBook laptop.

What do you consider to be the best piece of design since the millennium?
I guess most Apple products since they have helped create a new way of living that is very efficient for a very broad group of people.

Where do you think design is heading? Is there someone we should be watching out for?
Right now I'm living in China and am getting asked to design a lot for Chinese companies. I keep this in balance by helping European companies in Asia, but I expect others will be less thoughtful. Asian business and investment in design production is very fluid and not obstructed by over-zealous marketing teams such as the ones that tend to slow up European industrial implementation. Europe had better pull its finger from its ass pretty fast.

Is the cult of the personality taking over the design world?
I live in design exile. I don't know or care about such mechanics.

Watch, PXR-5
Michael Young
Steel, canvas
W: 3.5cm (1³/₈in)
L: 5cm (2in)
Dem Inc, Taiwan
www.dem.com.tw

Watch, Kaj
Karim Rashid
Polyurethane, crystal mineral
H: 24cm (9¹/₂in)
W: 13cm (5¹/₈in)
D: 4cm (1⁵/₈in)
Alessi SpA, Italy
www.alessi.com

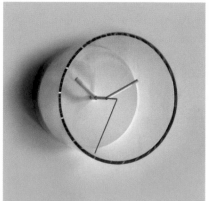

Clock, Space, Time
Sam Hecht
Acrylic, melamine
D: 17.5cm (6⁷/₈in)
Diam: 17.5cm (6⁷/₈in)
Habitat, UK
www.habitat.net

**Compass watch,
Altimer
(Oregon series)**
Scott Wilson and
Jason Martin
Solid forged aluminium
or titanium,
polyurethane,
mineral glass
D: 1.6cm (⅝in)
Diam: 5cm (2in)
Nike Inc, USA
www.nike.com

**Alarm clock and
weather station, the
Starck Collection**
Philippe Starck
Plastic, aluminium,
LCD screen
Various dimensions
Oregon Scientific,
France
www.oregonscientific.fr

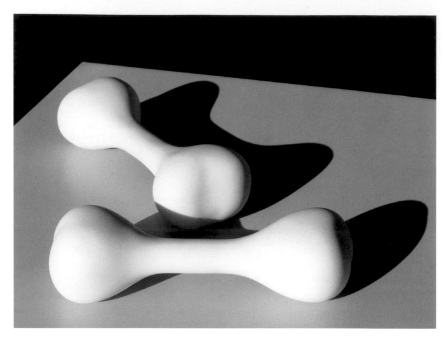

**Hand weights,
Foreveryoung**
Robert Stadler
Carrara statuario marble
3.5kg
Galerie Dominique Fiat,
France
www.radidesigners.com

**Entertainment robot,
AIBO ERS-7**
Yuka Takeda, Daisuke
Ishii, Taku Sugawara
and Jun Uchiyama
ABS, vegetable-based
plastic, silicone
H: 27.8cm (11in)
W: 18cm (7 ¹/₈in)
D: 31.9cm (12 ⁵/₈in)
Sony Corporation, Japan
www.sony.co.jp

Rather like a prostitute, '**AIBO ERS-7**' may greet you at your door with pre-programmed messages of welcome; it may cavort for pleasure with its many toys and will even preen under the caresses of your hand, but it will never love you. Although it is fine as a family pet or child's plaything, it is a rather negative comment on our technological, hectic (but ultimately rather lonely and alienating) twenty-first-century city existence. Sony describe their latest interactive robot in the following words: 'AIBO can see, hear, feel for itself and walk ... Through sharing your memories, learning your likes, getting to know your environment, AIBO will become in every way a truly unique individual. Entertaining and comforting you when you're glad, sad or angry. Reflecting a wide range of emotions through its uniquely LED-guided face, AIBO will become, in fact, your best friend.'

AIBO's 'character' is contained within its many cutting-edge software programs. It expresses itself through LEDs – blue for happy, red for angry – and lifelike body language. AIBO 'sees' due to a colour-vision camera mounted above its mouth. Equipped with face-recognition technology, the little robot will 'remember' your face and distinguish you from strangers. Infrared distance sensors next to the camera and on the main body help AIBO avoid obstacles and walk around your home. Your 'pet' feels through electric-static sensors on the crown of its head and will react to your strokes. Sensors on each paw enable AIBO to walk differently on different surfaces – it will even lift a paw to shake your hand. The chin is sensitive too, as is its back: stroke it and it will respond with its happy blue lights, tap it and its eyes will glow red. Stereo microphones mounted on either side help your little doggy listen and interact with you, and it will turn towards you when you issue a voice command. The centrepiece of AIBO's artificial intelligence is the 'MIND' software, located on a removable memory stick, which controls all behaviour as well as the applications that connect wirelessly with your PC or mobile. In short, there is little AIBO cannot do for you. It will take pictures either by transmitted command, or (more disturbingly) of its own accord, send e-mails and play back recorded messages to your family. It will reflect your own body rhythms and wake up and fall asleep when you do. It can locate its energy station and recharge without your help. It will entertain you with music and acrobatics and express its feelings with amusing sounds. What it will not do, however, is die for you, which of course is what we expect from man's best friend. AIBO is more likely to dance on your grave. Sadly, Sony have recently taken the decision to close their entire robot development department. After six years and sales of 150,000 units, AIBO is no longer in production. There's always eBay.

Marc Newson

Which of your designs to date would you like to be remembered by?
The completion of all the work I am doing for Qantas on the A380 fleet (the interiors, lounges and total design concept).

How do you think others view your work?
I guess someone likes it or clients wouldn't keep asking me to design stuff ...

Which designer has influenced you the most and why?
Bruno Munari.

If you were not a designer, what would you like to be and why?
I would have to make things – so I suppose a craftsperson.

What role do you think the designer has in society today?
To improve the quality of things.

Do you buy a lot of design pieces?
No.

Is there a design in your home that you couldn't live without?
No, not a design ... but many products I couldn't live without.

What do you consider to be the best piece of design since the millennium?
I don't know ... and I don't really care.

Where do you think design is heading?
It is difficult to look at design as an entity in itself. It is more appropriate to talk about the quality of design, and I'm not sure if it's getting any better. And it's so subjective anyway.

Is the cult of the personality taking over the design world?
No, I don't think so, although it is more prevalent than it was ten years ago. But I don't think it is overshadowing.

Vibrators

With Ann Summers and Agent Provocateur bringing female sexuality to the high street, the vibrator is no longer something that should be hidden away in the bedside cabinet but rather flaunted as art object on the dressing table. Both Tom Dixon's 'Bone' (is it a weight, a door stop or a piece of Brancusian sculpture?) and Marc Newson's 'Mojo' were designed for Myla, the UK-based chain of sex shops, and conceived for the design-savvy *Sex and The City* girl. 'If you're wearing Jimmy Choo shoes and carrying a Prada bag or using an orange press by Philippe Starck' said Charlotte Semlar, one of Myla's owners, 'why on earth would you want a conventional sex toy.' Seymour Powell's 'Little Gem' (discreetly intended to slip between the fingers and become an extension of the hand) is perhaps not quite so 'stylish' but its aesthetic still belies its function and it has lost all tacky reference to oversized male members. 'Objects like this should be precious, beautiful and hygienic, reflecting their intended purpose,' says Tom Dixon.

Sex toy, Mojo
Marc Newson
Silicone and ABS casting
H: 6cm (2 3/8in)
Diam: 10cm (4in)
Lilestone Plc, UK
www.myla.com

Vibrator, Bone
Tom Dixon
Hygienic resin
H: 5cm (2in)
W: 6cm (2 3/8in)
L: 22cm (8 5/8in)
Myla, UK
www.myla.com

Vibrator, Little Gem
Seymour Powell
Hypoallergenic silicone
rubber, ABS plastic
H (approx.): 5cm (2in)
W (approx.): 5cm (2in)
L (approx.): 10cm (3 7/8in)
Durex, UK
www.durex.co.uk

Dog toy, DXG BXNE
Karim Rashid
Non-toxic polymer
W: 16.5cm (6 ½in)
D: 2.5cm (1in)
For the dogs, Canada
www.karimrashid.com

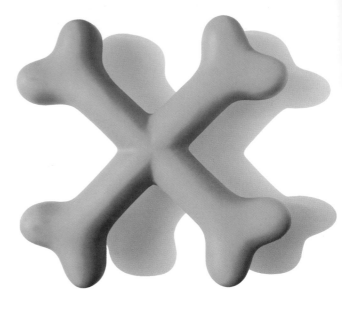

Karim Rashid

Which of your designs to date would you like to be remembered by?
My books, my writings, my lectures, my nihilistic contribution of my being in a conservative and monistic profession.

How do you think others view your work?
Love and hate. Good and evil. I am compared to Verner Panton in the sense of my fulgent, kaleidoscopic, orgiastic aesthetic, compared to Starck for my prolificness and broadness, and compared to everyone else; I was called best designer of the year by many magazines and worst designer of the year by *Wallpaper*. The public loves my work; the design community is very mixed, but we are here for the public.

Which designer has influenced you the most and why?
Luigi Colani, Dieter Rams, Isamu Noguchi, Marshall Macullan, David Bowie, Raymond Lowey, Victor Vaserley and Charles Eames all inspired me to crave for one rational, organic, digital, blobular, soft, perfect contemporary world.

If you were not a designer, what would you like to be and why?
I would like to be a space cowboy, musician, science-fiction filmmaker or philosopher, or all of them combined – a cult(ure) leader.

What role do you think the designer has in society today?
The designer is the liaison between the machine of capitalism and the human condition, a provocateur of the experience economy.

Do you buy a lot of design pieces?
No, they are given to me.

Is there a design in your home that you couldn't live without?
Yes, a sexy, intelligent, passionate, kinky, artistic, affectionate, inspiring woman.

What do you consider to be the best piece of design since the millennium?
The hydrogen car prototype just shown in Taiwan.

Where do you think design is heading?
To your home town soon.

Is there someone we should be watching out for?
Watch out for:
1. China.
2. Customization (variance and digital craft) where everyone designs their own things.
3. Neobaroque hell.
4. Designocracy (democratic design).
5. Pleasuretronics (where every low-tech object will have 'smart' technology embedded in it).
6. Desktop manufacturing (production on demand with no tools or dies).
7. Disposability.
8. Prime-time TV.
9. Perfect sustainability.
10. Robotics – craft is dead.
11. Rock stardom.

Is the cult of the personality taking over the design world?
The cult of the personality is not 'taking over'. It is just finally arriving and joining the design world!

Paperweight, Heavy Thing
Shinobu Ito
Crystal glass
H: 5cm (2in)
W: 9cm (3 ½in)
L: 9cm (3 ½in)
RC Ritzenhoff Cristal AG, Germany
www.ritzenhoff.de

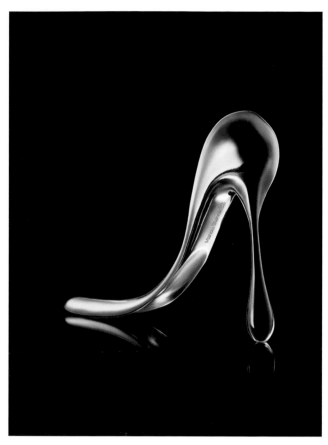

Table/tray, Volino
Michele De Lucchi and
Philippe Nigro
Moulded iron and
leather sheets
H: 61cm (24in)
W: 40cm (15 ³/₄in)
Diam: 40cm (15 ³/₄in)
Poltrona Frau srl, Italy
www.poltronafrau.it

Wine cooler stand
Jasper Morrison
18/10 stainless steel
H: 63cm (24 ³/₄in)
Diam: 28cm (11in)
Alessi SpA, Italy
www.alessi.com

**Shoehorn, Manolo
shoehorn
(for Habitat's VIP
Collection)**
Manolo Blanhik
Polished aluminium
H: 20cm (7 ⁷/₈in)
W: 30cm (11 ³/₄in)
D: 5cm (2in)
Habitat, UK
www.habitat.net

Habitat's VIP (Very Important Products) Collection
was launched in 2004 – a range of items designed
by a list of famous names in celebration of Habitat's
fortieth year in business. Rather than arranging a huge
celebration, Tom Dixon decided that it would be more
valid to plan an event that would last. He wanted to
introduce something of the flavour of the company
when it was first founded in the 1960s, a time when
Sir Terence Conran involved all his friends and
colleagues, no matter what their fields, to actively
participate in his nascent company and earliest
catalogues. 'It struck me that the whole thing of being
involved and engaged in other people's businesses,
fashion or food or whatever, was something that had
been forgotten a bit over the years,' writes Dixon.
His idea was to invite a range of people who were all
highly successful in their own fields, from actors to
athletes, to design a product for Habitat. The result
was twenty-two designs, including shoe storage
designed by Linford Christie, a yoga mat by Deepak
Chopra, a director's chair from Ewan McGregor,
a travelling case by Kristin Scott Thomas and,
most successfully as it turned out, the shoehorn by
shoe designer Manolo Blanhik that, if not literally,
figuratively 'walked' off the shelves.

Toshiyuki Yamanouchi
and Kanya Hiroi
ABS, polycarbonate,
PVC
H: 24cm (9 ½in)
W: 21cm (8 ¼in)
D: 14cm (5 ½in)
Toshiba Corporation,
Toshiba Consumer
Marketing
Corporation, Japan
www.toshiba.co.jp

**Pouf and hoover,
Airpouf**
Lorenzo Damiani
Lycra, polyurethane,
hoover 220V
Diam: 65cm (25 ⅝in)
Campeggi srl, Italy
www.campeggisrl.it

'Airpouf' is a seat-cum-
household appliance – a
fully upholstered sphere
with three holes filled
with contrasting
coloured balls. When in
use as a vacuum cleaner,
the balls fly out to reveal
a draft tube, start
button and air vent.

**Brush and dustpan,
Tokey**
Babled and Co.
Standard injection
H: 22cm (8 ⅝in)
W: 22cm (8 ⅝in)
D: 3cm (1 ⅛in)
Viceversa, Italy
www.viceversa.com

**Vacuum cleaner,
Trilobite**
Inez Ljunggren
ABS plastic
H: 13cm (5 ⅛in)
Diam: 35cm (13 ¾in)
Electrolux AB, Sweden
www.electrolux.com

Electrolux's 'Trilobite
2.0' robotic vacuum
takes just 40 minutes to
clean a 4 x 4.5m (14 x 15ft)
room, leaving the user
free to sit and relax.
Infrared and ultrasonic
sensors map out the
contours of the room,
avoiding obstacles; even
a wine glass is safe left
on the floor. Once
complete, or when the
batteries run low, the
vacuum cleaner will
automatically return
to its floor recharging
station.

Automatic battery lawnmower, Electrolux Automower
Stina Nilimaa Wickström
Painted ABS
H: 30cm (11 ³/₄in)
W: 55cm (21 ⁵/₈in)
D: 71cm (67in)
Electrolux AB, Sweden
www.electrolux.com

The 'Automower' lawnmower cuts grass so finely that the clippings can be left on the lawn to biodegrade and act as a fertilizer. However, this is not what makes this product so appealing. Completely free of wires and activated by sensors, this little green animal whizzes silently around the garden, grazing away at a rate of 75 square metres (807 square feet) per hour. Its intelligence is such that it can recognize where it should be working and avoid flowerbeds by keeping within an area designated by wire antennae, returning to a special battery pack to recharge when needed.

Fire dish, Qrater
Dirk Wynants
Cor-Ten steel
H: 45cm (17 ³/₄in)
Diam: 145cm (57in)
Extremis, Belgium
www.extremis.be

Grill, Outclass
Claus Jensen & Henrik Holbaek, Tools Design
Stainless steel
Diam: 49cm (19 ¹/₄in)
Eva Solo by Eva Denmark A/S, Denmark
www.evasolo.com

Security product design, Madame Buttly
Matthias Megyeri
Steel
L (min.): 400cm (158in)
Megyeri & Partners Ltd, UK
www.sweetdreams security.com

Sweet Dreams Security's products provide superb functional safety and mental well-being through non-threatening, contemporary design.

Security product design, Landscape
Matthias Megyeri
Glass
H (approx.): 10cm (3 $^7/_8$in)
W (approx.): 5cm (2in)
D (approx.): 2cm ($^3/_4$in)
Megyeri & Partners Ltd, UK
www.sweetdreams security.com

Jewel cases, Long-necked animals (giraffe, deer, goose)
Michele De Lucchi
Glass, metal
Diam: 13cm (5 $^1/_8$in)
Produzione Privata, Italy
www.produzioneprivata.it

Palm tree
Michele De Lucchi
Metal
H: 30cm (11 $^3/_4$in)
W: 32cm (12 $^5/_8$in)
D: 0.2cm ($^1/_4$in)
Produzione Privata, Italy
www.produzioneprivata.it

Pomegranate tree
Michele De Lucchi
Metal
H: 30cm (11 $^3/_4$in)
W: 32cm (12 $^5/_8$in)
D: 0.2cm ($^1/_4$in)
Produzione Privata, Italy
www.produzioneprivata.it

Maarten Baas

Which of your designs to date would you like to be remembered by?

That definitely would be 'Smoke'. But I think if I could choose, I would like to be remembered for my latest project: the 'Treasure' dining chair. It's because it's an even more personal concept than 'Smoke'. It's for many reasons: the concept, the way it's constructed, the spontaneous character and just how it looks: it's kind of an underdog, not a prestigious piece. That's something that I like very much, instead of a smooth, balanced rational piece. Since I like this kind of fresh air in the design world I would like my sweet little 'Treasure' chair to be my icon.

How do you think others view your work?

Opinions differ, and I like them all: from very short impulsive reactions like 'Cool!' to more over-thought opinions like 'Interesting because ...'. Both reactions are right; I even sometimes agree with 'negative' reactions. They're all in my head as well. I like it if my works give inspiration to others.

If you were not a designer, what would you like to be and why?

To be a cook. What I don't like about design is the fact that people's opinion on art or design is often very rational. Unfortunately, taste is not very subjective or emotional: there's often a rational reason why you like something or not. Experts, for example, want to see it in the context of their vision or of history, and non-experts are often influenced by status or general taste. People often think they should 'understand' design.

What I miss in design is the personal subjective aspect of the taste of food, for example. Just: do you like it or not? You don't need to understand food. Even if you always eat junk food you will have an opinion about haute cuisine. You would also never be influenced by the food taste of the direct neighbourhood. There's no explanation, it's just like that. If I don't like a certain food, I will not buy it. I know there are amateurs and experts who have different perceptions of something, but it's not rational. That's why I would like to be a cook: just making food that tastes good (or not).

What role do you think the designer has in society today?

I'm afraid that their role in general society is very small. There's much hypocrisy in it. Despite the fact that many designers pretend they have a social, ecological or whatever good reason to design, I don't believe design affects anything like that. I think the most I have done with my work is to tell some beautiful visual fairytales to people who see it, and to be able to pay the people who work for me. I would like to do more than that in the future. There are actually two Maartens in me: Maarten the newly graduated student is idealistic and observes the gigantic nonsensicality of the whole design circus; Maarten the professional designer likes designers to make beautiful things for the world. I don't know whether the first Maarten is 'still naive' or the other 'already blasé' ...

Do you buy a lot of design pieces?

No. I don't have any design pieces.

Where do you think design is heading? Is there someone we should be watching out for?

I have no idea and I'm generally not thinking of that kind of thing. I just make things that I like or consider to be interesting, without the context of where design generally should go. I think the designer to look at is Bertjan Pot.

Grandfather clock, Smoke
Maarten Baas
Burned wood finished off with epoxy
H: 180cm (71in)
W: 40cm (15 ³/₄in)
D: 50cm (19 ⁵/₈in)
Maarten Baas in collaboration with Moooi, the Netherlands
www.maartenbaas.com

Piano, Smoke
Maarten Baas
Burned wood finished off with epoxy
H: 130cm (51in)
W: 150cm (59in)
D: 50cm (19 ⁵/₈in)
Maarten Baas in collaboration with Moooi, the Netherlands
www.maartenbaas.com

'**Smoke**' is a range of timeless and poetic charcoaled objects preserved by a transparent epoxy coating.

Mikro-House (from the Mikro series)
Sam Buxton
0.15mm-thick hard-rolled stainless steel
Folded: 8 x 8 x 8cm
(3 ¹⁄₈ x 3 ¹⁄₈ x 3 ¹⁄₈in)
Worldwide Co., UK
www.sambuxton.com

The 'Mikro' series developed from a business card that Sam Buxton designed. Wanting to show his work directly from his pocket, this card transformed from flat item into a 3D object that could be kept. The process he uses is industrial acid etching. Commonly used in the electronics industry, it allows Sam to manufacture at high volume while also achieving fine detailing. The stainless steel sheet stays rigid when folded.

Umbrella stand, Paso Doble
Xavier Lust
Polyethylene
H: 47cm (18 ¹⁄₂in)
W: 49cm (19 ¹⁄₄in)
D: 27cm (10 ⁵⁄₈in)
Driade SpA, Italy
www.driade.com

Sport equipment, Airboard Classic
Joe Steiner
420 D Nylon with TPU coating
H (inflated): 25cm (9 ⁷⁄₈in)
L (inflated): 120cm (47in)
W (inflated): 72cm (28 ³⁄₈in)
Fun-care AG, Switzerland
www.airboard.com

The 'Airboard' weighs only 2.70 kilograms (6 pounds), yet has the same control as a pair of skis and has given rise to its own sport – snow body-boarding. Users lie chest down, reaching speeds of up to 126 kilometres (78 miles) an hour, shifting their body weight on to underside profile runners to change direction or stop (hopefully).

Magazine and firewood rack, Kanto
Pancho Nikander
Birch or oak veneer
H: 56.5cm (22 ¹⁄₄in)
W: 34cm (13 ³⁄₈in)
D: 28.3cm (11in)
Artek, Finland
www.artek.fi

DNA spiral staircase

Ross Lovegrove
Steps in bladder-
moulded GRP and
mono-directional
carbon fibre, handrail in
solid bladder-moulded
carbon fibre
H: 400cm (158in)
Diam: 240cm (94in)
Ross Lovegrove, UK
www.rosslovegrove.com

Ross Lovegrove's leitmotif staircase spirals like a double-helix from the top floor to the hollowed-out basement of his Notting Hill studio in London. Lovegrove is best known for his biomorphic designs and intelligent use of innovative materials, processes and technologies, and the staircase echoes the sensibilities of earlier designs, such as the bleached-bones 'Go' chair for Bernhardt and, even more so, his 2004 exhibition 'Designosaurus'. Taking what he refers to as 'organic minimalism' to the extreme, Lovegrove re-engineered the dinosaur skeleton as architecture, producing life-size models in lightweight polystyrene. Skeletally, the twisted spine of his studio staircase is obviously borrowed from the flowing forms of nature. Lovegrove makes collections of objects that he uses as source material and inspiration, including fossils, bones, castings and sculptures – 'fat-free forms', as he calls them.

Although the staircase is site specific, Lovegrove is researching ways of remodelling it to manufacture a product that could have other commercial applications. Creating the fragile, petal-shaped treads and the delicate outline of the original, however, involved a highly specialized process and the development of a unique material. The staircase is fabricated from an 8-millimetre (1/3-inch) deep matt fibreglass, reinforced by unidirectional carbon, while the high-quality finish was obtained by the bladder-moulding technique used on Formula One cars. This process involves a composite of gas and injection moulding, and Lovegrove also invested money in the creation of a specialized tool made from seven-part aluminium, into which an inflatable rubber membrane has been introduced. This forces the resin against the mould walls, creating an extra-smooth and even result. As is the case with many of his designs, the form was developed on a stereolithographic modelling machine, which enabled Lovegrove to visualize in three dimensions and to explore the holistic qualities of the object. This was followed up by a series of trial-and-error tests before the elegant profile, which has a delicacy that belies its strength, was reached. Each step, attached to the central steel post by a single nut, can carry 420 kilograms (924 pounds). The handrail runs independently of the main staircase and is made from carbon fibre. Lovegrove had initially shied away from a spiral, thinking the form 'banal'. In the end, after research into linear and other possibilities, he adopted this typology to make the most of the limited space available yet produce a feature staircase. Interviewed by Deyan Sudjic for *Domus*, Lovegrove pointed out, 'It has a practical value. The spiral could have been smaller and tighter and still worked, but because it saves space, you can afford to be much more generous.'

Thermometer, Clinical Thermometer

Fumie Shibata
(Design Studio S)
ABS
H: 12.5cm (4 7/8in)
W: 3.4cm (1 3/8in)
D: 1.5cm (5/8in)
Omron Healthcare
Co. Ltd, Japan
www.omron.co.jp

Ballpoint pen, Model 274 LAMY dialog 1

Richard Sapper
Brass, PVD,
titanium coating
L: 13.94cm (5 1/2in)
C. Josef Lamy GmbH,
Germany
www.lamy.com

Modular room divider, Eileen screen
Andrew Tye
Anodized aluminium, steel
H: 186cm (73in)
W: 175cm (69in)
D: 3.5cm (1 ³⁄₈in)
Andrew Tye, UK
www.tye3d.com

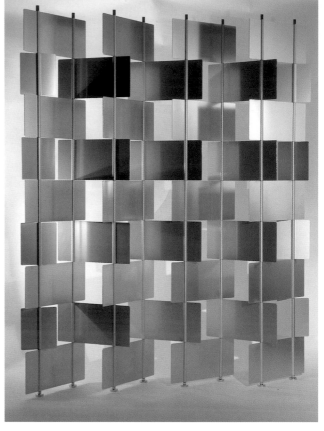

Space divider, Sticks
Hsu–Li Teo and Stefan Kaiser
Rubber, wood, solid timber, fibreglass
H: 180cm (71in)
W: 60cm (23 ⁵⁄₈in)
D: 30cm (11 ³⁄₄in)
Extremis, Belgium
www.extremis.be

Screen, UP
Paolo Ulian
Coverflex, plywood
H: 170cm (67in)
W: 35cm (13 ³⁄₄in)
L: 100cm (39 ³⁄₈in)
Bonacina Pierantonio srl, Italy
www.bonacina pierantonio.it

Due to the countless reinterpretations of the straight-backed minimalist chair, plywood is probably the most undervalued material on the market today. Yet handled intelligently, its simple, pared-down aesthetic allows the contemporary designer to exhibit his or her skill, the repeated folding of very thin sheets providing an opportunity to offer a delicate profile while retaining incredible weight-bearing properties.

Paolo Ulian's 'UP' screen is the result of his discovery of **Coverflex** – an extraordinarily flexible plywood 3.5 millimetres (¹⁄₈inch) thick that was patented in Italy in 1999 by the Jolando Eliseo Molteni company. The screen is sold flat packed, but with a simple action – the pushing in of the vertical sides – it transforms into a 3D object that can just as easily be restored to its flat form for transportation. The screen is soft, elastic and very light, weighing just 10 kilograms (22 pounds), but has a solid, almost monolithic presence once opened.

Screen, Hotel lounge screen
Robin McGrath
Birch ply, laminates, walnut and maple veneer
H: 150cm (59in)
W: 120cm (47in)
Robin McGrath, UK
Robin-mcgrath@excite.com

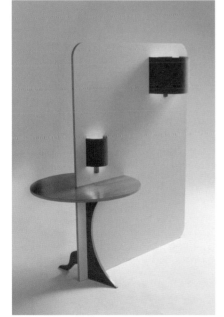

Screen, Traffic
Christopher Procter and Fernando Rihl
Acrylic
H: 180cm (71in)
W: 180cm (71in)
D: 40cm (15 ³/₄in)
Procter : Rihl, UK
www.procter-rihl.com

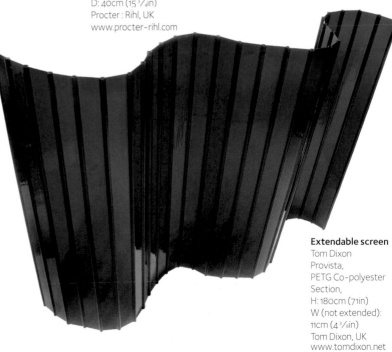

Extendable screen
Tom Dixon
Provista,
PETG Co-polyester
Section,
H: 180cm (71in)
W (not extended):
11cm (4 ³/₄in)
Tom Dixon, UK
www.tomdixon.net

Radiators are becoming fashionable. For a long time they have been at once intrusive yet 'invisible' in a room, ugly appendages taking up wall space, accepted but largely ignored. Now designers seem to be tackling the problem head on. Joris Laarman's concrete radiator (see page 334), initially a student project but now taken up by Droog Design in limited-batch production, seems to have started a trend that has seen King and Miranda following suit with their curtains of radiating aluminium. Franca Lucarelli and Bruna Rapisarda have coated steel heating elements with sheets of tempered coloured glass, creating a feature out of a necessity. The abstract forms of 'Vu' by Massimo Iosa Ghini spread across the wall, turning function into art, while Ludovica and Roberto Palomba's bright red 'sculpture' is exceptionally flat and is intended to be as uninvasive as possible. Satyendra Pakhalé's modular design (conceived in ceramic but now mass-produced in aluminium to comply with safety regulations) is an elegant and innovative addition to any interior. 'I wanted to develop a radiator that had personality and would fit into an interior with its own modest dignity ... ceramic seemed to be a great choice as it maintains its temperature and radiates heat for a long time.' His radiator is the first in a series of industrial design projects that will bring fresh perspectives to the field. He would like to create a range of electro-mechanical products that mix technically resolved design solutions with a warm, human sensorial aesthetic.

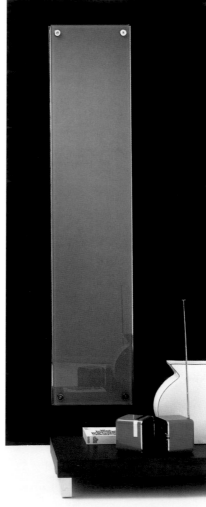

Mobile radiator, Ciussaì
Ad Hoc
Flexible stainless steel
Various dimensions
Ad Hoc, Italy
www.madeadhoc.com

Radiator, Square
Ludovica and
Roberto Palomba
Aluminium, steel
H: 140 or 200cm
(55 or 79in)
W: 31 or 61cm
(12 or 24in)
Tubes Radiatori srl, Italy
www.tubesradiatori.com

Radiator, Dress
Franca Lucarelli and
Bruna Rapisarda
Steel, glass/mirror sheet
H: 180cm (71in)
L: 40cm (15 ³/₄in)
Scirocco H srl, Italy
www.sciroccoh.it

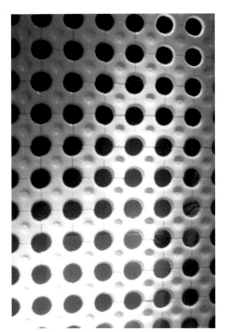

Radiator, Add-On
Satyendra Pakhalé
Die-cast aluminium
H: 102cm (40in)
W: 175cm (69in)
D: 8cm (3 ⅛in)
Tubes Radiatori srl, Italy
www.tubesradiatori.com

Satyendra Pakhalé

Which of your designs to date would you like to be remembered by?

It's a difficult question, because time will tell what will remain and what will be remembered. But what I could think of right now are probably two or three projects. The first that comes to mind is the 'Fish' chair, produced by Cappellini, as it is a resolved product, and works ergonomically, symbolically, as a piece of furniture.

Another one is 'Akasma' – a set of glass baskets and trays produced by RSVP, Italy. 'Akasma' is a technically resolved set of objects. It has the right balance of industrial production and craftsmanship – I mean industrial bent glass technology.

Last but not least is one of my recent projects, 'Add-On' radiator, produced by Tubes in Italy. It is a fresh, innovative way of looking at a typology that has been boring and neglected. I am glad at the way it has turned out, especially because I could take my first idea of making a radiator with its own dignity and personality, controlling all the stages of design and product development/product engineering to achieve the result I wanted. This is the kind of project I really love to work on, as it involves issues that are dear to my heart, such as a technological and manufacturing

challenges, and creating fresh, innovative, utilitarian products. By all means it's not an easy task, but I like it.

How do you think others view your work?

It is very difficult to know how others view my work. Dialogue for me is more important than understanding – often I don't expect anybody to understand me. Sometimes I don't understand what I have done, so how can I expect somebody else to!

However, what I know from the people with whom I collaborate closely from industry and cultural institutions, as well as colleagues, is that they see my work as universal yet unique, with a fine balance between soft and hard, archaic and contemporary, culture and commerce. It's work done with deep technical and cultural understanding of making things. Above all it is sensorial – it appeals to the senses and encourages people to touch and feel.

Which designer has influenced you the most and why?

There are many – many designers, engineers, architects and artists have influenced me, but one of the most influential designers that comes to my mind now is Issey Miyake. I have great admiration for Issey Miyake as a creator. If one looks at his unique creations such as 'Pleats Please' and 'A-Poc' it is very evident that they have universal appeal; however, it is also evident that they are deeply rooted in Japanese culture. For me, Issey Miyake has also been very important as an industrial designer. His approach to and understanding of traditions with a fresh perspective, and innovation in contemporary industrial products, has special meaning to me. His work is universal, without being nostalgic or regressive. He made me understand that there are no boundaries; boundaries are artificial and unnecessary man-made limitations.

If you were not a designer, what would you like to be and why?

I have never done anything except be involved in creating – I have been making things all my life since childhood. That's my preoccupation, which happens to be called the design profession. And people have started calling me a designer. Perhaps they take notice of it a bit more now, and I have the professional means and resources to get things done, but the process of creation and the will to create has always been more or less the same. It is a seductive idea – what if I were not a designer? Thinking now, I would have liked to be many things, perhaps a sculptor, a calligrapher, a martial artist, an inventor – someone with an absolute meditative dedication to a chosen way of life.

Do you buy a lot of design pieces?

I don't know how and when it started, but I hardly go shopping, which means I hardly buy any design pieces. I do often receive design pieces as gifts from friends who are active designers, or from companies with which I am collaborating. But most of the time I like to get items made – that's the way I had things when I grew up, so it is kind of normal for me.

Is there a design in your home you couldn't live without?

I'm sure I could live very well without anything around. It sounds a bit paradoxical, but I like the idea of living with almost nothing. Over time I have considerably reduced the number of things I have at home – the more I work, the more I feel the need to have nothing around in my living environment but simply to have space, open empty space, and lots of mental space.

So at home I live with bare, necessary things. However my studio in Amsterdam, where I often spend a good deal of time but sometimes am never there, is like a little personal museum, filled with a collection of things from all over the world. It is a sort of memory container filled with samples of materials, old and new objects, some from places I have visited, many books, items made from all sorts of materials in all different forms and with many different functions.

One piece of design in my home I couldn't live without is perhaps a wonderful 5 x 7ft (1.5 x 2m) aquarelle sketchpad that I get made whenever I visit the lovely handmade paper-manufacturing cottage industry in the southern part of our lovely earth.

What do you consider to be the best piece of design since the millennium?

I have no idea – I do not know. It is always not so easy to say what is simply best. In my mind there is no such thing as absolute best. Something could be relatively better than the other but best is something hypothetical and difficult for me to accept as the absolute best piece of design. One example of classic design that comes to mind now is the diamond-frame bicycle, a perfect example of design innovation from all perspectives. It is rooted in the culture of creation – technological, social and above all cultural. I'm not sure if it is the best, but I would like to do something that is equally significant as a piece of transportation design.

Where do you think design is heading? Is there someone we should be watching out for?

I have no idea where design is heading right now. I think we need to go towards humanizing our environment; to make design as a 'universal poetry'. We really need to look at the human, sensorial side of design/creation, before it's too late. In today's hyperactive information society it is more and more essential to make our man-made world a truly sensorial world. I think we should be watching those irresponsible imitative tendencies, which do not make sense from any perspective. We should be questioning those tendencies all the time.

Is the cult of the personality taking over the design world?

I think it has always existed all over the world during all times, but now is more visible, as obvious communication technology makes it accessible to everybody. I would say to negate personality in any creative field is an error; however, to remain satisfied with personality alone is a greater error. In the case of a really great individual the greatness lies in his/her having gone beyond his/her individualism. I feel design should not be impeded by individualism. Stress upon individualism alone is totally unsatisfactory, even though we designers all benefit by it sometimes. On the other hand where do we find true creation without individualism!!! So having no individuality and transcending it – these issues must not be confused.

What role do you think the designer has in society today?

Over a period of time, things have changed; now perhaps the objectives and intentions are different, but the major driving force remains almost unchanged, that is the primal will to express oneself. Through this, one should try to communicate what is appropriate in a given situation or time, try to create new associations, new cultural connections and above all innovate. Challenge industrial and socio-cultural stereotypes; try to create new ways of being and hopefully becoming.

Radiator
Joris Laarman
Concrete, plumbing
parts
H: 65cm (25 ⁵⁄₈in)
W: 250cm (98in)
D: 45cm (17 ³⁄₄in)
Joris Laarman, the
Netherlands
www.jorislaarman.com

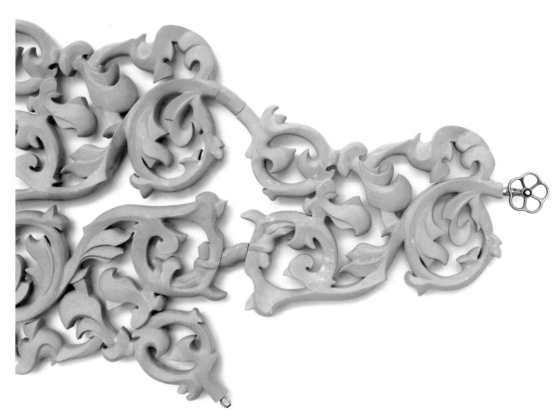

**Radiator system and
towel drier, Velum**
Perry King and Santiago
Miranda with C. Knox
Steel and extruded
aluminium
H: 45.4cm (17 ³⁄₄in)
W: 121cm (48in)
D: 10cm (3 ⁷⁄₈in)
Runtal (Zehnder Group),
Switzerland
www.runtal.com

Radiator, Domino
Matteo Thun
Aluminium
H: 20cm (7 ⁷⁄₈in)
W: 20cm (7 ⁷⁄₈in)
D: 5.5cm (2 ¹⁄₈in)
Tubor, Italy
www.tubor.com

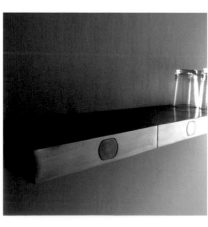

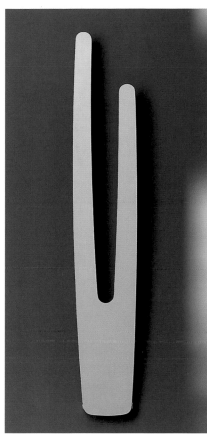

Radiator, Vu
Massimo Iosa Ghini
Steel
H: 168cm (66in)
W: 55cm (21 ⁵/₈in)
Antrax Art Heating, Italy
www.antrax.it

**Children's furniture,
Happy Horse (Black
Beauties Collection)**
Ineke Hans
Recycled plastic
H: 60cm (23 ⁵/₈in)
W: 28.5cm (11 ³/₈in)
D: 52.5cm (20 ⁷/₈in)
Ineke Hans/Arnhem,
the Netherlands
www.inekehans.com

'Black Beauties' is one of the most recent of **Ineke Hans**'s explorations of products in black, previous ranges that used this colour as a central theme being 'Black Gold' (porcelain) and 'Black Magic' (chairs). Ineke Hans trained in Arnhem, and then at the Royal College of Art in London. She worked for Habitat for three years before forming her own studio, returning to Arnhem in 1998. Her work is hard to categorize: it is design, yet it has sculptural qualities and relies heavily on collective consciousness and psychology; its appeal is largely generated by the powerful effect her products have on our imagination and behaviour. Basing her work on recognizable archetypes, she subtly shifts our preconceptions and associations, throwing us off balance by experimenting with materials, narrative, existing codes and colour. In her book *Black Bazaar: Design Dilemmas*, which she wrote in collaboration with the journalist Ed van Hinte, she explores the various connotations of the colour black, from the negative – occult (black magic), associations of evil and 'otherness', death and racism; to the more positive – black as the colour for the style conscious, sartorial elegance (black-tie event) and luxury (ebony). By playing with codes, we form our opinions and make our judgements. No colour is just a colour, especially black.

**Radiator, C-line,
type C-TA**
Wim Segers
Steel
Diam: 100 or 140cm
(39 or 55in)
Thermic, Belgium
www.thermic.be

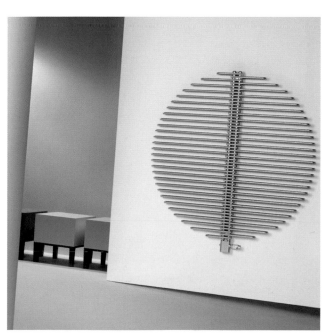

**Ironing board, Polder
Z-Series Ironing Board**
Scott Henderson, Scott Henderson Inc
Stamped sheet metal, injection-moulded polypropylene, silicon
H: 92cm (36in)
W: 140cm (55in)
D: 39cm (15 ³/₈in)
Polder Inc, USA
www.polder.com

Breathing new life into a boring and banal object, **Scott Henderson** has redesigned the ironing board. Apart from using a heat-resistant silicon pad and adding a rail around the generous cradle to hang shirts, the real innovation is in the overall shape, replacing the Y-profile tubular leg structure with a Z formation (so-called because stability comes from the way the legs crisscross on a diagonal). Add to this the fact that electrical wires run up through the board into a power outlet under the top surface, and tripping over ironing leads and legs becomes a thing of the past.

Mirror, Taylor Bird
Ed Annink,
Ontwerpwerk
Polished stainless steel
H: 87cm (34in)
W: 73.5cm (29 1/8in)
D: 4cm (1 5/8in)
Driade SpA, Italy
www.driade.com

Ed Annink's mirrors
in the shapes of two
different birds reflect the
colours of the interior,
and will appear to change
depending on the angle
you look at them.

Wall mirror, Hasami
Paolo Rizzatto
Curved glass
Diam: 96cm (38in)
Fiam Italia SpA, Italy
www.fiamitalia.it

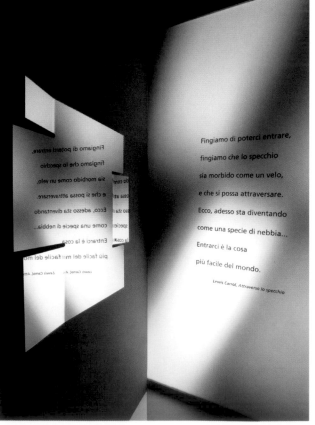

Mirror, Hiroshi
Paolo Rizzatto
Curved glass
H: 90cm (35 3/8in)
W: 90cm (35 3/8in)
D: 15cm (5 7/8in)
Fiam Italia SpA, Italy
www.fiamitalia.it

An articulated joint in
the rear allows the
mirror to be angled
as preferred.

Mirror, Ghost
Olivier Sidet
(RADI Designers)
Mirror, angled film
H: 80cm (31½in)
L: 130cm (51⅛in)
Glace Control, France
lb@toolsgalerie.com

Wall mirror that is able to receive SMS messages sent from a mobile phone, +336
Robert Stadler
Mirror, electronics
H: 70cm (27¼in)
W: 55cm (21⅝in)
Galerie Dominique Fiat, France
www.radidesigners.com

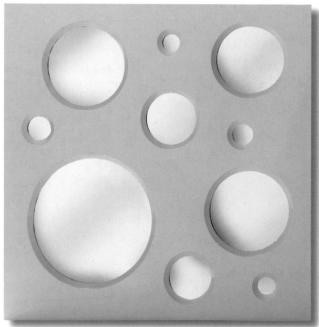

Mirror, Versailles
Marco Romanelli
and Marta Laudani
Mirror, MDF
H: 100cm (39in)
W: 100cm (39in)
D: 4cm (1⅝in)
Montina srl, Italy
www.montina.it

Pushchair, Xplory
Stokke
Plastic
H: 81–130cm (32–51in)
W: 57cm (22½in)
D: 72–130cm (28⅜–51in)
Stokke, Norway
www.stokke.com

Self-watering flowerpot, Flower Power

Claus Jensen and Henrik Holbaek, Tools Design
Glass container and ceramic pot
H: 14 or 18cm
(5 ¹⁄₂ or 7in)
Diam: 11 or 13cm
(4 ³⁄₈ or 5 ¹⁄₈in)
Eva Solo by Eva Denmark A/S, Denmark
www.evasolo.com

Eva Solo (the one and only) has added to its range of innovative yet simple household designs. The **self-watering flowerpot** consists of two parts: an outer glass vase that functions as a reservoir for the water and a ceramic pot in which the potted plant is grown. Nylon threads act as an extension of the plant's roots, reaching down into the water and drawing it up to feed the plant.

Glass, Sbic

Lorenzo Damiani
Plastic
H: 10cm (3 ⁷⁄₈in)
Diam: 8cm (3 ¹⁄₈in)
Lorenzo Damiani Studio, Italy
lorenzo.damiani@tin.it

Watering can

Nicolas Le Moigne
Polypropylene
H: 26.4cm (10 ¹⁄₄in)
L: 24.2cm (9 ¹⁄₂in)
Viceversa, Italy
www.viceversa.com

The idea of this **watering can** is to reuse PET and glass bottles. A closing piece is able to fit different shapes of bottle and to change them into watering cans.

Series of containers, Nox Magnum

Raul Barbieri
Stainless steel
Various dimensions
Rexite, Italy
www.rexite.it

Can of gold

Marcel Wanders
Gold-plated tin
H: 12cm (4 ¾in)
Diam: 7cm (2 ¾in)
Marcel Wanders,
the Netherlands
www.marcelwanders.com

Conceived to celebrate the first anniversary of Galerie Xpressions, a small venue for young artists in Hamburg, **Marcel Wanders** has found a way of linking the art world, the consumer and the local homeless. The gallery purchased 100 cans of soup, the contents were distributed and the cans were then washed, gilded, distinctively labelled and sold. The proceeds generated enough capital for the local welfare institution to reinvest the following year for the benefit of the homeless. Marcel sees the concept being taken up by different cities, each sealing the product with their individual labels to create an international philanthropic series of precious containers.

Pot plant holder, Plant Cup

Gitta Gschwendtner
Ceramic
H: 27cm (10 ⅝in)
Diam (cup): 31cm (12 ¼in)
Diam (saucer): 49cm (19 ¼in)
Thorsten van Elten, UK
www.thorstenvanelten.com

Flowerpot, Kew

Vico Magistretti
Linear polyethylene
H: 40cm (15 ¾in)
Diam: 73cm (28 ¾in)
P. Serralunga, Italy
www.serralunga.it

Expandable outdoor pot-planter, Top-Pot

Ron Arad
Polyethylene
H: 108cm (42 ½in)
Diam: 73cm (28 ¾in)
P. Serralunga, Italy
www.serralunga.it

Ron Arad has elevated the humble flowerpot using the technology of rotation moulding. The volume of the container is broken by the contracting bellow action of the zigzag section. A valve in the double-skin pot controls the amount of air trapped in the bellow and so freezes the height and inclination of the '**Top-Pot**' at any given position. Alternatively, you can cut off the inner skin and let the earth that fills the pot act as a fixative for the volume and position. A variant of the design is now available as a giant garden light (see page 263).

Saddle, Rebel
Propeller
Thermo-moulded
carbon fibre, expanded
PVC, leather, titanium
Various dimensions
Linear, Sweden
www.linear.se

Working in collaboration with a Swedish saddle manufacturer and veterinary surgeons, Propeller have created a whole new concept in saddle design – the '**Rebel Saddle**'. Ergonomically suited to both rider and horse, it was devised to cut down on the problem of musculo-skeletal-related injury to the animal. Saddlery is traditionally a very conservative industry, so it was initially difficult to get the manufacturer to accept the cutting-edge new materials and streamlined motorcycle aesthetic, but once that hurdle had been jumped, the obvious advantage of using a lightweight carbon fibre composite frame could not be denied. The new frame offers even weight distribution, strength and stability. This frame is in turn joined to an exchangeable seat pad in PU-foam with a range of finishes from leather to textile. These modules can be swapped depending on the rider's age, size, needs and preferred sport. Rather than maintaining the usual forward position of the stirrups, Propeller have now attached these to both the front and back of the saddle in a Y-shaped configuration which distributes the weight evenly over the contact surface of the horse's back. The advantages of this new saddle system are that the horse can be under saddle without prolonged rest periods, the life span of the horse is doubled, it never needs to be refitted and, as a plus to the manufacturer, the profitability of the company increased exponentially with orders for 300,000 units placed in the first three months.

Landscape for domestic cats, Nowhere
Robert Stadler
Plywood, carpet, PVC
H: 93cm (37in)
W: 80cm (31in)
D: 34.4cm (13 ³/₈in)
Galerie Dominique Fiat, France
www.radidesigners.com

Dog house, Magis Dog House
Michael Young
Rotational moulded polyethylene, stainless steel, brass
H: 75.5cm (29 ⁷/₈in)
W: 48.5cm (19 ¹/₄in)
D: 89cm (35in)
Magis SpA, Italy
www.magisdesign.com

Bird table, Pip-Pip
Stina Sandwall
Metal
H: 16cm (6 ¼in)
W: 26cm (10 ¼in)
D: 12.5cm (4 ⅞in)
SMD Design AB,
Sweden
www.smdoffice.se

Bird feeder, Egg
Jim Schatz
Glossy ceramic
earthenware, aluminium
H: 22cm (8 ⅝in)
W: 15cm (5 ⅞in)
J Schatz, USA
www.jschatz.com

**Bird table,
Self-Service**
Claus Jensen and Henrik
Holbaek, Tools Design
Hand-blown glass,
stainless steel
H: 150cm (59 ⅛in)
Diam: 40cm (15 ¾in)
Eva Solo by Eva
Denmark A/S, Denmark
www.evasolo.com

There is no reason whatsoever why a contemporary design aesthetic should not be applied to something as banal as animal husbandry. Matali Crasset has just rejuvenated the ancient art of pigeon racing with a biomorphic yellow dovecote that dominates the French countryside around Beauvois-en-Cambrésis. On a much smaller and more domestic level, Royal College of Art industrial design graduates Simon Nicholls, William Windham, Johannes Paul and James Tuthill are about to make names for themselves with their equally colourful 'Eglu' chicken coop, which sold over 1200 units in the first six months of production. As more and more upwardly mobile thirty-somethings are leaving their urban domains for a more pastoral existence, those who cannot do so try to add a little of the countryside to their city environments. 'Eglu' is constructed in polyethylene and can accommodate two medium-sized hens. It consists of a slatted roosting area, nesting box, sliding droppings tray and back-door egg port. It is not cheap at £330 ($615), but does include an attachable predator-safe run, feed and water containers, a shade and, for an extra £35 ($65) for UK customers only, two Gingernut Ranger or Miss Pepperpot hens and a six-week supply of chicken feed.

Chicken coop, Eglu
Omlet
Polyethylene
H: 70cm (27 ½in)
W: 80cm (31in)
D: 80cm (31in)
Omlet, UK
www.omlet.co.uk

Retail Stores
Max Fraser

Australia:

Collect
88 George Street
The Rocks, Sydney
New South Wales 2000
+61 2 9247 7984
www.object.com.au
Collect is the retail arm of
Object, Australia's craft and
design centre, where one
can find contemporary
glass, ceramics, jewellery,
tableware and gifts by
Australian designers
and makers.

Dedece
263 Liverpool Street
Darlinghurst, Sydney
New South Wales 2010
+61 2 9360 2722
www.dedece.com
Dedece has been selling
European furniture and
lighting brands since 1978
and now runs three stores,
in Sydney, Melbourne and
Brisbane. Brands include
Cappellini, Knoll, Moooi,
Extremis, MDF Italia, de
Padova, Paola Lenti and
Minotti.

ECC Lighting + Living
111 Flinders Street
Darlinghurst, Sydney
New South Wales 2010
+61 2 9380 7922
www.ecc.com.au
ECC specializes in European
furniture and lighting and
carries numerous leading
brands in its Sydney,
Melbourne, Brisbane, Perth,
Adelaide, Canberra and
Northern Territory
showrooms.

Scandinavium
200 Campbell Street
Darlinghurst, Sydney
New South Wales 2010
+61 2 9332 4660
www.scandinavium.com.au
Well-lit showroom
importing Scandinavian
brands such as Swedese,
Skandiform, David Design,
CBI, Iittala and Louis Poulsen.

Space Furniture
84 O'Riordan Street
Alexandria, Sydney
New South Wales 2015
+61 2 8339 7588
www.spacefurniture.com.au
Space Furniture dominates
the contemporary design
retailing market in Australia
with showrooms in Sydney,
Melbourne and Brisbane
selling Boffi, Porro, B&B
Italia, Cassina, Kartell,
Edra, Zanotta, Driade,
Fiam, XO, Living Divani,
Ingo Maurer and Alias,
amongst others.

Austria:

B-Line
Imbergstraße 43
A-5020 Salzburg
+43 662 87 39 82
www.b-line.at
Placing a strong onus
on Kartell and USM
concessions, this retailer
also stocks Artemide,
Danerka, Fasem, Rexite,
Steelcase and Belux.

Henn
Naglergasse 29
A-1010 Vienna
+43 1 533 83 82
www.henn-design.com
Stockist of classic and
contemporary furniture
and lighting products
from Europe.

Prodomo
Michael-Bernhard-
Gasse 12–14
A-1120 Vienna
+43 1 982 16 11
www.prodomowien.at
This showroom, established
over 30 years ago, stocks
the A–Z of leading brand
names, from Alias to Zanotta.

Silenzio
Salzgries 2
A-1010 Vienna
+43 1 535 67 50
www.silenzio.at
Every conceivable leading
manufacturer for the home,
the office, eating and
sleeping has its products
in this Viennese design
showroom.

Belgium:

Dominique Rigo
210 rue de Stalle
1180 Brussels
+32 2 649 95 94
www.dominiquerigo.be
Poliform, Vitra, MDF Italia,
Kartell, Ligne Roset, Ingo
Maurer, Flos, Foscarini,
Artemide, Cassina and Knoll
are some of the brands sold
in this outlet's two stores
in Brussels.

Donum
Havermarkt 31/33
3500 Hasselt
+32 11 22 83 36
www.donum.be
Light and spacious lifestyle
store stocking international
brands, while also placing
particular attention on
Belgium's homegrown
talents such as Dirk Wynants,
Xavier Lust, Maarten Van
Severen, Piet Stockmans
and Vincent Van Duysen.

Scoonwoon
Gemeentestraat 1
2060 Antwerpen
+32 3 232 45 72
www.scoonwoon.be
For more than 35 years,
this family run business
has occupied this six-floor
showroom selling major
labels including Kartell,
B&B Italia, Driade, Ligne
Roset, Artelano, Molteni,
Cinna, Magis, MDF Italia,
Moroso, Porro, Vitra
and Zanotta.

Visa-versa
Wijnveld 4/6
9112 Sinaai Waas
+32 3 772 70 64
www.visaversa.be
Fresh showroom featuring
furniture, lighting and
accessories from Turkish
brand Derin, as well as
Elmar Flotötto, Authentics,
Loom, Eurolounge,
Mathmos and IQ Light.

Brazil:

BYDESIGN
Shopping Rio Design Barra
Avenida das Americas,
7.777 – lj.220
Rio de Janeiro
+55 21 3328 8690
www.bydesign.com.br
BYDESIGN has several
stores and concessions
across Brazil, with a
particular fondness for
colour in their selections
from the likes of Alessi,
Magis and Kartell.

Inove Store
Rua Castro, 197
Curitiba
Paraná
+55 41 342 5446
www.inovestore.com.br
Retailer of contemporary
furniture for home, office,
garden and sleeping.

Canada:

Inform Interiors
97 Water Street
Vancouver
British Columbia
V6B 1A1
+1 604 682 3868
www.informinteriors.com
Inform Interiors has been
running for over 20 years,
selling every major brand
of furniture, lighting and
accessories, as well as
design books.

Latitude Nord
4400 Saint-Laurent
Boulevard
Montreal, Quebec
H2W 1Z5
+1 514 287 9038
www.latitudenord.com
Founded in 1995, Latitude
Nord sells a fine selection
of furniture, lighting and
accessories of Scandinavian,
Italian, Swiss, Spanish and
Canadian origins. Dismo
International is their sister
company.

Living Space Interiors
188 Kingsway (at Broadway)
Vancouver, British Columbia
V5T 3J2
+1 604 683 1116
www.livingspace.com
An impressive converted
warehouse that is now home
to brands such as Artelano,
e15, Coro, Heller, Kartell,
Magis, MDF Italia and
Minotti, to mention a few.

Quasi Modo
789 Queen Street West
Toronto, Ontario
M6J 1G1
+1 416 703 8308
www.quasimodo
modern.com
Since 1981, Quasi Modo
has specialized in retailing
modern furniture and
lighting for the home and
office from leading suppliers
around the world.

Robert Sweep
739 11th Avenue SW
Calgary, Alberta
T2R 0E3
+1 403 262 8525
www.robertsweep.com
Established in 1980, Robert
Sweep was the first to
introduce Ligne Roset and
B&B Italia to Calgary. He
now supplies other favourite
brands Flos and Serralunga.

Triede Design
385 Place D'Youville, no.15
Montreal, Quebec
H2Y 2B7
+1 514 845 3225
www.triede.com
Triede Design has over
20 years of experience
selling brands such as
Herman Miller, Cappellini,
Luceplan, Flexform, Molteni,
Driade, Ingo Maurer,
Gervasoni, Serralunga
and Zanotta.

Void
334 King Street East
Toronto, Ontario
M5A 1K8
+1 416 868 6600
www.voidint.com
Supplier of MDF Italia, La
Palma, Fritz Hansen, Pallucco,
Living Divani, Magis and
Walter Knoll furniture.

Czech Republic:

Konsepti
Komunardů 32
170 00, Prague 7
+420 222 326 928
www.konsepti.cz
Prague's best design store
selling Kartell, Cappellini, Vitra,
Moroso, Driade, Cassina,
Amat and B&B Italia.

Ranný Architects
Thámova 11
Prague 8
+420 221 729 222
www.ranny.cz
Retail and contract supplier
of many leading brands such
as Cappellini, Fiam, Frighetto,
Segis, Rexite and Magis.

Vincent Interier
Údolní 16
Brno 602 00
+420 541 240 444
www.vincent.cz
Supplier of Vitra, Bulo,
Cappellini, Cassina, Driade,
Kartell, La Palma, Iittala,
Porsche Design plus more.

Denmark:

Casa Shop
Store Regnegade 2
1110 Copenhagen K
+45 33 32 70 41
www.casagroup.com
Spacious design store
benefiting from plenty of
natural light plays host to
designs from brands such

as Foscarini, Santa & Cole, Mobles 114, Flos, Pallucco, Zanotta, Fritz Hansen, David design, Arper, Edra, Minotti, e15 and Flexform.

Hay
Pilestræde 29–31
1112 Copenhagen K
+45 99 42 44 00
www.hay.dk
Hay is a recent Danish furniture brand that has been enjoying much success across the world since their inception in 2003. They display their collection with other complementing accessory designs in this Copenhagen showroom.

Normann Copenhagen
Trianglen, Østerbrogade 70
2100 Copenhagen
+45 35 55 44 59
www.normann-copenhagen.com
Normann Copenhagen produces its own range of products designed principally by Danish talents. Their showroom also houses other complementing brands such as Moooi, Kartell, Magis, Stelton, Flos, Artemide, Alessi and Mandarina Duck.

Paustian
Paustian Copenhagen.
Kalkbrænderiløbskaj 2,
2100 Copenhagen East
+45 39 16 65 65
Paustian Aarhus
Skovvejen 2
8000 Aarhus C.
+45 86 20 89 89
www.paustian.dk
Paustian is a large established retail/contract business selling home and office furniture from the likes of Vitra, Arper, de Padova, Kartell and Walter Knoll, as well as own production.

France:

Artelano
54 rue de Bourgogne
75007 Paris
+33 1 44 18 00 00
www.artelano.com
Artelano has been producing its own range of sofas, tables, chairs and storage since 1972. They work with talents such as Piero Lissoni, Pascal Mourgue, Christophe Pillet, Emmanuel Dietrich,

EOOS, Patricia Urquiola and Marco Zanuso. whose work can be viewed in the showroom.

Cinna
Stores across France, Belgium and Luxembourg
www.cinna.fr
This vast network of stores carries interior products designed by over 30 French and international designers including Arik Levy, Didier Gomez, Pascal Mourgue, Jean-Marie Massaud, Francois Bauchet and Eric Jourdan, with an impressive selection of furniture, rugs, lighting and decorative objects.

Forum Diffusion
55 rue Pierre Demours
75017 Paris
+33 1 43 80 62 00
www.forumdiffusion.fr
Founded in 1977, this large showroom is an established destination for contemporary furniture and lighting, for both public and trade buyers. A few classics are mixed in with creations from Alias, Cappellini, Cassina, Edra, Flexform, Moooi, Moroso and Zeus, to mention a few.

Meubles et Fonction – MFI
135 boulevard Raspail
75006 Paris
+33 1 45 48 55 74
www.meubles-fonction.com
A retailer since 1959, MFI is practiced at selling furniture and lighting from leading brands including B&B Italia, Alias, Fritz Hansen, Driade and Tisettanta.

Sentou
29 rue François Miron
75004 Paris
+33 1 42 78 50 60
www.sentou.fr
New design merged with classic creations is the order in this shop, plus its four other sister shops in the area. Think Eames with Arik Levy, Noguchi with Marc Newson, Yanagi with Jasper Morrison.

Silvera
58 avenue Kleber
75016 Paris
+33 1 53 65 78 78
www.silvera.fr
An immense showroom selling the most beautiful

interior creations from Alessi, Flos, B&B Italia, Moroso, Vitra, Cappellini, Cassina, Artemide, Magis, Zanotta, Driade, Edra, Moooi, Kartell and MDF Italia, amongst others.

Tools Galerie
119 rue Vielle-du-Temple
75003 Paris
+33 1 42 77 35 80
An innovative store mixing both known and unknown designers. They specialize in objects and small furniture from the likes of Radi Designers, Marcel Wanders, Hella Jongerius, Tom Dixon, Ron Arad, Konstantin Grcic and Jurgen Bey.

Germany:

Dopo Domani
Kantstraße 148
10623 Berlin
+49 30 882 22 42
www.dopo-domani.de
Supplier of the best international brands of furniture and lighting such as B&B Italia, Boffi, Cappellini, Driade, Droog, Edra, Flos, Kartell, Luceplan, MDF Italia, Molteni, Moroso, Vitra and Zanotta.

pesch wohnen
Kaiser-Wilhelm-Ring 22
50672 Cologne
+49 221 161 30
www.pesch-wohnen.de
One of the most established large design stores in Germany, stocking everything contemporary for the home from a plethora of leading international brands.

Roomservice
Lehmweg 56, Eppendorf
20251 Hamburg
+49 480 86 72
One of the leading contemporary design stores in Hamburg, selling brands such as Droog Design, Moooi and Cordula Kafka.

Scala Wohnen
Ludwig-Erhard-Straße 6
20459 Hamburg
+49 37 51 98 81
www.scala-wohnen.de
Comprehensive store selling Alias, Bulo, Cappellini, Driade, Droog, Edra, Gervasoni, Kartell, Living Divani, Minotti, Neotu, XO, Ycami and Zanotta, to name a few.

Stilwerk Berlin
Kantstraße 17,
Charlottenburg
10623 Berlin
+49 315 156 20
www.stilwerk.de
One of the largest centres of interior design, selling over 400 international brands. 'Design + Handwerk Plattform' on the fourth floor is dedicated to young designers from Berlin. Also large stores in Hamburg, Düsseldorf and Stuttgart.

Hong Kong:

Louvre Gallery
Shop B, LG/Floor
The Design Showcase
Ruttonjee Centre
11 Duddell Street
+852 2762 2393
www.louvre.com.hk
Substantial showroom specializing in furniture, lighting and decorative items by European designers, including collections from Artelano, Artifort, Bellato, Kartell, Pallucco, Rolf Benz, Stua, Montis and Knoll.

Israel:

Tollmans
72 Hey Be-Iyar
Kikar Hamedina, Tel Aviv
+972 03 60 55 659
www.tollmans.co.il
With showrooms in Tel Aviv, Jerusalem and Haifa, Tollmans has long been considered one of the leading retailers of contemporary furniture and lighting from the likes of Magis, Cassina, Cappellini, Herman Miller, Alessi and Extremis.

Italy:

Italy is awash with great design stores. Here is a pick of some of the top branded stores in their design capital, Milan.

Alessi
Corso Matteotti 9
Milano
+39 02 79 57 26
www.alessi.com

Artemide
Corso Monforte 19

Milano
+39 02 76 00 69 30
www.artemide.com

B&B Italia
Via Durini 14
Milano
+39 02 76 44 42 22
www.bebitalia.it

Cappellini
Via Santa Cecilia 4
Milano
+39 02 76 00 38 89
www.cappellini.it

Cassina
Via Durini 18
Milano
+39 02 76 02 07 58
www.cassina.it

Dadriade
Via Manzoni 30
Milano
+39 02 76 02 03 59
www.driade.com

De Padova
Corso Venezia 14
Milano
+39 02 77 72 01
www.depadova.it

Dovetusai
Via Sigieri 24
20135 Milano
+39 02 59 90 24 32
www.dovetusai.it

Edra
Via Ciovasso 11
Milano
+39 02 86 91 57 20
www.edra.com

Flos
Corso Monforte 9
Milano
+39 02 76 00 36 39
www.flos.com

Fontana Arte
Via Santa Margherita 4
Milano
+39 02 86 46 45 51
www.fontanaarte.com

Kartell
Via Carlo Porta 1
@ via Turati
Milano
+39 02 65 97 79 16
www.kartell.it

MDF Italia
Via della Chiusa
@ via Crocefisso
Milano
+39 02 58 31 71 68
www.mdfitalia.it

Moroso
Via Pontaccio 8/10
Milano
+39 02 72 01 63 36
www.moroso.it

Poltrona Frau
Via della Moscova 58
Milano
+39 02 65 71 205
www.poltronafrau.it

Sawaya & Moroni
Via Manzoni 15
Milano
+39 02 87 45 49
www.sawayamoroni.it

Zanotta
Piazza Tricolore 2
Milano
+39 02 76 01 64 45
www.zanotta.it

Japan:

Cassina IXC.
2-12-14 Minamiaoyama
Minato-ku
Tokyo 107-0062
+81 3 5474 9001
www.cassina-ixc.jp
Italian brand Cassina's
Japanese division, including
collections from Europe as
well as designs generated in
Asia such as the aluminium
'Air Frame' furniture by
David Chipperfield. Also
stores in Fukuoka, Osaka,
Sapporo and Nagoya.

Cîbone
Aoyama Bell Commons B1F
2-14-6 Kita-aoyama
Minato-ku
Tokyo
+81 3 3475 8017
www.cibone.com
Leading lifestyle store, home
to contemporary home
products from designers such
as Marcel Wanders, Nendo,
Piet Hein Eek, Claesson
Koivisto Rune, Monica
Forster and Patricia Urquiola.

hhstyle.com
6-14-2 Jingumae
Shibuya-ku
Tokyo 150-0001
+81 3 3400 3434
www.hhstyle.com
Slick, internationally-driven
showroom and one of the
main outlets for a plethora
of European brands such as
Cappellini and Vitra, with a
stunning sister shop next
door by Tadao Ando.

Idée
6-1-16 Minami-Aoyama
Minato-ku
Tokyo
+81 3 3409 6581
www.idee.co.jp
Established retail and
manufacturing network
founded by design
entrepreneur Teruo Kurosaki,
responsible for launching the
career of Marc Newson in
the late 80s. Diverse in its
approach, one can find
modern furniture, lighting,
accessories and books –
many items unseen
elsewhere in the world.

Sfera
17 Benzaiten-cho
Higashiyama-ku
Kyoto 605-0086
+81 7 5532 1139
www.ricordi-sfera.com
Minimal lifestyle store
spread over four floors
designed by Swedish trio
Claesson Koivisto Rune,
comprising restaurants as
well as a design store of
furniture, lighting, books
and accessories.

Trico
www.bytrico.com
Small but enterprising
retailer and manufacturer
of quirky, concept-driven
designs by the likes of
Michael Marriott, Electricwig
and El Ultimo Grito. Sell
designs by Thorsten Van
Elten, Richard Hutten, Details
and Dovetusai.

Zero First Design
Kosugi Building Robadai
2-3-1 Robadai, Meguro-ku
Tokyo 153-0042
+81 3 5489 6101
www.01st.com
A buzzy store selling
Artifort, Derin, Offecct,
Rosendahl and Yamagiwa
amongst other brands.

The Netherlands:

The Frozen Fountain
Prinsengracht 629
1016 HV Amsterdam
+31 20 622 9375
www.frozenfountain.nl
One of Holland's best design
stores selling items by
leading international brands
as well as being the launch
pad for many conceptual
projects by Dutch designers

such as Hella Jongerius,
Marcel Wanders, Jurgen Bey
and Piet Hein Eek.

Droog @ Home
Staalstraat 7B
1011 JJ Amsterdam
+31 20 523 5059
www.droogdesign.nl
The quirky dry humour is a
firm fixture of contemporary
Dutch design and is the
mainstay of Droog's
collection of furniture,
lighting and home
accessories. See and
purchase the range at this
store, which is attached to
their headquarters.

Vivid
William Boothlaan 17a
3012 VH Rotterdam
www.vividvormgeving.nl
A leading centre for design,
selling names such as Hella
Jongerius, Konstantin Grcic,
Ineke Hans, MNO, Gijs
Bakker, Richard Hutten,
Marcel Wanders and Studio
Job alongside a changing
programme of exhibitions.

Vorm Vast
Liesboslaan 291
4838 EV Breda
+31 76 520 1620
www.vormvast.nl
The list of international
suppliers to this showroom
is extensive – a veritable
home to contemporary
design for the home
and office.

Norway:

Black & White Studio
Kong Oscarsgate 18
5017 Bergen
+47 55 33 62 55
Øvre Holmegate 11
4006 Stavanger
+47 51 54 88 10
www.black-white.no
All items for the home from
leading contemporary
design manufacturers are
available, from the timeless
to the more avant-garde.

Expo Nova
Bygdøy allé 69
Pb 554 Skøyen, 0214 Oslo
+47 23 13 13 40
www.expo-nova.no
Major retailer of Cassina,
Cappellini, ClassiCon,
B&B Italia, Kartell, Magis,
Driade, Flexform, Plank,

La Palma and Varenna, to
name a few.

Kiil
Snekkerveien 4
2619 Lillehammer
+47 61 24 73 80
www.kiil.no
Founded in 1994, Kiil has
a well-displayed and
professional showroom that
houses many Nordic brands
with other well-known
European counterparts.

TiT
Teatergaten 35 4
Engen
5010 Bergen
+47 44 31 57 08
www.titnett.no
A wide range of European
furniture brands from
Moooi, Zanotta, Alias and
others available from a
sizeable showroom.

Poland:

MM Idea
Ul. Duchnicka 3
01-796 Warsaw,
+48 22 322 50 00
www.mmidea.pl
Opened in 1990, this
showroom introduces
furniture from the likes
of MDF Italia, Moroso,
Cappellini, Porro, Cassina,
Vitra, Kartell, ClassiCon,
Boffi and Driade to the
Polish capital.

Zoom
Ul. Nowogrodzka 84/86
02-018 Warsaw
+48 22 816 20 65
www.zoom.waw.pl
Alias, B&B Italia, Bulthaup,
Giorgetti, Maxalto, Poltrona
Frau, Rimadesio, Artemide,
Fontana Arte, Ingo Maurer
and Penta are some of the
European brands available.

Portugal:

Aveiro Meu Amor
Rua de São Martinho 13
Glória
3810-184 Aveiro
+351 23 44 23 514
www.amadesio.net
Once a soap factory, then a
porcelain factory, now this
large space is home to a
design store with soul, mixing
international brands with
Portuguese art and design.

Empatias
Rua da Piedade, 37–41
4050-481 Porto
+351 22 60 08 271
www.empatias.pt
Smart, elegant displays of
timeless designs mixed with
more funky alternatives
from brands such as
Driade, Kartell, Flos,
and Moooi.

Galante
Rua Mouzinho da Silveira,
27C
1250-166 Lisbon
+351 21 35 12 440
www.galante.pt
Ingo Maurer, Fontana Arte,
Vitra, Wogg are just some of
the brands that are presented
with such professionalism
at this store.

In a In
Rua João de Deus, 753
4100-462 Porto
+351 22 60 84 830
www.inain.com
Very light and airy
showroom that plays
host to simple displays of
mainly furniture and lighting
from the likes of Segis,
Vitra, Luceplan, Living
Divani, Fontana Arte, Flos,
Sawaya & Moroni and
Minotti.

Paris-Sete
Largo de Santos, 14 D
1200-808 Lisbon
+351 21 39 33 170
www.paris-sete.com
Housed beneath the arched
ceilings of this store are
classic and contemporary
furniture and lighting designs
from the world's premier
designers and brands.

Russia:

Neuhaus
Leningradskiy Prospect 64
125829 Moscow
+7 095 780 4747
Novosmolenskaja Nab. 1/4
199397 St Petersburg
+7 812 324 4455
www.galerie-neuhaus.ru
A slightly conservative
retailer of modern interior
products, in particular
furniture, storage, lighting,
kitchens and bathrooms
from brands such as
Wittmann, Tonon, Magis,
Cor, Walter Knoll, iGuzzuni
and Ingo Maurer.

Solo
Bolshaya Dorogomilvskaya 9A
Moscow
+7 095 105 5055
www.solo.ru
Solo has several stores in Moscow selling furniture and lighting from such brands as Alias, ICF, Kartell, Poltrona Frau, Walter Knoll and Bulo.

Singapore:

Lifestorey
02-33D Great World City
1 Kim Seng Promenade
Singapore 237994
+65 6732 7362
www.lifestorey.com
Brightly-lit and upbeat showroom selling furniture, lighting and accessories from Bontempi, Kartell, Porada, Cattalan, Jongform and more.

Space Furniture
Millenia Walk Level 2
9 Raffles Boulevard
Singapore 039596
+65 6415 0000
www.spacefurniture.com.au
An impressive store housing the best European furniture and lighting brands. Spacious and beautifully displayed. Sister company to stores of the same name in Australia.

X-tra Living
#9 Penang Road
01-01 Park Mall
Singapore 238459
+65 336 0688
www.xtra.com.sg
A sizeable showroom dedicated to leading edge designs from Moroso, Lema, Montis, Andreu World, Magis, Foscarini, Kundalini and Artemide, amongst others.

South Africa:

Limeline
4 Jarvis Street
Green Point
Cape Town
+27 (21) 421 3545
www.limeline.co.za
Limeline stocks a wide variety of local and imported design products from the likes of Driade, Cassina, Leolux, Magis, Knoll, Kartell, Cor, and Vilagrasa.

Twiice International
5 Winchester Road
Parktown
Johannesburg 2193
+27 (11) 727-8800
70-2 Bree Street
Cape Town 8001
+27 (21) 487-9060
www.twiice.com
Classic and contemporary seating, systems, storage and accessory items from designers including Jasper Morrison, Alberto Meda, Antonio Citterio and Mario Bellini.

South Korea:

Hanlux Co. Ltd
441-4 Taejeon Dong
Gwangju, Gyeonggi-Do
+82 31 761 5887
www.hanlux.co.kr
The principal retailer of Alessi, Magis and Flos in the region.

Spain:

BD
C/ Mallorca, 291
08037 Barcelona
+34 934 586 909
www.bdbarcelona.com
BD's impressive Barcelona showroom houses BD Ediciones' own collections as well as those of other complimentary brands including Driade. Also stores in Madrid, Girona and Zaragoza.

Espai Pilma
37 Santa Amèlia street
08084 Barcelona
+34 932 060 099
www.pilma.com
Pilma has a long history of retailing behind it, and now operates three stores in Barcelona selling modern interior products, while representing MDF Italia as the Spanish agent.

Mosel
Gran Via, 53
Bilbao
+34 944 41 78 35
www.mosel.es
An established retailer, carrying brands such as Alessi, Kartell, Magis, Flexform, de Padova, Driade, Molteni, Artemide, Flos and Luceplan. Also a store in Vitoria.

Punto Luz
Pau Claris, 146
08009 Barcelona
+34 932 160 393
www.punto-luz.com
Flos, Fontana Arte, Artemide, Ingo Maurer, Santa & Cole, Luceplan, Pallucco, Metalarte, Foscarini, Oluce and Droog Design are just a handful of the lighting brands available here.

Vinçon
Passeig de Gràcia. 96
Barcelona
+34 932 15 60 50
Castéllo, 18
Madrid
+34 915 78 05 20
www.vincon.com
Formerly specializing in crockery, Vinçon now presents a variety of contemporary furniture, lighting, accessories, kitchenware, tableware, bedroom and outdoor furniture from across the world.

Sweden:

Asplund
Sibyllegatan 31
114 42 Stockholm
+46 8 662 52 84
www.asplund.org
Asplund is a reputed producer of contemporary rugs, furniture and accessories designed by Swedish and international names. Their collection is sold in this shop alongside other complimentary brands, notably Cappellini.

Dahl Agenturer
Strandvägen 7B
114 56 Stockholm
+46 8 665 70 41
www.dahlagenturer.se
Dahl Agenturer represents Europe's leading design companies, showing designers such as Terence Woodgate, Arne Jacobsen and Miguel Milá.

Ekerö Möbler
Malmvik
178 24 Ekerö
+46 8 560 340 40
www.ekeromobler.se
This family business has been selling quality Scandinavian and Italian furniture for over 25 years from their showroom in

an old, renovated barnhouse just outside Stockholm.

Källemo
Skeppargatan 4
114 52 Stockholm
+46 8 665 19 89
www.kallemo.se
Unusual and inimitable furniture art by Mats Theselius, Mattias Ljunggren, Anna Kreitz, John Kandell and Jonas Bohlin, amongst others.

Nordiska Galleriet
Nybrogatan 11
Stockholm
+46 8 442 83 60
www.nordiskagalleriet.se
High end furniture, lighting and gifts from leading brands such as Cappellini, Cassina, Flexform, Vitra, Fritz Hansen, Artek, Flos and Foscarini.

Orrefors
Birger Jarlsgatan 15
111 45 Stockholm
+46 8 545 040 84
www.orrefors.se
Flagship showroom for all collections by leading Swedish glass producer Orrefors and sister company Kosta Boda from designers such as Lena Bergström, Ingegerd Råman, Per Söderberg and Martti Rytkönen.

Svenskt Tenn
Strandvägen 5
114 84 Stockholm
+46 8 670 16 00
www.svenskttenn.se
The famous 80-year-old company represents all that is great about Swedish design, selling classic fabrics by the likes of Josef Frank alongside new furniture designs by architect and designer Thomas Sandell and other young design talent.

Switzerland:

Form + wohnen
Rathausgasse 24
CH 5400 Baden
+41 56 200 93 00
www.form-wohnen.ch
Every imaginable current brand is sold here across the fields of furniture, lighting, homewares, floors and blinds.

Holm
Brandschenkestrasse 130
CH 8002 Zurich
+41 44 201 44 05
www.holmsweetholm.com
A store dedicated to Nordic design from such talents as Claesson Koivisto Rune, Thomas Sandell, Ingegerd Raman, Louise Campbell, Mats Theselius and Pia Wallen.

Marghitola
Metzgerrainle 6
CH 6004 Luzern
+41 41 419 70 10
www.marghitola.ch
Spread across 8 floors, this store boasts an impressive selection of modern and contemporary design items. Most large manufacturing brands are available.

sitz&co
Kauffmannweg 22
CH 6003 Luzern
+41 41 210 82 22
www.sitzco.ch
sitz&co carries a good selection of chairs, stools, tables and sofas from the likes of Ligne Roset, Kartell, Magis, Stua, Baleri, Arper and Bonaldo.

Teo Jakob
Gerechtigkeitsgasse 25
CH 3000 Berne 8
+41 31 327 57 00
www.teojakob.ch
A network of design stores across Switzerland that sells a well-presented selection of innovative furniture, lighting, kitchens and bathrooms from national and international brands.

UK:

Aram
110 Drury Lane
London WC2B 5SG
+44 20 7557 7557
www.aram.co.uk
An immense design emporium spread across five floors in central London, selling leading European brands such as Alias, Artek, Cassina, Edra, Flexform, Fritz Hansen, Knoll, Moroso and Vitra.

The Conran Shop
Michelin House
81 Fulham Road
London SW3 6RD
+44 20 7589 7401
www.conran.com

Terence Conran's flagship store selling a vast variety of design items for the home, with designs by luminaries such as Dieter Rams, Jasper Morrison, Jorge Pensi, Mario Bellini, Marcel Wanders, Philippe Starck, Ron Arad and the Azumis. Other stores in London as well as Paris, New York, Tokyo and Fukuoka.

Geoffrey Drayton
85 Hampstead Road
London NW1 2PL
+44 20 7387 5840
www.geoffrey-
drayton.co.uk
Geoffrey Drayton was one of the first people to introduce contemporary furniture and lighting to London in 1962. He is still trading today with an impressive list of suppliers, in particular Cassina.

Purves & Purves
222 Tottenham Court Road
London W1T 7QE
+44 20 7580 8223
www.purves.co.uk
Located on a busy London shopping street, Purves & Purves opens up high-end brands such as B&B Italia, Driade, Edra, MDF Italia, Kartell and Magis to the general public, offering furniture, lighting, rugs, tableware, accessories and books.

SCP
135–9 Curtain Road
London EC2A 3BX
+44 20 7739 1869
www.scp.co.uk
SCP started out manufacturing their own brand of furniture designed by the likes of Jasper Morrison, Konstantin Grcic, Terence Woodgate, Matthew Hilton and Michael Sodeau. There is now a shop with complimenting items to accompany the brand.

Skandium
86 Marylebone High Street
London W1U 4QS
+44 20 7935 2077
www.skandium.com
A haven for anyone interested in classic and contemporary Scandinavian design for the home, including iittala, Boda Nova, Orrefors, Kosta Boda, Stelton, Asplund,

Fritz Hansen, Swedese, Marimekko, plus much more.

Twentytwentyone
274 Upper Street
London N1 2UA
+44 20 7288 1996
www.twentytwentyone.com
Originally founded selling twentieth-century classics, the business moved towards contemporary designs more recently with brands such as Moroso, Cappellini, Vitra, Zanotta, Nola, David Design, Moooi, Isokon and Tom Dixon gracing the displays.

Vessel
114 Kensington Park Road
London W11 2PW
+44 20 7727 8001
www.vesselgallery.com
Vessel is must for anyone after leading tablewares, glass and ceramics from Salviati, Orrefors, Rosenthal, Stelton, Venini, Nymphenburg, littala, De Vecchi and Driade, plus many more special pieces.

Viaduct
1–10 Summer's Street
London EC1R 5BD
+44 20 7278 8456
www.viaduct.co.uk
Viaduct occupies a sizeable showroom representing Driade, e15, MDF Italia, Montis, XO and Zeus as their UK agent. Other brands are sold too, such as Cappellini, Arper, Magis, Vitra and Established & Sons.

USA:

Apartment Zero
406 7th Street NW
Washington DC 20004
+1 202 628 4067
www.apartmentzero.com
Founded in 1999 focusing mainly on American and Canadian design, the store has expanded its offerings to include Dutch, German, Italian and Scandinavian furnishings from the likes of Moooi, Foscarini, e15, littala, Flos, Vitra and Magis.

Arango
7519 SW 88 Street
Dadeland Mall
Miami, Florida 33156
+1 305 661 4229
www.arango-design.com

Arango was founded in 1959 and has become somewhat of an institution, selling and supporting international design innovation via its store, exhibitions, workshops, the design studio and the Arango Design Foundation.

Design Within Reach
Stores nationwide
www.dwr.com
Design Within Reach is a fast expanding retail network selling furniture and lighting from the Modernist masters as well as timeless contemporary pieces from Jasper Morrison, Karim Rashid, Terence Woodgate, Frank Gehry, the Azumis, Blu Dot and Philippe Starck.

Limn
San Francisco showroom
290 Townsend Street
San Francisco, CA 94107
+1 415 543 5466
Sacramento showroom
501 Arden Way
Sacramento, CA 95815
+1 916 564 2900
www.limn.com
Two showrooms selling clean-lined interior items as well as more avant-garde furniture from Moroso, B&B Italia, Cappellini, Foscarini, Moooi, Paola Lenti, Sawaya & Moroni, Driade and MDF Italia.

Linea
8843–49 Beverly Blvd.
Los Angeles, CA 90048
+1 310 273 5425
www.linea-inc.com
Large showroom specializing in sharp, clean-lined and timeless designs for home and office from brands including Ligne Roset, Driade, MDF Italia, Arper, Baleri, de Padova.

Luminaire
Coral Gables showroom
2331 Ponce de Leon Blvd
Coral Gables, FL 33134
+1 305 448 7367
Chicago showroom
301 West Superior
Chicago, IL 60610
+1 312 664 9582
www.luminaire.com
Luminaire comprises both retail and contract divisions, selling contemporary design items from leading designers including Philippe Starck, Antonio Citterio and

Konstantin Grcic and a plethora of top brands.

Montage
75 Arlington Street
Boston, MA 02116
+1 617 451 9400
www.montageweb.com
Montage opened in 1959 by introducing the best of European design to Boston. Their showroom includes brands such as Alias, B&B Italia, Cassina, DeSede, Zanotta and Poltrona Frau.

Moss
146 Greene Street
New York, NY 10012
+1 212 204 7100
www.mossonline.com
Widely considered to be one of the most exciting design stores in the world, Moss presents a beautifully presented selection of cutting-edge furniture, lighting, ceramics, glass and accessories sourced from across the globe by visionary owner Murray Moss.

Property
14 Wooster Street
New York, NY 10013
+1 917 237 0123
www.propertyfurniture.com
Eclectic mix of slick and colourful design items such as furniture from LaPalma, Emmemobili and Casamilano, alongside lighting and accessories from Tom Dixon, Bosa, Pallucco and Kundalini.

Troy
138 Greene Street
New York, NY 10012
+1 212 941 4777
www.troysoho.com
Modern retail store representing key European and American furniture lines, including Fritz Hansen, Living Divani, e15, Carl Hansen and Porro along with choice accessories and lighting.

Twentieth
8057 Beverly Blvd,
Los Angeles, CA 90048
+1 323 904 1200
www.twentieth.net
Stunning showroom merging art with design from the likes of Tom Dixon, Venini, Moooi, Derin, Quinze & Milan and Royal Tichelaar Makkum.

Photo credits

The publisher and editor would like to thank the designers, the manufacturers and the following photographers, for the use of their material.

p.8 Thomas Peter (Tantalight); p.23 Alexander Tsoehler (Scissor); p.24 Frank Stolle (Breeding); p.25 Marc Eggimann (Wood table); p.27 Daniele Oberrauch (Più); p.29 Maarten van Houten (Two Tops); p.34 Doppio (Solitaire); p.36 Marc Eggimann (Hocker); p.38 Anders Kjaergaard (Qoffee); Harri Kosenen (Pony), p.40 Tom Vack (Lo-rez-dolores); p.41 Tom Vack (MT Rocker); p.47 John Ross (Go); p.48 Bitotto Chimenti (S.T.); p.50 Donato de Bello (Fjord); p.52 Patricia von Ah (Fish Net); p.58 Walter Gumerio (Rive Droite); p.65 Pelle Wahlgren (Hug); p.66 Yoneo Kawabe (NextMaruni); p.69 Erik Brahl (Non); p.74 Walter Gumiero (Lac); p.77 Walter Gumiero (Tate); p.87 Andrés Otero (Humble), Walter Gumiero (Oblong), Marc Eggimann (Late Sofa); p.88 Tommaso Sartori (M.I.S.S.); p.91 Maarten van Houten (Barbarella); p.96 Neal Oshima (Paloma), Patrick Gries (Pools & Pouf!); p.101 Luciano Svegliado (Volta); p.102 Carlo Lavatori (Shadow); p.103 Hans Hansen (MVS); p.105 Tom Vack (Tokyo Pop); p.106 Carlo Lavatori (AND); p.108 Jason Tozer (Snoozy); p.113 Brahl Fotografi (Grandlit); p.130 Bitotto E Chimenti (Avio); p.131 Neal Oshima (Kabuki); p.132 Maarten van Houten (Eek); p.138 Santi Caleca (Tri); p.158 Frédéric Gooris/Rodrigo Torres (Floor-standing WC); p.164 Augusto Naldoni (Morode); p.169 Luis Silva Campos (mvb); p.174 Erwin Olaf (Salvation); p.180 Bianca Pilet (do break); p.183 Mathias Nero (Bamboo); p.186 Carlo Lavatori (Ken Kuts/Cylinders/Serie Vegetali); p.189 Santi Caleca (Primaire); p.191 Carlo Lavatori (Hypnos); p.193 Tiziano Rossi (Mickey); p.194 Roland

Persson (Slowfox); p.195 Goran Tacevski (Twig); p.197 Geoff Crowther (Not Made by Hand, Not Made in China); p.203 Erwin Olaf (Flames); p.207 Toine van den Nieuwendijk (Corale); p.209 Erwin Olaf (Kiki); p.212 Bart Nieuwenhuijs (Salto); p.213 Anna Tiedink (Sunflower); p.220 Mario Di Biasi (Air); p.222 Maarten van Houten (Pantheon/Flower/July); p.226 Paul Tahon (Algue); p.232 William Wegman (Posey); p.240 Tom Vack (Big Dish); p.243 Andrea Ferrari (Mini Blossom); p.244 Maarten van Houten (Dandelion); p.245 Maarten van Houten (Fringe); p.247 Andrea Ferrari (Mini Ball); p.248 Andrea Ferrari (Nova), Toine van den Nieuwendijk (Loom); p.254 Kozo Takayama (Flow); p.257 Tom Vack (Topolino); p.258 Tobias Grau/Michael Wurzbach (Soon); p.259 Hiro Zagnoli (Kaio/Duck Light); p.262 Lyn Gardiner (Kovac); p.270 Javier Tles/Mauricio Salinas (Waterproof), David Steets (Flapflap); p.274 Javier Tles (Inout); p.275 Angelo Caligaris (Ufosausoo); p.276 Tom Vack (Satel.light); p.283 Oliver Mesnage (Handy Light); p.285 Toine van den Nieuwendijk (Fruit); p.287 Inga Knölke (Martí Guixé portrait), Bianca Pilet (do scratch); pp.302–3 Maarten van Houten (HE Electronics); p.303 Hidetoyo Sasaki (Plusminuszero); p.307 Hidetoyo Sasaki (Plusminuszero); p.311 Mark Serr (Netgear); p.313 Sven Wiederholt (Yves Béhar portrait); p.319 Holger Lübbe (Altimer); p.320 Patrick Gries (Foreveryoung); p.321 David Chancellor (Marc Newson portrait); p.323 Santi Caleca (Volino); p.328 Jonathan Heyer (Airboard); p.334 Anita Star (Laarman); p.335 Andrea Zani (Velum); p.337 Patrick Gries (Wall mirror)